10 0067134 5

KU-546-321

A SYSTEM OF SOCIAL SCIENCE

A SYSTEM OF SOCIAL SCIENCE

Papers Relating to Adam Smith

Second Edition

ANDREW STEWART SKINNER

NOTTINGHAM UNIVERSITY LIBRARY

CLARENDON PRESS · OXFORD
1996

Oxford University Press, Walton Street, Oxford OX2 6DP
Oxford New York
Athens Auckland Bangkok Bombay
Calcutta Cape Town Dar es Salaam Delhi
Florence Hong Kong Istanbul Karachi
Kuala Lumpur Madras Madrid Melbourne
Mexico City Nairobi Paris Singapore
Taipei Tokyo Toronto
and associated companies in
Berlin Ibadan

Oxford is a trade mark of Oxford University Press

Published in the United States
by Oxford University Press Inc., New York

© Andrew Stewart Skinner, 1996

All rights reserved. No part of this publication may be reproduced,
stored in a retrieval system, or transmitted, in any form or by any means,
without the prior permission in writing of Oxford University Press.
Within the UK, exceptions are allowed in respect of any fair dealing for the
purpose of research or private study, or criticism or review, as permitted
under the Copyright, Designs and Patents Act, 1988, or in the case of
reprographic reproduction in accordance with the terms of the licences
issued by the Copyright Licensing Agency. Enquiries concerning
reproduction outside these terms and in other countries should be
sent to the Rights Department, Oxford University Press,
at the address above

British Library Cataloguing in Publication Data
Data available

Library of Congress Cataloging in Publication Data
Skinner, Andrew S.
A system of social science: papers relating to Adam Smith/
Andrew S. Skinner. – 2nd ed.
Includes bibliographical references and index.
ISBN 0–19–823334–5
1. Smith, Adam, 1723–1790. I. Title.
HB103.S6S56 1996 95–40597
300'.92–dc20

1 3 5 7 9 10 8 6 4 2

Typeset by J&L Composition Ltd, Filey, North Yorkshire
Printed in Great Britain
on acid-free paper by
Bookcraft (Bath) Ltd., Midsomer Norton, Avon

1000671345

Preface

The first edition of this book was published by Oxford University Press in 1979. It contained nine essays, all of which were the by-products of editorial work done on the Glasgow edition of Smith's *Works and Correspondence* (Oxford, 1976–83).

Subsequently, the original papers were used as the basis of a lecture course entitled 'The Age and Ideas of Adam Smith' which was designed for senior undergraduates and for postgraduates taking classes in Political Economy. The organization and content of the present volume reflects what I have learned from the students I have been privileged to teach, and is aimed at the same audience.

This introductory text is divided into six parts and eleven chapters.

Part I addresses those essays that bear upon the exercise of the human understanding as illustrated by Smith's treatment of the theory of communication of ideas in *LRBL* and by his analysis of the 'principles which lead and direct' philosophical enquiries (*EPS*).

Part II contains essays that deal with the treatment of ethics and of the emergence of the 'present establishments' in Europe, both of which prepare the way for a discussion of political economy which is introduced via an examination of the contributions of some of Smith's predecessors.

Part III contains an essay on Francis Hutcheson, in which emphasis is placed on the contribution to the theory of value, and an essay concerning Smith's account of the Physiocratic system and the influence that it may have had upon his thought.

Part IV consists of a single chapter and aims to provide a summary account of Smith's 'conceptual system' i.e. his vision of a theoretical structure which provided a basis for the classical system.

Part V features essays that address Smith's treatment of the functions of government and his critique of the mercantile system as illustrated by the colonial relationship with America. It is argued in the latter case that there is a rhetorical dimension to Smith's argument, which returns us to themes examined in Chapter 1. Smith's analysis is also interesting in that it emphasizes the problems presented by differential rates of growth, a theme that was developed more systematically by Hume and Steuart.

Part VI comprises papers on David Hume and Sir James Steuart. The latter paper is concerned to expound Steuart's system as a subject that is important in its own right. But the argument also explores the link with Hume, who exerted a marked influence on his two friends. The argument taken as a whole is designed to provide an opportunity further to

vi   *Preface*

explore parallels and contrasts with the position adopted by Smith, thus throwing more light upon its content. Chapters 1, 5, 10, and 11 are new to this edition. The remaining chapters have been rewritten.

Acknowledgements

Chapter 1 is based upon two contributions: 'Lectures on Rhetoric and the Considerations Concerning the First Formation of Languages' as contained in chapter 7 of *Adam Smith* with R. H. Campbell (Croom Helm, London, 1982), and 'Adam Smith: Rhetoric and the Communication of Ideas' in *Methodological Controversy in Economics: Historical Essays in Honour of T. W. Hutchison* (J. A. I. Press, 1983). The version of the argument of Chapter 3 that is included here first appeared as 'Adam Smith: Ethics and Self Love' in *Adam Smith Reviewed*, ed. with P. Jones (Edinburgh University Press, 1992). Sections of Chapter 4 are drawn from 'A Scottish Contribution to Marxist Sociology', as published in *Classical and Marxian Political Economy*, ed. I. Bradley and M. Howard (Macmillan, 1982). Chapter 5 is drawn from a lecture given on the occasion of the Francis Hutcheson Tricentenary Conference (Glasgow, 1994), and has been published in the *Scottish Journal of Political Economy* (1995). Chapter 10 is drawn from *The Cambridge Companion to Hume*, ed. David Fate Norton (Cambridge University Press, 1993). Chapter 11 is based on 'Sir James Steuart: Author of A System, *Scottish Journal of Political Economy* (1981), and on my introduction to the *Principles* (Edinburgh and Chicago, 1966).

The provenance of the remaining articles, which appeared in the first edition, is given in the notes to each. In quoting from the various texts used, I have followed the spelling and punctuation of the originals.

A. S. S.

Glasgow, 1995

Contents

Contents
PART VI

Abbreviations and References

Works of Adam Smith

Corr.	*Correspondence*
Early Draft	'Early Draft' of *The Wealth of Nations*
EPS	*Essays on Philosophical Subjects*, included among which are:
Ancient Logics	'The History of the Ancient Logics and Metaphysics'
Ancient Physics	'The History of the Ancient Physics'
Astronomy	'The History of Astronomy'
English and Italian Verses	'Of the Affinity between certain English and Italian Verses'
External Senses	'Of the External Senses'
Imitative Arts	'Of the Nature of that Imitation which takes place in what are called the Imitative Arts'
Letter	'Letter to the Authors of the *Edinburgh Review*'
Stewart	Dugald Stewart, 'Account of the Life and Writings of Adam Smith'
Languages	*Considerations Concerning the First Formation of Languages*
LJ(A)	*Lectures on Jurisprudence*, Report of 1762–3
LJ(B)	*Lectures on Jurisprudence*, Report dated 1766
LRBL	*Lectures on Rhetoric and Belles Lettres*
TMS	*The Theory of Moral Sentiments*
WN	*The Wealth of Nations*

References to *Corr.* give the number of the letter (as listed in the volume of Smith's *Correspondence* in the Glasgow edition). References to *LJ* and *LRBL* give the volume (where applicable) and the page number of the manuscript (shown in the printed texts of the Glasgow edition). References to the other works listed above locate the relevant paragraph, not the page, in order that any edition may be consulted. (In the Glasgow edition, the paragraph numbers are printed in the margin.) Thus:

Astronomy II. 4	'History of Astronomy', Sect. II, para. 4
Stewart I. 12	Dugald Stewart, 'Account of the Life and Writings of Adam Smith', Sect. I, para. 12
TMS I. i. 5. 5	*The Theory of Moral Sentiments*, Part I, Sect. i, Chap. 5, para. 5
WN v. i. f. 26	*The Wealth of Nations*, Book v, Chap. i, sixth division, para. 26

In the Glasgow edition *WN* was edited by R. H. Campbell, A. S. Skinner, and W. B. Todd; *TMS* by D. D. Raphael and A. L. Macfie (1976); *Corr.* by E. C. Mossner and I. S. Ross (1977); *EPS* by W. P. D. Wightman (general editors, D. D. Raphael and A. S. Skinner, 1980); *LJ* by R. L. Meek, D. D. Raphael and P. G. Stein (1978), and *LRBL* by John Bryce (general editor, A. S. Skinner, 1983).

Other Works

ASSP	W. R. Scott, *Adam Smith as Student and Professor* (1937).
EAS	*Essays on Adam Smith*, ed. A. S. Skinner and T. Wilson (1975).
ECPM	David Hume, *Enquiry Concerning the Principles of Morals* (1751)
EHU	David Hume, *An Enquiry Concerning Human Understanding* (1748)
Essays	David Hume, *Essays Moral, Political and Literary*, ed. E. F. Miller (1987).
EW	*David Hume, Writings on Economics*, ed. E. Rotwein (1955).
History	David Hume, *The History of England*, 6 vols. (1778)
HL	*Letters of David Hume*, ed. J. Y. T. Greig, 2 vols. (1932)
THN	David Hume, *Treatise of Human Nature* (1739–40)
HV	John Millar, *Historical View of the English Government*, 4 vols. (1803)
Principles	Sir James Steuart, *An Inquiry into the Principles of Political Economy*, ed. A. S. Skinner (1966)
Works	*The Works of Sir James Steuart*, 6 vols. (1805)
Rae	John Rae, *Life of Adam Smith* (1895)

Introduction

On 9 January 1751 Adam Smith was elected to the Chair of Logic in the University of Glasgow. In the following year he was translated to the Chair of Moral Philosophy. As his pupil John Millar recalled:

His course of lectures on this subject was divided into four parts. The first contained Natural Theology; in which he considered the proofs of the being and attributes of God, and those principles of the human mind upon which religion is founded. The second comprehended Ethics strictly so called, and consisted chiefly of the doctrines which he afterwards published in his *Theory of Moral Sentiments*. In the third part, he treated at more length of that branch of morality which relates to *justice*, and which, being susceptible of precise and accurate rules, is for that reason capable of a full and particular explanation. (Stewart I. 18).

In the last part of his lectures, he examined those political regulations which are founded, not upon the principle of *justice*, but that of *expediency*, and which are calculated to increase the riches, the power, and the prosperity of a State. . . . What he delivered on these subjects contained the substance of the work he afterwards published under the title of *An Inquiry into the Nature and Causes of The Wealth of Nations*. (Stewart, I. 20).

Following the publication of *The Theory of Moral Sentiments*, it appears that Smith gave greater emphasis to jurisprudence and economics, at the expense of the ethical material (Stewart, III. 1).

While the lectures on theology have not been discovered as yet, it is at least possible that Smith's position would have shown agreement with that of Newton, who 'infers from the structure of the visible world, that it is governed by *One Almighty and All Wise Being*. Colin MacLaurin, one of Newton's most influential expositors, continued to state quite baldly that 'The plain argument for the existence of the Deity, obvious to all . . . is from the evident contrivance and fitness of things for one another . . . There is no need for nice and subtle reasonings in this matter: a manifest contrivance immediately suggests a contriver.'

While Smith seems unlikely to have agreed with this entire statement, there is no doubt that he did make use of a number of Newtonian analogies whose implications are not inconsistent with the view of God as the Divine Architect or Great Superintendent of the Universe. He made wide use of mechanistic (and other) analogies, seeing in the universe a 'great machine' wherein we may observe 'means adjusted with the nicest artifice to the ends which they are intended to produce'

(*TMS* II. ii. 3. 5). In the same way, he noted that 'Human society when we contemplate it in a certain abstract and philosophical light, appears like a great, an immense machine' (*TMS* VII. iii. 1. 2)—a position that leads quite naturally to a functionalist thesis and to Smith's distinction between efficient and final causes (*TMS* II. ii. 3. 5). In fact, as we shall see, Smith argues that over almost the whole range of human activity man is led *as if* 'by an invisible hand to promote an end which was no part of his intention' (*WN* IV. ii. 9; cf. *TMS* IV. i. 10).

The remaining parts of Smith's lectures—that is, the ethics, jurisprudence, and economics—may all be seen not only to share a common methodology, but also to employ analogies of the kind we have just been considering. Moreover, each area of interest may be regarded, like the rhetoric, as a system of thought—a concept which, interestingly enough, Smith also illustrated in terms of a mechanistic analogy, remarking that:

Systems in many respects resemble machines. A machine is a little system, created to perform, as well as to connect together, in reality, those different movements and effects which the artist has occasion for. A system is an imaginary machine invented to connect together in the fancy those different movements and effects which are already in reality performed. (Astronomy, IV. 19).

But the ethics, jurisprudence, and economics were also seen by Smith as the parts, separate but interconnected, of an even wider system of social science, a point that emerges clearly from the advertisement to the sixth edition of *The Theory of Moral Sentiments*, published in the year of Smith's death. In this advertisement, Smith observed:

In the last paragraph of the first Edition of the present work, I said, that I should in another discourse endeavour to give an account of the general principles of law and government, and of the different revolutions which they had undergone in the different ages and periods of society; not only in what concerns justice, but in what concerns police, revenue, and arms, and whatever else is the object of law. In the *Enquiry concerning the Nature and Causes of the Wealth of Nations*, I have partly executed this promise; at least so far as concerns police, revenue, and arms. What remains, the theory of jurisprudence, which I have long projected, I have hitherto been hindered from executing, by the same occupations which had till now prevented me from revising the present work. Though my very advanced age leaves me, I acknowledge, very little expectation of ever being able to execute this great work to my own satisfaction; yet, as I have not altogether abandoned the design, and as I wish still to continue under the obligation of doing what I can, I have allowed the paragraph to remain as it was published more than thirty years ago, when I entertained no doubt of being able to execute every thing which it announced. (para. 2).

The 'occupations' to which Smith referred were connected with his duties as a Commissioner of Customs and of the Salt Duties in Scotland;

offices to which he was preferred in 1778 and which caused him to take up residence in Edinburgh. In fact, the theory of jurisprudence was never completed, although generous traces of the historical perspective to which Smith referred appear in books III and v of the *Wealth of Nations*, and in the two sets of lectures on jurisprudence which have so far been discovered.

The links between the parts of this great plan are many and various. The *TMS*, for example, may be regarded as an exercise in social philosophy, which was designed in part to show the way in which so self-regarding a creature as man erects (by natural as distinct from artificial means) barriers against his own passions, thus explaining the observed fact that he is always found in 'troops and companies'. The argument places a good deal of emphasis on the importance of general rules of behaviour which are related to experience and which may thus vary in respect of content.

The historical analysis, with its four socio-economic stages, complements this argument by formally considering the origin of government and by explaining to some extent the forces that cause variations in accepted standards of behaviour over time. Both are related in turn to Smith's treatment of political economy. The historical argument explains the origins and nature of the particular type of socio-economic structure with which the economic analysis of the *Wealth of Nations* is concerned, while *The Theory of Moral Sentiments* provides an account of the psychological assumptions upon which both analyses depend. It is this view of the interconnections that exist between the parts of Smith's system which in the main explains the focus of the papers in Parts I–V, and the order in which they are placed. But it should be made clear at the outset that this collection of papers is concerned primarily with Smith's scientific works in so far as they throw light on his contribution to the development of political economy.

PART I

1
Language, Rhetoric, and the Communication of Ideas

In his *Memoirs of the Life and Writings of Lord Kames*, A. F. Tytler remarked that:

It was by his persuasion that Mr. Adam Smith, soon after his return from Oxford, and when he had abandoned all views towards the Church, for which he had been originally destined, was induced to turn his early studies to the benefit of the public, by reading a course of Lectures on Rhetoric and *Belles Lettres*. He delivered these lectures at Edinburgh in 1748, and the following two years, to a respectable auditory, chiefly composed of students in law and theology. (Tytler 1814: i. 266).

The lectures, of a broadly extramural kind, were evidently successful. They brought Smith an income of some £100 per annum and were to be continued after his departure, first by Robert Watson and then by Hugh Blair, who became Professor of Rhetoric in 1762 (Lothian 1963: pp. xiii–xiv).

In 1751 Smith removed to Glasgow, where he used at least some part of the Edinburgh material in developing a course whose distinctive character was recalled by John Millar:

In the Professorship of Logic, to which Mr. Smith was appointed on his first introduction into this University, he soon saw the necessity of departing widely from the plan that had been followed by his predecessors, and of directing the attention of his pupils to studies of a more interesting and useful nature than the logic and metaphysics of the schools. Accordingly, after exhibiting a general view of the powers of the mind, and explaining so much of the ancient logic as was requisite, to gratify curiosity with respect to an artificial method of reasoning, which had once occupied the universal attention of the learned, he dedicated all the rest of his time to the delivery of a system of rhetoric and belles-lettres. The best method of explaining and illustrating the various powers of the human mind, the most useful part of metaphysics, arises from an examination of the several ways of communicating our thoughts by speech, and from an attention to the principles of those literary compositions which contribute to persuasion or

The material in this paper is drawn in part from chapter 7 of *Adam Smith* (with R. H. Campbell, London, 1982) and 'Adam Smith: Rhetoric and the Communication of Ideas', in *Methodological Controversy in Economics: Historical Essays in Honour of T. W. Hutchison* (Greenwich, Conn., 1983). I am grateful to both publishers for permission to reproduce certain passages.

entertainment. By these arts, every thing that we perceive or feel, every operation of our minds, is expressed and delineated in such a manner, that it may be clearly distinguished and remembered. There is, at the same time, no branch of literature more suited to youth at their first entrance upon philosophy than this, which lays hold of their taste and feelings. (Stewart, I. 16).

It is interesting that Smith chose to continue the course after he moved to the Chair of Moral Philosophy in 1752.

The notes, dated 1762–3 amply confirm Millar's claim with regard to Smith's originality, and at the same time clearly reflect what must have been the substance of some parts of the Edinburgh lectures (1748–51).

LANGUAGE AND STYLE

One of the first major problems that Smith addressed in the *Rhetoric* was that of language. The subject was taken up in Lecture 3 in the midst of the related discussion of grammar, and subsequently was expanded into the printed version, *Considerations concerning the First Formation of Languages*, which appeared in the *Philological Miscellany* in 1761 and in the third edition of *The Theory of Moral Sentiments* in 1767. Dugald Stewart was correct in saying that Smith 'set a high value' on the piece, although many modern commentators would probably agree with Stewart's judgement that 'it deserves our attention less on account of the opinions which it contains, than as a specimen of a particular sort of inquiry, which, so far as I know, is entirely of modern origin, and which seems, in a peculiar degree to have interested Mr. Smith's curiosity' (Stewart, II. 44). The reference is to Smith's interest in *conjectural* history, to that form of historical investigation where in the absence of direct evidence 'we are under a necessity of supplying the place of fact by conjecture; and when we are unable to ascertain how men have actually conducted themselves upon particular occasions, of considering in what manner they are likely to have proceeded, from the principles of their nature, and the circumstances of their external situation' (Stewart II. 46). Smith provided early evidence of the technique, opening his treatment of the development of language by supposing two 'savages, who had never been taught to speak, but had been bred up remote from the societies of men' (*Languages*, 1).

The conjectural technique is useful in some stages of the inquiry into the origin and development of language. A more telling criticism is that Smith's account is based upon insufficient data. He concentrates chiefly on the classical languages, together with French, Italian, and English, and his argument rests upon the view that linguistic structures can be discussed basically in terms of parts of speech. Smith's treatment is 'genetic', thus placing him in the 'organic school' (Land 1977). His argument is also distinguished by the emphasis given to those psychological characteristics that help to explain the origin and development of languages that, once formed, serve further to enhance our capacity for expression. Smith gave particular emphasis to man's capacity for comparison and systematization, and a growing capability for acts of abstraction (see Chapter 2).

The points at issue can be conveyed by taking some examples from the *Languages*. Although Smith stated that 'Verbs must necessarily have been coeval with the very first attempts towards the formation of language', he opened the published version of the argument with the suggestion that a hypothetical group of isolated savages would institute nouns substantive as 'one of the first steps towards the formation of language' (*Languages*, 1). Initially they would ascribe particular names to familiar objects of immediate relevance, such as the cave which gave them shelter, or the fountain which provided water, before extending these terms to cover the whole class of things to which these objects were eventually perceived to belong. Once this step had been taken, Smith observed that the savage would face the need to distinguish one particular object from others of the same general species, by reference either to its peculiar *qualities*, or to the specific *relation* which it might bear to other things: hence the origin of nouns adjective which express a quality, e.g. the *green* tree, and of prepositions, which express a relation, e.g. the green tree *of* the meadow.

It was Smith's contention that the emergence of both nouns adjective and prepositions involved a considerable effort of abstraction and therefore that they would be preceded by simpler responses to the problems raised. For example, it was argued that: 'The man who first distinguished a particular object by the epithet of *green*, must have observed other objects that were not *green*, from which he meant to separate it by this appellation. The institution of this name, therefore, supposes comparison. It likewise supposes some degree of abstraction.' He continues:

The person who first invented this appellation must first have distinguished the quality from the object to which it belonged, and must have conceived the object as capable of subsisting without the quality. The invention, therefore, even of the simplest nouns adjective, must have required more metaphysics than we are apt to be aware of. The different mental operations, of arrangement or classing, of comparison, and of abstraction, must all have been employed, before even the names of the different colours, the least metaphysical of all nouns adjective, could be instituted. From all of which I infer, that when languages were beginning to be formed, nouns adjective would by no means be the words of the earliest invention. (*Languages*, 7).

Smith suggested that variation in nouns substantive would probably precede the emergence of nouns adjective, pointing to the fact that 'in many languages, the qualities both of sex and of the want of sex, are expressed by different terminations in the nouns substantive, which denote objects so qualified . . . Julius, Julia; Lucretius, Lucretia, etc.' (*Languages*, 8). Smith believed that the different formations of nouns substantive might forestall the need for nouns adjective at least for some time, and that,

When nouns adjective came to be invented, it was natural that they should be formed with some similarity to the substantives, to which they were to serve as epithets or qualifications. Men would naturally give them the same terminations with the substantives to which they were first applied, and from that love of similarity of sound, from that delight in the returns of the same syllables, which is the foundation of analogy in all languages they would be apt to vary the termination of the same adjective, according as they had occasion to apply it to a masculine, to a feminine, or to a neutral substantive. They would say, *magnus lupus, magna lupa, magnum pratum*, when they meant to express a great *he wolf*, a great *she wolf*, a great *meadow*' (*Languages*, 10).

The preposition suggests the need for an even greater effort of abstraction than that involved in the development of nouns adjective. Smith offered three reasons in support of this contention. First, was the tenet that 'relation is, in itself, a more metaphysical object than a quality'. Secondly,

though prepositions always express the relation which they stand for, in concrete with the co-relative object, they could not have originally been formed without a considerable effort of abstraction. A preposition denotes a relation, and nothing but a relation. But before men could institute a word, which signified a relation, and nothing but a relation, they must have been able, in some measure, to consider this relation abstractedly from the related objects: since the idea of those objects does not, in any respect, enter into the signification of the preposition . . . a preposition is from its nature a general word, which, from its very institution, must have been considered as equally applicable to denote any other similar relation. The man who first invented the word *above*, must not only have distinguished in some measure, the relation of *superiority* from the objects which were so related, but he must also have distinguished this relation from other relations, such as, from the relation of *inferiority* denoted by the word *below*, from the relation of *juxta-position*, expressed by the word *beside* and the like. (*Languages*, 12).

Smith concluded, as in the case of nouns adjective, that the problem could be temporarily avoided by using apparently simpler devices, such as the invention of *cases*. For example, he suggested that the use of the genitive and dative cases in Greek and Latin in effect supplied the place of the preposition, as in the example *fructus arboris* (fruit of the tree). Therefore the development of language would feature the appearance of nouns substantive, with different terminations, prior to the appearance of nouns adjective and of the preposition, a process that leads to the emergence of a language that employs all these parts of speech.

Smith then took his argument a stage further and suggested that the perception of a complex whole will lead to its simplification. He availed himself of the analogy of the machine in suggesting that, initially, languages are 'extremely complex in their principles' until succeeding 'improvers observe, that one principle may be so applied as to produce several' of the 'movements' required:

In language, in the same manner, every case of every noun, and every tense of every verb, was originally expressed by a particular distinct word, which served for this purpose and for no other. But succeeding observation discovered, that one set of words was capable of supplying the place of all that infinite number, and that four or five prepositions, and half a dozen auxiliary verbs, were capable of answering the end of all the declensions, and of all the conjugations in the ancient languages. (*Languages*, 41).

But, whereas the simplification of machines is of advantage in terms of their efficiency, the same was not true of language in Smith's view. Apart from the fact that the simplification of languages renders them less agreeable to the ear, the major problem is found in the fact that they become more prolix in the sense that several words become necessary to express what could have been conveyed by a single word before. Or, as Smith put it by way of example, 'What a Roman expressed in the single word *amavissem*, an Englishman is obliged to express by four different words, *I should have loved*' (*Languages*, 43).

Three points should be noted before going further. First, there is Smith's belief that the parts of speech should be studied in an analytical manner, a perspective that led him to praise Dr Johnson for the care he had taken in collecting examples of particular usages. But Smith drew attention to what he took to be a defect in a plan 'which appears to us not to be sufficiently grammatical. The different significations of a word are indeed collected; but they are seldom digested into general classes, or ranged under the meaning which the word principally expresses' (*EPS* 232).

Secondly, we should observe Smith's argument that the development of the means of communication reveals important features of human nature, most notably with regard to the role of analogy, the capacity for classification, abstraction, and reflection. It was Smith's contention that the actual (as distinct from the conjectural) record of developing linguistic capacity was of great importance from this point of view—a belief that was neatly expressed in a letter to George Baird, dated 7 February 1763, where Smith commented on William Ward's projected *Essay on Grammar* (1765). Smith wrote:

I have read over the contents of your friend's work with very great pleasure, and heartily wish it was in my power to give or to procure him all the encouragement which his ingenuity and industry deserve. I think myself greatly obliged to him for the very obliging notice he has been pleased to take of me, and should be glad to contribute anything in my power towards completing his design. I approve greatly of his plan for a Rational Grammar and am convinced that a work of this kind executed with his abilities and industry, may prove not only the best System of Grammar, but the best System of Logic in any Language, as well as the best History of the natural progress of the Human mind in forming the most important abstractions upon which all reasoning depends. (*Corr.* 69).

The letter is also interesting for the attention given to the articles on grammar in the French *Encyclopédie* and for the fact that Smith drew attention to the Abbé Girard's *Les Vrais principes de la Langue Française* (1747) as the work 'which first set me thinking upon these subjects . . . I have received more instruction from it than from any other I have yet seen upon them' (*Corr.* 69).

Thirdly, it will be observed that Smith's interest in language effectively illustrates his own preoccupation with grammar. As he remarked in the *Rhetoric*: 'After language had made some progress it was natural to imagine that men would form some rules according to which they should regulate their language. These rules are what we call Grammar' (*LRBL* I.v.53). In this connection, Smith drew attention not merely to parts of speech but also to the constituent elements of the sentence. In particular, he drew attention to the emergence of *figures of speech* which constitute departures from general rules, or usages that cannot be reduced to rule—topics that 'naturally lead to the consideration of what I call style'.

Smith believed that the 'plain style' was the only acceptable modern form for a rhetoric that was committed to communication, and he proceeded to advise his students accordingly in Lectures 6, 7, 8, and 11. He warned that words must be 'put in such order that the meaning of the sentence shall be quite plain' and that a 'natural order of expression free of parentheses and superfluous words is likewise a great help towards perspicuity' (*LRBL* i. 10). Short sentences are recommended as 'generally more perspicuous than long ones as they are most easily comprehended in one view' (*LRBL* i. 11). Smith's students were also taught that the words used 'should be natives . . . of the language we speak in' and that they should conform 'to the custom of the country' at least as established by 'men of rank and breeding' (*LRBL* i. 5). Smith also recommended that the writer should seek harmony of sound 'by avoiding harsh clashings of consonants or the hiatus arising from the meeting of many vowels' (*LRBL* i. v. 51), concluding this section with the confident remark that 'Many other rules for arrangement have been given but they do not deserve attention' (*LRBL* i. v. 52^b). But Smith's main point was to instruct his hearers that:

perfection of style consists in expressing in the most concise, proper and precise manner the thought of the author . . . This, you'll say, is not more than common sense: and indeed it is no more. But if you'll attend to it, all the Rules of Criticism and morality when traced to their foundation, turn out to be some Principles of Common Sence which every one assents to . . . (*LRBL* i. 133).

Earlier he noted that:

When the sentiment of the speaker is expressed in a neat, clear, plain and clever manner, and the passion or affection he is possessed of and intends, *by sympathy*, to communicate to his hearer, is plainly and cleverly hit off, then and only then the expression has all the force and beauty that language can give it. It matters not the least whether figures of speech are introduced or not. (*LRBL* i. v. 56).

The reference to figures of speech is particularly important. Smith recognized that figures of speech could give 'life' to the expression of an idea, but his position is distinctive in that he believed 'that the most beautiful passages are generally the most simple' and that figures of speech 'have no intrinsic worth of their own'. This argument marks Smith's break with at least one rhetorical tradition, as evidenced by his remark that it is 'from the consideration of these figures, and the divisions and subdivisions of them, that so many systems of rhetorick, both ancient and modern have been formed. They are generally a very silly set of Books and not at all instructive' (*LRBL* i. v. 59). Smith went on to note that three elements are needed in a sound author:

1st—That he have a complete knowledge of his Subjects; 2ndly That he should arrange all the parts of his Subject in their proper order; 3rdly, That he paint or describe the Ideas he has of these severall in the most proper and expressive manner; this is the art of painting or imitation. (*LRBL* i. 104–5).

THE FORMS OF DISCOURSE

Having disposed of the issues of language and style, Smith then proceeded to consider the forms of discourse that were employed in the communication of ideas through the medium of the spoken or written word. In Smith's view, all examples of the written word could be reduced to four broad types: the poetical, where the purpose is to entertain; the historical, which is intended to relate some fact or facts; the didactic, where the purpose is to prove some proposition; and the oratorical. These different types of discourse, in Smith's view, had some common elements although differing in purpose and therefore in organization. Thus for example he suggested that the rules of narrative (i.e.

historical) discourse were the same for the poetical, even though the purpose of poetical discourse was entertainment while historical discourse aimed to instruct. In the same way, he suggested that, while both didactic (i.e. scientific) and rhetorical discourse were intended to prove some proposition, they differ in that the former 'proposes to put before us the arguments on both sides of the question in their true light, giving each its proper degree of influence, and has it in view to perswade no further than the arguments themselves appear convincing'. That is, he suggests that didactical discourse seeks to persuade 'only so far as the strength of the argument is convincing' (*LRBL* i. 150).

It will be useful to say a little about each of these three types of discourse to which Smith devoted the bulk of the lectures–the narrative (historical), didactic, and oratorical (rhetorical) forms.

On Smith's argument, the purpose of *historical* discourse is to 'narrate transactions as they happened, without being inclined to any part' (*LRBL* ii. 13). The author must then be objective so far as possible and also concern himself with matters of fact. The facts in question may be either internal (such as the thoughts and sentiments of the actor) or external, and may be described either directly or indirectly (as for example when we describe the effects produced by some event on 'those who behold it', as distinct from simply describing the event itself). Moreover, Smith argued that the facts reviewed should be arranged in a particular way, preferably chronologically, in that 'In general the narration is to be carried on in the same order as that in which the events themselves happened.' But where chronology cannot be observed, the best method, Smith believed, 'is to observe the connection of place'. In particular, the lecturer advised his hearers that the narrative should be continuous and that 'we should never leave any chasm or gap in the thread of the narration, even though there are no remarkable events to fill up that space'–the reason being that the 'very notion of a gap makes us uneasy'.

Yet, important as the connections of time and place may be: 'There is another connection still more striking than any of the former: I mean that of cause and Effect. There is no connection with which we are so much interested as this of cause and effect' (*LRBL* ii. 32). These causes, in turn, were separated into the remote or immediate and, as Smith went on to argue, could be defined as internal or external–where the former refer to the passions or sentiments of the actor. Smith argued that writers such as Thucydides and Julius Caesar, who actually witnessed the events recorded in their histories, tended to explain them by reference to their external causes (the terrain for example, or the disposition of troops), in contrast to Tacitus, who leads us

so far into the sentiments and mind of the actors, that they are some of the most striking and interesting passages to be met with in any history. In describing the more important actions he does not give us an account of their externall causes, but only of the internall ones, tho this perhaps will not tend so much to instruct us in the knowledge of the causes of events, yet it will be more interesting and lead us into a science no less usefull, to wit, the knowledge of the motives by which men act' (*LRBL* ii. 67).

For Smith, historical or narrative writing quite clearly involved discipline and has something of a scientific character, in that such writing 'sets before us the more interesting and important events of human life, points out the causes by which these events were brought about, and by this means points out to us by what manner and method we may produce similar good effects or avoid similar bad ones'.

Didactic writing, on the other hand, must obviously require similar qualities of mind in that the writer should aspire to be objective in the handling of facts and to be interested in the causal processes involved. Yet for Smith this form of discourse was more complex than the narrative and the rules of organization correspondingly more extensive.

Smith addressed himself to the question of didactic writing in a lecture dated 24 January 1763, apparently delivered '*sine libro*, except what he read from Livy'. In this lecture he suggested that didactic writing could have one of two aims: either to 'Lay Down a proposition and prove this by the different arguments which lead to that conclusion', or to deliver a system in any science (*LRBL* ii. 125). In the first case, the writer may seek to prove a single proposition or present a complex proposition which requires proof of several subordinate ones. In this context, Smith recommended that 'these subordinate propositions should not be above 5 at most. When they exceed this number the mind cannot easily comprehend them at one view; and the whole runs into confusion. Three, or there-about, is a very proper number' (*LRBL* ii. 126).

The second function of didactic discourse, namely the delivery of a system in any science, also presents the writer with a choice. As Smith put it,

in Naturall Philosophy, or any other Science of that Sort, we may either like Aristotle go over the Different branches in the order they happen to cast up to us, giving a principle commonly a new one for every phaenomenon; or, in the manner of Sir Isaac Newton, we may lay down certain principles known or proved in the beginning, from whence we account for the severall Phenomena, connecting all together by the same Chain. This Latter, which we may call the Newtonian method is undoubtedly the most Philosophical, and in every science, whether of Moralls or Naturall Philosophy, etc., is vastly more ingenious, and for that reason more engaging than the other. (*LRBL* ii. 133).

Oratorical discourse, which Smith divided into the demonstrative, the deliberative, and the judicial (or forensic), is the subject of the last nine lectures in the series and brought Smith to what had formerly been the sole concern of the rhetorician. In Smith's view, this type of discourse was still more complex than either the narrative or the didactic, being further distinguished from the latter by the fact that such discourses were solely designed to persuade. As he put it,

The Rhetoricall . . . endeavours by all means to perswade us; and for this purpose it magnifies all the arguments on the one side and diminishes or conceals those that might be brought on the side conterary to that which it is designed that we should favour. Persuasion which is the primary design in the Rhetoricall, is but the secondary design in the Didactick. It endeavours to persuade us only so far as the strength of the arguments is convincing: instruction is the main End. (*LRBL* i. 150).

The point is repeated in an even clearer form later in the argument, where it is noted:

But when we propose to persuade at all events, and for this purpose adduce those arguments that make for the side we have espoused, and magnify those to the utmost of our power; and on the other hand make light of and extenuate all those which may be brought on the other side, then we make use of the Rhetorical stile. (*LRBL* ii. 12).

All three forms of the rhetorical (or oratorical) discourse have the same basic purpose while differing in their objectives and therefore in terms of their organization. *Demonstrative* eloquence was for Smith the simplest of the three types of oratorical discourse 'not because it was that sort which is used in mathematical demonstrations' but because:

The subjects of such discourses were generally the Praises or the discommendation of some particular persons, communities or actions, exhorting the people to or deterring them from some particular conduct. As it was more safe to commend than to discommend men or actions, these discourses generally turned that way. (*LRBL* i. 152).

Deliberative eloquence differs from the demonstrative in that it is designed to be used in councils and assemblies in regard to matters of public consequence, whereas the judicial is used in proceedings before a court of justice. But once again, Smith drew attention to the importance of the psychology of the audience. In the case of deliberative eloquence, for example, he suggested that the orator faced a choice of two methods:

The 1st may be called the Socratick method . . . In this method we keep as far from the main point to be proved as possible, bringing on the audience by slow and imperceptible degrees to the thing to be proved, and by gaining their consent to some things whose tendency they cant discover, we force them at last either to deny what they had before agreed to, or to grant the Validity of the Conclusion. This is the smoothest and most engaging manner.
    The other is a harsh and unmannerly one where we affirm the things we are to prove, boldly at the Beginning, and when any point is controverted, begin by

proving that very thing and so on, this we may call the Aristotelian method, as we know it was that which he used. (*LRBL* ii. 136).

Smith again went on to note that the choice of method would depend on the orator's judgement of his audience, the Socratic being used where the audience needs to be persuaded, the Aristotelian where it is basically convinced that the case is sound and merely needs confirmation (cf. Eltis 1993).

While such recommendations may also apply to *judicial* oratory, Smith added a different point with regard to the ordering and structure of the parts of the orator's argument:

These when placed separately have often no great impression, but if they be placed in a naturall order, one leading to the other, their effect is, greatly increased . . . By this means, tho he can bring proof but of very few particulars, yet the connection there is makes them easily comprehended and consequently agreeable, so that when the adversary tries to contradict any of these particulars it is pulling down a fabric with which we are greatly pleased and are very unwilling to give up. (*LRBL* ii. 197).

Smith regarded this point as one of some importance, remarking later in the argument that

by this means tho we can prove but a very small part of the facts yet those which we have proved give the others by the close connection they have with them a great appearance of truth and the whole Story has the appearance, at least, of considerable probability. (*LRBL* ii. 207).

THE RHETORIC AND OTHER ASPECTS OF SMITH'S SYSTEM

The text of Smith lectures on rhetoric was discovered by John Lothian in 1958 and ably introduced in setting them in the context of an 'age of improvement'. W. S. Howell, on the other hand, made a more deliberate attempt to place the lectures in the context of the history of rhetoric, elucidating by this means the areas in which Smith sought to claim some degree of originality (Howell 1975).

Once pointed out, the clues are obvious—perhaps no more so than in Smith's claim that existing 'systems' of rhetoric showed a preoccupation with figures of speech. Equally interesting is Smith's insistence that 'perfection of style consists in expressing in the most concise, proper, and precise manner the thought of the author'. For Smith, the 'plain style' was the most appropriate for the modern world, a point that is illustrated by a comparison of Shaftesbury and Jonathan Swift. In Smith's view, Shaftesbury was much preoccupied with 'ornaments in language'. The lecturer concluded somewhat harshly that 'As he was of no great depth in Reasoning he would be glad to set off by the ornament of language what was deficient in matter' (*LRBL* i. 145). Swift, in contrast, was a master of his subject matter, partly in consequence of which he had a style 'so plain that one partly asleep may carry the sense along with him' (*LRBL* i. 10).

Smith's students would no doubt find the lectures interesting because they provided not only a critique of literary composition but also a set of criteria against which his own literary performances could be judged. At the same time, they would be left in little doubt as to the areas in respect of which Smith was claiming some degree of originality. Moreover, given that the rhetoric lectures would overlap with Smith's treatment of ethics and jurisprudence, the students could hardly fail to be struck by evidence of linkages between the different parts of the course.

For example, the attention devoted to the influence of environment in *The Theory of Moral Sentiments* and in the historical treatment of jurisprudence finds a reflection in the lectures on rhetoric. Students of Smith's teaching on jurisprudence would also discover an echo of his preoccupation with the role of economic factors. It is noted in the rhetoric, for example, that the quality of prose would be affected by that opulence that commonly attends the introduction of commerce:

Opulence and Commerce commonly precede the improvement of arts, and refinement of every Sort. I do not mean that the improvement of arts and refinement of manners are the necessary consequences of Commerce, the Dutch and the Venetians bear testimony against me, but only that it is a necessary requisite. Wherever the Inhabitants of a city are rich and opulent, where they enjoy the necessaries and conveniencies of life in ease and Security, there the arts will be cultivated and refinement of manners a never failing attendant. (*LRBL* ii. 115).

Smith also noted that the deliberative eloquence of Demosthenes and Cicero was affected not merely by the different political climates that prevailed at the time of writing but also by the fact that the economic circumstances of Greece and Rome were different. In Athens commerce and luxury 'gave the Lowest an opportunity of raising themselves to an equality with the nobles, and the nobles an easy way of reducing themselves to the state of the meanest citizen' (*LRBL* ii. 144), whereas in Rome a considerable degree of inequality prevailed–with consequent effects on style: 'These considerations may serve to explain many of the differences in the manners and Stile of Demosthenes and Cicero. The latter talks with the Dignity and authority of a superior and the former with the ease of an equall' (*LRBL* ii. 165).

This type of perspective reminds us of that 'relativity' which runs through Smith's historical work in all its manifestations. As Howell

has observed, in making a wider point which is also more specific to
the rhetoric:

Another point to be emphasised in this analysis of Smith's view of oratorical
composition is that he regarded the oratory of one cultural establishment to be
unsuited to a different establishment, and that as a consequence, the rhetorical
theory calculated to produce oratory under one set of conditions would not
necessarily be the theory which ought to prevail when the conditions change.
This idea is a characteristic of the new rhetoric. . . . Boyle had already stressed it.
(Howell 1975: 37).

However, interesting as these assessments are, attention should be
drawn to further areas where links are to be found between the lectures
on rhetoric and other parts of Smith's thought. Looked at from one point
of view, the lectures on rhetoric amply illustrate many of the psychological judgements that are employed in the ethics. In the context of his
lectures on deliberative eloquence, Smith recommended that the writer
should concentrate on the great, on the ground that we are typically
more interested in their condition. In the same vein, he warned the
authors of oratorical discourses who sought to strike a sympathetic
chord in their readers that 'there is nothing which is more apt to raise
our admiration and gain our applause than the hardships one has
undergone with firmness and constancy'. He added that there are
some virtues which 'attract our respect and admiration, and others
which we love and esteem'–just as there are vices which 'we contemn
and despise and others which we abominate and detest' (*LRBL* ii. 102).
All these represent opinions that would be familiar to students of
Smith's ethics, as well as to readers of the *Moral Sentiments*.

Similarly, it could be claimed that the arguments developed in the
lectures on rhetoric complement the analysis of the *Moral Sentiments*,
where it is remarked that:

We may judge of the propriety or impropriety of the sentiments of another
person by their correspondence or disagreement with our own, upon two
different occasions; either first, when the objects which excite them are considered without any peculiar relation, either to ourselves or to the person whose
sentiments we judge of; or, secondly, when they are considered as peculiarly
affecting one or other of us. (*TMS*, i. i. 4. 1).

Objects that lack a 'peculiar' relation include 'the expression of a
picture, the composition of a discourse . . . all the general subjects of
science and taste'. For Smith, the characteristic feature of such judgement is that we look at 'a picture, a poem, or a system of philosophy'
from the 'same station' (*TMS*, i. i. 4. 5): 'We look at them from the same
point of view, and we have no occasion for sympathy, or for that
imaginary change of situations from which it arises, in order to
produce, with regard to these, the most perfect harmony of sentiments

and affections' (*TMS*, I. i. 4. 2). Yet at the same time he noted a similarity with the nature of *moral* judgement, arising from the fact that to 'approve of another man's opinions is to adopt those opinions, and to adopt them is to approve of them' (*TMS*, I. i. 3. 2). He further observed that:

There are some very noble and beautiful arts, in which the degree of excellence can be determined only by a certain nicety of taste, of which the decisions, however, appear always, in some measure, uncertain. There are others, in which the success admits, either of clear demonstration, or very satisfactory proof. Among the candidates for excellence in those different arts, the anxiety about the public opinion is always much greater in the former than in the latter. (*TMS* III. 2. 18).

The contrast is between the young poet, uncertain in his reception, and the great mathematician, confident of his results (Cf. *TMS* III. II. 20–3). Yet both are 'candidates for excellence', and both are likely to be conscious of literary or scientific reputation as a source of social distinction. As Smith remarked, when the opinions of another person

not only coincide with our own, but lead and direct our own; when in forming them he appears to have attended to many things which we had overlooked, and to have adjusted them to all the various circumstances of their objects; we not only approve of them, but wonder and are surprised at their uncommon and unexpected acuteness and comprehensiveness, and he appears to deserve a very high degree of admiration and applause. For approbation heightened by wonder and surprise, constitutes the sentiment which is properly called admiration, and of which applause is the natural expression. (*TMS* I. i. 4. 3).

While these themes are only incidental to the main drift of the *Moral Sentiments*, Smith's students would be well aware that they were central to the lectures on rhetoric with their attendant emphasis on the theory of communication and persuasion.

But for the historian of ideas with an interest in methodology, some of the most interesting points arise from Smith's decision to extend the boundaries of the traditional rhetoric to include not only oratorical discourse (demonstrative, deliberative, and judicial) but also narrative or historical writing (*LRBL*, lectures 16–19). The lectures on the history of classical writers such as Herodotus, Thucydides, Polybius, and Livy are especially striking. Here it is of particular interest to recall Smith's point that the purpose of historical writing is to 'set before us the more interesting and important events of human life' and to 'point out the causes by which these events were brought about'. With such a definition in mind, it is hardly surprising to find Smith agreeing with David Hume's admiration for Thucydides, while suggesting that: 'Machiavelli is of all Modern Historians the only one who has contented himself with that which is the chief purpose of History, to relate events and connect them with their causes, without becoming a party on either side' (*LRBL* ii. 70).

Such a point reminds the reader, as Smith explicitly does, that historical discourses frequently have something of the character of scientific (or didactic) writing. As we have already noted, there are two methods in which a didactical writing, containing an account of some system, may be delivered. The first, which Smith described as the 'Newtonian method', is 'without doubt, the most philosophical one'. He continued:

'It gives us a pleasure to see the phaenomena which we reckoned the most unaccountable all deduced from some principle (commonly a well-known one) and all united in one chain, far superior to what we feel from the unconnected method where everything is accounted for by itself without any reference to the others. We need not be surprised then that the Cartesian philosophy (for Descartes was in reality the first who attempted this method), though it does not perhaps contain a word of truth, and to us who live in a more enlighten'd age and have more enquired into these matters, it appears very Dubious, should nevertheless have been so universally received by all the Learned in Europe at that time. The Great Superiority of the method over that of Aristotle, the only one then known, and the little enquiry that was then made into those matters, made them greedily receive a work which we justly esteem one of the most entertaining Romances that has ever been wrote. (*LRBL* ii. 134).

There are perhaps two points arising from this statement which deserve more than a passing mention. First, it will be observed that Smith credits both Newton and Descartes with the same method of exposition, even although a more 'enlightened' age had now perceived that the Cartesian system of physics was no more than an entertaining romance. Smith was well aware of the point that the principles governing the organization of didactic or scientific discourse are distinct from those rules of procedure that constitute scientific method properly so called. In fact, the Newtonian method, in the latter sense of the term, was aptly described by Colin McLaurin in recommending that

we should begin with phenomena, or effects, and from them investigate the powers or causes that operate in nature; that from particular causes we should proceed to the more general ones, till the argument end in the most general: this is the method of *analysis*. Being once possessed of these causes, we should then descend in a contrary order, and from them as established principles, explain all the phenomena that are their consequences, and prove our explications; and this is the *synthesis*. It is evident that, as in mathematics, so in natural philosophy, the investigation of difficult things by the method of *analysis*, ought ever to precede the method of composition, or the *synthesis*. (McLaurin 1775: 9).

Secondly, it should be observed that Smith's statement raises the issue of those links that exist between the rhetoric and the *Essays on Philosophical Subjects*, most notably the 'Astronomy'. Some of these links are obvious enough, for example the judgements that emerge from the study of language, illustrating man's capacity for acts of abstraction, reflection, and generalization. To these must be added Smith's emphasis on the point that 'the very notion of a gap', or lack of connection in the materials studied, 'makes us uneasy'–a proposition that is illustrated in the discussion of narrative and judicial writing and which is also central to the treatment of the 'principles which lead and direct' philosophical study (see Chapter 2 below, and Longuet-Higgins 1992).

Smith's discussion of the sources of stimulus to philosophical or scientific study as developed in the 'Astronomy' suggests that men are prompted to seek explanations for the jarring and discordant appearances which may be observed with a view to restoring the mind to a state of tranquility. In this connection, he emphasized the pleasure that may be derived from simplicity, coherence, and order in theoretical work, making the point that, since the contemplation of beauty is a source of pleasure, we may unwittingly give the products of the intellect a form that satisfies purely aesthetic criteria (cf. Jones 1992). Hence the Newtonian 'method' as described in the *Lectures on Rhetoric and Belles Lettres* may be used *because* it is more ingenious, and for that reason 'more engaging', than the alternative. It is also worthy of note that Smith should have likened the system of thought to an 'Imaginary machine' (Astronomy, IV. 19). In the Imitative Arts he also likened the pleasure to be derived from the contemplation of a great system of thought to that acquired from listening to a 'well composed concerto of instrumental music', remarking that:

In the contemplation of that immense variety of agreeable and melodious sounds, arranged and digested, both in their coincidence and in their succession, into so complete and regular a system, the mind in reality enjoys not only a very great sensual, but a very high intellectual, pleasure, not unlike that which it derives from the contemplation of a great system in any other science. (Imitative Arts, II. 30).

While such points are important in themselves, they have relevance outside the study of rhetoric and of the 'Astronomy'. The distinction between scientific method and the method used in expounding a system of thought reminds the historian of ideas that use of the 'Newtonian method' in the latter sense does not of itself confirm or deny that the thinker in question is employing a scientific method of the kind described by McLaurin. In the same way, the emphasis that Smith gave to 'subjective' elements in science reminds us of the tensions that frequently exist between the obligations of 'scientific' work and the subjective preferences of the thinker–tensions that exist, and whose consequences may be concealed, even in the works of those who claim to be employing the experimental method.

Smith's awareness of the fact that scientific discourse is only one of a number of forms of communication also encourages vigilance in the interpretation of ideas, thus helping us to identify an author's changing purposes (cf. Endres 1991). Clearly the historian should not neglect the point that, while different types of discourse (didactic, oratorical, narrative) have different purposes and hence different rules of composition, the individual thinker may employ the techniques of demonstration and persuasion in the context of a single work. It is argued elsewhere that Smith's treatment of the alleged contradictions of mercantile policy in the context of the American Colonies may be plausibly interpreted as an illustration of Smith's forensic, as distinct from his scientific, skills (see Chapter 9 below).

REFERENCES

Bevilacqua, V. M. (1965), 'Adam Smith's *Lectures on Rhetoric and Belles Lettres'*, *Studies in Scottish Literature*, 3.

Berry, C. J. (1974), 'Considerations', *Journal of the History of Ideas*, 35.

Brown, V. (1994), *Adam Smith's Discourse: Canonicity, Commerce and Conscience* (London).

Bryce, J. C. (1983), 'Introduction' to the Glasgow edition of the *LRBL* (Oxford).

—— (1992), 'Adam Smith's Rhetoric', in *Adam Smith Reviewed*, ed. P. Jones, and A. S. Skinner, (Edinburgh).

Eltis, W. (1993), 'France's Free Market Reforms in 1774–6 and Russia's in 1991–3: The Immediate Relevance of L'Abbe de Condillac's Analysis', *European Journal of the History of Economic Thought*, 1 (Autumn).

Endres, A. M. (1991), 'Adam Smith's Rhetoric of Economics', *Scottish Journal of Political Economy*, 38.

Howell, W. S. (1975), 'Adam Smith's Lectures on Rhetoric: An Historical Assessment', in *Essays on Adam Smith*, ed. A. S. Skinner, and T. Wilson, (Oxford).

Jones, P. (1992), 'The Aesthetics of Adam Smith', in *Adam Smith Reviewed*, ed P. Jones and A. S. Skinner, (Edinburgh).

Land, S. K. (1977), 'Adam Smith's Concerning the First Formation of Languages', *Journal of the History of Ideas*, 38.

Longuet-Higgins, H. C. (1992), 'The History of Astronomy: A Twentieth Century View', in *Adam Smith Reviewed*, ed. P. Jones, and A. S. Skinner, (Edinburgh).

Lothian, J. M. (1963), 'Introduction' to his edition of the *Lectures on Rhetoric and Belles Lettres* (Edinburgh).

McLaurin, C. (1748), *An Account of Sir Isaac Newton's Philosophical Discoveries* (Edinburgh; 3rd edn. 1775).

Plank, F. (1992), 'Adam Smith: Grammatical Economist', in *Adam Smith Reviewed*, ed. P. Jones, and A. S. Skinner, (Edinburgh).

Redman, D. A. (1993), 'Adam Smith and Isaac Newton', *Scottish Journal of Political Economy*, 40.

Tytler, A. F. (1814), *Memoirs of the Life and Writings of Henry Home of Kames* (Edinburgh).

2
Early Writings:
Science and the Role of the Imagination

INTRODUCTION

The *Lectures on Rhetoric* clearly illustrate the truth of Millar's claim with regard to Smith's interest in the principles of human nature. Even the brief account that is offered in the previous chapter attests to the emphasis that Smith placed upon the faculties of reason and imagination, together with man's propensity to discover patterns of causality or to classify phenomena. While these faculties and propensities are illustrated by reference to a wide range of literary works, they are further illustrated by writings of a more philosophical or scientific kind.

It is probable that Smith's essay on the 'External Senses' dates from the early 1750s, and it is known that at least part of his study of the 'Imitative Arts' was read to a society in Glasgow. As Dugald Stewart was to point out, it is possible that Smith's interest in these arts was cultivated 'less . . . with a view to the particular enjoyments they convey (though he was by no means without sensibility to their beauties) than an account of their connection with the general principles of the human mind' (Stewart, III. 13).

But it is also interesting to note that Smith had a very wide knowledge of scientific literature.[1] His 'Letter to Authors of the *Edinburgh Review*' for 1756, for example, contains not only a plea for a wide coverage of all branches of literature, but also references to the French *Encyclopédie* as well as to the specific works of Buffon, Daubenton, and Réamur. In addition, it is known that Smith owned copies of the works of D'Alembert, Diderot, and Maupertuis—all writers who made important

---

This chapter is a modified version of three previous attempts to deal with 'The History of Astronomy': 'Adam Smith: Philosophy and Science', *Scottish Journal of Political Economy*, 19 (1972), 'Adam Smith: Science and the Role of the Imagination', in W. B. Todd (ed.), *Hume and the Enlightenment: Essays Presented to Ernest Campbell Mossner* (1974), and the chapter on 'Early Writings' as published in *Adam Smith* (1982; with R. H. Campbell).

[1] Dugald Stewart referred to Smith's early interest in mathematics: 'Dr Maclaine of the Hague, who was a fellow-student of Mr Smith's at Glasgow, told me some years ago, that his favourite pursuits while at that University were mathematics and natural philosophy; and I remember to have heard my father remind him of a geometrical problem of considerable difficulty, about which he was occupied at the time when their acquaintance commenced, and which had been proposed to him as an exercise by the celebrated Dr Simson' (Stewart, I. 7).

contributions to early theories of biology. The work of men such as these was of profound importance, associated as it is with the introduction of the 'great chain' thesis and of those theories of 'transformism' that were being developed in the late 1740s and early 1750s. Such theories may well have affected the way in which research was conducted in other fields, and it has in fact been suggested that they were 'intimately related to the entrance of historicism into the European intellectual outlook'.[2] As Dugald Stewart pointed out in commenting on the 'Letter', 'The observations on the state of learning in Europe are written with ingenuity and elegance; but are chiefly interesting, as they shew the attention which the Author had given to the philosophy and literature of the Continent, at a period when they were not much studied in this island' (Stewart I. 25). Smith extended his list to include English writers such as Bacon and Boyle.

One of Smith's purposes was to contrast the 'genius' of France and England by reference to their different preferences. In literary merit, 'Imagination, genius and invention, seem to be the talents of the English; taste, judgement, propriety and order, of the French', while in natural philosophy 'all the great discoveries, which have not come from Italy or Germany, have been made in England. France has scarce produced any thing very considerable in that way' (Letter, 5). In a lengthy discussion of the *Encyclopédie*, Smith continued to drive home the distinction between the two nations in remarking that:

It seems to be the peculiar talent of the French nation, to arrange every subject in that natural and simple order, which carries the attention, without any effort, along with it. The English seem to have employed themselves entirely in inventing, and to have disdained the more inglorious but not less useful labour of arranging and methodizing their discoveries, and of expressing them in the most simple and natural manner. (Letter, 5).

'The original and inventive genius of the English' was also to be found in 'morals, metaphysics, and part of the abstract sciences' (Letter, 10). In one specific illustration, which occupies most of this section of the article, Smith points out, as a representative example of the way in

---

[2] By mid-century, work in biology had produced two main theses: the first, that of the 'great chain of being', the second, a theory of evolution which was associated with Diderot and Maupertuis. The latter had been influenced by Réaumur, and was one of the first avowed disciples of Newton in France; see Lovejoy (1936), Glass (1959) and Crocker (1959). In the same volume ('Buffon and the Problem of Species'), Lovejoy suggested that the 'Leibnitian calculus' which brought the 'notion of the continuum into fashion' was one of the forces that prepared men's minds for the concept of evolution. In the *Great Chain* (1936), Lovejoy pointed out that evolutionary theses were 'becoming familiar in very widely recognised writings before the middle of the eighteenth Century' and cited as examples Young's poem *Night Thoughts* (1742–4) and Mark Akenside's *The Pleasures of Imagination* (1744). Lovejoy also drew attention to the importance of Epicurean-inspired accounts of evolution in the third of his *Essays in the History of Ideas* (1948).

which original English ideas have been transported to France, how the principle in the second volume of Mandeville's *Fable of the Bees* 'has given occasion to the system of Mr Rousseau, in whom however the principles of the English author are softened, improved and embellished, and stript of all that tendency to corruption and licentiousness which have disgraced them in their original author' (Letter, 11). Or, later, ' the principles and ideas of the profligate Mandeville seems in him to have all the purity and sublimity of the morals of Plato, and to be only the true spirit of a republican carried a little too far' (Letter, 12).

But in many respects the most remarkable of Smith's essays on philosophical subjects are those concerned with the 'Principles which lead and direct Philosophical Enquiries' illustrated by reference to the Histories of Astronomy, Ancient Physics, and Ancient Logics and Meta-physics. The last two pieces are scarcely more than fragments, but the Astronomy is a truly remarkable piece of work which was composed before 1758, thus confirming the quite astonishing range and level of intellectual activity that Smith sustained in this period. Smith himself took the essay seriously, as is attested by a letter written to David Hume on the eve of his departure to London in 1773:

As I have left the care of all my literary papers to you, I must tell you that except those which I carry along with me there are none worth the publishing, but a fragment of a great work which contains a history of the Astronomical Systems that were successively in fashion down to the time of Des Cartes. Whether that might not be published as a fragment of an intended juvenile work, I leave entirely to your judgement; tho I begin to suspect myself that there is more refinement than solidity in some parts of it. This little work you will find in a thin folio paper book in my writing desk in my bedroom. All of the other loose papers which you will find either in that desk or within the glass folding doors of a bureau which stands in My bedroom together with about eighteen thin paper folio books which you will likewise find within the same glass folding doors I desire may be destroyed without examination. Unless I die very suddenly I shall take care that the Papers I carry with me shall be carefully sent to you. (*Corr.* 137).[3]

There are two broad features of 'The History of Astronomy' in particular which command attention. In the first place, Smith was concerned with the 'principles which lead and direct' philosophical (that is scientific) study. In this section Smith addressed himself to the psychological stimuli to study as they affect both the ordinary man and the philosopher or scientist, thus elaborating on one of the problems that had been touched upon in the lectures on didactic discourse as contained in the *Lectures on Rhetoric*. The second section illustrates these principles

[3] In the last year of Smith's life, Lord Loughborough wrote to David Douglas indicating that Smith had been engaged in 'correcting' the essay (*ASSP* 313).

by reference to 'The History of Astronomy' and provides us with a further example of philosophical or conjectural history. As Dugald Stewart observed:

The mathematical sciences, both pure and mixed, afford, in many of their branches, very favourable subjects for theoretical history; and a very competent judge, the late M. D'Alembert, has recommended this arrangement of their elementary principles, which is founded on the natural succession of inventions and discoveries, as the best adapted for interesting the curiosity and exercising the genius of students. The same author points out as a model a passage in Montucla's History of Mathematics, where an attempt is made to exhibit the gradual progress of philosophical speculation, from the first conclusions suggested by a general survey of the heavens, to the doctrines of Copernicus. It is somewhat remarkable, that a theoretical history of this very science (in which we have, perhaps, a better opportunity than in any other instance whatever, of comparing the natural advances of the mind with the actual succession of hypothetical systems) was one of Mr Smith's earliest compositions, and is one of the very small number of his manuscripts which he did not destroy before his death. (Stewart, II. 49).[4]

While it is important to remember that others were working in the same general field, it seems unlikely that Montucla could have influenced Smith since the former's History of Mathematics first appeared in 1758.

THE ASSUMPTIONS

The psychological assumptions that Smith employed in the essays under discussion are fundamentally simple: he assumes that man is endowed with certain faculties and propensities such as reason, reflection, and imagination, and that he is motivated by a desire to acquire or to avoid the sources of pleasure or pain.[5] In this context pleasure relates to a state of the imagination, or 'What may be called the natural state of the mind, the state in which we are neither elated nor dejected, the state of sedateness, tranquility, and composure . . .' (Imitative Arts, II. 20). Such a state of mind may be attained where we contemplate objects that satisfy certain conditions, conditions that are quite well expressed in a passage from the *Theory of Moral Sentiments*, where it is pointed out that 'Connected variety, in which each new appearance seems to be introduced by

---

[4] A further example is provided by the economist A. R. J. Turgot in 'A Discourse at the Sorbonne', which was delivered in December 1750. This work, entitled 'A Philosophical Review of the Successive Advances of the Human Mind', appears in Meek (1973) and was previously noted by Stephens (1895: 164).

[5] For comment see Moscovici (1956); Becker (1961–2); Thomson (1965); Lindgren (1969); Campbell (1971: pt I); Lindgren (1973: ch. 1); Wightman (1975), and Foley (1977: ch. 2).

what went before it, and in which all the adjoining parts seem to have some natural relation to one another, is more agreeable than a disjointed and disorderly assemblage of unconnected objects' (*TMS* V. 1. 9). We derive a feeling of pleasure, Smith argues, from the contemplation of relation, similarity, or order; from a certain association of ideas. As Smith remarked, in a passage that clearly shows the influence of Hume,

When two objects, however unlike, have often been observed to follow each other, and have constantly presented themselves to the senses in that order, they come to be so connected together in the fancy, that the idea of the one seems, of its own accord, to call up and introduce that of the other. If the objects are still observed to succeed each other as before, this connection, or, as it has been called, this association of their ideas, becomes stricter and stricter, and the habit of the imagination to pass from the conception of the one to that of the other, grows more and more rivetted and confirmed . (Astronomy, II. 7).[6]

He added that under such circumstances 'There is no break, no stop, no gap, no interval. The ideas excited by so coherent a chain of things seem, as it were, to float through the mind of their own accord, without obliging it to exert itself, or to make any effort in order to pass from one of them to another' (II. 7).[7] While emphasizing that the imagination *is* indolent, and that men find no stimulus to thought under such conditions, Smith struck a more original note in going on to argue that this would not be the case where the 'appearances' were in any way irregular or unexpected:

But if this customary connection be interrupted, if one or more objects appear in an order quite different from that to which the imagination has been accustomed, and for which it is prepared, the contrary of all this happens. We are at first surprised by the unexpectedness of the new appearance, and when that momentary emotion is over, we still wonder how it came to occur in that place. (Astronomy, II. 8).[8]

In other words, we feel *surprise* when some object (or number of objects) is drawn to our attention which does not fall into an expected pattern; a sentiment quickly followed by that of *wonder*, where the latter is defined in these terms: 'The stop which is thereby given to the career of the imagination, the difficulty which it finds in passing along such

---

[6] Cf. Hume, 'Of the Connection and Association of Ideas' (*THN* I. i. 4. For comment on the relationship between Smith and Hume, see Raphael (1977).

[7] A similar passage occurs in *TMS* (V. 1. 2), where it is stated that 'When two objects have frequently been seen together, the imagination acquires a habit of passing easily from the one to the other.' Smith emphasizes that it is 'the unusualness alone of the succession' that occasions some stop or interruption in the 'progress of the imagination' (Astronomy, II. 11). J. R. Lindgren in particular has emphasized that Smith's interest in conventional knowledge has often been underestimated (1973: 6).

[8] Cf. Hume: 'There is commonly an astonishment attending everything extraordinary' (*THN* I. iii. 14. 24).

disjointed objects, and the feeling of something like a gap or interval betwixt them, constitute the whole essence of this emotion' (Astronomy, II. 9). Wonder, in short, involves a source of pain (or disutility), a feeling of discomfort which gives rise to 'uncertainty and anxious curiosity', to 'giddiness and confusion', which can in extreme cases lead to mental derangement. Smith made much of this point, to the extent of illustrating his case by reference to the rational individual 'all at once transported alive to some other planet, where nature was governed by laws quite different from those which take place here' (II. 10).

The response to this situation then involves the pursuit of some explanation, with a view to relieving the mind of a state of disequilibrium; a natural psychological reaction designed to eliminate the sense of wonder by providing some appropriate ordering of the phenomena in question. As Smith put it, the imagination 'endeavours to find out something which may fill up the gap, which, like a bridge, may so far at least unite those seemingly distant objects, as to render the passage of the thought betwixt them smooth, and natural, and easy' (II. 8).[9]

Before going further, it may be useful to elaborate on Smith's argument by reviewing the two types or species that he used to illustrate the procedures above described. In the first case, Smith considered objects where the link was provided by similarity rather than relation, suggesting in this instance that we would naturally tend to place such objects in certain 'sorts' or 'categories'.[10] 'It is evident that the mind takes pleasure in observing the resemblances that are discoverable betwixt different objects. It is by means of such observations that it endeavours to arrange and methodise all its ideas, and to reduce them into proper classes and assortments' (II. 1). He also added that we take pleasure in referring a particular object: 'to some species or class of things, with all of which it has a nearly exact resemblance; and though we often know no more about them than about it, yet we are apt to fancy that by being able to do so, we show ourselves to be better acquainted with it, and to have a more thorough insight into its nature' (II. 3).

---

[9] Smith makes a related point in *LRBL* (ii. 36), in remarking that: 'We should never leave any chasm or Gap in the thread of the narration, even though there are no remarkable events to fill up that space. The very notion of a gap makes us uneasy . . .' Similar points are made at ii. 196, 205–6. See ch. 1 above.

[10] Smith makes much of this point in his work on language, where it is pointed out that 'The different mental operations, of arrangement or classing, of comparison, and of abstraction, must all have been employed, before even the names of the different colours, the least metaphysical of all nouns adjective, could be instituted' (*Languages*, 7). Smith also refers to 'that love of analogy and similarity of sound, which is the foundation of by far the greater part of the rules of grammar' (16, 25). Similar arguments appear in the *LRBL* (i. v. 25). It is interesting to observe that Smith's main objection to Johnson's Dictionary related to a plan which struck him as insufficiently 'grammatical'. 'The different significations of a word are indeed collected; but they are seldom digested into general classes' (*Edinburgh Review*, 1755–6).

Now, so long as the individual objects that are presented to us fall within some existing classification, the mind can retain a position of equilibrium. 'But when something quite new and singular is presented, we feel ourselves incapable of doing this. The memory cannot, from all its stores, cast up any image that nearly resembles this strange appearance' (II. 3). Hence the feelings of surprise and wonder, together with the response to them, as the individual struggles to connect the object in question to some known class of objects. The observer 'must find out some resemblance or other, before he can get rid of that Wonder, that uncertainty and anxious curiosity excited by its singular appearance, and by its dissimilitude with all the objects he had hitherto observed' (II. 4). Smith also made the interesting point that new appearances would often lead to new classifications, and that 'The further we advance in knowledge and experience, the greater number of divisions and subdivisions of those Genera and Species we are both inclined and obliged to make' (II. 2).

In the second case, Smith argued that when some relation of things strikes the observer as unusual he will also be subject to the emotions above mentioned. For example:

The motion of a small piece of iron along a plain table is in itself no extraordinary object, yet the person who first saw it begin, without any visible impulse, in consequence of the motion of a loadstone at some little distance from it, could not behold it without the most extreme Surprise; and when that momentary emotion was over, he would still wonder how it came to be conjoined to an event with which, according to the ordinary train of things, he could have so little suspected it to have any connection. (Astronomy, II. 6).

Once again the mind suffers a disturbance, and once again it responds by endeavouring to find some train of intermediate events that will satisfy the need for explanation.

Thus, when we observe the motion of the iron, in consequence of that of the loadstone, we gaze and hesitate, and feel a want of connection betwixt two events which follow one another in so unusual a train. But when, with Des Cartes, we imagine certain invisible effluvia to circulate round one of them, and by their repeated impulses to impel the other, both to move towards it, and to follow its motion, we fill up the interval betwixt them, we join them together by a sort of bridge, and thus take off that hesitation and difficulty which the imagination felt in passing from the one to the other. (Astronomy, II. 8).

The argument then proceeds along exactly similar lines to the previous case, although it may be useful to take this opportunity to emphasize two aspects of it. First, it will be noted that man is impelled to seek an explanation for observed appearances as a result of some subjective feeling of discomfort, and that the resulting explanation is therefore designed to meet some *psychological* need. Secondly, Smith argues that the explanation offered can satisfy the mind only if it is coherent, capable of accounting for observed appearances, and stated in terms of 'familiar' or plausible principles–requirements satisfied by the Cartesian argument above mentioned, since 'Motion after impulse is an order of succession with which of all things we are most familiar' (Astronomy, II. 8). It will be noted that, for a theory to be acceptable to the mind, it need not be 'true'.

Although the examples so far used are drawn from the reactions of the casual observer to the phenomena he contemplates, the main point of Smith's argument is to show that the philosopher or scientist is also subject to the same basic universal principles of human nature.[11] Indeed, from one point of view the main difference between the philosopher and the non-philosopher is to be found in the type and range of problems with which the two parties are concerned. For nature as a whole, Smith suggested, 'seems to abound with events which appear solitary and incoherent' and which therefore 'disturb the easy movement of the imagination' (II. 12). Under these circumstances, the philosopher feels the disutility involved in the sentiments of surprise and wonder, and reacts to them by endeavouring to find some explanation. As Smith puts it: 'Wonder, therefore, and not any expectation of advantage from its discoveries, is the first principle which prompts mankind to the study of Philosophy, of that science which pretends to lay open the concealed connections that unite the various appearances of nature' (III. 3).

Philosophy in all its forms, natural as well as moral, emerges as 'the science of the connecting principles of nature' (II. 12), with, as its ultimate end, 'the repose and tranquility of the imagination' (IV. 13). Although these motives are of universal relevance, the purposes of philosophy are made especially clear in Smith's discussion of astronomy, where he argues that the task of theory is to introduce 'order into this chaos of jarring and discordant appearances, to ally this tumult of the imagination, and to restore it, when it surveys the great revolutions of the universe, to that tone of tranquility and composure, which is both most agreeable in itself, and most suitable to its nature' (II. 12).

The similarities between the philosopher and the non-philosopher are therefore emphasized, although Smith did take considerable pains to bring out a number of important differences between them. For example, he pointed out that in any developed society philosophy would tend to emerge as a distinct trade like any other, and its practitioners as 'men of speculation, whose trade it is, not to do any thing, but to observe every thing; and who, upon that account, are often capable of combining together the powers of the most distant and

[11] As Campbell points out, the words 'philosophy' and 'science' were at this time used almost interchangeably (1971: 25).

dissimilar objects' (*WN* I. i. 9). As a result, certain differences emerge between the two groups, which 'arise not so much from nature, as from habit, custom, and education' (I. ii. 4). These differences involve knowledge, and powers of observation, and are important in that they permit the philosopher to perceive problems of connection to which the non-philosopher may be insensible. For example, Smith cites the case of artisans such as dyers, brewers, and distillers, who handle processes that strike the skilled observer as complex, but do not seem so to the artisan himself 'who has been for many years familiar with the consequences of all the operations of his art'. In a passage that may reflect his own experience, Smith records the amusement that such questions often excite, since the artisan 'cannot conceive what occasion there is for any connecting events to unite those appearances, which seem to him to succeed each other very naturally. It is their nature, he tells us, to follow one another in this order, and that accordingly they always do so' (Astronomy, II. 11). In the same way, Smith points out that men are so familiar with the conversion of food into flesh and bone that they do not (typically) think about the processes involved; that ordinary men 'have seldom had the curiosity to inquire by what process of intermediate events this change is brought about. Because the passage of the thought from the one object to the other is by custom become quite smooth and easy' (II. 11). Similarly, Smith remarked that 'After a little use and experience . . . looking-glasses cease to be wonders altogether; and even the ignorant become so familiar with them, as not to think that their effects require any explication' (Imitative Arts, I. 17). But, just as the botanist differs from the casual gardener, or the musician from his auditor, so the philosopher,

who has spent his whole life in the study of the connecting principles of nature, will often feel an interval betwixt two objects, which, to more careless observers, seem very strictly conjoined. By long attention to all the connections which have ever been presented to his observation, by having often compared them with one another, he has, like the musician, acquired, if one may say so, a nicer ear . . . (Astronomy, II. 11).

This is an important point, because it also means that the philosopher is less likely to be completely reassured by the 'explanations' offered (by himself or others) for jarring and discordant appearances and, therefore, that speculation need not cease after a generally acceptable solution has been found for a particular problem. Or, as Smith remarked in referring to the simpler problem of explaining the movement of scenery on a stage, 'In the Wonders of nature . . . it rarely happens that we can discover so clearly this connecting chain' (Astronomy, II. 9).

A second major difference between the philosopher and the non-philosopher is to be found in the *pleasure* to be derived, directly or indirectly, from the exercise of the intellectual faculties. Smith devoted a good deal of attention to the 'pleasing satisfaction of science', while indicating that it had many sources. He pointed out that, once we have succeeded in providing an acceptable and coherent account of some observed phenomena, the very existence of that explanation may heighten our appreciation of the 'appearances' themselves, thus representing a source of satisfaction in addition to that acquired from the explanation itself. In this way, for example, we may learn not only to understand, but also to admire a complex social structure once its 'hidden springs' have been exposed; we understand and thus admire the animal body once we know something of its structure; the theory of astronomy helps us to admire the heavens through presenting the 'theatre of nature' as a 'coherent, and therefore a more magnificent spectacle' (II. 12). Smith also adverted to the pleasure to be derived from effort of a philosophical kind, in suggesting that men 'pursue this study for its own sake, as an original pleasure or good in itself, without regarding its tendency to procure them the means of many other pleasures' (III. 3).[12]

We may therefore conclude that, if the principles of human nature are to be regarded as constant, the philosopher emerges as a very different creature from the unskillful spectator. Yet at the same time, Smith evidently believed that the popular reception of scientific work could have an important influence on its future course, in arguing: 'we observe, in general, that no system, how well soever in other respects supported, has ever been able to gain any general credit in the world, whose connecting principles were not such as were familiar to all mankind' (II. 12).[13]

THE ASTRONOMY

Most of the points just mentioned find further illustration in 'The History of Astronomy', where Smith reviewed four main systems of thought, not with a view to judging their 'absurdity or probability, their

---

[12] Cf. Hume: 'the pleasure of study consists chiefly in the action of the mind, and the exercise of the genius and understanding in the discovery or comprehension of any truth (*THN*, II. iii. 10. 6, 'Of Curiosity, or the Love of Truth'). Smith's old teacher, Francis Hutcheson, had also emphasized that we 'have delight in exercising our own rational, inventive and active powers; we are pleased to behold the like exercises in others, and the artful effects of them' (*System of Moral Philosophy*, 1755: II. 2). James Hutton also gave prominence to the theme: 'The proper object of science is truth, and the motive of it is pleasure' his (*Investigations of the Principles of Knowledge*, 1794: II. i. 4).

[13] Smith uses this point to explain why the 'chemical philosophy' had in all ages 'crept along in obscurity, and been so disregarded by the generality of mankind' (Astronomy, II. 12).

agreement or inconsistency with truth and reality', but rather with the intention of considering how far each of them was fitted to 'sooth(e) the imagination'–'that particular point of view which belongs to our subject' (Astronomy, II. 12). Looked at in this way, the analysis has a 'comparative' aspect, at least in so far as it is designed to show the extent to which each of the four systems reviewed actually did succeed in 'soothing' the imagination. But Smith goes further than his stated object in noting that the theories which he reviewed had followed each other in a certain sequence, and in exposing the causal links which, he felt, might explain that sequence.

The essence of Smith's argument would seem to be that each system at the time of its original statement satisfied the needs of the imagination, but that each was subject to a process of modification as new problems came to light, a process that eventually resulted in a degree of complexity which ultimately became unacceptable to the imagination. This in turn paves the way for a new kind of response—the production not just of a particular account, but of an alternative account (in this case of the heavens); a new thought-system, designed to explain the same problems as the first, at least in its most complex form, but in a different and more acceptable form.

From one point of view this is the classic pattern of cultural history; human activity released within a given environment ultimately causes a qualitative change in that environment—as illustrated, say, by the development of language or the transition from feudalism to the commercial stage (see Chapters 1 and 4). But there is a difference, partly because 'environment' here refers to a state of knowledge, and partly because the reactions of individuals are now described as self-conscious–that is, as deliberately designed to modify an existing thought-system or to replace it with a more acceptable alternative.

We may usefully illustrate the burden of Smith's argument by commenting on the rise, progress, and decline of the first great astronomical system, that of Concentric Spheres. As Smith presents the case, the first astronomers were faced with the need to explain the movements of three different types of object: Sun, Moon, and Stars. This was effected, he suggests, in terms of a theory of Solid Spheres, each one of which was given a circular but regular motion, for two reasons. First, he suggested that 'A circle, as the degree of its curvature is everywhere the same, is of all curve lines the simplest and the most easily conceived' (Astronomy, IV. 51). Secondly, he considered that 'The equality of their motions was another fundamental idea, which, in the same manner, and for the same reason, was supposed by all the founders of astronomical systems. For an equal motion can be more easily attended to, than one that is continually either accelerated or retarded' (IV. 52). In the first system, the sky was regarded as the roof of the universe, while the stars, being apparently static in respect of their relative positions, 'were naturally thought to have all the marks of being fixed, like so many gems, in the concave side of the firmament, and of being carried round by the diurnal revolutions of that solid body' (IV. 1).

Given this explanation, Smith argued, it was equally natural to explain the movements of the Sun and Moon in terms of a hypothesis of the same kind, thus rendering the 'theory of the heavens more uniform' than would otherwise have been the case. In this instance, since the Sun and Moon change their relative positions, each was given a sphere of its own, one inside the other (in order to account for the eclipse), and was supposed 'to be attached to the concave side of a solid and transparent body, by whose revolutions they were carried round the earth' (IV. 2). Additional spheres were subsequently added in order to account for the movement of the five planets or 'wandering stars', until a system emerged which represented the earth as 'self-balanced and suspended in the centre of the universe, surrounded by the elements of Air and Ether, and covered by eight polished and cristalline Spheres, each of which was distinguished by one or more beautiful and luminous bodies, and all of which revolved round their common centre, by varied, but by equable and proportionable motions' (IV. 5). As Smith pointed out, such a system of thought appealed to the imagination by apparently providing a coherent explanation of the 'different movements and effects already in reality performed', and connected, by simple and familiar processes, the 'grandest and most seemingly disjointed appearances in the heavens'. He added: 'If it gained the belief of mankind by its plausibility, it attracted their wonder and admiration; sentiments that still more confirmed their belief, by the novelty and beauty of that view of nature which it presented to the imagination' (IV. 5).[14]

Indeed, even if some contemporaries recognized that such a system did not account for all appearances, the degree of completeness was such that the generality of men would be tempted to 'slur over' (IV. 6) such problems. Smith went on to suggest that this beautiful and appealing construction of the intellect might 'have stood the examination of all ages, and have gone down triumphant to the remotest posterity', had there been 'no other bodies discoverable in the heavens' (IV. 4). But such bodies were discovered, and this, together with the fact that Eudoxus was not one of the 'generality of men', led to the need to modify the existing system, and to the addition of more spheres, as a means of accounting for changes in the relative positions of the planets. As a result, Eudoxus raised the total number of spheres to 27, Callippus to

---

[14] It is remarked in *TMS* (I. i. 4. 3) that 'approbation heightened by wonder and surprise, constitutes the sentiment which is properly called admiration'.

34, until Aristotle 'upon a yet more attentive observation' increased the number to 56.

In short, the existing, relatively simple, system of Eudoxus was gradually modified in order to meet the needs of the imagination when faced with new problems to be explained, until a situation was reached where the explanation offered actually violated the basic prerequisite of simplicity. As Smith put it: 'This system had now become as intricate and complex as those appearances themselves, which it had been invented to render uniform and coherent. The imagination, therefore, found itself but little relieved from that embarrassment, into which those appearances had thrown it, by so perplexed an account of things' (IV. 8). In consequence, another system was developed by Apollonius (subsequently refined by Hipparchus and Ptolemy) which distinguished between the 'real and apparent motion of the heavenly bodies' and which solved the problem of changes in relative position by supposing that 'the Sun and the other Planets revolved in circles, whose centres were very distant from the centre of the earth'.

At the same time, the adherents of this system attempted to account for the irregular movements of the planets: 'By supposing, that in the solidity of the Sphere of each of the Five Planets there was formed another little Sphere, called an Epicycle, which revolved round its own centre, at the same time that it was carried round the centre of the Earth by the revolution of the great Sphere, betwixt whose concave and convex sides it was inclosed' (IV. 10).

Once again, we face a system that was designed to 'introduce harmony and order into the mind's conception of the movements of those bodies', and which once again succeeded to a degree. However, the same argument is advanced: namely, that a gradual (and inevitable) process of modification to the system involved a progressive increase in its degree of complication, until a situation was reached where 'this imaginary machine, though, perhaps, more simple, and certainly better adapted to the phaenomena than the Fifty-six Planetary Spheres of Aristotle, was still too intricate and complex for the imagination to rest in it with complete tranquility and satisfaction' (IV. 19). Indeed, Smith argued that the situation became even more complex with the work done by the Schoolmen, and especially Purbach, who laboured to reconcile the Aristotelian doctrine of Solid Spheres with the later system of Eccentric Spheres and Epicycles in the form given it by Ptolemy. As Smith suggested, Purbach, 'as well as all those who had worked upon the same plan before him, by rendering this account of things more complex, rendered it still more embarrassing than it had been before' (IV. 25).

It will be observed that this illustration introduces a new element into Smith's discussion, namely, the attempt made not merely to explain observed events, but to find consistency between conflicting accounts of those events. But the (modified) system of Eccentric Spheres was to suffer the same fate as its predecessor, and for the same reason, being ultimately replaced by the Copernican. Indeed, Copernicus provides a good example of Smith's reliance on the role of the imagination, in that 'The confusion, in which the old hypothesis represented the motions of the heavenly bodies, was, he tells us, what first suggested to him the design of forming a new system, that these, the noblest works of nature, might no longer appear devoid of that harmony and proportion which discover themselves in her meanest productions' (IV. 28).

Like the system it was to replace, the Copernican managed to account for observed appearances, in the manner of a 'more simple machine' requiring 'fewer movements'. It represented 'the Sun, the great enlightener of the universe, whose body was alone larger than all the Planets taken together, as established immoveable in the centre, shedding light and heat on all the worlds that circulated around him in one uniform direction, but in longer or shorter periods, according to their different distances' (IV. 32). It was to prove an attractive hypothesis to some, not merely because of the beauty and simplicity of the system, but also because the novelty of the view of nature thus provided excited a certain feeling of wonder and surprise:

For, though it is the end of Philosophy, to ally that wonder, which either the unusual or seemingly disjointed appearances of nature excite, yet she never triumphs so much, as when, in order to connect together a few, in themselves, perhaps, inconsiderable objects, she has, if I may say so, created another constitution of things, more natural indeed, and such as the imagination can more easily attend to, but more new, more contrary to common opinion and expectation, than any of those appearances themselves. (Astronomy, IV. 33).

This was emphatically the case with a system that 'moved the earth from its Foundations, stopt the revolution of the Firmament, made the sun stand still'.

Yet at the same time, Smith argued that the system was by no means acceptable to all, or even to those who confined their attention to astronomical matters, the difficulty being that Corpernicus had invested the earth with a velocity that was 'unfamiliar', and ran counter to normal experience. The imagination, Smith suggested, tended to think of the earth as ponderous 'and even averse to motion' (Astronomy, IV. 38), and it was this difficulty that led to the formulation of the alternative system of Tycho Brahe–a system partly prompted by jealousy of Copernicus, but none the less a system to some extent compounded of that of the latter and of Ptolemy. In this system, 'the Earth continued to be, as in the old account, the immoveable center of the universe' (IV. 42). Smith added that Brahe's account was 'more complex and more incoherent than that of Copernicus. Such, however, was the difficulty that mankind felt in conceiving the motion of the Earth, that it long balanced the reputation of that otherwise more beautiful system' (IV. 43).

In other words, the coherence and simplicity of the Copernican system was qualified by the unfamiliarity of one of its central principles, a problem that was so important as to render a relatively complex account more acceptable than it could otherwise have been. Interestingly enough, Smith represents subsequent developments as involving an attempt to make the more elegant system (of Copernicus) acceptable to the imagination by removing the basic difficulty—that is, by providing a plausible explanation for the movement of the earth. In this connection, he argued that the astronomical work done by Kepler contributed to the completion of the system, while research on the problem of motion by Galileo had helped to remove some of the more telling objections to the idea of a moving earth. However, in terms of the general acceptance of the idea of the earth spinning at high velocity, Smith gave most emphasis to the work of Descartes, who had represented the planets as floating in an immense ocean of ether containing 'at all times, an infinite number of greater and smaller vortices, or circular streams' (IV. 62). Once the imagination accepted a hypothesis based on the familiar principle of motion after impulse, it was a short step to the elimination of the central difficulty, since 'it was quite agreeable to its usual habits to conceive' that the planets 'should follow the stream of this ocean, how rapid soever' (IV. 65). He added, in a significant passage, that under such circumstances 'the imaginations of mankind could no longer refuse themselves the pleasure of going along with so harmonious an account of things. The system of Tycho Brahe was every day less and less talked of, till at last it was forgotten altogether' (IV. 65).

Yet, as Smith went on to note, the modifications introduced by Descartes were not prompted by astronomical knowledge so much as by a desire to produce a plausible explanation for the Copernican thesis. Moreover, Smith noted that further observations, especially those of Cassini, supported the authority of laws first discovered by Kepler for which the Cartesian 'theory' could provide no explanation. Under such circumstances, the latter system, while it 'might continue to amuse the learned in other sciences . . . could no longer satisfy those that were skilled in Astronomy' (IV. 67).

The Copernican system, if apparently complete, was still cumbersome, and destined in due time to give way to yet another, capable of accounting more adequately for observed appearances, in terms of a smaller number of basic principles, and of successfully predicting their future movement. This was the system of Newton: 'a system whose parts are all more strictly connected together, than those of any other philosophical hypothesis. Allow his principle, the universality of gravity, and that it decreases as the squares of the distance increase, and all the appearances, which he joins together by it, necessarily follow' (IV. 76). Moreover, the basic principles involved could be regarded as familiar, since: 'The gravity of matter is, of all its qualities, after its inertness, that which is most familiar to us. . . . The law too, by which it is supposed to diminish as it recedes from its centre, is the same which takes place in all other qualities which are propagated in rays from a centre, in light, and in every thing else of the same kind' (IV. 76).

While Smith wrote with real enthusiasm about Newton's contribution and its current reception in France, he added a characteristic warning in stating that:

even we, while we have been endeavouring to represent all philosophical systems as mere inventions of the imagination, to connect together the otherwise disjointed and discordant phaenomena of nature, have insensibly been drawn in, to make use of language expressing the connecting principles of this one, as if they were the real chains which Nature makes use of to bind together her several operations. Can we wonder then, that it should have gained the general and complete approbation of mankind, and that it should now be considered, not as an attempt to connect in the imagination the phaenomena of the Heavens, but as the greatest discovery that ever was made by man, the discovery of an immense chain of the most important and sublime truths, all closely connected together, by one capital fact, of the reality of which we have daily experience. (Astronomy, IV. 76).

CONCLUSIONS

As noted earlier, Adam Smith had read D'Alembert's *Preliminary Discourse*, the first part of which is relevant for the student of Smith's essay.

The differences between the two men are obvious. Unlike Smith, D'Alembert argued that men would first seek useful knowledge and then, having developed techniques such as the mathematical, proceed to subjects such as astronomy, 'the study of which, next to the study of ourselves, is most worthy of our application because of the magnificent spectacle which it presents to us'. Yet at the same time there are interesting parallels, especially in respect of D'Alembert's emphasis on the imagination, which he defined as 'the talent of creating by imitating' and as a 'creative faculty'. He also adverted to the fact that the principles used in any form of explanation will be the more fertile the fewer they are in number, and added: 'in the hierarchy of our needs and of the objects of our passions, pleasure holds one of the highest places, and curiosity is a need for anyone who knows how to think, especially when this restless desire is enlivened with a sort of vexation at not being able to satisfy itself entirely'.[15]

Smith's discussion of the principles that lead and direct philosophical inquiries also concentrates, as we have seen, on the needs of the imagination–on broadly psychological needs–so that, as Richard Olson has recently pointed out:

The great significance of Smith's doctrine is that since it measures the value of philosophical systems solely in relation to their satisfaction of the human craving for order, it sets up a human rather than an absolute or natural standard for science, and it leaves all science essentially hypothetical. Furthermore, Smith implied that unceasing change rather than permanence must be the characteristic of philosophy.(Olson 1975: 123).[16]

It was exactly this perspective that led Smith to utter the warning that was quoted in the conclusion of the preceding section and that led him to take the bold and novel step, in an age dominated by Newton, of reminding his readers that the content of that system was not necessarily 'true'.

While this position does seem accurately to express the burden of Smith's argument, three points might be suggested by way of qualification. First, the argument of 'The History of Astronomy' could be taken to imply that, once the nature of intellectual activity is understood, it may become possible to control its subjective elements.[17] Secondly, it should be recalled that Smith did not claim an exclusive role for the sentiments of surprise, wonder, and admiration, but rather asserted that the role fulfilled by them was 'of far wider extent that we should be apt upon a careless view to imagine'. Thirdly, it is worth remarking that, while Smith regarded all intellectual constructions as products of the imagination and designed to meet its needs, he also indicated that there were differences between the natural and moral sciences arising from the contrasting problems of verification. As he put the point in *The Theory of Moral Sentiments*,

A system of natural philosophy may appear very plausible, and be for a long time very generally received in the world, and yet have no foundation in nature, nor any sort of resemblance to the truth. The vortices of Des Cartes were regarded by a very ingenious nation, for near a century together, as a most satisfactory account of the revolutions of the heavenly bodies. Yet it has been

---

[15] *The Preliminary Discourse to the Encyclopedia of Diderot*, translated by R. N. Schwab (1963: 16).

[16] The hypothetical element in Smith's thought was also emphasized by Moscovici (1956). For an interesting comparison, see Kuhn (1962: 169).

[17] Given the importance of such elements, it is interesting to note that C. West Churchman should have unwittingly suggested a new role for the 'impartial spectator' as expounded in the *Theory of Moral Sentiments* in observing that 'no observation can become objective unless the observer is also observed objectively' (Churchman 1971: 150; ch. 7).

demonstrated, to the conviction of all mankind, that these pretended causes of those wonderful effects, not only do not actually exist, but are utterly impossible, and if they did exist, could produce no such effects as are ascribed to them. But it is otherwise with systems of moral philosophy, and an author who pretends to account for the origin of our moral sentiments, cannot deceive us so grossly, nor depart so very far from all resemblance to the truth. (*TMS VII. ii.* 4. 14).[18]

Yet Smith had earlier remarked that some philosophers, notably mathematicians, 'are frequently very indifferent' about the reception they may meet with from the public, enjoying as they do the 'most perfect assurance, both of the truth and of the importance of their discoveries'. He added:

The great work of Sir Isaac Newton, his *Mathematical Principles of Natural Philosophy*, I have been told, was for several years neglected by the public. The tranquillity of that great man, it is probable, never suffered, upon that account, the interruption of a single quarter of an hour. Natural philosophers, in their independency upon the public opinion, approach nearly to mathematicians, and, in their judgments concerning the merit of their own discoveries and observations, enjoy some degree of the same security and tranquillity. (TMS III. 2. 20).

But there can be no doubt that Smith did as a matter of fact draw attention to the importance of the 'subjective side of science',[19] both in emphasizing the role of the imagination when reviewing the basic principles of human nature and in illustrating the working of these principles by reference to the history of astronomy. Thus, for example, when speaking of the introduction of the ingenious 'equalizing circle' in the system of eccentric spheres, he noted that 'Nothing can more evidently show, how much the repose and tranquillity of the imagination is the ultimate end of philosophy' (Astronomy, IV. 13) than this device, and later he commented on the ease with which 'the learned give up the evidence of their senses to preserve the coherence of the ideas of their imagination' (IV. 35). In the same way, he emphasized the pleasure to be derived from simplicity, order, and coherence and indicated that, because men find beauty to be a source of pleasure, they may unwittingly give the products of the intellect a form that satisfies purely aesthetic criteria.[20] Hence the Newtonian 'method' as described in the *Lectures on Rhetoric and Belles Lettres* may be used *because* it is 'more ingenious and for that reason more engaging' than any other. In the same vein, it is interesting to note that Smith should have referred to a

---

[18] Cf. D'Alembert: 'If one judges impartially those vortices which today seem almost ridiculous, it will be agreed, I daresay, that at that time nothing better could be imagined' (*Preliminary Discourse*, ed. Schawb (1963): 79).

[19] Mitroff (1974); see especially ch. 7, 'Objectivity in Science'.

[20] In 'Imitative Arts' (II. 30), Smith likened the pleasure to be derived from the contemplation of a great system of thought to that acquired from listening to a 'well composed concerto of instrumental music' (see ch. 1 above).

propensity, natural to all men, 'to account for all appearances from as few principles as possible' *(TMS vii. ii. 2. 14)*.

It was also in this connection that he recognized the importance of analogy in suggesting that philosophers, in attempting to explain unusual 'appearances', often did so in terms of knowledge gained in unrelated fields.[21] In this way, Smith suggested that reasoning by analogy might affect the nature of the work done, in the manner of the Pythagoreans who first studied arithmetic and then explained 'all things by the properties of numbers'–or the modern physician who 'lately gave a system of moral philosophy upon the principles of his own art' (Astronomy, ii. 12). 'In the same manner also, others have written parallels of painting and poetry, of poetry and music, of music and architecture, of beauty and virtue, of all the fine arts; systems which have universally owed their origin to the lucubrations of those who were acquainted with the one art, but ignorant of the other.' Indeed, Smith went further in noting that in some cases the analogy chosen could become not just a source of 'ingenious similitudes' but even 'the great hinge upon which every thing turned' (ii. 12).

This then leads on to the discussion of another side of the problem, again illustrated by 'The History of Astronomy', namely that different types of philosopher may produce conflicting accounts of the same thing, without any real possibility of communication. Smith noted that at a certain stage of development the Cartesian system 'might continue to amuse the learned in other sciences, but could no longer satisfy those that were skilled in Astronomy' (iv. 67); that the Copernican system had been adopted by astronomers even though inconsistent with the laws of physics as then known (iv. 35); that the system of eccentric spheres had been accepted by astronomers and mathematicians, but not by philosophers in general: 'Each party of them too, had . . . completed their peculiar system or theory of the universe, and no human consideration could then have induced them to give up any part of it' (iv. 18). As this implies, there may be a certain unwillingness to accept ideas formulated in a particular way, and even resistance to the reception of new ones, as a result of certain 'prejudices'. Some of these are obvious: for example, the 'natural prejudices of the imagination' (iv. 52) which partly explained the original resistance to the idea of a moving earth. Others are more complex, especially those that Smith described as prejudices of

---

[21] Cf. Meek (1973: 46) 'The senses constitute the unique source of our ideas: the whole power of our mental faculties is restricted to combining the ideas which they have received from the senses: hardly ever can they form combinations of ideas of which the senses do not provide them with a model. Hence that almost irresistible tendency to judge of what one does not know by what one knows; hence those delusive analogies to which the first men in their immaturity abandoned themselves with such little thought.'

education.[22] Smith pointed out that resistance to the acceptance of Copernican ideas was partly explained by the 'Peripatetic Philosophy, the only philosophy then known in the world' (IV. 38), and added, with reference to the system as a whole, that 'When it appeared in the world, it was almost universally disapproved of, by the learned as well as by the ignorant. The natural prejudices of sense confirmed by education, prevailed too much with both, to allow them to give it a fair examination' (IV. 35). In the same way, the immediate followers of Copernicus were held to have faced objections that were 'necessarily connected with that way of conceiving things, which then prevailed universally in the learned world' (IV. 39).

Smith also noted the constraint on the development of new knowledge represented by reverence for the past (IV. 20), and made a good deal of national prejudice in the 'Letter to the Authors of the Edinburgh Review', observing that the attachment of French philosophers to the system of Descartes had for a time 'retarded and incumbered the real advancement of the science of nature' (para. 5).

All of these points relate to the role of the subjective in science and suggest difficulties with regard to both the formulation and the communication of ideas. It is therefore particularly interesting to observe, as a matter of fact, that points such as those made by Smith have often been 'confirmed' by those whose business it has been to examine the *behaviour* of philosophers (in Smith's sense of the term).[23] It is equally striking that T. S. Kuhn's work on scientific revolutions should also have emphasized the problems of communication that exist (Smith's 'prejudices of education') between the proponents of conflicting systems. It is also noteworthy that another writer interested in a branch of applied mathematics (such 'favourable subjects for theoretical history') should have reached conclusions on the basis of developments in the 1930s which are, in appearance, even closer to Smith's than those of Kuhn. In his *Years of High Theory*, G. L. S. Shackle drew attention to the thinker's search for 'consistency, coherence, order', and, while noting that 'Theoretical advance can spring only from theoretical crises', also confirmed that the 'scientist's ultimate aim is to see everything as an illustration of a very few basic principles incapable of further unification'. There is an even more dramatic parallel in the following statement, which could well serve as a summary of Smith's whole thesis:

---

[22] Cf. Hume (*THN* I. iii. x. 1): 'But though education be disclaimed by philosophy, as a fallacious ground of assent to any opinion, it prevails nevertheless in the world, and is the cause why all systems are apt to be rejected at first as new and unusual.'

[23] It is for example one of the themes of Israel Scheffler's study, *Science and Subjectivity*, that the orthodox or 'standard view' of science is 'coming increasingly under fundamental attack' (Scheffler 1967: 7).

The chief service rendered by a theory is the setting of minds at rest. So long as we have a satisfying conceptual structure, a model or a taxonomy which provides for the filing of all facts in a scheme of order, we are absolved from the tiresome labour of thought, and the uneasy consciousness of mystery and a threatening unknown ... Theory serves deep needs of the human spirit: it subordinates nature to man, imposes a beautiful simplicity on the unbearable multiplicity of fact, gives comfort in the face of the unknown and the unexperienced, stops the teasing of mystery and doubt which, though salutary and life-preserving, is uncomfortable, so that we seek by theory to sort out the justified from the unjustified fear. Theories by their nature and purpose, their role of administering to 'a good state of mind', are things to be held and cherished. Theories are altered or discarded only when they fail us. (Shackle 1967: 288–9).

But perhaps the most striking parallel is with Karl Popper's *Logic of Scientific Discovery* (1959), in so far as he emphasized the importance of psychological elements and rejected the role commonly ascribed to the 'legendary method' of science; the 'myth of a scientific method that starts from observation and experiment and then proceeds to theories' (1972 edn.: 279). Smith's emphasis on the principles that lead and direct philosophical inquiries may also seem to imply that the Newtonian method as described by Colin MacLaurin cannot explain the origin of theories.

Points such as these may lend some support to Smith's assessment of the principles of human nature and to his belief that these principles were constant through time. It was of course this belief that made it possible to conceive of the moral sciences as being on a par with the natural, thus matching the achievements of Newton in this field. For Dugald Stewart, the application of this 'fundamental and leading idea' to the various branches of theoretical history was to become 'the peculiar glory of the latter half of the eighteenth century, and forms a characteristic feature in its philosophy'. (Stewart 1858: i. 70). What Smith does is to leave the reader of these essays in some doubt as to wherein exactly that glory is to be found: in a contribution to knowledge or to the composure of the imagination, or both.

Smith's essay on 'The History of Astronomy' may also reveal a great deal about his own drives as a thinker. His marked predilection for systematic argument may be especially significant in that this feature of his thought may be found in all his major works—ethics, jurisprudence, and economics—and in the interconnections that link them. In all these cases, Smith revealed his appreciation of the 'beauty of a systematical arrangement of different observations connected by a few common principles' (*WN*, v. i. f. 25). It is to these areas of Smith's thought that we now turn.

REFERENCES

Becker, J. F., (1961–2), 'Adam Smith's Theory of Social Science', *Southern Economic Journal*, 28.

Brown, Maurice (1988), *Adam Smith's Economics* (London).

Campbell, T. D. (1971), *Adam Smith's Science of Morals* (London).

Churchman, C. W. (1971), *The Design of Enquiring Systems* (New York).

Cremaschi, Sergio (1989),'Adam Smith: Sceptical Newtonianism, Disenchanted Republicanism, and the Birth of Social Science', in *Knowledge and Politics: Case Studies in the Relationship between Epistemology and Political Philosophy*, ed. M. Dascal and O. Gruengard (London).

Crocker, L. G. (1959), 'Diderot and Eighteenth Century Transformism', in *Forerunners of Darwin*, ed. B. Glass, O. Temkin, and W. L. Strauss, (Baltimore).

Foley, V. (1977), *The Social Physics of Adam Smith* (Durham, NC).

Glass, B. (1959), 'Maupertuis, Pioneer of Genetics and Evolution', in *Forerunners of Darwin*, ed. B. Glass, O. Temkin, and W. L. Strauss, (Baltimore).

Kuhn, T. S. (1962), *The Structure of Scientific Revolutions* (Chicago).

Lindgren, J. R. (1969), 'Adam Smith's Theory of Enquiry', *Journal of Political Economy*, 77.

———(1973), *The Social Philosophy of Adam Smith* (The Hague).

Longuet-Higgins, C. (1992), 'The History of Astronomy: A Twentieth Century View', in P. Jones, and A.S. Skinner, (eds.), *Adam Smith Reviewed* (Edinburgh).

Lovejoy, A. O. (1936), *The Great Chain of Being* (Cambridge, Mass.).

———(1948), *Essays in the History of Ideas* (Baltimore).

Meek, R. L. (1973), *Turgot on Progress, Sociology and Economics* (Cambridge).

Mitroff, I. I. (1974), *The Subjective Side of Science* (New York).

———and Mason, R. O. (1974), 'On Evaluating the Scientific Contribution of the Apollo Moon Missions via Information Theory: A Study of the Scientist–Scientist Relationship', *Management Science*, 20.

Moscovici, S. (1956), 'A propos de quelque travaux d'Adam Smith sur l'histoire et la philosophie des sciences', *Revue d'Histoire des Sciences et de leur applications*, 9.

Olson, R. (1975), *Scottish Philosophy and British Physics, 1750–1880* (Princeton/London, 1975).

Popper, K. (1959), *The Logic of Scientific Discovery* (London, 2nd edn., 1972).

Rae, J. (1895), *Life of Adam Smith* (London).

Raphael, D.D., 'The Impartial Spectator', in *EAS*.

———(1977), 'The True old Humean Philosophy and its Influence on Adam Smith', in *David Hume: Bicentenary Papers*, ed. S. P. Morice, (Edinburgh).

Redman, D. A. (1991), *Economics and the Philosophy of Science* (Oxford, 1991).

———(1995), 'Adam Smith and Isaac Newton', *Scottish Journal of Political Economy*, 40.

Scheffler, I. (1967), *Science and Subjectivity* (Indianapolis).

Schwab, R. N. (trans.)(1963), *The Preliminary Discourse to the Encyclopedia of Diderot* (Library of Liberal Arts).

Shackle, G. L. S. (1967), *The Years of High Theory* (Cambridge).

Shepherd, C. M. (1982), 'Newtonianism in Scottish Universities in the Seventeenth Century', in R. H. Campbell and A. S. Skinner (eds.), *The Origins and Nature of the Scottish Enlightenment* (Edinburgh).

Skinner, A. S. (1979), *A System of Social Sciences: Papers Relating to Adam Smith* (Oxford).

Stephens, W. W. (1895), *The Life and Writings of Turgot* (London).

Stewart, D. (1858), *Works*, ed. W. Hamilton (Edinburgh).

Thomson, H. F. (1965). 'Adam Smith's Philosophy of Science', in *Quarterly Journal of Economics*, 79.

Wightman, W. P. D. (1975), 'Adam Smith and the History of Ideas', in *EAS*.

Part II

3
Moral Philosophy and Civil Society: Ethics and Self-Love

Smith's work on moral philosophy has a great deal in common with that of other members of the Scottish School[1] and especially with Hutcheson and Hume. Smith described his teacher as the 'never to be forgotten' Hutcheson, and it is well known that he regarded Hume as 'by far the most illustrious philosopher and historian of the present age' (*WN*, v. i. g. 3). The three have much in common, in respect of methodology, their interest in human nature, and the attempt made by each to elucidate the features of those bonds that make life in society possible.

HISTORICAL INTRODUCTION

In part vii of *The Theory of Moral Sentiments*, Smith commented at length on the work of other thinkers who had addressed the two main questions which he considered to fall within the proper province of the moral philosopher:

First, wherein does virtue consist? Or what is the tone of temper, and tenour of conduct, which constitutes the excellent and praise-worthy character which is the natural object of esteem, honour, and approbation? And, secondly, by what power or faculty in the mind is it, that this character, whatever it be, is recommended to us? Or in other words, how and by what means does it come to pass, that the mind prefers one tenour of conduct to another, denominates the one right and the other wrong; considers the one as the object of approbation, honour, and reward, and the other of blame, censure, and punishment?. (*TMS* vii. i. 2).

In each case, Smith showed that a number of authors had attained some part of the truth, while rejecting other features of their work—a characteristic of his commentary which suggests that he set out to

---

This chapter is based on an essay in Skinner (1979) but also draws on a different version which was published in Jones and Skinner (1992).

[1] Commentaries that I have found most helpful include: Morrow (1928); Macfie (1967); Stewart (ii), and T. D. Campbell (1971); see also Lindgren (1973), and Foley (1977). McCosh (1875) remains a helpful commentary on the School as a whole. The introduction to the Glasgow edn. of the *TMS* has valuable sections on the influence of Stoic philosophy and on Smith's relation to contemporary thinkers.

resolve the 'jarring and discordant' appearances which the different philosophical traditions seemed to present, and that his own work had a synthetic character at least to some extent. We may take the two questions in turn.

In dealing with the first question, Smith suggested that all previous systems of moral philosophy could be placed within three broad categories (itself an interesting example of his capacity for classification) according as they found virtue to consist in propriety, prudence, or benevolence: 'Besides these three, it is scarce possible to imagine that any other account can be given of the nature of virtue' (*TMS* vii. ii. 4).

By *propriety* Smith means something very like a kind of balance, and he groups under this head all those systems that found virtue to consist not in the exercise of any particular 'affection' or disposition 'but in the proper government and direction of all our affections, which may be either virtuous or vicious according to the objects which they pursue, and the degree of vehemence with which they pursue them' (vii. ii. 1). Plato, Aristotle, and Zeno are cited as the main classical examples, Clarke, Woollaston, and particularly Shaftesbury[2] as the most important modern authors. However, although Smith did agree that propriety is an essential ingredient in every virtuous action, he also felt that it is not always the sole ingredient (vii. ii. 1. 50). Moreover, the existing systems were rejected on the ground that they did not provide 'any precise or distinct measure by which this fitness or propriety of affection can be ascertained or judged of' (vii. ii. 1. 49), and also because, in emphasizing the importance of a balance of expression, they gave undue weight to the 'awful' and respectable virtues, such as self-command, at the expense of milder but no less important virtues, such as benevolence.

The chief representative of the second system, which found virtue in *prudence*, is Epicurus, who, Smith suggests, rested his case on two main propositions: first, that in 'ease of body . . .and in security or tranquility of mind, consisted . . . the most perfect state of human nature' (vii. ii. 2. 7) and, second, that bodily pleasure and pain were the sole ultimate objects of natural desire or aversion. In this system temperance can be seen as prudence with regard to pleasure, and justice as prudence with regard to tranquility—a state of mind that is attainable only in so far as our actions do not cause others to regard us with indignation.

Smith accepted that 'Our success or disappointment in our undertakings must very much depend upon the good or bad opinion which is commonly entertained of us, and upon the general disposition of those

---

[2] Samuel Clarke, *Discourse of Natural Religion* (7th edn., 1728); William Wollaston, *Religion of Nature Delineated* (1724); Anthony Ashley Cooper, 3rd Earl of Shaftesbury, 'Inquiry Concerning Virtue', in *Characteristics of Men, Manners, Opinions, Times* (1711).

we live with, either to assist or to oppose us' (vii. ii. 2. 13). But at the same time, he rejected the general tenor of the approach partly on the ground that it gave too little emphasis to the 'soft and amiable' virtues, in celebrating the importance of 'the habits of caution, vigilance and sobriety'. Smith also rejected an argument that seemed to suggest that an action could be regarded as virtuous only in so far as it contributes to some end, thus echoing the earlier criticism (*TMS* iv) of Hume's alleged reliance on utility as the basis of approbation.

The third system was that which found virtue in *benevolence*. Here the main classical examples were the Eclectics, the more important modern authorities being Ralph Cudworth and especially Francis Hutcheson, who, 'of all the patrons of this system, ancient or modern . . . was undoubtedly, beyond all comparison, the most acute, the most distinct, the most philosophical, and what is of the greatest consequence of all, the soberest and most judicious' (vii. 3. 3).[3] Smith clearly recognized that benevolence was a virtue, while pointing out that the defect of Hutcheson's account lay in its emphasis on the amiable virtues and in the corresponding neglect of the awful and respectable virtue of self-command (featured by the proponents of propriety) and of the inferior virtues of prudence and temperance (as noted by Epicurus and his followers).[4]

In dealing with the second major question, Smith once again concentrated on three main groups: namely, those who approached the study of the 'means by which' judgements are formed by emphasizing the importance of self-love, reason, or sentiment. As in the previous case, a threefold classification is used, although here there is one important difference: in dealing with the initial problem, Smith considered three distinct approaches ancient *and* modern to the definition of virtue, whereas in the second case he deals with different theories which follow each other in sequence. Hobbes is described as representative of the first 'school' and is alleged to have adopted the position that 'The very ideas of laudable and blamable, ought to be the same with those of obedience and disobedience' (*TMS* vii. iii. 2. 1). Cudworth is cited as representative of the second school, that is, as one who found the origin of judgement in reason, and who was critical of writers, such as Hobbes, who 'affirm justice and injustice to be only by law and not by nature'.

Smith accepted Cudworth's contention that law could not be the source of the distinction between right and wrong, while rejecting the

---

[3] Ralph Cudworth, *A Treatise Concerning Eternal and Immutable Morality* (1731); Francis Hutcheson, *Inquiry Concerning Moral Good and Evil*, iii. i; Raphael (1969: 328).

[4] Hutcheson also argued that self-interested activities did not command moral approbation as distinct from approval—a theme that is developed at some length in his *System of Moral Philosophy* (1755: bk i. ch.8).

view that our first perceptions can be attributed to reason. As Smith noted: 'If virtue . . . in every particular instance, necessarily pleases for its own sake, and if vice as certainly displeases the mind, it cannot be reason, but immediate sense and feeling, which . . . reconciles us to the one, and alienates us from the other' (vII. iii. 2. 7). In this Smith followed the lead of Hutcheson, who had the merit, as he was quick to admit, 'of being the first who distinguished with any degree of precision in what respect all moral distinctions may be said to arise from reason, and in what respect they are founded upon 'immediate sense and feeling' (vII. iii. 2. 9). In fact, Hutcheson placed most stress on the latter, ascribing our capacity to distinguish between right and wrong to a special (internal) sense, the moral sense, which was held to be analogous to (external) senses such as sight, sound, or taste. To this Hutcheson added a sense of honour and of shame, a public sense, and a sympathetic sense, 'by which, when we apprehend the state of others, our hearts naturally have a fellow feeling with them'.[5] Smith thoroughly approved of Hutcheson's emphasis on immediate sense and feeling in regard to moral judgement, to the extent of stating that:

In his illustrations upon the moral sense he has explained this so fully, and, in my opinion, so unanswerably that, if any controversy is still kept up about this subject, I can impute it to nothing, but either to inattention to what that gentleman has written, or to a superstitious attachment to certain forms of expression, a weakness not very uncommon among the learned. (*TMS* vII. iii. 2. 9).

Yet at the same time Smith rejected the basis of Hutcheson's explanation of the moral sentiments:

Against every account of the principle of approbation, which makes it depend upon a peculiar sentiment, distinct from every other, I would object; that it is strange that this sentiment, which Providence undoubtedly intended to be the governing principle of human nature, should hitherto have been so little taken notice of, as not to have got a name in any language. The word moral sense is of very late formation, and cannot yet be considered as making part of the English tongue. (*TMS* vII. iii. 3. 15).

Hume (whose doctrines are reviewed in *TMS* IV) was in broad agreement with Hutcheson at least to the extent of agreeing with the latter that 'Morality, according to your Opinion as well as mine, is determin'd merely by Sentiment'.[6] At the same time, Hume comes even closer to the position later adopted by Smith in suggesting that we must begin with 'the nature and force of sympathy' (*THN* III. i. 7), a force that allows the observer to approve or disapprove, for example, of situations that

[5] Ibid. i. 19; see generally bk I. chs. 2 and 3.
[6] Quoted in Smith (1966: 20). There is an interesting account of the influence of Hutcheson on Hume at pp. 12–20.

contribute to feelings of pleasure or pain as expressed by another party. We may derive some satisfaction from the pleasure manifested by the possessor of an object: 'Here the object . . . pleases only by its tendency to produce a certain effect. That effect is the pleasure or advantage of some other person. Now, the pleasure of a stranger for whom we have no friendship, pleases us only by sympathy.' (*THN* III. i. 8). Hume went on to argue that the same principle (utility) explains our feelings with regard to beauty, as well as morals, enabling Smith to conclude that 'No qualities of the mind, he observes, are approved of as virtuous, but such as are useful or agreeable either to the person himself or to others; and no qualities are disapproved of as vicious but such as have a contrary tendency' (*TMS* IV. 2. 3).

In fact, there was a good deal in Hume's position that Smith could accept, such as his emphasis on sentiment rather than reason, and (again in the manner of Hutcheson) the importance that he ascribed to sympathy and fellow-feeling. Smith also agreed that perception of the 'utility' of an action added a 'new beauty' to it, and accepted Hume's argument that moral judgement was typically disinterested. But he rejected Hume's reliance on utility as the *initial* ground of approval, partly because 'the sentiment of approbation always involves in it a sense of propriety quite distinct from the perception of utility' (IV. 2. 5).

Smith's achievement was to produce a system of thought that answered both of the major questions with which moral philosophy was concerned, by taking a route that differed from the one chosen by his two Scottish contemporaries, even if it did follow the same general direction. In handling the question as to the means by which the mind forms judgements concerning what is fit to be done or to be avoided, Smith greatly developed mechanisms, already mentioned by Hutcheson and Hume, that involved the use of sympathy, reason, imagination, and the concept of the observer or spectator. At the same time, he succeeded in producing an argument that gave due weight to the amiable virtues such as benevolence, to the 'awful' virtues such as self-command, and to the 'inferior' virtues such as prudence—thus including certain elements from each of the three traditions that he had initially identified. It may be of more importance to note that Smith developed his argument in the context of a discussion which was designed to explain the manner in which men erect effective barriers against their own passions, by natural, as distinct from artificial, means—thus bringing us to the main theme of this chapter.[7]

---

[7] Cf. Goldberg (1959: 11–13).

THE PROCESS OF MORAL JUDGEMENT

Smith's own theory might well be regarded as an extensive commentary on the text: 'There is no virtue without propriety, and wherever there is propriety some degree of approbation is due. But . . . though propriety is an essential ingredient in every virtuous action, it is not always the sole ingredient' (*TMS* vii. ii. 1. 50). In expounding on this text, Smith first explains what is meant by the concept of propriety before going on to draw a distinction between propriety and virtue, and propriety and merit. In fulfilling these tasks, he first considers actions or expressions of feeling that do not have consequences for others, then proceeds to examine the more complex case where a judgement has to be formed with regard both to the actions of the agent and the reactions of the subject. We may take these in turn.

On Smith's argument, the process by which we distinguish between objects of approval or disapproval involves a complex of abilities and propensities that include sympathy, imagination, reason, and reflection. To begin with, he states that man is possessed of a certain 'fellow-feeling': 'How selfish soever man may be supposed, there are evidently some principles in his nature, which interest him in the fortune of others, and render their happiness necessary to him, though he derives nothing from it except the pleasure of seeing it' (i. i. 1. 1). This fellow-feeling, or interest in the fortune of others, permits us to feel joy or sorrow as it were on their behalf, and to form a judgement as to whether or not the circumstances faced by an individual contribute to a state of pleasure or of pain. An expression of sympathy (broadly defined) for another person thus involves an act of reflection and imagination on the part of the observer or spectator, in the sense that we can form a judgement with respect to the situation faced by another person only 'by changing places in the fancy' with him.

The question of *propriety* becomes relevant when we go beyond the consideration of the circumstances facing the subject, to examine the extent to which his actions or 'affections' (i.e. expressions of feeling) are appropriate to the conditions prevailing or to the objects they seek to attain. Smith thus defined propriety or impropriety as consisting in 'the suitableness or unsuitableness, in the proportion or disproportion which the affection seems to bear to the cause or object which excites it' (i. i. 3. 6).

Given the principles so far established, it follows that, where the spectator of another man's conduct seeks to form an opinion as to its propriety, he must 'bring home to himself' both the circumstances and the 'affections' of the person judged. As before, Smith argued that such a judgement on the part of the spectator must involve an effort of the imagination, since 'When we judge in this manner of any affection, as proportioned or disproportioned to the cause which excites it, it is scarce possible that we should make use of any other rule or canon but the correspondent affection in ourselves' (I. i. 3. 9).

Now this argument means that the actions of all men are judged by the real spectator of their conduct, and that, 'When the original passions of the person principally concerned are in perfect concord with the sympathetic emotions of the spectator, they necessarily appear to this last just and proper' (I. i. 3. 1). The argument in fact raises two distinct but connected problems, affecting the person judged and the person who judges. In the first place, it is evident that the actual, or real, spectator can 'enter into' the situation of another person only to a limited degree, the problem being that we have 'no immediate experience of what other men feel'. As Smith pointed out: 'Mankind, though naturally sympathetic, never conceives, for what has befallen another, that degree of passion which naturally animates the person principally concerned' (I. i. 4. 7). It was in recognition of this point that Smith went on to argue that the *degree* to which the spectator can 'enter into' the feelings of the subject can involve a virtue—the 'soft and amiable' virtue of sensibility or humanity.

Secondly, it is evident that, if the reactions of the spectator provide the means by which the conduct of others is judged, and if the spectator has no immediate experience of what other men feel, then it follows that an action that is considered to be 'proper' by the spectator must involve an element of restraint on the part of the agent. In other words, the person judged *of* can attain the agreement, and thus the approval, of the spectator only 'by lowering his passion to that pitch, in which the spectators are capable of going along with him. He must flatten, if I may be allowed to say so, the sharpness of its natural tone, in order to reduce it to harmony and concord with the emotions of those who are about him' (I. i. 4. 7).

It thus follows that, before actions or expressions of feeling can be approved of by the spectator, an element of restraint must be present, a certain mediocrity of expression with which Smith associated the 'awful and respectable' virtue of self-command.[8] In this way Smith made due allowance for both sets of virtues, and in so doing illustrated what he meant by saying that propriety was an essential, but not the sole, ingredient of virtue. As he noted, 'the virtues of sensibility and self-command are not apprehended to consist in the ordinary, but in the uncommon degrees of those qualities' (I. i. 5. 6). There is, in short, a considerable difference between those qualities and actions that deserve

---

[8] Ralph Anspach (1972) has recently emphasized the pleasure to be derived from 'role-switching' as described above and from the process of attaining a concordance of view between subject and observer.

to be admired and celebrated, and those that simply deserve to be approved of' (ɪ. i. 5. 7):

In cases of this kind, when we are determining the degree of blame or applause which seems due to any action, we very frequently make use of two different standards. The first is the idea of complete propriety and perfection ... The second is the idea of that degree of proximity or distance from this complete perfection, which the actions of the greater part of men commonly arrive at. Whatever goes beyond this degree, how far soever it may be removed from absolute perfection, seems to deserve applause; and whatever falls short of it, to deserve blame. (*TMS* ɪ. i. 5. 9).

Smith went on to observe that the *point of propriety*, that is 'the degree of any passion which the spectator approves of', is 'differently situated in different passions'; and that the point of propriety stands high in the case of those passions where

the immediate feeling or sensation is more or less agreeable to the person principally concerned: and that, on the contrary, the passions which the spectator is least disposed to sympathize with, and in which, upon that account, the point of propriety may be said to stand low, are those of which the immediate feeling or sensation is more or less disagreeable, or even painful, to the person principally concerned. This general rule, so far as I have been able to observe, admits not of a single exception. (*TMS* vɪ. iii. 14).

Thus, for example, the disposition 'to the affections which tend to unite men in society—to humanity, kindness, natural affections—are more apt to offend by their defect than their excess', while 'the disposition to the affections which drive men from one another, and which tend, as it were, to break the bands of human society; the disposition to anger, hatred, envy, malice, revenge; is, on the contrary, much more apt to offend by its excess than by its defect' (*TMS* vɪ. iii. 16).

The latter points serve to introduce the second side of Smith's account, namely, his interest in the judgement of an action not merely in relation to the 'cause or object which excites it' but also in relation to the end proposed or the effects produced. In this connection, Smith argued that the *merit* or *demerit* of an action would depend on the beneficial or hurtful effects it tended to produce, and that judgement in such cases would involve framing an opinion about the propriety of the action of the agent and of the reaction of the subject. More specifically, Smith argued that our sense of the merit of an action 'seems to be a compounded sentiment, and to be made up of two distinct emotions; a direct sympathy with the sentiments of the agent, and an indirect sympathy with the gratitude of those who receive the benefit of his actions' (ɪɪ. i. 5. 2). It then follows that 'In the same manner as our sense of the impropriety of conduct arises from a want of sympathy, or from a direct antipathy to the affections and motives of the agent, so our sense of its demerit arises from what I shall here . . . call an indirect sympathy with the resentment of the sufferer' (II. i. 5. 4).

Smith emphasizes two points that derive from this argument. He argues, first, that our estimate of the merit or demerit of an action must be linked to our understanding of the *motives* of the agent and not merely of its consequences. 'We do not . . . thoroughly and heartily sympathize with the gratitude of one man towards another, merely because this other has been the cause of his good fortune, unless he has been the cause of it from motives which we entirely go along with' (II. i. 4. 1). Nor, he points out, can we sympathize entirely with the resentment that one man feels for another 'unless he has been the cause of it from motives which we cannot enter into'.

Secondly, Smith argues that actions that are judged to have the quality of 'merit' dispose us to *reward*, by virtue of our fellow-feeling with both the agent and the subject;

But when to the hurtfulness of the action is joined the impropriety of the affection from whence it proceeds, when our heart rejects with abhorrence, all fellow-feeling with the motives of the agent, we then heartily and entirely sympathize with the resentment of the sufferer. Such actions seem then to deserve, and, if I may say so, to call aloud for, a proportionable punishment; and we entirely enter into, and thereby approve of, that resentment which prompts to inflict it. (*TMS* II. i. 4. 4).

It will be evident that Smith's argument is in large measure designed to explain the manner in which we form judgements as to the propriety or merit of actions taken by ourselves or others, and that such judgements always have a 'social' reference. Or, as Smith put it,

Were it possible that a human creature could grow up to manhood in some solitary place, without any communication with his own species, he could no more think of his own character, of the propriety or demerit of his own sentiments and conduct, of the beauty or deformity of his own mind, than of the beauty or deformity of his own face. . . . Bring him into society, and he is immediately provided with the mirror which he wanted before. (*TMS* III. 1. 3).

The basic point is that individuals react to the images thus presented in a way which suggests that they are important to them; it is for this reason that we seek a certain mediocrity of expression in our affections and to conform to the different 'points of propriety' that are associated with the 'social' and 'unsocial' passions. As Smith said, 'Without the restraint which this principle imposes, every passion would, upon most occasions, rush headlong, if I may say so, to its own gratification' (*TMS* VI. concl. 2). Yet at the same time, Smith observed that this general disposition may be insufficient of itself to secure adequate levels of control over our passions or expressions of feeling, for reasons that are connected with the basic mechanisms whose deployment enables us to form judgements.[9]

In the case of the actual or real spectator, it is evident that the accuracy of judgement must be a function of the information available, and that information with respect to the feelings of a person external to him can never be complete. Smith's point is that we can generally acquire a level of information which is at least sufficient to permit us to arrive at a considered judgement, when contemplating the observed circumstances of an individual or his reaction to them. But at the same time, there is evidently one area where it is particularly difficult to get access to the necessary information, namely, that relating to the *motives* that prompt a person to act in a particular way. This is obviously an important problem, given Smith's contention that knowledge of motive is essential to the decision as to whether or not an action partakes of any degree of merit or demerit. Smith formally recognized the point in the discussion of justice when noting that men typically judge 'by the event and not by the design', observing that in this lay some advantage: 'That necessary rule of justice . . . that men in this life are liable to punishment for their actions only, not for their designs and intentions, is founded upon this salutary and useful irregularity in human sentiments concerning merit or demerit, which at first sight appears so absurd and unaccountable' (II. iii. 3. 2). Yet at the same time, it is evident that, while this 'irregularity' may be useful in one sense, in another it may have a contrary tendency in that it constitutes a 'great discouragement' to virtue. The problem thus raised was in fact solved in Smith's model by the use of an additional hypothesis, namely, that individuals desire not only the approval of their fellows but also to be worthy of that approval; as Smith expressed it:

this desire of the approbation, and this aversion to the disapprobation of his brethren, would not alone have rendered him fit for that society for which he was made. Nature, accordingly, has endowed him, not only with a desire of being approved of, but with a desire of being what ought to be approved of; or of being what he himself approves of in other men. The first desire could only have made him wish to appear to be fit for society. The second was necessary in order to render him anxious to be really fit. (*TMS* III. 2. 7).

Hence the importance in later editions of Smith's theory of the 'supposed' or 'ideal' spectator of our own conduct (that is, that spectator who is always well informed with regard to our own motives). As Smith put it,

We can never survey our own sentiments and motives, we can never form any judgement concerning them, unless we remove ourselves, as it were, from our

[9] For specialized comment on the 'spectator' concept, see especially the articles by T. D. Campbell and D. D. Raphael in *EAS*.

own natural station, and endeavour to view them as at a certain distance from us. But we can do this in no other way than by endeavouring to view them with the eyes of other people, or as other people are likely to view them' (*TMS* III. 1. 2).

Hence too the argument that we are really subject to two sources of judgement—that of the 'man without' and that of 'the man within'. 'The jurisdiction of the man without, is founded altogether in the desire of actual praise, and in the aversion to actual blame. The jurisdiction of the man within, is founded altogether in the desire of praise-worthiness, and in the aversion to blame-worthiness' (*TMS* III. 2. 32). It is not then the 'soft power of humanity' that ensures that we impose some control over our own passions or activities, but 'reason, principle, conscience, the inhabitant of the breast, the man within, the great judge and arbiter of our conduct' (III. 3. 4). It is moreover the expected judgement of the ideal spectator which supports us in the path of virtue when our just rewards are denied us, or our title to them unknown. Thus,

The man who is conscious to himself that he has exactly observed those measures of conduct which experience informs him are generally agreeable, reflects with satisfaction on the propriety of his own behaviour. . . . He looks back upon every part of it with pleasure and approbation, and though mankind should never be acquainted with what he has done, he regards himself, not so much according to the light in which they actually regard him, as according to that in which they would regard him if they were better informed. (*TMS* III. 2. 5).

While this argument seems to suggest that the judgement of the man within is independent of the man without, Smith took notice of two qualifications. First, he observed that the judgements of the man within could be 'so much shaken' in their steadiness and firmness 'that their natural effect, in securing the tranquility of the mind, is frequently in a great measure destroyed' (*TMS* III. 2. 32). Secondly, he noted that the judgement of the man within, 'the abstract and ideal spectator of our sentiments and conduct, requires often to be awakened and put in mind of his duty, by the presence of the real spectator' (III. 3. 38).

SELF-LOVE, APPROBATION, AND CONSTRAINT: THE PROBLEM OF IMPARTIALITY

Having introduced the concept of the ideal spectator, which 'solves' the problem of knowledge, Smith still confronted a problem that arises from the fact that man is presented as an active and frequently self-regarding being, who is unlikely to be wholly impartial in judging his own actions. There are two stages in the argument.

1. Self-Love and Approbation

Self-love represents a thread which runs through the argument we have just considered and reflects Smith's recognition of the point that 'Every man, as the Stoics used to say is first and principally recommended to his own care' (*TMS* VI. ii. 1. 1). Smith objected to Francis Hutcheson's assertion that self-love was a principle 'which could never be virtuous in any degree or in any direction' (VII. ii. 3. 12). Against this position, Smith argued that a regard 'to our own private happiness and interest . . . appear upon many occasions very laudable principles of action' (VII. ii. 3. 16), and added that,

whatever may be the case with the Deity, so imperfect a creature as man, the support of whose existence requires so many things external to him, must often act from many other motives. The condition of human nature were peculiarly hard, if those affections, which, by the very nature of our being, ought frequently to influence our conduct, could upon no occasion appear virtuous, or deserve esteem and commendation from anybody. (*TMS* VII. ii. 3. 18).

Major applications of Smith's psychological assumptions are to be found in his treatment of questions which are often explicitly economic in character.[10] To begin with, Smith addressed the issue of utility or the sources of satisfaction which are attainable by virtue of man's command over resources. In *The Wealth of Nations*, for example, he drew attention to the fact that beauty and scarcity help to explain the value we place upon commodities such as the precious metals or stones: 'The demand for the precious stones arises altogether from their beauty. They are of no use, but as ornaments; and the merit of their beauty is greatly enhanced by their scarcity' (*WN*, I. xi. c. 32).[11] The argument builds upon that of the *Lectures on Jurisprudence*, where Smith drew attention to the 'taste of beauty, which consists chiefly in the three following particulars, proper variety, easy connexion, and simple order' and elaborated on the significance of qualities such as colour and imitation.[12] He summarized the argument in the following statement:

These qualities, which are the ground of preference and which give occasion to pleasure and pain, are the cause of many insignificant demands which we by no means stand in need of. The whole industry of human life is employed, not in procuring the supply of our three humble necessities, food, cloaths, and lodging,

---

[10] Recent articles which explore the links between the *TMS* and the economic work include W. F. Campbell (1967); Evensky (1987), and Gee (1968). Others that bear directly upon the argument include Anspach (1972), Coase (1976); Danner (1976); Gramp (1948), Hollander (1977), and see especially Oakley (1994).

[11] Smith stated the famous paradox of value in *WN* I. iv. 13. For comment, see n. 31 to ch. iv in the Glasgow edn.

[12] See also Smith's essay, 'Of the Nature of that Imitation which takes place in what are called the Imitative Arts', in *EPS*.

but in procuring the convenience of it according to the nicety and delicacy of our taste. To improve and multiply the materials which are the principal objects of our necessities, gives occasion to all the variety of the arts. (*LJ*(B) 209).

But the argument was stated most fully in *The Theory of Moral Sentiments*, part IV, and especially in chapter 1, which is entitled 'Of the Beauty which the Appearance of Utility Bestows upon all the Productions of Art, and of the Extensive Influence of this Species of Beauty'. In this chapter Smith accepted Hume's suggestion that the utility of any object 'pleases the master by perpetually suggesting to him the pleasure or conveniency which it is fitted to promote . . .The spectator enters by sympathy into the sentiments of the master, and necessarily views the object under the same agreeable aspect' (*TMS* IV. 1. 2). But Smith felt that the point could be further developed:

But that this fitness, this happy contrivance of any production of art, should often be more valued, than the very end for which it was intended; and that the exact adjustment of the means for attaining any conveniency or pleasure, should frequently be more regarded, than that very conveniency or pleasure, in the attainment of which their whole merit would seem to consist, has not, so far as I know, been yet taken notice of by any body (*TMS* IV. 1. 3).

As the editors of the *Moral Sentiments* have observed, Smith 'sets great store by this observation not only for its originality but also because it forms a link, in his view, between ethics and political economy'.

There are two links with the economic analysis that may be noted here. First, Smith uses the argument further to explain the demand for commodities or for 'conveniences' (*TMS* IV. i. 6). Secondly, he employs the argument to illustrate the point that: 'Power and riches appear then to be, what they are, enormous and operose machines contrived to produce a few trifling conveniencies to the body, consisting of springs the most nice and delicate' (IV. 1. 8).

Smith went on to make two points, both of which are associated with the argument developed thus far. He suggests that the 'rich' have an important function with regard to the distribution of the product. In a passage that contains a notable reference to the invisible hand, Smith remarked that:

The homely and vulgar proverb, that the eye is larger than the belly, never was more fully verified than with regard to him. The capacity of his stomach bears no proportion to the immensity of his desires, and will receive no more than that of the meanest peasant. The rest he is obliged to distribute among those, who prepare, in the nicest manner, that little which he himself makes use of . . . They consume little more than the poor, and in spite of their natural selfishness and rapacity, tho' they mean only their own convenience, tho the sole end which they propose from the labour of all the thousands whom they employ, be the gratification of their own vain and insatiable desires, they divide with the poor the produce of all their improvements. They are led by an invisible hand to make nearly the same distribution of the necessaries of life, which would have been made, had the earth been divided into equal portions among all its inhabitants, and thus without intending it, without knowing it, advance the interest of the society, and afford means to the multiplication of the species. (*TMS* iv. 1. 10).

It should also be noted that Smith attached great importance to the point that the active pursuit of riches and of the imagined conveniences of wealth is a self-sustaining process which involves a deception, in the sense that realized satisfaction rarely equals that which had been expected. He added:

It is well that nature imposes upon us in this manner. It is this deception which rouses and keeps in continual motion the industry of mankind. It is this which first prompted them to cultivate the ground, to build houses, to found cities and commonwealths, and to invent and improve all the sciences and arts, which ennoble and embellish human life, which have entirely changed the whole face of the globe, have turned the rude forests of nature into agreeable and fertile plains, and made the trackless and barren ocean a new fund of subsistence, and the great high road of communication to the different nations of the earth. The earth, by these labours of mankind has been obliged to redouble her natural fertility, and to maintain a greater number of inhabitants. (*TMS* iv. 1. 10).

The references offered so far concentrate on motives that relate to *self* and trace some of their consequences. But Smith went further in arguing that the self-interested pursuit of wealth has a *social* reference. In this context, he contended that 'A person appears mean-spirited' who does not pursue the 'more extraordinary and important objects of self-interest', and he contrasted the 'man of dull regularity' with the 'man of enterprise', going on to remark that 'Those great objects of self-interest, of which the loss or acquisition quite changes the rank of the person, are the objects of the passion properly called ambition' (iii. 6. 7). He concluded:

it is chiefly from this regard to the sentiments of mankind, that we pursue riches and avoid poverty. For to what purpose is all the toil and bustle of this world? What is the end of avarice and ambition, of the pursuit of wealth, of power, and preheminence [sic]? Is it to supply the necessities of nature? The wages of the meanest labourer can supply them. . . . From whence, then, arises that emulation which runs through all the different ranks of men, and what are the advantages which we propose by that great purpose of human life which we call bettering our condition? To be observed, to be attended to, to be taken notice of with sympathy, complacency, and approbation, are all the advantages which we can propose to derive from it. It is the vanity, not the ease, or the pleasure, which interests us. But vanity is always founded upon the belief of our being the object of attention and approbation (*TMS* I. iii. 2. 1).[13]

The reference to vanity reminds us that *The Theory of Moral Sentiments* affords some interesting (if 'splenetic') perspectives on a basic human drive. In at least one place, Smith cited the case of the individual 'whom heaven in its anger has visited with ambition' (IV. I. 8). Elsewhere he drew attention, with ironic wit, to 'place, that great object which divides the wives of aldermen', as being the 'end of half the labours of human life' (I. iii. 2. 8).

2. Self-Love and Constraint

What is most interesting about the argument is the repeated emphasis on the point that the fundamental drive to better our condition is rooted in a desire to be approved of or at least to be admired. But Smith made a different if related point when he repeated that the individual in the pursuit of his own ends must take account of the interests and opinions of his fellows. If the individual

would act so that the impartial spectator may enter into the principles of his conduct, which is what of all things he has the greatest desire to do, he must, upon this, as upon all other occasions, humble the arrogance of his self-love, and bring it down to something which other men can go along with. They will indulge it so far as to allow him to be more anxious about, and to pursue with more earnest assiduity, his own happiness than that of any other person. Thus far, whenever they place themselves in his situation, they will readily go along with him. In the race for wealth, and honours, and preferments, he may run as hard as he can, and strain every nerve and every muscle, in order to outstrip all his competitors. But if he should justle, or throw down any of them, the indulgence of the spectators is entirely at an end. It is a violation of fair play, which they cannot admit of. (*TMS* II. ii. 2. 1).

Smith added a further gloss to the argument in suggesting that the objectives of actions based upon self-love could be realized by practising the virtue of prudence, which is essentially rational self-love. Yet, as he observed,

---

[13] Cf. *TMS* VI. i. 3: 'Though it is to supply the necessities and conveniencies of the body, that the advantages of external fortune are originally recommended to us, yet we cannot live long in the world without perceiving that the respect of our equals, our credit and rank in the society we live in, depend very much upon the degree in which we possess, or are supposed to possess, these advantages. The desire of becoming the proper objects of this respect, of deserving and obtaining this credit and rank among our equals, is, perhaps, the strongest of all our desires, and our anxiety to obtain the advantages of fortune is accordingly much more excited and irritated by this desire, than by that of supplying all the necessities and conveniences of the body, which are always very easily supplied.'

Prudence, . . . when directed merely to the care of the health, of the fortune, and of the rank and reputation of the individual, though it is regarded as a most respectable, and even, in some degree, as an amiable and agreeable quality, yet it is never conceived as one, either of the most endearing or of the most ennobling of virtues. It commands a certain cold esteem, but seems not entitled to any very ardent love or admiration. (*TMS* vi. i. 14).

A general desire to avoid being treated with 'indignation' or to be approved of by others is, however, unlikely to be sufficient to ensure an adequate level of control, especially given the assumption that men are above all active in the pursuit of their own interests. The basic problem that arises is that we may on particular occasions fail to judge our own actions with the required degree of impartiality. As Smith put it,

There are two different occasions upon which we examine our own conduct and endeavour to view it in the light in which the impartial spectator would view it: first, when we are about to act; and secondly, after we have acted. Our views are apt to be very partial in both cases; but they are apt to be most partial when it is of most importance that they should be otherwise. (*TMS* ii. 4. 2).

First, 'When we are about to act, the eagerness of passion will seldom allow us to consider what we are doing, with candour of an indifferent person' (*TMS* iii. 4. 3). Secondly, Smith noted that, while we are likely to be able to judge our own actions in a clearer light after the event, this is of little benefit to those who may suffer from them, and that even here 'It is so disagreeable to think ill of ourselves, that we often purposely turn away our view from those circumstances which might render that judgement unfavourable' (iii. 4. 4). The argument suggests that there will be many occasions on which men are unlikely to be able to form accurate judgements with respect to their own activities, and that they would therefore be unlikely to be able to impose on themselves the kind of restraint that the 'inhabitant within the breast' would normally recommend. As Smith remarked, in a passage that is likely to have attracted the attention of Robert Burns: 'this self-deceit, this fatal weakness of mankind, is the source of half the disorders of human life. If we saw ourselves in the light in which others see us, or in which they would see us if they knew all, a reformation would generally be unavoidable. We could not otherwise endure the sight' (iii. 4. 6).[14]

---

[14] Cf. Macfie (1967: 66), 'To a Louse':

> O wad some Power the giftie gie us
> To see oursels as ithers see us!
> It wad frae mony a blunder free us,
> An' foolish notion;
> What airs in dress an' gait wad lea'e us,
> An' ev'n devotion!

Smith's solution to the problem just identified involves no principle in addition to those already considered:

Nature . . . has not left this weakness, which is of so much importance, altogether without a remedy; nor has she abandoned us entirely to the delusions of self-love. Our continual observations upon the conduct of others, insensibly leads us to form to ourselves certain general rules concerning what is fit and proper either to be done or to be avoided. (*TMS* III. 4. 7).

In short, Smith suggests that our capacity to form judgements in particular cases permits us to frame general rules by the process of induction:

It is thus that the general rules of morality are formed. They are ultimately founded upon experience of what, in particular instances, our moral faculties, our natural sense of merit and propriety, approve, or disapprove of. We do not originally approve or condemn particular actions; because, upon examination, they appear to be agreeable or inconsistent with a certain general rule. The general rule, on the contrary, is formed, by finding from experience, that all actions of a certain kind, or circumstanced in a certain manner, are approved or disapproved of (*TMS* III. 4. 8).

Reason, it will be observed, is not the *original* source of the distinction between what is fit and proper to be done or to be avoided, but merely the means of elucidating general principles from a number of particular judgements, each one of which initially depends on the exercise of our moral sentiments.

These general principles or rules become, in turn, yardsticks against which we can judge our own conduct under all circumstances, and are thus of 'great use in correcting the misrepresentations of self-love concerning what is fit and proper to be done in our particular situation' (*TMS* III. 4. 12). Indeed, Smith went so far as to argue that, without a regard to general rules of behaviour, 'there is no man whose conduct can be much depended upon' (III. 5. 2).

Given that general rules may be formulated in the way described, Smith went on to argue that men would be disposed to obey them for two reasons. First, he re-affirmed that the voice which commands obedience is that of conscience or duty: 'a principle of the greatest consequence in human life, and the only principle by which the bulk of mankind are capable of directing their actions' (III. 5. 1). Secondly, it is suggested that our disposition to obey is 'still further enhanced by an opinion which is first impressed by nature, and afterwards confirmed by reasoning and philosophy, that those important rules of morality are the commands or laws of the Deity, who will finally reward the obedient, and punish the transgressors of their duty' (III. 5. 3). Smith added that: 'The sense of propriety too is here well supported by the strongest motives of self-interest. The idea that, however we may escape the observation of man, or be placed above the reach of human punishment, yet we are always acting under the eye, and exposed to the punishment of God . . . is a motive capable of restraining the most headlong passions' (III. 5. 12).

The rules of behaviour that Smith identifies vary in character. Those that are related to justice may often hinder us 'from hurting our neighbour'; they may only involve restraint from injury and may thus be fulfilled by 'sitting still and doing nothing', while other rules may embody a more comprehensive and positive guide. The essential difference that emerges is between the negative and positive virtues of justice and beneficence. As Smith put it,

The rules of justice may be compared to the rules of grammar; the rules of the other virtues to the rules which critics lay down for the attainment of what is sublime and elegant in composition. The one, are precise, accurate, and indispensable. The other, are loose, vague and indeterminate, and present us rather with a general idea of the perfection we ought to aim at, than afford us any certain and infallible directions for acquiring it. (*TMS* III. 6. 11).

It thus appears that, while both sets of rules are useful to society, they must each, taken separately, be compatible with different levels of social experience. Smith notes that, where men act with an eye to the positive rules of moral conduct, where their behaviour is marked by beneficence with regard to others (which is perfectly consistent with the pursuit of the objects of self-interest), then that society 'flourishes and is happy'. If on the other hand justice alone is the rule, then life in society may be characterized by nothing more than 'a mercenary exchange of good offices according to an agreed valuation' (*TMS* II. ii. 3. 2). Smith plainly regarded the first situation as the more typical and as involving a higher level of achievement than the second, although he was in no doubt as to which set of rules was the most important from the standpoint of social order:

Though Nature, therefore, exhorts mankind to acts of beneficence, by the pleasing consciousness of deserved reward, she has not thought it necessary to guard and enforce the practice of it by the terrors of merited punishment in case it should be neglected. It is the ornament which embellishes, not the foundation which supports the building, and which it was, therefore, sufficient to recommend, but by no means necessary to impose. Justice, on the contrary is the main pillar that upholds the whole edifice. If it is removed, the great, the immense fabric of human society, that fabric which to raise and support seems in this world, if I may say so, to have been the peculiar and darling care of Nature, must in a moment crumble into atoms. (*TMS* II. ii. 3. 4).

He continued:

Men, though naturally sympathetic, feel so little for another, with whom they have no particular connexion, in comparison of what they feel for themselves; the misery of one, who is merely their fellow creature, is of so little importance to them in comparison even of a small conveniency of their own; they have it so much in their power to hurt him, and may have so many temptations to do so, that if this principle did not stand up within them in his defence, and overawe them to a respect for his innocence, they would, like wild beasts, be at all times ready to fly upon him; and a man would enter an assembly of men as he enters a den of lions. (*TMS* II. ii. 3. 4).

Smith added a further condition in noting that:

As the violation of justice is what men will never submit to from one another, the public magistrate is under a necessity of employing the power of the commonwealth to enforce the practice of this virtue. Without this precaution, civil society would become a scene of bloodshed and disorder, every man revenging himself at his own hand whenever he fancied he was injured (*TMS* VII. iv. 36).

CONCLUSION

There are a number of points arising from the previous argument which are worth noting.

There is undoubtedly a certain elegance and ingenuity about the argument of *The Theory of Moral Sentiments* which is nowhere more obvious than in the way in which Smith made allowances for certain features of the three main types of theory that he reviewed (that is, those that emphasized prudence, benevolence, and self-command). The same features are evident in the way in which he developed concepts, often found in Hutcheson and Hume, when addressing himself to the question concerning the manner in which moral judgements are formed. But, undoubtedly, the best example is to be found in the structure of Smith's own argument. As we have seen, Smith initially considered the concepts of propriety and merit, leading to the development of the spectator thesis and to the proposition that men will typically conform to the judgement of the spectator because the opinions of their fellows are thought to be important. The problems that then emerge are that the judgement of the spectator must be well informed and impartial, with the first resolved by the introduction of the *ideal* spectator and the second by reference to general rules, or standards, of behaviour. The rules themselves emerge as the result of man's capacity to frame judgements in particular cases; they are obeyed because men are held to seek to be worthy of approval, while those that relate to justice are buttressed by the approval of punishment. In this way, Smith represents social order as a balance of opposed forces, where that balance, in the shape of general rules of conduct, is attained by natural as distinct from artificial means. Whatever may be thought of its content, and the argument is often very plausible, there can be little doubt that the model developed in *The Theory of Moral Sentiments* possesses a certain elegance and economy of expression.

The argument is also of interest in respect of the links it provides with two other aspects of Smith's system, namely the treatment of economics and of jurisprudence. As far as the economic analysis is concerned, some areas of interest are immediately obvious, most notably the attention given to the analysis of the sources of utility in *TMS* part IV, which throws important light on the issue of subjective preference as it affects the problem of the demand for commodities. Equally significant is the fact that it is in *The Theory of Moral Sentiments* rather than the *Wealth of Nations* that Smith fully explained the psychological drives which support man's desire to better his condition, an argument that is linked in turn to the pursuit of wealth, the desire for status, and the admiration of our fellows.

Equally important is Smith's analysis of self-interest and the need for constraint, where he established the point that men are led as if by an invisible hand to generate barriers against their unsocial passions by natural as distinct from artificial means. It will be noted that man's capacity to erect barriers against his self-interested passions, which is so essential for the orderly conduct of *economic* affairs, depends critically on his capacity for *moral* judgement.

In *The Theory of Moral Sentiments* Smith also described a wide range of human behaviour. He offers, for example, an account of the prudent, the vain, and the proud man (notably in part VI) but really intended to make the point that men typically manifest both selfish and other-regarding propensities (cf. Wilson 1976), which find expression as it were at one and the same time. The point is clearly made when Smith remarked that:

Concern for our own happiness recommends to us the virtue of prudence; concern for that of other people, the virtue of justice and benificence; of which, the one restrains us from hurting, the other prompts us to promote that happiness. Independent of any regard either to what are, or what ought to be, or to what upon a certain condition would be, the sentiments of other people, the first of these three virtues is originally recommended to us by our selfish, the other two by our benevolent affections (*TMS*, VI, conclusion).

The student of Smith's economics is thus reminded that our selfish affections represent only one facet of human nature. Even if it is useful to be able to concentrate on the self-regarding propensities in some spheres of economic analysis, Smith does not rule out the possibility that the butcher, the brewer, or the baker may, as men, be capable of acts of benevolence in ways that could affect the conduct of their economic affairs. (see also Chapter 7).

The ethics, in short, remind us that there is a moral dimension to Smith's treatment of (economic) man in society, a point that has enabled Donald Winch and others to argue that Smith's political economy is informed throughout by this consideration (cf. Winch 1978; Billet 1976; Teichgraeber 1986; and V. Brown 1994).

Smith stated, but did not develop, the interesting possibilities that are presented by this argument. But he did make use of related points in dealing effectively with an important problem of the time, namely Bernard Mandeville's 'licentious' doctrine (cf. W. F. Campbell 1967; Macfie 1967: 81). *The Fable of Bees*, first published in 1714, had advanced a doctrine that caused uproar. As F. B. Kaye remarked:

The *Fable* was twice presented by the Grand Jury as a public nuisance; ministers alike denounced it from the pulpit. The book, indeed, aroused positive consternation, ranging from the indignation of Bishop Berkeley to the horrified amazement of John Wesley, who protested that not even Voltaire could have said so much wickedness. In France the *Fable* was actually ordered to be burned by the common hangman. (Kaye 1924: p. cxvi).

Yet as Hume observed, 'To imagine, that the gratifying of any sense, or the indulging of any delicacy in meat, drink, or apparel, is of itself a vice, can never enter a head, that is not disordered by the frenzies of enthusiasm' (1955: 19; 1987: 268). Smith echoed his friend's calm assessment of Mandeville's position:

If the love of magnificence, a taste for the elegant arts and improvements of human life, for whatever is agreeable in dress, furniture or equipage, for architecture, statuary, painting and music, is to be regarded as luxury, sensuality and ostentation, even in those whose situation allows, without any inconveniency, the indulgence of these passions, it is certain that luxury, sensuality and ostentation are public benefits; since without these qualities upon which he thinks it proper to bestow such opprobious names, the arts of refinement could never find encouragement and must languish for want of employment. Some popular ascetic doctrines which had been current before his time, and which placed virtue in the entire extirpation and annihilation of all our passions, were the real foundation of this licentious system. It was easy for Dr Mandeville to prove, first, that this entire conquest never actually took place among men; and secondly, that, if it was to take place universally, it would be pernicious to society, by putting an end to all industry and commerce, and in a manner to the whole business of human life. By the first of these propositions he seemed to prove that there was no real virtue, and that what pretended to be such, was a mere cheat and imposition upon mankind; and by the second, that private vices were public benefits, since without them no society could prosper or flourish. (*TMS* vii. ii. 4. 12).

While admitting that Mandeville's argument 'could never have imposed upon so great a number of persons, nor have occasioned so great an alarm among those who are friends of better principles, had it not in some respects bordered upon the truth' (*TMS* vii. ii. 4. 14), Smith's point was a simple one: namely, that the pursuit of gratification is not inconsistent with *propriety*—and indeed should be consistent with it. It was an important point to make in the sense that the whole process of economic development was seen to be inextricably linked with the natural and insatiable wants of man, a thesis that was central to the explanation of growth in the eighteenth century and in respect of which it was necessary to defend the high moral ground which Mandeville's attack had threatened.

A second link emerges in connection with Smith's treatment of private and public law in the *Lectures on Jurisprudence*. As we have seen, Smith's analysis of general rules of behaviour suggests that they emerge in part as a result of our capacity to form judgements concerning what is fit and proper to be done or to be avoided on particular occasions. Smith suggests that his account of the way in which we arrive at judgements is of universal validity. But rules must be regarded as being based upon experience, and thus may vary between different societies at the same point in time and in the same society at different points in time. In this way Smith managed to remain within the framework of Montesquieu's emphasis on the variability of human experience, and drew from Edmund Burke the perceptive comment that 'A theory like yours founded on the Nature of man, which is always the same, will last, when those that are founded on his opinions, which are always changing, will and must be forgotten.'[15]

Variations in standards or patterns of behaviour were recognized by Smith to be important. In commenting on the role of custom and fashion, he observed that their effects 'upon the moral sentiments of mankind, are inconsiderable, in comparison of those which they give occasion to in some other cases; and it is not concerning the general style of character and behaviour, that those principles produce the greatest perversion of judgement, but concerning the propriety or impropriety of particular usages' (*TMS* v. 2. 12). And yet, he continued, particular usages could be of great significance, in that custom 'is capable of establishing, as lawful and blameless, particular actions, which shock the plainest principles of right and wrong' (v. 2. 14). In this connection Smith cited as an extreme example the classical practice of exposing children—a practice once based on necessity but which was still in force long after the circumstances which had first given occasion to it were no more.

In fact, Smith gave a good deal of attention to one particular set of rules, namely those relating to justice, and noted that 'Every system of positive law may be regarded as a more or less imperfect attempt towards a system of natural jurisprudence, or towards an enumeration

---

[15] Edmund Burke, addressed to Smith, dated Westminster, 10 Sept. 1759 (*Corr.* 38).

of the particular rules of justice' (VII. iv. 36). At the same time, he observed that 'the interest of the government; sometimes the interest of particular orders of men who tyrannize the government, warp the positive laws of the country from what natural justice would prescribe', thus ensuring that 'Systems of positive law . . . though they deserve the greatest authority, as the records of the sentiments of mankind in different ages and nations . . . can never be regarded as accurate systems of the rules of natural justice' (VII. iv. 36).

The argument points in two directions, only one of which is examined here. First, Smith believed that, despite variations in accepted patterns of behaviour or in the content of general rules, common elements could be found as a consequence of studies of a comparative kind. He clearly believed that studies of jurisprudence, on the model of Grotius, of what 'were the natural rules of justice independent of all positive institutions' (VII. iv. 37), could and should be undertaken. Indeed, he announced his intention to write such a book in the conclusion to the first edition of his work on ethics. Secondly, Smith was profoundly interested in the *causes* of variation in patterns of behaviour.

Central to the argument is Smith's deployment of the now-famous four stages of society: hunting, pasture, agriculture, and commerce. Smith used these distinct socio-economic stages in the *Lectures on Jurisprudence* in addressing the subjects of private and of public law. In the first case, where the link with the analysis of *The Theory of Moral Sentiments* is most direct, he considered man's rights as a member of the family, as an individual, and as a citizen. In particular, he traced the historical changes that had taken place in the laws governing property to changes in the mode of subsistence, and later extended his coverage to include voluntary transference, servitudes, pledges, contract, and delinquency. In the following chapter, however, the focus will be more upon the associated treatment of the history of civil society and upon Smith's examination of the emergence of the 'present establishments' in Europe—economic, social, and political—in the context of his treatment of public (or constitutional) law.

REFERENCES

Anspach, R. (1972), 'The Implications of the *Theory of Moral Sentiments* for Adam Smith's Economic Thought', *History of Political Economy*, 4; reprinted in Wood (1983: i. 438).

Billet, L. (1976), 'The Just Economy: The Moral Basis of the *Wealth of Nations*', *Review of Social Economy*, 34; reprinted in Wood, (1983: ii. 205).

Brown, Maurice, (1988), *Adam Smith's Economics: Its Place in the Development of Economic Thought* (Beckenham).

Brown, V. (1994), *Adam Smith's Discourse: Canonicity, Commerce and Conscience* (London).

Campbell, T. D. (1971), *Adam Smith's Science of Morals* (London).

Campbell, W. F. (1967), 'Adam Smith's Theory of Justice, Prudence and Beneficence', *American Economic Review*, 57; reprinted in Wood, (1983: i, 351).

Coase, R. H. (1976), 'Adam Smith's View of Man', *Journal of Law and Economics*, 19; reprinted in Wood, (1983: i. 546).

Danner, P. L. (1976), 'Sympathy and Exchangeable Value: Keys to Adam Smith's Social Philosophy', *Review of Social Economy*, 34; reprinted in Wood, (1983: i. 628).

Etzioni, Amitai, (1988), *The Moral Dimension: Towards a New Economics* (London).

Evensky, J. (1987), 'The Two Voices of Adam Smith: Moral Philosopher and Social Critic', *History of Political Economy*, 19.

Foley, V. (1977), *The Social Physics of Adam Smith* (Durham, NC).

Freeman, R. D. (1969), Adam Smith: Education and Laisser-Faire', *History of Political Economy*, i; reprinted in Wood, (1983: i. 378).

Gee, A. (1968), 'Adam Smith's Social Welfare Function', *Scottish Journal of Political Economy*, 15; reprinted in Wood, (1983: iv. 84).

Goldberg, M. A. (1959), *Smollett and the Scottish School* (Albuquerque).

Gramp, W. (1948), 'Adam Smith and the Economic Man', *Journal of Political Economy*, 56; reprinted in Wood, (1983: i. 250).

Haakonssen, K. (1980), *The Science of the Legislator* (Cambridge).

Heilbroner, R. L. (1982), 'The Socialisation of the Individual in Adam Smith', *History of Political Economy*, 14.

Hollander, S. (1977), 'Adam Smith and the Self-Interest Axiom', *Journal of Law and Economics*, 20; reprinted in Wood, (1983: i. 680).

Hume, David, (1955), *Economic Writings*, ed. E. Rotwein (London).

——(1987), *Essays Moral Political and Literary*, ed. E. Miller (Indianapolis).

Jones, P., and Skinner, A. S. (eds.) (1992), *Adam Smith Reviewed* (Edinburgh).

Kaye, F. B. (1924), ed., *The Fable of the Bees* (Oxford).

Lindgren, R. (1973), *The Social Philosophy of Adam Smith* (The Hague).

Macfie, A. L. (1967), *The Individual in Society* (London).

McCosh, J. (1875), *The Scottish Philosophy* (New York).

Morrow, G. (1928), 'Adam Smith: Moralist and Philosopher', in *Adam Smith, 1776–1926* (Chicago).

Myers, M. L. (1983), *The Soul of Economic Man* (Chicago).

Oakley, A., (1994), *Classical Economic Man* (Aldershot).

Raphael, D. D. (1969), *British Moralists 1650–1800* (Oxford).

——(1985), *Adam Smith* (Oxford).

Skinner, A. S. (1979), *A System of Social Science* (Oxford).

——(1982), 'A Scottish Contribution to Marxist Sociology?' in *Classical and Marxian Political Economy*, ed. I. Bradley and M. Howard (London).

Smith, Norman Kemp, (1966), *The Philosophy of David Hume* (London).

Teichgraber, R. (1986), *Free Trade and Moral Philosophy: Rethinking the Sources of Adam Smith's Wealth of Nations* (Durham).

Urquhart, R. (1994), 'Reciprocating Monads', *Scottish Journal of Political Economy*, 41.

Wilson, T. (1976), 'Sympathy and Self-Interest', in *The Market and the State*, ed. T. Wilson and A. S. Skinner (Oxford).

Winch, D. (1978), *Adam Smith's Politics* (Cambridge).

——(1983), 'Science and the Legislator: Adam Smith and After', *Economic Journal*, 93.

Wood, J. C. (1984), *Adam Smith: Critical Assessments* (Beckenham).

4
Historical Theory

INTRODUCTION:

We should recall at the outset that Smith's interest in social history found a number of precedents and parallels on the Continent. It is interesting to note, in this connection, that, as Quaestor for the University Library, Smith made purchases including the works of Giannonne, Daniel, and Brosse, and that he owned copies of works by Fénelon, Fontenelle, Rollin, Raynal, Mably, Duclos, and Chastellux, to name but a few (see e.g. Becker 1932: Sect. 3).

Such writers are associated with something of a revolution in historical writing, a revolution whose nature is aptly expressed in Voltaire's comment that 'My principal object is to know, as far as I can, the manners of peoples, and to study the human mind. I shall regard the order of succession of kings and chronology as my guides, but not as the objects of my work.' (quoted in Black 1926: 4). Writing much earlier, the Italian Giannonne felt able to state that his *History of Naples*, 'wherein the Policy, Laws and Customs of so noble a Kingdom, shall be treated separately', could be regarded for this reason as being altogether new.[1] But of course it was Giannonne's pupil, Montesquieu, who 'first showed that laws were not the arbitrary fiat of their makers' and who now seems to stand at the beginning of a major change in historical writing.[2] As John Millar often said, it was Montesquieu who first pointed out the way, and the acknowledgement finds an echo in Dugald Stewart's generous assessment of his influence (Stewart II. 50).

Smith's own work on the history of civil society is particularly noteworthy, and is among the first subjects that he appears to have addressed. Even if we exclude the Edinburgh Lectures, it is now well

This chapter is a modified version of a paper entitled 'An Economic interpretation of History' which originally appeared in *Essays on Adam Smith* (*EAS*). The modifications take account of points made in Skinner (1982) but do not supersede that article.

[1] Pietro Giannonne, *The Civil History of the Kingdom of Naples: Where the Author Clearly Demonstrates, that the Temporal Dominion and Power exercis'd by the Popes, has been altogether owing to the Ignorance, and Connivance of, or Concessions extorted from Secular Princes during the Dark Ages*, trans. by James Ogilvy 1729).

[2] Martin (1954: 152). In Scottish circles at least, the emphasis given to physical factors was widely discounted; see e.g. Hume's essay 'Of National Characters' and John Millar's introduction to his *Origin of the Distinction of Ranks* (1771).

known, from the account supplied by John Millar, that the third part of Smith's lecture course delivered from the Moral Philosophy chair had been concerned with 'that branch of morality which relates to justice', and that:

Upon this subject he followed the plan that seems to be suggested by Montesquieu; endeavouring to trace the gradual progress of jurisprudence, both public and private, from the rudest to the most refined ages, and to point out the effect of those arts which contribute to subsistence, and to the accumulation of property, in producing correspondent improvements or alterations in law and government. (Stewart, 1. 19).[3]

The reference to 'arts which contribute to subsistence' is particularly striking when we reflect that Smith managed to isolate four distinct modes of subsistence to which there corresponded four types of social structure: the stages of 'hunting, pasturage, farming, and commerce' (*LJ*(B) 149).[4]

Yet despite Millar's reference, the sociological and historical dimension of Smith's work was noticed only relatively recently. For our present purposes, it would appear that Roy Pascal's 1938 article, 'Property and Society: The Scottish Contribution of the Eighteenth Century', provided the groundwork for a debate that has come to feature both Marxist and non-Marxist interpretations of the Scottish School. In view of subsequent developments, it may therefore be useful to recall some of the major points that Pascal made.

To begin with, Pascal identified the main members of the 'School' (Smith, Ferguson, Miller, and Robertson) and drew attention to their interest in what could be called a 'new science of civil society'. The emergence of this science was ascribed to a number of forces, such as Scotland's isolation from the seat of government, and the nature and position of her universities, but Pascal emphasized two elements in particular. He drew attention first to the consequences of a rapid rate of economic and social change in the eighteenth century, and secondly to the importance of that information concerning primitive peoples which was available to the members of the School. Particular reference was made to contemporary knowledge of the North American Indians; knowledge that gave 'a real basis to speculations deriving from the contrast between a primitive and an advanced civilisation'.

Having drawn attention to the origin and nature of the new theory, Pascal then went on to review its content. In this connection he chose to

---

[3] The most complete account of the whole argument is to be found in *LJ*(A) iv, which corresponds to the briefer treatment 'Of Public Jurisprudence' offered in *LJ*(B), pt 1. It is interesting to note that, while *LJ*(A) deals with private, domestic, and public law in that order, *LJ*(B) reverses the sequence.
[4] The same division of stages appears in *LJ*(A) i. 27.

emphasize the importance of property relations and of the use made
of 'four types of society differentiated by different modes of production', points that led to the conviction that Adam Smith saw the
development of civil society as 'a completely secular, material process' (Pascal 1938: 170–1). In Pascal's eyes, Smith emerges as the
founder of a 'new interpretation of society which is undoubtedly
materialistic, and which his contemporaries and disciples . . . elaborate' (1938: 173). Leading on from this, Pascal was able to place the
Scottish writers in the general context of the history of political
theory, in arguing that Adam Smith and his contemporaries are to
be seen as the critics of the tradition associated with Hobbes and
Locke, i.e. as critics of a political science whose 'basic conceptions . . .
were abstract, speculative, and rationalistic; abstract and speculative
in that it postulated man living in a "state of nature", and rationalistic in that it ascribed the establishment of society to a voluntary act
(1938: 167).

Pascal was correct. Smith's historical account of the rise and progress
of government amounted to a denial that it could be the work of artifice,
i.e. the result of the kind of contract that is associated with John Locke.
Smith made this point quite explicitly in the *Lectures* (following Hume),
in arguing that the doctrine seemed to be peculiar to Great Britain and
that it was one of which the greater part of mankind were entirely
ignorant. As he said, the 'foundation of a duty cannot be a principle
with which mankind is entirely unacquainted' (*LJ*(B) 16). The same point
was also made in another way when Smith argued that government
originated with the first division of property and the appearance of
subordination, a situation that 'introduces some degree of that civil
government which is indispensably necessary for its own preservation:
and it seems to do this naturally, and even independent of the consideration of that necessity' (*WN* v. i. b. 12). In the same way, Smith's social and
historical argument led him to dismiss the Hobbesian state of nature as
an irrelevance, since 'there is no such state existing' (*LJ*(B) 3), and, while
agreeing with Locke that 'Men may live together in society with some
tolerable degree of security, though there is no civil magistrate' (*WN* v. i.
b. 2), he confined this judgement to the first and rudest state (the North
American Indian), which, however, he denied could be defined as a
'state of nature'. The reason is obvious, since, if we define human
experience as something that is subject to a process of continuous
change, then every state can be regarded as natural. The point was
neatly put by Adam Ferguson when he enquired, 'If we are asked,
therefore, Where the state of nature is to be found? we may answer, It
is here; and it matters not whether we are understood to speak in the

island of Great Britain, at the Cape of Good Hope, or the Straits of Magellan.'[5]

The first article which might be seen to build upon the basis provided by Pascal, but without adopting a Marxist stance, is Duncan Forbes's 'Scientific Whiggism: Adam Smith and John Millar', published in the *Cambridge Journal* for 1953–4. Pascal is shown to have developed Sombart's suggestive remarks with regard to the School's anticipation of 'the historical materialism of Marx', while in the case of Millar it is confirmed that 'everything is explained in terms of the progress of society, and the economic interpretation is basic' (Forbes 1953/4: 663–4). In Smith's case especially, attention was drawn to the importance of the four-stages thesis as providing the organizing principle behind the treatment of progress, as well as to his use of the doctrine of 'unintended outcomes': a point also emphasized by Pascal.

But there is one very important difference, as compared with Pascal, arising from the fact that Forbes was concerned not so much with placing Smith and Millar in the history of political *theory* as with the attitudes adopted by these men to questions that are more directly related to political *science* (in an institutional sense). This theme was to be continued in 'Sceptical Whiggism: Commerce and Liberty' published in 1975. But as early as 1954 Forbes was arguing that the attitudes that Smith and Millar adopted to matters of contemporary debate were informed by an understanding of underlying historical processes, and that:

The 'scientific' nature of the Whiggism of Smith and Millar is thrown into relief when it is contrasted with other historical attitudes, especially liberal ones, in England in the later eighteenth century. In relation to the appeal to history by the political reformers of the 70s and 80s, for instance, it may almost be said to stand as Marxian to pre-Marxian socialism, so crude, utopian and mentally parochial is one, so wide in the sweep of its historical survey, and so self-consciously 'scientific' is the other. (Forbes 1953/4: 661).

But, whereas Forbes's first contribution to the debate pursued an *analogy* with Marx, Ronald Meek's opening article of the same year reflected a growing conviction that the Scottish contribution to 'Marxist sociology' was 'greater in degree, and to some extent different in kind, from what has commonly been imagined' (Meek 1954: 34). In developing this theme, Meek neglected the 'political' dimension of Pascal's essay while starting from the point at which he had left off, namely, the statement that 'Marx's first thorough exposition of historical materialism, the *German Ideology* . . . builds on the ground work laid by Smith and his contemporaries' (Pascal 1938: 178).

[5] Forbes (1967: 8). See generally pt I, § 1, where Ferguson deals at some length with 'the question relating to the State of Nature'.

It was certainly Meek's firm view that the stadial thesis provides the basic conceptual framework within which the major part of Smith's argument is set. In fact, there are two dimensions to Smith's argument: first, the statement of certain 'sociological' propositions which are related to the 'four stages', and secondly, the application of these propositions to the interpretation of specific areas of historical experience. The main propositions are of continuing interest because of the relationships that were established between economic forces and other areas of activity; the historical aspects, because it is here that these relationships are lent a dimension of greater complexity than their formal sociological statement might imply.

THE STAGES OF SOCIETY

The first stage of society was represented as the 'lowest and rudest' state, such 'as we find it among the native tribes of North America' (*WN* v. i. a. 2). In this case, life is maintained through gathering the spontaneous fruits of the soil, and the dominant activities are taken to be hunting and fishing—a mode of acquiring subsistence that is antecedent to any social organization in production. As a result, Smith suggested that such communities would be small in size and characterized by a high degree of personal liberty—due of course to the absence of any form of economic dependence. Smith also observed that in the absence of private property, which was also capable of accumulation, disputes between different members of the community would be minor, 'so there is seldom any established magistrate or any regular administration of justice' in such states. He added that 'Universal poverty establishes there universal equality, and the superiority, either of age, or of personal qualities, are the feeble, but the sole foundations of authority and subordination. There is therefore little or no authority or subordination in this period of society' (*WN* v. i. b. 7).

The second social stage is that of pasture, which Smith represented as a 'more advanced state of society, such as we find it among the Tartars and Arabs' (v. i. a. 3). Here the use of cattle is the dominant economic activity, and the mode of subsistence meant, as Smith duly noted, that life would tend to be nomadic and the communities would be larger in size than had been possible in the preceding stage. More dramatically, Smith observed that the appropriation of herds and flocks, which introduced an inequality of fortune, was what first gave rise to regular government. We also find here a form of property that can be accumulated and transmitted from one generation to another, thus explaining a change in the main sources of authority as compared with the previous period. As Smith put it,

The second period of society, that of shepherds, admits of very great inequalities of fortune, and there is no period in which the superiority of fortune gives so great authority to those who possess it. There is no period accordingly in which authority and subordination are more perfectly established. The authority of an Arabian scherif is very great; that of a Tartar khan altogether despotical. (*WN* v. i. b. 7).

At the same time, it is evident that the mode of subsistence involved ensured a high degree of dependence of those who must acquire the means of subsistence through the exchange of personal service on those who, owning the means of subsistence, have no other way of expending it save on the maintenance of dependants, who at the same time contribute to their military power. Smith added that while the distinction of birth, being subsequent to the inequality of fortune, can have no place in a nation of hunters, this distinction 'always does take place among nations of shepherds' (*WN* v. i. b. 10). Since the great families lack, in this context, the means of dissipating wealth, it follows that 'there are no nations among whom wealth is likely to continue longer in the same families' (v. i. b. 10).

The third and fourth stages in Smith's scheme are much more complex than the first two, and for this reason a fuller treatment of them will be postponed until the next section of the argument. However, enough may be said at this point to confirm the basic principles that Smith ought to establish.

In the agrarian case, for example, there are many obvious differences compared with the pasturage economy. The most important form of property is now land (rather than cattle), while in addition some form of tillage will be practised—all of which indicates that societies will no longer be nomadic and that they are likely to be still larger in size. Yet in a sense Smith chose to emphasizes *similarities* with the previous stage: for here too property is likely to be distributed in a markedly unequal way, and to be transmitted from one member of a family to another through a number of generations. Here too the economy is designed basically for subsistence rather than exchange, so that those who lack the means of subsistence can acquire it only through the provision of personal service. In this way those who own property acquire power by virtue of that fact, while those who have 'no equivalent to give in return for their maintenance' become members of a group who must obey their superiors 'for the same reason that soldiers must obey the prince who pays them' (III. iv. 5).

In the case of the stage of 'commerce', many of the principles so far mentioned also apply: wealth and birth remain important sources of distinction, as a result of the basic 'irregularity' in our moral sentiments of which Smith made so much in *The Theory of Moral Sentiments*. Property too remains an important source of power, and Smith was certainly aware of the 'oppressive inequality' that was to be found even in the most advanced states. But here he chose to emphasize two important *contrasts* with the previous stages, especially with those of pasture and agriculture, differences that reflect the fact that the fourth stage features the production of goods with a view to exchange. In the first place, he argued that property derived from 'commercial' activity was likely to be more equally distributed and unlikely to be kept within particular families over long periods of time. Secondly, Smith suggested that, where goods and services generally command a price, the direct dependencies of the second stage could no longer apply. As he put it,

In a country where there is no foreign commerce, nor any of the finer manufactures, a man of ten thousand a year cannot well employ his revenue in any other way than in maintaining, perhaps, a thousand families, who are all of them necessarily at his command. In the present state of Europe, a man of ten thousand a year can spend his whole revenue, and he generally does so, without directly maintaining twenty people, or being able to command more than ten footmen not worth the commanding. (*WN* III. iv. 11).

By purchasing the products of other men's labour, the 'rich' contribute to their maintenance, while 'Each tradesman or artificer derives his subsistence from the employment, not of one, but of a hundred or a thousand different customers. Though in some measure obliged to them all, therefore, he is not absolutely dependent upon any one of them' (*WN* III. iv. 12).

Perhaps enough has been said to indicate that for Smith the relations of authority and dependence were of striking importance, that the relationships involved will manifest themselves in different ways in different situations, and that the operation of the same basic principles will generate the sharpest contrasts when comparing the third and fourth stages. The point was neatly put by Smith's contemporary, Sir James Steuart (Steuart 1966: i. 208–9: see Chapter 11 below).

Looked at in this way, the analysis may be seen to employ the technique of comparative statics, at least in the sense that it provides a means of contrasting and comparing different forms of economic and social organization that may be found to exist at a particular point in time, and of fulfilling a like role when comparing the different forms of socio-economic organization that a particular society may have attained at different points in time. While there is a good deal of evidence to suggest that the 'stadial' thesis was used in exactly this way it is equally true that Smith's deployment of the thesis also supports Meek's view that 'The four stages, at any rate at the outset of its career, usually took the form of a *theory of development*, embodying the idea of some "natural" or "normal" movement through a succession of different modes of subsistence' (Meek 1976: 225). Smith was well aware that the sequence of hunting, pasture, agriculture, and commerce need not always unfold in the order suggested. For example, the North American Indians constitute an 'objection to this rule', in that 'They, tho they have no conception of flocks and herds, have nevertheless some notion of agriculture' (*LJ*(A) i. 29). He also pointed out that the process depended on the satisfaction of certain physical preconditions, such as fertility of the soil and access to good communications:

Tartary and Araby labour under both these difficulties. For in the first place their soil is very poor and such as will hardly admit culture of any sort. . . . Neither have they any opportunity of commerce, if it should happen that they should make any advances in arts and sciences. . . . In these countries therefore little or no advances can be expected, nor have any yet been made. But in Greece all the circumstances necessary for the improvement of the arts concurred. The several parts were separated from each other by mountains and other barriers, no less than Arabia, but [it] is far more adapted to culture. They would therefore have many inducements to cultivate the arts and make improvements in society. The lands would be divided and well improved and the country would acquire considerable wealth. (*LJ*(A) iv. 62).

In short, where the necessary conditions were satisfied, a certain sequence of stages could be expected:

If we should suppose 10 or 12 persons of different sexes settled in an uninhabited island, the first method they would fall upon for their subsistence would be to support themselves by the wild fruits and wild animals which the country afforded. . . . This is the age of hunters. In process of time, as their numbers multiplied, they would find the chase too precarious for their support. . . . The contrivance they would most naturally think of would be to tame some of those wild animals they caught, and by affording them better food than what they could get elsewhere they would enduce them to continue about their land themselves and multiply their kind. Hence would arise the age of shepherds. They would more probably begin first by multiplying animals then vegetables, as less skill and observation would be required. . . . We find accordingly that in almost all countries the age of shepherds preceded that of agriculture. . . .

But when a society becomes numerous they would find a difficulty in support-ing themselves by herds and flocks. Then they would naturally turn themselves to the cultivation of land and the raising of such plants and trees as produced nourishment fit for them . . . And by this means they would gradually advance into the Age of Agriculture. As society was farther improved, the severall arts, which at first would be exercised by each individual as far as was necessary for his welfare, would be separated; some persons would cultivate one and others others, as they severally inclined. They would exchange with one another what they produced more than was necessary for their support, and get in exchange for them the commodities they stood in need of and did not produce themselves. This exchange of commodities extends in time not only betwixt the individualls of the same society but betwixt those of different nations. . . . Thus at last the Age of commerce arises. (*LJ*(A) i. 27–32).

A HISTORICAL APPLICATION: THE FALL OF THE ROMAN EMPIRE

The sequence stated implies a certain progression through time, while seeming to suggest that there is a sense in which the development of productive forces is to be associated with certain social (or qualitative) changes. Yet at the same time, it is clear that statements of the kind just quoted do not of themselves constitute an explanation of the process of transition between stages. Smith was well aware of this problem, and it is noteworthy that his treatment of public jurisprudence, with its attendant use of the 'four stages', in fact unfolded within the framework of a *historical* account of the origins and nature of the present 'establishments' in Europe.

It is now well known that this account opens with the first beginnings of civilization in Greece before passing on to Rome and to the eventual emergence of the modern European state. It is the latter subject that is our main concern here.

The nations that overran the Western Empire were represented by Smith as having been at exactly that stage of development which had been attained by the early inhabitants of Greece. Primitive peoples whose military power was of the awesome proportions appropriate to the second stage are thus shown to have come into contact with a much more sophisticated society, but one whose power was already on the decline. The result, as Smith duly noted, was the destruction of civilization as then known, a step backwards.

When the German and Scythian nations over-ran the western provinces of the Roman empire, the confusions which followed so great a revolution lasted for several centuries. The rapine and violence which the barbarians exercised against the antient inhabitants, interrupted the commerce between the towns and the country. The towns were deserted, and the country was left uncultivated, and the western provinces of Europe, which had enjoyed a considerable degree of opulence under the Roman empire, sunk into the lowest state of poverty and barbarism. (*WN* III. ii. 1).

At the same time, however, Smith argued that the domination of the barbarian nations had generated not only a desert, but also an environment from which a higher form of European civilization was ultimately to emerge.[6] Smith's explanation of this general trend begins with the fact that the primitive tribes that overran the Roman Empire had already attained a relatively sophisticated form of the pasturage economy, with

---

[6] Almost exactly this point was made by Dugald Stewart, in *Works*, x. 147.

some idea of agriculture and of property in land.[7] He argued that they would therefore naturally use existing institutions in their new situation and that in particular their first act would be a division of the conquered territories: 'the chiefs and principal leaders of those nations, acquired or usurped to themselves the greater part of the lands . . . A great part of them was uncultivated; but no part of them, whether cultivated or uncultivated, was left without a proprietor. All of them were engrossed, and the greater part by a few great proprietors' (*WN* III. ii. 1).

In this way we move in effect from a developed version of one economic stage to a primitive version of another; from the state of pasture to that of 'agriculture'. Under the circumstances outlined, property in land became the great source of power and distinction, with each estate assuming the form of a separate principality. As a result of this situation, Smith argued, a gradual change took place in the laws governing property, featuring the introduction of primogeniture and entails, designed to protect estates against division and to preserve a 'certain lineal succession'. The basic point emphasized was that in such periods of disorder 'The security of a landed estate . . . the protection which its owner could afford to those who dwelt on it, depended upon its greatness. To divide it was to ruin it, and to expose every part of it to be oppressed and swallowed up by the incursions of its neighbours' (III. ii. 3).

Such institutions as these quite obviously reflect a change in the mode of subsistence and in the form of property, thus presenting some important contrasts with the previous stage. On the other hand, the great proprietor still has nothing on which to expend his surpluses other than the maintenance of dependants—and at the same time has a positive incentive to support them since they contribute to his military power and hence his security. While Smith carefully distinguished between *retainers* and *cultivators* in this context, he took pains to emphasize that the latter group was in every respect as dependent on the proprietor as the first, and added that 'Even such of them as were not in a state of villanage, were tenants at will, who paid a rent in no respect equivalent to the subsistence which the land afforded them' (III. iv. 6).[8]

In short, the period was marked by clear relations of power and dependence—but above all by disorder and conflict, and it was from

---

[7] Smith commented briefly on the implied sequence of stages when he stated that men would 'naturally turn themselves to the cultivation of land' once the growth of population had put pressure on supplies derived from pasturage. He added: 'The only instance that has the appearance of an objection to this rule is the state of the North American Indians. They, tho they have no conception of flocks and herds, have nevertheless some notion of agriculture' (*LJ*(A) i. 29). Similar points are made in *LJ*(B) 150.

[8] It is pointed out in *LJ*(A) i. 119 that those who used the land initially 'paid a small rent to the possessor, rather as an acknowledgment of their dependence than as the value of the land'. Cf. the remarks made by Steuart as cited above, see generally the *Principles* (Skinner 1966: 206–17 and p. xiii–lxviii).

this source that the first important changes in the outlines of the system were to come. As Smith put it by way of summary: 'In those disorderly times, every great landlord was a sort of petty prince. His tenants were his subjects. He was their judge, and in some respects their legislator in peace, and their leader in war. He made war according to his own discretion, frequently against his neighbours, and sometimes against his sovereign' (III. ii. 3)

It was this state of conflict, Smith suggests, that gave the proprietors some incentive to alter the pattern of landholding, in two quite different ways. First, he argued that the heavy demands that were inevitably made on the immediate tenants (as distinct from villeins) for military service would inevitably change the quit-rent system in terms of which land was normally held. Smith argued in effect that the great lords would naturally begin to grant leases for a term of years, and then in a form that gave security to the tenant's family and ultimately to his posterity. In this way, land came to be held as *feuda* rather than *munera*, being designed to give both parties a benefit: the lord, a supply of military service, and the tenant, security in the use of land. Smith also noted certain consequential developments reflecting the basic purpose of the arrangement, which improved and protected the power of the great proprietor, in describing what he called the feudal *casualities*.[9]

Secondly, Smith argued that the same need for protection that altered the relationship between the great lord and his tenants would also lead to patterns of alliance between members of the former group, and therefore to arrangements that gave some guarantee of mutual service and protection. It was for these reasons, Smith argued, that the lesser landowners entered into feudal arrangements with those greater lords who could ensure their survival (thus enhancing their ability to do so), just as the great lords would be led to make similar arrangements among themselves and with the king. These changes took place about the ninth, tenth, and eleventh centuries, and, by imposing some constraints on the freedom of the proprietors, contributed thereby to the emergence of a more orderly form of government.

However, while Smith did describe the feudal as a higher form of the agrarian economy than the allodial, he also took some pains to emphasize the limited possibilities for economic growth that it presented; limitations which were themselves the reflection of the political institutions prevailing. He argued that the quit-rent system, so far as it survived, gave no incentive to industry, and that the institution of slavery ensured that it was in the interest of the ordinary individual to 'eat as much, and to labour as little as possible' (*WN* III. ii. 9). In the same way, he also cited the disincentive effects of the arbitrary services and

---

[9] See *LJ*(A) iv. 127 ff.; *LJ*(B) 53–7, and *WN* III. iv. 9; v. ii. h. 5, 6.

feudal taxes that were imposed at this time. But, undoubtedly, Smith placed most emphasis on the continuing problem of political instability:

The authority of government still continued to be, as before, too weak in the head and too strong in the inferior members, and the excessive strength of the inferior members was the cause of the weakness of the head. After the institution of feudal subordination, the king was as incapable of restraining the violence of the great lords as before. They still continued to make war according to their own discretion, almost continually upon one another, and very frequently upon the king; and the open country still continued to be a scene of violence, rapine, and disorder. (*WN* III. iv. 9).

Once again, a state of instability was to produce some change in the outlines of the social system, and once again the motive behind it was *political* rather than *economic* - this time with the kings rather than the great lords as the main actors in the drama.[10]

EMERGENCE OF THE EXCHANGE ECONOMY

The kind of economy that Smith described as appropriate to the agrarian state is fundamentally a simple one. It consists of the usual division between town and country, that is between those who produce food and those who make the manufactured goods without which no large country could subsist—the critical point being, however, that such an economy was not wholly based on exchange. The cities that Smith described were small, and composed of those merchants, tradesmen, and mechanics who were not bound to a particular place and who might find it in their (economic) interest to congregate together. Smith had in fact relatively little to say about the historical origins of such groupings, but he did emphasize that the inhabitants of the towns were in the same servile condition as the inhabitants of the country, and that the wealth that they did manage to accumulate under such unfavourable conditions was subject to the arbitrary exactions of those lords on whose territories they might happen to reside (*WN* III. iii. 2).

But evidently some development must have been possible, for Smith examines the role of the city from that point in time when three distinctive features of royal policy with regard to them were already in evidence. First, he noted that cities had often been allowed to farm the taxes to which they were subject, the inhabitants thus becoming 'jointly and severally answerable' for the whole sum due (*WN* III. iii. 3). Secondly, he noted that in some cases these taxes, instead of being farmed for a given number of years, had been 'let in fee', that is 'for ever,

[10] Smith also stressed the importance of the Church as a source of instability in *WN* v. i. g. 17, 22.

reserving a rent certain never afterwards to be augmented' (III. iii. 4). Thirdly, Smith observed that the cities 'were generally at the same time erected into a commonality or corporation, with the privilege of having magistrates and a town-council of their own, of making bye-laws for their own government, of building walls for their own defence, and of reducing all their inhabitants under a sort of military discipline, by obliging them to watch and ward . . .' (*WN* III. iii. 6).

It was as a result of following these policies that some kings had achieved the apparently remarkable result of freezing the very revenues that were most likely to increase over time, and at the same time had apparently curtailed their own power by erecting 'a sort of independent republicks in the heart of their own dominions' (*WN* III. iii. 7). Smith advanced two main reasons to explain the apparent paradox: he argued, first, that by encouraging the cities the king made it possible for a group of his subjects to defend themselves against the power of the great lords where he personally was unable to do so, and, secondly, that by imposing a limit on taxation 'he took away from those whom he wished to have for his friends, and, if one may say so, for his allies, all ground of jealousy and suspicion that he was ever afterwards to oppress them, either by raising the farm rent of their town, or by granting it to some other farmer' (*WN* III. iii. 8). The encouragement given to the cities represented in effect a tactical alliance which was beneficial to both parties, and in speaking of the burghers Smith remarked that 'Mutual interest . . . disposed them to support the king, and the king to support them against the lords. They were the enemies of his enemies, and it was his interest to render them as secure and independent of those enemies as he could' (III. iii. 8).

Smith also noted that this development was directly related to the weakness of kings, so that it was likely to be more significant in some countries than in others, and that in general the policy had been successful where employed.[11] He also remarked that the granting of powers of self-government to the inhabitants of the cities had set in motion forces that were ultimately to weaken the authority of the kings through creating an environment within which the forces of economic development could, for the first time, be effectively released. In Smith's own words,

---

[11] In *LJ*(A) iv. 154, Smith also associated this trend with the military ambition of certain kings such as Edward I and Henry IV, 'the two most warlike of the English Kings'. It is also pointed out in *WN* III. iii. 11 that, while the cities in England did not become so powerful as to be virtually independent (as in Italy and Switzerland, where the physical size and nature of the country made this possible), 'They became, however, so considerable that the sovereign could impose no tax upon them, besides the stated farm-rent of the town, without their own consent. They were, therefore, called upon to send deputies to the general assembly of the states of the kingdom.'

Order and good government, and along with them the liberty and security of individuals, were, in this manner, established in cities at a time when the occupiers of land . . . were exposed to every sort of violence. But men in this defenceless state naturally content themselves with their necessary subsistence; because to acquire more might only tempt the injustice of their oppressors. On the contrary, when they are secure of enjoying the fruits of their industry, they naturally exert it to better their condition, and to acquire not only the necessaries, but the conveniencies and elegancies of life. (*WN* III. iii. 12).

The stimulus to economic growth and to further social change was thus seen to emanate from the cities, institutions that had themselves been developed and protected in an attempt to solve a political problem. From this point, Smith's attention shifted to the analysis of the process of economic growth in the manufacturing and trading sector, before going on to examine its impact on the agrarian sector.

Smith clearly recognized that growth was limited by the size of the market, and, since the agrarian sector was relatively backward, that the main stimulus to economic growth would have to come from foreign trade. He therefore concluded that cities such as Venice, Genoa, and Pisa, all of which enjoyed ready access to the sea, had provided the models for the process, while noting that their development had been further accelerated by particular 'accidents' such as the Crusades. In general however Smith laid most emphasis on three sources of encouragement to the development of trade and manufactures. First, he argued that in many cases agrarian surpluses could be acquired by the merchants and used in exchange for foreign manufactures, and suggested as a matter of fact that the early trade of Europe had largely consisted in the exchange 'of their own rude, for the manufactured products of more civilized nations'. Secondly, he argued that over time the merchants would naturally seek to introduce manufactures at home with a view to saving carriage. Such manufactures, it was suggested, would require the use of foreign materials, thus inducing an important change in the general pattern of trade. Thirdly, he argued that some manufactures would develop 'naturally', that is through the gradual refinement of the 'coarse and rude' products that were normally produced at home and were, therefore, based on domestic materials. Smith suggested that such developments were normally found in those cities that were 'not indeed at a very great, but at a considerable distance from the sea coast, and sometimes even from all water carriage' (*WN* III. iii. 20). That is, he suggested that manufactures might well develop in areas to which artisans had been attracted by the cheapness of subsistence, thus allowing trade to develop within the locality. Once some progress had been made in this way, foreign trade became possible:

The manufacturers first supply the neighbourhood, and afterwards, as their work improves and refines, more distant markets. For though neither the rude produce, nor even the coarse manufacture, could, without the greatest difficulty, support the expence of a considerable land carriage, the refined and improved manufacture easily may. In a small bulk it frequently contains the price of a great quantity of rude produce. (*WN* III. iii. 20).

Smith cited the silk manufacture at Lyons and Spitalfields as examples of the first category of manufactures, and those of Leeds, Halifax, Sheffield, Birmingham, and Wolverhampton as examples of the second, the natural 'offspring of agriculture' (*WN* III. iii. 19, 20). He also added that manufactures of the latter kind were generally posterior to those 'which were the offspring of foreign commerce', and that the process of development just outlined made it perfectly possible for the city within which growth took place to 'grow up to great wealth and splendor, while not only the country in its neighbourhood, but all those to which it traded, were in poverty and wretchedness' (III. iii. 13).

In the next stage of the analysis, however, it was argued that the development of manufactures and trade within the cities was bound to impinge on the agrarian sector and, ultimately, to destroy the service relationships that still subsisted within it.[12] As Smith put it,

commerce and manufactures gradually introduced order and good government, and with them, the liberty and security of individuals, among the inhabitants of the country, who had before lived almost in a continual state of war with their neighbours, and of servile dependency upon their superiors. This, though it has been the least observed, is by far the most important of all their effects. (*WN* III. iv. 4).[13]

Essentially, this process may be seen to stem from the fact that the development of trade and manufactures had given the proprietors a means of expending their wealth, other than in the maintenance of dependents. The development of commerce and manufactures 'gradually furnished the great proprietors with something for which they could exchange the whole surplus produce of their lands, and which they could consume themselves without sharing it either with tenants or

---

[12] It is interesting to note that P. M. Sweezy should have rejected Maurice Dobb's thesis that feudalism broke down as a result of *internal* pressures in emphasizing the importance of foreign trade (i.e. an *external* force), both with regard to induced changes in taste and as an explanation for the fact that the cities 'became generators of commodity production in their own right' (Sweezy 1976: 42).

[13] Smith went on to add that 'Mr. Hume is the only writer who, so far as I know, has hitherto taken any notice of it.' See especially Hume's essay 'Of Refinement in the Arts' and Duncan Forbes's introduction to Hume's *History* (Forbes 1970: 38–43). Smith's statement is interesting when we recall that Steuart, Ferguson, Millar, and Kames had all published prior to the appearance of the *Wealth of Nations*. Since Smith can hardly have been unaware of these facts, it seems likely that his citation of Hume alone simply provided further evidence as to the age of this section of the work.

retainers. All for ourselves, and nothing for other people, seems, in every age of the world, to have been the vile maxim of the masters of mankind' (*WN* III. iv. 10).

This situation generated two results. First, since the proprietor's object was now to increase his command over the means of exchange, it would be in his interest to reduce the number of retainers, 'till they were at last dismissed altogether. The same cause gradually led them to dismiss the unnecessary part of their tenants. Farms were enlarged, and the occupiers of land, notwithstanding the complaints of depopulation, reduced to the number necessary for cultivating it, according to the imperfect state of cultivation and improvement in those times' (III. iv. 13).

Secondly, since the object was now to maximize the disposable surplus, it was in the proprietor's interest to change the forms of leasehold in order to encourage output and increase his returns. In this way, Smith traced the gradual change from the use of slave labour on the land,[14] to the origin of the 'metayer' system, where the tenant had limited property rights, until the whole process finally resulted in the appearance of farmers properly so called, 'who cultivated the land with their own stock, paying a rent certain to the landlord' (III. ii. 14). Smith added that the same process would over time tend to lead to an improvement in the conditions of leases, until the tenants could be 'secured in their possession, for such a term of years as might give them time to recover with profit whatever they should lay out in the further improvement of the land. The expensive vanity of the landlord made him willing to accept of this condition . . .' (III. iv. 13).

As a result of these two general trends, the great proprietors gradually lost their powers, both judicial and military,[15] until a situation was reached where 'they became as insignificant as any substantial burgher or tradesman in a city. A regular government was established in the country as well as in the city, nobody having sufficient power to disturb its operations in the one, any more than in the other' (III. iv. 15).

Smith thus associated the decline in the feudal powers of the great proprietors with three general trends, all of which followed on the introduction of commerce and manufactures: the dissipation of their

[14] Smith argued in effect that slavery was undermined because of economic forces and thus rejected the claims of the Church (*WN* III. ii. 12); see also *LJ*(A) iii. 121. He also pointed out that slavery still subsisted in large parts of Europe, especially 'Russia, Poland, Hungary, Bohemia, Moravia, and other parts of Germany. It is only in the western and south-western provinces of Europe, that it has gradually been abolished altogether' (*WN* III. ii. 8); see also *LJ*(A) iii. 122 and *LJ*(B) 134.

[15] In *WN* v. i. g. 25, Smith ascribed the decline in the temporal powers of the clergy to the same basic forces. In this connection he pointed out that, although the clergy as a group had exerted greater power than the Lords, owing to their greater cohesion, none the less, their authority declined rather sooner owing to the fact that in general the benefices of the clergy were smaller than the fortunes of the barons.

fortunes,[16] the dismissal of their retainers, and the substitution of a cash relationship for the service relationships that had previously existed between the owner of land and those who cultivated it. The trend was further supported by changes in the law which facilitated the aquisition of estates by the mercantile group.

As a result, we face a system where the disincentives to 'industry' had been removed from the agrarian sector, and where both sectors were, for the first time, fully interdependent at the domestic level. Smith thus argues in effect that the *quantitative* development of manufactures based on the cities eventually produced an important *qualitative* change in creating the institutions of the exchange economy, i.e. of the fourth economic stage. It is in this situation that the drive to better our condition, allied to the insatiable wants of man (referred to in *The Theory of Moral Sentiments*), provides the maximum possible stimulus to economic growth, and ensures that the gains accruing to town and country are both mutual and reciprocal (*WN* III. i. 1). The emergence of the fourth stage effectively eliminated the direct dependence of the previous period. In this situation, each productive service commands a price and therefore ensures that, while the farmer, tradesman, or merchant must depend upon his customers, yet 'Though in some measure obliged to them all . . . he is not absolutely dependent upon any one of them' (III. iv. 12).

It will be noted that the whole process of change, and especially that involved in the transition from the feudal to the commercial state, depends on the activities of individuals who are themselves unconscious of the ultimate end towards which such activities contribute. Or, as Smith put it in reviewing the actions of the proprietors and merchants during the latter stages of the historical process which we have outlined,

A revolution of the greatest importance to the publick happiness, was in this manner brought about by two different orders of people, who had not the least intention to serve the publick. To gratify the most childish vanity was the sole motive of the great proprietors. The merchants and artificers, much less ridiculous, acted merely from a view to their own interest, and in pursuit of their own pedlar principle of turning a penny wherever a penny was to be got. Neither of them had either knowledge or foresight of that great revolution which the folly of the one, and the industry of the other, was gradually bringing about. (*WN* III. iv. 17).[17]

[16] Smith did note however that this general trend had not been matched in Germany owing to the size of the country and the extent of the estates that were held by individuals. As he pointed out in *LJ*(A) iv. 166, the German nobles 'could not possibly by any personall luxury, consume all their revenues; they therefore contrived to have a great number of retainers and dependents, and have accordingly become absolute'. Similar points are made in *LJ*(B) 60–1.
[17] The first printing of the Glasgow edition of *WN* has 'out' for 'about' in III. iv. 17.

It should also be noted that, while Smith regarded the processes of history as inherently complex, he did none the less associate these processes with certain definite trends.[18] As we have seen, the growth of 'luxury and commerce' is represented as the inevitable outcome of normal human drives, and is associated with the appearance of new sources of wealth together with a particular type of economy: an economy composed of interdependent sectors within and among which all goods and services command a price.

These new forms of wealth, allied to the high degree of personal liberty appropriate to the new patterns of dependence also brought with them a new social and political order—a form of 'constitution'[19] which was often cited as an explanation for the English Revolution Settlement. In this way, Whig principles could be put on a sound historical basis, a point that is neatly illustrated by Ramsay's comment on Lord Kames's abandonment of his early Jacobite leanings. Ramsay expressed no surprise that Kames should have finally concluded that the Revolution was 'absolutely necessary' after 'studying history and conversing with first rate people'—no doubt including Smith.[20] Rather similar sentiments were expressed by John Millar when he remarked that 'When we examine historically the extent of the tory, and of the whig principle, it seems evident, that from the progress of arts and commerce, the former has been continually diminishing, and the latter gaining ground in the same proportion' (*HV*, iv. 304).[21] The point at issue had already been stated by David Hume (see Chapter 10 below) when commenting on the impact of 'commerce and industry' on the distribution of political power. At least in England, he wrote, 'the lower house is the support of our popular government, and all the world acknowledges, that it owed its chief influence and consideration to the encrease of commerce, which threw such a balance into the hands of the commons' (*Essays*, 277–8).

---

[18] The Marxist view is also a qualified one: in a letter to J. Bloch, dated September 1890, Engels wrote that, 'According to the materialist conception of history, the *ultimately* determining element in history is the production and reproduction of real life. More than this neither Marx nor I have ever asserted. Hence if somebody twists this into saying that the economic element is the *only* determining one, he transforms that proposition into a meaningless, abstract, senseless phrase' (in Marx and Engels 1955: ii. 488).

[19] 'Upon the manner in which any state is divided into the different orders and societies which compose it, and upon the particular distribution which has been made of their respective powers, privileges, and immunities, depends, what is called, the constitution of that particular state' (*TMS* VI. ii. 2. 8). [20] John Ramsay, (1888: i. 191).

[21] In *LJ*(A) v. 124, Smith associated the 'bustling, spirited, active folks' with the Whig interest, and the 'calm, contented folks of no great spirit and abundant fortunes' with the Tories. He also argues in this place that, while the Tories favour the principle of authority, the Whig interest favoured that of utility in matters of government.

CONCLUSIONS

While it is hoped that the brief account offered of Smith's argument is sufficient to delineate its major features, it may be appropriate to add some comment with regard to its general character and content, in terms of two broad areas.

Methodological

Perhaps the most striking feature of the analysis which we have considered is that it purports to place the study of history on the same level as other social sciences.

We are reminded that the claim to scientific status often implied that philosophical history was in some respects superior to other forms of historical writing–and in particular to the orthodox or narrative type. The terms used often invite this conclusion, as for example when Dugald Stewart referred to the 'habits of scientific disquisition' that were required of the natural historian, while expressing regret that William Robertson, perhaps the leading orthodox historian of his own time and country, had not prepared himself more for his incursions into this field. A rather similar impression is left by John Millar's statement that he would seek to 'point out the chief incidents of a constitutional history, lying in a good measure beneath that common surface of events which occupies the details of the vulgar historian' (*HV,* iv. 101).

But whatever points Stewart or Millar may have intended to convey in making such remarks, it should be noted that Smith himself was very careful in his comments—as befits one who broke new ground in lecturing on the history of historians.[22] While we cannot fully examine these lectures here (see Chapter 1 above), it should be noted that Smith at no time expressed contempt for those historians who worked in different fields. He pointed out for example that the first historians—the poets, who had concerned themselves with the 'marvellous'—provide valuable evidence as to the times in which they lived, and he went on to argue that, if Herodotus had many defects as a historian, yet 'We can learn from him rather the customs of the different nations and the series of events . . . in this way, too, we may learn a great deal' (*LRBL,* ii. 47–8). In addition, Smith observed that historians such as Thucydides and Tacitus were particularly informative, not only because of the way in which they recorded facts, but also because they tended to emphasize the psychological pressures to which the main figures involved were

---

[22] See *LRBL,* lects. 16–19 and especially the latter. Smith's classification of types of historical writing affords an interesting parallel with Hegel's introduction to the lectures on the philosophy of history; see Chapter 1.above.

subjected. He added that, 'though this perhaps will not tend so much to instruct us in the knowledge of the causes of events yet it will be more interesting and lead us into a science no less useful, to wit, the knowledge of the motives by which men act' (ii. 66). Smith, in short, quite clearly recognized that the narrative historian often supplied the materials on which the work of the philosophical historian was based.

We should also recall that Smith did not himself claim that philosophical history had an exclusive title to be described as *scientific* in character. For example, he referred to the objectivity or 'impartiality' that the orthodox historian has to maintain, in remarking that he fulfils his duty only when he 'sets before us the more interesting and important events of human life, points out the causes by which these events were brought about, and by this means points out to us by what manner and method we may produce similar good effects or avoid similar bad ones' (ii. 17–18). In short, the historian must bring to his study a critical awareness of facts; he must study these facts objectively; and he must seek to elucidate their causes—qualities which led Smith to give particular praise to Thucydides, who reported events of which he was the witness, and Tacitus, who recorded the history of a nation. Of the modern historians, Smith considered Machiavelli to be incomparably the best, in the sense that he was the only one 'who has contented himself with that which is the chief purpose of history, to relate events and connect them with their causes, without becoming a party on either side' (ii. 68).

Machiavelli is an interesting choice, in that his example also reminds us that use of the 'constant principles of human nature' in the interpretation of events was not of itself the distinguishing feature of 'philosophical history' as written by Smith. For Machiavelli too employed exactly this hypothesis in seeking to provide a science of history. As he put it in a characteristic passage: 'If the present be compared with the remote past, it is easily seen that in all cities and in all peoples, there are the same desires and the same passions as there always were'. (Walker 1950: i. 302).[23] It was because of the similarity of human nature that Machiavelli felt able to generalize on the basis of experience past and present and to project his results into the future. It follows that if human nature remains the same, and if a state of conflict is a constant, then men will behave in predictable ways despite other changes in the environment. The same point was made by Thucydides in reviewing the tragedy of Melos during *The Peloponnesian War* (chapter 17), where he makes the Athenian envoys remark that 'right, as the world goes, is only a question between equals in power, while the strong do what they can and the

---

[23] Cf. C. Montesquieu, *Considerations of the Causes of the Greatness of the Romans and their Decline*, (Lowenthal 1965: 26).

weak suffer what they must'. As Thucydides, who was warmly admired by Hume and Smith, noted:

The absence of romance in my history, will, I fear, detract from its interest; but if it be judged useful by those enquirers who desire an exact knowledge of the past as an aid to the interpretation of the future, which in the course of human things it must resemble, if it does not reflect it, I shall be content. In fine, I have written my work, not as an essay with which to win the applause of the moment, but as a possession for all time. (*Peloponnesian War* I. 1).

Even if we were to confine attention to classical sources, it is readily apparent that philosophical history as understood by Smith was hardly unique in the attempt made to treat historical materials scientifically or in respect of the desire to treat history as science.

The distinguishing feature of the type of philosophical history that engaged Smith's attention is to be found in the question posed, a question that was stated neatly and exactly by Dugald Stewart (surely the most perceptive of contemporary commentators), when he remarked:

When, in such a period of society as that in which we live, we compare our intellectual acquirements, our opinions, manners, and institutions, with those which prevail among rude tribes, it cannot fail to occur to us as an interesting question, by what gradual steps the transition has been made from the first simple efforts of uncultivated nature, to a state of things so wonderfully artificial and complicated. Whence has arisen that systematical beauty which we admire in the structure of a cultivated language . . . Whence the origin of the different sciences and of the different arts . . . Whence the astonishing fabric of the political union; the fundamental principles of which are common to all governments . . . ?' (Stewart, II. 45).

Stewart recognized that Smith's historical work was concerned primarily with the analysis of change over time. His description of the approach as 'theoretical' or 'philosophical' history draws attention to Smith's interest in 'fundamental principles'. Stewart's other term, namely 'conjectural history', refers in part to Smith's practice of using facts that were known to be valid in respect of primitive societies, but could be used to reconstruct a version of the social stages through which modern nations might reasonably be supposed to have passed in ages when written records were unavailable.

In this want of direct evidence, we are under a necessity of supplying the place of fact by conjecture; and when we are unable to ascertain how men have actually conducted themselves upon particular occasions, of considering in what manner they are likely to have proceeded, from the principles of their nature, and the circumstances of their external situation. (Stewart II. 46).

Stewart was also correct in suggesting that studies of a philosophical (and dynamic) nature seems 'in a peculiar degree, to have interested Mr. Smith's curiosity', and that something 'very similar to it may be traced in all his different works' (Stewart II. 44).

We are reminded that 'philosophical' history is in no sense confined to the area of enquiry that has been the main subject of this chapter. Smith's editors, Black and Hutton, also referred to 'a plan he had once formed for giving a connected history of the liberal sciences and elegant arts' (advertisement to *Essays on Philosophical Subjects*). Dugald Stewart mentioned Smith's essay on the Origin of Languages as a 'very beautiful specimen of theoretical history' (II. 55) and took notice of the fact that the mathematical sciences 'afford very favourable subjects' for treatment of this kind (II. 49). Indeed, it is probably true that Smith's history of astronomy is one of the most perceptive and complete versions of the thesis that he left us, starting as it does from a statement of the principles of human nature as relevant to a work of scientific or speculative thought, and going on to trace the development of knowledge in terms of four major astronomical systems, which culminate in the work of Newton (see Chapter 2 above).

Analytical

It is appropriate to observe that the interest that Smith showed in economic forces also featured largely at the time. For example, Harrington was widely recognized as a 'profound political writer' and as one who showed a 'thorough acquaintance with the true principles of democracy'.[24] Montesquieu too had shown an interest in the role of time in his *Considerations* (1752),[25] and had given some attention to economic factors in the *Esprit*, especially in book xx, where he examined the problem of 'How Commerce Broke Through the Barbarism of Europe'. The same basic theme is featured in Rousseau's *Origin of Inequality*, in Hutcheson's *System*, and especially in Hume's *History*, where he relates the increasing significance of that middling rank of men 'who are the best and firmest basis of public liberty' to the growth of commerce and industry.[26] Another notable figure in this general area is Lord Kames, who as early as 1747 had quite unequivocally linked the decline of feudal institutions to the appearance of arts and industry, in

---

[24] Kames, *Sketches* (1774: ii. 197); *HV* iii. 286. Harrington's *Oceana* (1656; 3rd edn. 1747) was also praised in Hume's essay on 'The Idea of a Perfect Commonwealth' and was given considerable attention by Francis Hutcheson in his *System of Moral Philosophy* (1755: bk 3, ch. 6: 'The Several Forms of Polity, with their Principal Advantages and Disadvantages'.

[25] Perhaps the best example of a truly dynamic theory of historical change is provided by Vico's remarkable *New Science* (1725). This work does not, however, seem to have had much direct impact, at least in this country.

[26] For comment, see Forbes (1970: 39).

remarking that, 'after the arts of Peace began to be cultivated, Manufactures and trade to revive in Europe, and Riches to increase, this Institution began to turn extremely burdensome. It first tottered and then fell by its own Weight, as wanting a solid foundation.'[27]

While it is not so much our purpose here to assess the extent of Smith's intellectual debts as to report on the existence of a climate of opinion, it should also be noted that the idea of distinct socio-economic stages was also entering the literature on quite a wide front. It is found, for example, in the first two books of Sir James Steuart's *Principles*,[28] first published in 1767 but completed in outline by 1759, and also in Kames's *Historical Law Tracts*, printed a year earlier.[29]

As noted above, Ronald Meek's work has also drawn attention to the French contribution, a development which was first noted in the *Economics of Physiocracy*, part I of which is was devoted to translations of Quesnay and Mirabeau, with reference to those works which 'seemed . . . to require special attention, if only because of their striking resemblance to the doctrines of the Scottish Historical School' (Meek 1962: 38). The argument was later extended to include Turgot (following Forbes) in an article published in 1971, and further developed in *Turgot on Progress Sociology and Economics* (1973). Here the stadial thesis was traced to fragments such as 'Universal History' (1750), 'Political Geography', 'Successive Advancements of the Human Mind', and the more complete *Reflections on the Formation and Distribution of Riches* (1766). Meek's research helped to make obvious 'the crucial role which the "four stages" theory must have played in the emergence of the new Franco-Scottish view of socio-economic development' (Meek 1971: 22). In *Social Science and the Ignoble Savage*, the point was put in an even more explicit form:

For better or for worse, this 'four stages' theory . . . was destined not only to dominate socio-economic thought in Europe in the latter half of the eighteenth century, but also to become of crucial significance in the subsequent development of economics, sociology, anthropology, and historiography, right down to our own time' (Meek 1976: 2).

However, it would appear that Smith must be regarded as a particularly influential figure in the development of this general line of thought, one who appears to have been especially dominant among Scottish writers at this time. It was in recognition of this point that Dugald

---

[27] Kames, *Essays Upon Several Subjects concerning British Antiquities* (1747); For comment see Ross (1973).

[28] These points are made in Skinner (1966: p.pxii and n.); see also Meek (1971, 1973).

[29] The stadial argument figures especially in Tract I, 'Criminal Law', and Tract II, 'Promises and Covenants'. Dugald Stewart considered that Kames's *Law Tracts* provided some 'excellent specimens' of philosophical history (Stewart II. 51).

Stewart felt moved to remark, in the course of an address to the Royal Society of Edinburgh, that:

It will not, I hope, be imputed to me as a blamable instance of national vanity, if I conclude this Section with remarking the rapid progress that has been made in our own country during the last fifty years, in tracing the origin and progress of the present establishments in Europe. Montesquieu undoubtedly led the way, but much has been done since the publication of his works, by authors whose names are enrolled among the members of this Society. Stewart 1858: x.147).

Even if the work done by Smith and his Scottish contemporaries finds parallels and precedents, it nevertheless appears to have been remarkable for the weight of emphasis that was placed on economic factors. As we have seen, there were really two applications of the general thesis. First, there is the argument that the development of productive forces ultimately depended on the 'natural wants' of man; the point being that man is first subject to certain basic needs which, once satisfied, allow him to pursue more complex goals (*WN* III. iii. 12). The same point was made by Adam Ferguson when he remarked that 'refinement and plenty foster new desires, while they furnish the means, or practice the methods, to gratify them'.[30] John Millar also linked these natural and insatiable desires to the development of productive forces, and even went so far as to argue that the latter would emerge in a sequence that corresponded to the four socio-economic stages. (Lehmann 1960: 176; cf. 224).

The second application of the thesis is to be found in the link that Smith established between economic organization and the social structure, particularly with regard to the classes involved and the relations of power and dependence likely to exist between them. As we have seen, the link that was established between the form of economy and the social and political structure was remarkably explicit, so much so indeed as to permit William Robertson to state the main propositions with economy and accuracy. First, he noted that 'In every enquiry concerning the operations of men when united together in society, the first object of attention should be their mode of subsistence. According as that varies, their laws and policy must be different'. Secondly, Robertson drew attention to the relationship between property and power, noting for example that, 'Upon discovering in what state property was at any particular period, we may determine with precision what was the

---

[30] *History of Civil Society* (Forbes 1967: 216–17); see also Ferguson's *Principles of Moral and Political Science* (1792); ch. 3, § ix. The thesis is a feature of Smith's *Lectures* e.g. *LJ*(B) 206–11) and of *TMS* IV. i. i, 'Of the Beauty which the Appearance of Utility bestows upon all the Productions of Art, and of the extensive Influence of this Species of Beauty'. See Ch. 2 above.

degree of power possessed by the king or by the nobility at that juncture'.[31]

While such statements apply equally to Smith's approach to the history of society, they should not be taken to imply that Smith was an economic determinist. Three points may be noted by way of illustration.

First, while Smith did argue that the 'commercial' stage of socio-economic growth would have certain recognizable features, he did not suggest that it was incompatible with 'absolutist' government. For example, both France and Spain could be regarded as 'developed' economies from a historical point of view, yet both were associated with monarchical systems which pretended to be absolutist.[32] Smith also made this point with respect to England, in arguing that the first effect of a developing manufacturing sector had been to *increase* the power of her kings (for example the Tudors) at the expense of the lords;[33] the point being that the decline in the power of the lords had taken place before the same underlying causes elevated the House of Commons to a superior degree of influence.[34]

Secondly, Smith argued that England was really a special case, and that she alone had escaped from absolutism.[35] To a great extent this was the reflection of her own natural economic advantages (*WN* III. iv. 20), but Smith also emphasized other factors, many of which were of an extra-economic type. For example, he argued that Great Britain's situation as an island had obviated the need for a standing army,[36] and thus denied her kings an important instrument of oppression. He added that Elizabeth I had also helped to weaken the position of her successors by selling off Crown lands, a policy that was not unconnected with the fact that she had no direct heirs. As Smith presents the case, it was the growing weakness of the Stuart kings (reflecting in part their own

---

[31] Robertson, (1777: i. 324; 1769: i. 222). The significance of these statements was first noted by Pascal (1938: 117).

[32] Smith comments in *WN* I. xi. n. 1 that, though 'the feudal system has been abolished in Spain and Portugal, it has not been succeeded by a much better'.

[33] This point is made in *LJ*(A) iv. 159 and *LJ*(B) 59–60, where it is stated that, as a result of the growth of manufactures, etc., 'the power of the nobility was diminished, and that too before the House of Commons had established its authority, and thus the king became arbitrary. Under the House of Tudor the government was quite arbitrary, the nobility were ruined, and the boroughs lost their power.'

[34] Smith considers the rise of the House of Commons in *LJ*(A) iv. 148 ff; *LJ*(B) 58–9.

[35] Smith emphasized England's position as a special case at some length; see especially *LJ*(A) iv. 168, where it is stated that 'In England alone a different government has been established from the naturall course of things. The situation and circumstances of England have been altogether different.' Cf. *HV* iv. 102–4, and Forbes's edition of Hume's *History*, (Forbes 1970: 23).

[36] The same arguments are considered in the opening lecture of *LJ*(A) v, where Smith also includes a review of the constitutional guarantees of English liberties. Similar arguments are stated in *LJ*(B) 61–4, although at rather less length.

peculiarities of character), and the growing significance of the Commons, that had ultimately combined to produce that particular system of liberty that was now found in England. In England alone, he emphasized, liberty is secured by 'an assembly of the representatives of the people, who claim the sole right of imposing taxes' (*WN* IV. vii. b. 51). Smith was to deploy the principles involved in his treatment of the American question (see Chapter 9 below).

But if Smith preferred the English model, he was very far from suggesting that this model represented the best of all possible worlds. In his 'Early Draft' especially, Smith adverted to the 'oppressive inequality' of the modern economy,[37] and elsewhere he drew attention to the fact that the House of Commons, whose power provided the foundation and protection of the liberty of the subject, could easily become a clearing-house for those sectional interests on which that power was collectively based (*WN* I. xi. p. 10). Smith was also well aware of corruption in politics and of the fact that the institutions of British government were markedly unrepresentative.[38] 'It is in Britain alone that any consent of the people is required, and God knows it is but a very figurative metaphoricall consent which is given here. And in Scotland still more than in England, as but very few have a vote for a member of Parliament who give this metaphoricall consent' (*LJ*(A) v. 134).

Yet if Smith did notice many of the defects of modern society, and some of the problems that were to arise in the future, the general tenor of his argument must be said to be broadly optimistic with regard to the possibilities of economic and political development. In this respect his position is perhaps adequately summarized in the remarks of his pupil, Millar,[39] who wrote that, when we contemplate the 'crowds of people . . . continually rising from the lower ranks . . . how habits of industry, have banished idleness . . . and have put it into the power of almost every individual by the exertion of his own talents, to earn a comfortable subsistence', then 'We cannot entertain a doubt of their powerful efficacy to propagate corresponding sentiments, of personal independence, and to instill higher notions of general liberty' (HV, iv. 124–5). Stewart concurred (Stewart IV. 9). Nor was the point lost on the French revolutionary, Barnave, who, writing quite independently of Smith and his contemporaries, reached the conclusion that:

---

[37] The 'Early Draft' opens ch. 2 with a long statement concerning the problem of inequality in the modern state.

[38] The distinction between personal and political freedom is a major feature of Duncan Forbes's article, 'Sceptical Whiggism, Commerce, and Liberty' (1975); see also Winch (1978: 40). One of the most interesting features of this valuable study is the attention given to Francis Hutcheson and to the contrast between his political views and those of Smith.

[39] This view is contested, at least to some extent, in Winch (1978: 100–2).

As soon as the arts and commerce succeed in penetrating the life of the society, and of opening up a new source of wealth for the labouring class, a revolution is prepared in political laws; a new distribution of wealth produces a new distribution of power. Just as the possession of land created aristocracy, so industrial property gives rise to the power of the people. It acquires liberty; it grows in numbers, it begins to influence affairs. (quoted in Laski 1936: 232).[40]

LINKS WITH SMITH'S POLITICAL ECONOMY

The arguments just reviewed are important in their own right as a contribution to an influential history of the development of civil society. The approach is based upon the treatment of public law as developed in the *Lectures on Jurisprudence*, although it should be noted that the treatment of the rise and fall of the feudal system offered above is based largely upon the content of book III of the *Wealth of Nations*. The model there outlined is economical and formal, suggesting that this area of analysis represents Smith's mature version of a much older analysis.

The location of book III is interesting. In the *Lectures* the analysis of the origins of the 'present establishments' in Europe provides the preface, or one of the prefaces, to the systematic treatment of political economy. In the *Wealth of Nations*, book III can be seen either as providing a retrospective view of the origins of a new institutional structure or as an introduction to the critique of the mercantile system that was to follow. The latter view is supported by the fact that Smith chose to preface his historical analysis with a statement of his thesis regarding the natural progress of opulence: 'according to the natural course of things, . . . the greater part of the capital of every growing society, is, first, directed to agriculture, afterwards to manufactures, and last of all to foreign commerce. This order of things is so very natural, that in every society that had any territory, it has always, I believe, been in some degree observed' (*WN* III. i. 8).

But, he continued, 'though this natural order of things must have taken place in some degree in every such society, it has, in all the modern states of Europe, been, in many respects, entirely inverted' (III. i. 9). Smith believed that the policy of Europe had introduced an 'unnatural and retrograde order' (III. i. 9) which had caused commerce to introduce manufactures, which in turn had given 'birth to the principal improvements of agriculture' (III. i. 9), thus explaining the 'slow progress of opulence' in European nations. Or, as he put it: 'Had human

---

[40] The socio-economic content of Steuart's *Principles* prompted the editor of the French translation (1789) to remark that of the advantages to be derived from reading the book: '*Le premier sera de convaincre, sans doute, que le revolution qui s'opere sous nos yeux etait dans l'ordre des choses necessaires.*' (Skinner 1966: 24n).

institutions, therefore, never disturbed the natural course of things, the progressive wealth and increase of the towns would, in every political society, be consequential, and in proportion to the improvement and cultivation of the territory or country' (III. i. 4).

The historical record, on the other hand, suggested that, 'through the greater part of Europe the commerce and manufactures of cities, instead of being the effect, have been the cause and occasion of the improvement and cultivation of the country. This order, however, being contrary to the natural course of things, is necessarily both slow and uncertain' (III. iv. 18, 19).

Smith's views as to the causes of the slow progress of opulence (as developed in *WN* III. ii) would be familiar to those who had heard his *Lectures on Jurisprudence*. What would have been new (and possibly strange) was the suggestion that the *actual* historical record as explained in the *Lectures* (and in *WN* III), was now to be regarded in some sense as an *unnatural* progression. The version of the argument presented in the *Lectures*, on the other hand, provides a useful guide to Smith's original intention in the sense that he set out to provide his students with the means of understanding the origins and nature of the fourth stage, that stage which it was his business to examine from the standpoint of the treatment of political economy. In the context of the *Lectures*, the historical material provides a necessary introduction to the treatment of political economy. In the context of the *Wealth of Nations*, the analysis of book III can be read as a retrospective account of the emergence of the exchange economy, presented not as a model to be designed and possibly imposed, but as the product of a long period of historical evolution. The exchange economy was presented by Smith as an institutional structure with a past.

On the other hand, *The Theory of Moral Sentiments* provides, as we have seen, an account of the way in which men form moral judgements and further explains the way in which they erect, in effect, barriers against their own passions, thus explaining the emergence of those conditions that make possible an ordered social structure. The principles involved could be presented as having an universal validity (see Chapter 3 above). But it is clear that many of the judgements Smith offered in *The Theory of Moral Sentiments* with regard to human behaviour may be regarded as specific to the economic, social, and cultural environment that corresponds to the fourth stage. We refer here to Smith's emphasis on an environment based on exchange, the pursuit of status, admiration for the 'habits of oeconomy, industry, discretion and application of thought' (*TMS*, IV. 2. 8) and to the esteem in which 'all men naturally regard a steady perseverance in the practice of frugality, industry and application, though directed to no other purpose than the acquisition of fortune'. These are hardly patterns of behaviour that would have commanded universal approbation in earlier cultural environments.

In speaking of *The Theory of Moral Sentiments*, Nicholas Phillipson has recently argued that Adam Smith is best understood as a writer who was offering a response to matters of contemporary relevance, in presenting him as 'a practical moralist who thought that his account of the principles of morals and social organisation would be of use to responsibly-minded men of middling rank, living in a modern, commercial society'. Indeed Dr Phillipson has gone so far as to suggest that Smith's ethical theory 'is redundant outside the context of a commercial society with a complex division of labour' (Phillipson 1983: 179, 182; cf. Dwyer 1987).

For his part, Professor Pocock has concluded that:

A crucial step in the emergence of Scottish social theory is, of course, that elusive phenomenon, the advent of the four-stages scheme of history. The progression from hunter to shepherd to farmer to merchant offered not only an account of increasing plenty, but a series of stages of increasing division of labour, bringing about in their turn an increasingly complex organisation of both society and personality. (1983: 242).

Professor Pocock has associated these trends with the emergence of what may be described as a bourgeois ideology.

Before proceeding to Smith's more formal analysis of a modern system of political economy, it may be convenient to consider the contributions of some of his predecessors to this field.

REFERENCES

Becker, C. (1932), *The Heavenly City of the Eighteenth Century Philosophers* (New Haven).

Black, J. F. (1926), *The Art of History* (London).

Bryson, G. (1945), *Man and Society* (Princeton).

Dwyer, J. (1987), *Virtuous Discourse* (Edinburgh).

Forbes, D. (1953–4), 'Scientific Whiggism: Adam Smith and John Millar', *Cambridge Journal*, 7.

——— (1967), ed. Adam Ferguson's *History of Civil Society* (Edinburgh).

——— (1970), *David Hume: The History of Great Britain* (Harmondsworth).

——— (1975), 'Sceptical Whiggism, Commerce and Liberty', in *EAS*.

Hont, I., and Ignatieff, M. (eds.) (1983), *Wealth and virtue: The Shaping of Political Economy in the Scottish Enlightenment* (Cambridge).

Kames, H. (1774), *Sketches of the History of Man* (Edinburgh).

Laski, H. (1936), *The Rise of European Liberalism* (London).

Lehmann, W. (1960), *John Millar of Glasgow* (London).

Lowenthal, D. (ed.) and (trans.) (1965), Montesquieu's *Considerations of the Causes of the Greatness of the Romans and their Decline* (London).

Martin, Kingsley, (1954), *French Liberal Thought in the Eighteenth Century*, ed. J.P. Mayer (London).

Marx, K., and Engels, F. (1955), *Karl Marx and Frederick Engels: Selected Works* (Moscow and London).

Meek, R. L. (1954), 'The Scottish Contribution to Marxist Sociology, in *Democracy and the Labour Movement*, ed. J. Saville (London); reprinted with amendments in Meek (1967).

——(1962), *The Economics of Physiocracy* (London).

——(1967), *Economics and Ideology and Other Essays* (London).

——(1971), 'Smith, Turgot and the Four Stages Theory', *History of Political Economy*, 3.

——(1973), *Turgot on Progress, Sociology and Economics* (Cambridge).

——(1976), *Social Science and the Ignoble Savage* (Cambridge).

Pascal, R. (1938), 'Property and Society: The Scottish Contribution of the Eighteenth Century', *Modern Quarterly*, 1.

Phillipson, N. (1983), 'Adam Smith as a Civic Moralist', in Hont and Ignatieff, (1983).

Pocock, J. G. A. (1983), 'Cambridge Paradigms and Scotch Philosophers', in Hont and Ignatieff, (1983).

Ramsay, J. (1888), *Scotland and Scotsmen*, ed. A. Allardyce, from the Ochtertyre MS, i. 191 (Edinburgh).

Robertson, W. (1769), *The History of the Reign of the Emperor Charles V* (Edinburgh).

——(1777), *The History of America* (Edinburgh).

Ross, I. (1973), *Lord Kames and the Scotland of his Day* (Oxford).

Skinner, A. S. (1982), 'A Scottish Contribution to Marxist Sociology?' *Classical and Marxian Political Economy*, ed. I. Bradley and M. Howard (London).

Steuart, Sir James, (1966), *Principles of Political Oeconomy*, ed. A. S. Skinner (Edinburgh).

Stewart, Dugald, (1854–60), *Works*, ed. Sir Williams Hamilton, 10 vols. (Edinburgh).

Sweezy, P. M. (1976), contribution to 'The Debate on the Transition', in *The Transition from Feudalism to Capitalism*, ed. R. Hilton (London).

Walker, L. J. (1950), ed. *The Discourses of Niccolo Machiavelli* (London).

Webster, A. (1993), 'J. Barnave: Philosopher of a Revolution', *History of Economic Ideas*, 17.

Winch, D. N. (1978), *Adam Smith's Politics: An Essay in Historiographical Revision* (Cambridge).

PART III

5

Some Principles of Political Economy:
Pufendorf, Hutcheson, and Adam Smith

INTRODUCTION

In a recent study entitled *Before Adam Smith: The Emergence of Political Economy 1662–1776*, Terence Hutchison reminded his readers that:

> The University of Glasgow was one of the first and most important of the founts and origins of the Scottish Philosophical Enlightenment, and especially of its contribution to political economy. But, in this great, meteoric intellectual movement, outstandingly the most brilliant and original thinker and writer . . . was neither a Glaswegian nor an academic. Though, as a boy, he studied for a time at Edinburgh University, David Hume never obtained a degree. Subsequently, hardly to the credit of those celebrated institutions, he failed to obtain either of the chairs he sought, one at Edinburgh in 1744–45, and one at Glasgow in 1751. (Hutchison 1988: 199).

Seen in retrospect, and from the vantage point of a different cultural environment, Glasgow may be thought to have lost an opportunity to establish a link with all three major figures of the Scottish Enlightenment, even if it is also evident that this deficiency did not impede the emergence of a period of 'ascendancy', notably in the period 1756–76.

Terence Hutchison was writing a history of economic thought which gave due attention to Francis Hutcheson even if he excluded his work from the list of those that contributed to the period of Scottish dominance. For the point remains that Hutcheson exerted a great influence on Smith, as indeed did the 'most illustrious philosopher and historian of the present age' (i.e. Hume (*WN* v. i. g. 3).

Francis Hutcheson, Smith, and Hume should be of continuing interest to the student of political economy, not least because they did not see themselves as economists so much as philosophers who placed the study of economic phenomena in a broad social context. All three start from a

This paper formed the basis of a lecture delivered at a conference held in Glasgow to celebrate the tricentenary of the birth of Francis Hutcheson (1694–1746), the second incumbent of the Chair of Moral Philosophy in the University. The purpose of the present argument is to convey something of the flavour of Hutcheson's teaching in economics and to confirm his debt to one of *his* teachers, Gerschom Carmichael (1672–1729), his predecessor in the philosophy chair, and, through Carmichael a further debt to Pufendorf. It was first published in the *Scottish Journal of Political Economy*, **42** (1995).

position that was neatly stated by Hutcheson's correspondent, Adam Ferguson, when he noted that 'both the earliest and the latest accounts collected from every quarter of the globe, represent mankind as assembled in troops and companies'. The basic task was to explain how it was that a creature endowed with both self and other-regarding propensities was fitted for the social state. The responses, which varied in character, were to be found in the way in which Hutcheson, Hume, and Smith addressed the central question which was so neatly posed by the latter, namely: 'how and by what means does it come to pass, that the mind prefers one tenor of conduct to another, denominates the one right and the other wrong; considers the one as the object of approbation, honour and reward, and the other of blame, censure and punishment?' (*TMS* vii. i. 2). In dealing with this question, both Hume and Smith agreed with Hutcheson's emphasis on immediate sense and feeling as distinct from reason (see Chapter 3 above).

When we turn to Hutcheson, it is to discover marked similarities with the work of his successor, especially in the context of his belief that 'We may see in our species, from the very cradle, a constant propensity to action and motion' (Hutcheson 1755: 21). But in some respects the position is subtler than that stated by Smith. To begin with, Hutcheson argued that man has powers of perception which 'introduce into the mind all the materials of knowledge' and which are associated with 'acts of the understanding' (1755: 7). Acts of the understanding assist in the isolation of objects to be attained (e.g. sources of pleasure) or avoided, and culminate in acts of will.

Acts of will, which may be calm or turbulent, were divided in turn into the selfish or the benevolent. Benevolent acts of will, which may be described as calm, tend towards the 'universal happiness of others', while the turbulent include 'pity, condolence, congratulation, gratitude'. Acts of will that are selfish but calm include 'an invariable constant impulse towards one's own perfection and happiness of the highest kind' (1755: 9) and do not rule out 'deliberate purposes of injury' (1755: 73). The turbulent and selfish embrace 'hunger, thirst, lust, passions for sensual pleasure, wealth, power or fame' (1755: 11–12). In Hutcheson's case, the problem is that of attaining a degree of balance between the turbulent and the calm, the selfish and the benevolent: 'the general tenor of human life is an incoherent mixture of many social, kind, innocent actions, and of many selfish, angry, sensual ones; as one or other of our natural dispositions happens to be raised, and to be prevalent over others' (1755: 37).

While Smith was correct in identifying Hutcheson with that school of thought that found virtue to consist in benevolence, there is equally no doubt that Hutcheson gave a prominent place to self-love:

Our reason can indeed discover certain bounds, within which we may not only act from self-love consistently with the good of the whole; but every mortal's acting thus within these bounds for his own good, is absolutely necessary for the good of the whole; and the want of self-love would be universally pernicious . . . But when self-love breaks over the bounds above mentioned, and leads us into actions detrimental to others, and to the whole; or makes us insensible of the generous kind affections; then it appears vicious, and is disapproved. (Hutcheson 1725: III. v).

As in the case of Smith, what is critically important is man's desire to be approved of: 'an high pleasure is felt upon our gaining the approbation and esteem of others for our good actions, and upon their expressing their sentiments of gratitude; and on the other hand, we are cut to the very heart by censure, condemnation, and reproach' (Hutcheson 1755: 25). On Hutcheson's argument, an important source of control is represented by a capacity for judgement, including moral judgement, which is linked to man's deployment of internal senses such as the 'sympathetic', which differ from external senses such as sight, sound, or taste, and 'by which, when we apprehend the state of others, our hearts naturally have a fellow-feeling with them' (1755: 19).

In practice Hutcheson places most emphasis on the moral sense whose exercise (reinforced by the senses of honour and of shame) encourages the individual to virtuous action, and to the practice of restraint. It was Hutcheson's contention that men were inclined to, and fitted for, society: 'their curiosity, communicativeness, desire of action, their sense of honour, their compassion, benevolence, gaiety and the moral faculty, could have little or no exercise in solitude' (1755: 34).

This discussion was to lead to Hutcheson's treatment of natural rights and of the state of nature in a manner that is reminiscent of Locke. He also advances the Lockean claim that the state of nature is a state not of war but of inconvenience which can be resolved only by the establishment of government in terms of a complex double contract. This has been described as the 'Real Whig position' (Winch 1978: 46; Robbins 1968) and may explain the considerable influence of Hutcheson's political ideas in the American Colonies (Norton 1976). Hutcheson's 'warm love of liberty' was attested by Principal Leechman in his introduction to the *System* (1755: pp. xxxv–xxxvi), a sentiment that was echoed by Hugh Blair (Winch 1978: 47–8) in a contemporary review of the book.

While agreeing that an essential precondition of social stability is some system of 'magistracy' (*TMS* VII. iv. 36), Adam Smith (like Hume) was to emerge as a critic of the contract theory. It is also well known that he rejected the idea of a moral sense as a 'peculiar sentiment, distinct from every other' (VII. iii. 3. 15). In addition, he criticized Hutcheson for seeming to imply that self-love was 'a principle which could never be virtuous in any degree or in any direction' (VII. ii. 3. 12). But for the economist, it is important to note that Hutcheson distinguished often more clearly than did Smith between approval and moral approbation. As Hutcheson put it:

The calm desire of private good, tho' it is not approved as a virtue, yet it is far from being condemned as vice. And none of the truly natural and selfish appetites are of themselves condemned as evil, when they are within certain bounds, even tho' they are not referred by the agent to any public good. It was necessary for the general good that all such affections should be implanted in our species; and therefore it would have been utterly unnatural to have made them a matter of disapprobation. (Hutcheson 1755: 65).

Elsewhere he noted that:

A penetrating genius, capacity for business, patience of application and labour . . . are naturally admirable and relished by all observers, but with quite a different feeling from moral approbation. (Hutcheson 1755: 28).

Whatever the differences of emphasis and of analysis that are disclosed in the writings of Hutcheson and Smith, the arguments reviewed in this section are or should be important to the economist for three reasons. First, it appears that social order as a basic precondition for economic activity depends in part upon a capacity for moral judgement. Secondly, it is alleged that the psychological drives that explain economic activity must be seen in a context wider than the economic. Finally, the argument suggests that all forms of activity are subject to the scrutiny of our fellows. Economic choices may be socially constrained (see Chapter 3 above and Chapter 7 below).

HUTCHESON'S ECONOMIC ANALYSIS

There are five major topics covered in Hutcheson's *System*, which is generally assumed to follow closely the content of his lecture course as a whole. The economic analysis is not given in the form of a single coherent discourse, but rather is woven into the broader treatment of jurisprudence. Perhaps for this reason, Hutcheson's work did not attract a great deal of attention from early historians of economic thought. But the situation was transformed as a result of Edwin Cannan's discovery of Smith's *Lectures on Jurisprudence*. Cannan recalled that:

On April 21, 1895, Mr Charles C. Maconochie, Advocate, whom I then met for the first time, happened to be present when, in course of conversation with the literary editor of the Oxford Magazine, I had occasion to make some comment about Adam Smith. Mr Maconochie immediately said that he possessed a manuscript report of Adam Smith's lectures on jurisprudence, which he regarded as of considerable interest. (Cannan 1896: p. xv).

While Cannan's reaction may be imagined, the lectures had the effect of confirming Hutcheson's influence upon his pupil on a broad front, but especially in the area of economic analysis (as distinct from policy). For what Cannan discovered was that the *order* of a large part of Smith's course and its content corresponded closely with what Hutcheson was believed to have taught. It is this correspondence that served to renew interest in Hutcheson's economics with remarkable speed. Quite apart from Cannan's introduction to the *Lectures*, the same theme is elaborated in his introduction to the *Wealth of Nations* (1904 edn.). The link had also been noted, following the publication of the *Lectures*, in Palgrave's *Dictionary of Political Economy* (1899) and received its most elaborate statement in W. R. Scott's *Francis Hutcheson* (1900). The most modern treatment of this kind is to be found in W. L. Taylor's influential work, *Francis Hutcheson and David Hume as Predecessors of Adam Smith* (1965).

But Cannan noted something else, namely that it may be that the 'germ of the *Wealth of Nations*' is to be found in Hutcheson's treatment of value (Cannan 1896: p. xxvi). It is this topic that forms the central feature of the remainder of the present argument, although it will be convenient to begin with Hutcheson's views on the division of labour where his influence on Smith may be particularly obvious.

Before we pass on to these subjects, however, it should be noted that Hutcheson's work on economic topics has its own history. It is evident that he admired the work of his immediate predecessor in the Chair of Moral Philosophy, Gershom Carmichael (1672–1729), and especially his translation of, and commentary on, Samuel Pufendorf. In Hutcheson's address to the 'students in Universities' the *Introduction to Moral Philosophy* (1742) is described thus:

The learned will at once discern how much of this compeund is taken from the writing of others, from Cicero and Aristotle, and to name no other moderns, from Pufendorf's smaller work, *De Officio Hominis et Civis Juxta Legem Naturalem* which that worthy and ingenious man the late Professor Gerschom Carmichael of Glasgow, by far the best commentator on that book, has so supplied and corrected that the notes are of much more value than the text. (Taylor 1965: 25).

Carmichael's influence as a student of ethics and of jurisprudence has been frequently celebrated, notably by Sir William Hamilton, who stated that he may be regarded 'on good grounds, as the true founder of the Scottish school of philosophy' (Taylor 1965: 253). But it is to W. L. Taylor that we are indebted for the reminder that Carmichael (and Pufendorf) may have shaped Hutcheson's economic ideas. Taylor concluded that:

The interesting point for the development of economic thought in all this is the very close parallelism between Pufendorf's *De Officio* and Hutcheson's *Introduction to Moral Philosophy*. Each man covered almost exactly the same field . . . The inescapable conclusion is that Francis Hutcheson took over almost in whole, from Carmichael, the economic ideas of Pufendorf. (Taylor 1965: 28–9).

The Division of Labour

A key issue for both arose from the comparison of the social as distinct from the solitary state; or, as Pufendorf put it,

it would seem to have been more wretched than that of any wild beast, if we take into account with what weakness man goes forth into this world, to perish at once, but for the help of others; and how rude a life each would lead, if he had nothing more than what he owed to his own strength and ingenuity. On the contrary, it is altogether due to the aid of other men, that out of such feebleness, we have been able to grow up, that we now enjoy untold comforts, and that we improve mind and body for our own advantage and that of others. And in this sense the natural state is opposed to a life improved by the industry of men. (Pufendorf 1927 edn.: ii. 89).

This broad line of argument was developed in the *System* (Hutcheson 1755: bk 2, ch. 4), where Hutcheson offered two specific economic applications. First, he noted that the 'joint labours of twenty men will cultivate forests, or drain marshes, for farms to each one, and provide houses for habitation, and inclosures for their stocks, much sooner than the separate labours of the same number' (1755: 289). Secondly, Hutcheson drew attention to the importance of the division of labour:

Nay 'tis well known that the produce of the labours of any given number, twenty, for instance, in providing the necessaries or conveniences of life, shall be much greater by assigning to one, a certain sort of work of one kind, in which he will soon acquire skill and dexterity, and to another assigning work of a different kind, than if each one of the twenty were obliged to employ himself, by turns in all the different sorts of labour requisite for his subsistence, without sufficient dexterity in any. In the former method each procures a great quantity of goods of one kind, and can exchange a part of it for such goods obtained by the labours of others as he shall stand in need of. One grows expert in tillage, another in pasture and breeding cattle, a third in masonry, a fourth in the chace, a fifth in iron-works, a sixth in the arts of the loom, and so on throughout the rest. Thus all are supplied by means of barter with the works of complete artists. In the other method scarce any one could be dextrous and skillful in any one sort of labour. (Hutcheson 1755: 288–9).

Property

The discussion of the division of labour implied that members of society are interdependent in respect of the satisfaction of their wants. It also led to two further analytical developments; security of property, and the problem of value in exchange (see especially Brown 1987).

Much of the discussion in book 2, chapter 6, of the *System* is concerned with 'the right of property'. But Hutcheson also noted that:

If we extend our views further and consider what the common interest of society may require, we shall find the right of property further confirmed. Universal industry is plainly necessary for the support of mankind. Tho' men are naturally active, yet their activity would rather turn toward the lighter and pleasanter exercises, than the slow, constant, and intense labours requisite to procure the necessaries and conveniences of life, unless strong motives are presented to engage them to these severer labours. Whatever institution therefore shall be found necessary to promote universal diligence and patience, and make labour agreeable or eligible to mankind, must also tend to the public good; and institutions or practices which discourage industry must be pernicious to mankind. Now nothing can so effectually excite men to constant patience and diligence in all sorts of useful industry, as the hopes of future wealth, ease, and pleasure to themselves, their offspring, and all who are dear to them, and of some honour too to themselves on account of their ingenuity, and activity, and liberality. All these hopes are presented to men by securing to every one the fruits of his own labours, that he may enjoy them, and dispose of them as he pleases. . . .
Nay the most extensive affections could scarce engage a wise man to industry, if no property ensued upon it. (Hutcheson 1755: 320–1).

Hutcheson attached a great deal of importance to freedom of choice, and in fact concluded this phase of the argument by rejecting any suggestion that 'magistrates' may be involved, passages that may well have attracted the attention of the youthful Smith (Hutcheson 1755: 322–3).

The Theory of Value

It is Hutcheson's treatment of value that shows most clearly the influence of Pufendorf and of Carmichael, where the latter observed that:

In general we may say that the value of goods depends upon these two elements, their *scarcity*, and the difficulty of acquiring them . . . Furthermore, *scarcity* is to be regarded as combining two elements, the number of those demanding, and the usefulness thought to adhere in the good or service, and which can add to the utility of human life. (quoted in Taylor 1965: 65; cf. Naldi 1993).

Pufendorf's analysis received its most elaborate statement in the *De Jure*, in the long chapter 'On Price' (bk 5, ch. 1). The most succinct statement, on which Carmichael commented, is to be found in the *De Officio* (bk 1, ch. 14), where Pufendorf observed:

Of common value the foundation as such is that aptitude of the thing or service, by which it can contribute something directly or indirectly to the necessities of human life, and to make it more comfortable or agreeable. Hence we usually call things that serve no *use* at all things of no value. Yet there are some things most useful for human life, upon which no definite value is understood to have been set, either because they do not admit of ownership, and necessarily so, or because they are unsuited for exchange, and hence withdrawn from trade, or because in trade they are never considered otherwise than as an addition to something else [e.g. the ether, the heavenly bodies, the ocean, sunlight, clear, pure air, the fair face of the earth, the wind and shade] . . . For in this matter the necessity of the thing, or its exalted usefulness, are so far from always holding the first place, that we rather see men hold in lowest esteem the things with which human life cannot dispense. And this because nature, not without the singular providence of God, pours fourth a bountiful *supply* of them. *Hence an increase of value tends to be produced especially by scarcity* . . . For articles in everyday use prices are raised especially when their *scarcity* is combined with *necessity or want* . . . (Pufendorf 1927 edn.: 70–3).

To this Pufendorf added two important points which relate to what may be termed the supply price and to associated matters affecting the rate of exchange:

In the case of artificial commodities, scarcity apart, the price is chiefly raised by the fineness and elegance of the workmanship which they display, sometimes too by the fame of the artificer, also the difficulty of the work, the scarcity of artisans and workmen, and so forth. As for services and arts, difficulty enhances their price, as do also skill, utility, necessity, the scarcity or rank or freedom of the agents, and finally even the reputation of the art, as being accounted noble or ignoble. The opposite of these things usually lowers the price. (Pufendorf 1927 edn.: 71; cf. *De Jure*, bk 5, ch. 1).

Secondly, Pufendorf seems to have distinguished between the utility of the commodity to be acquired in exchange and our perception of the value of the good *to be* exchanged:

as a rule, people who possess a thing do not set the same value on it as people who wish to acquire it, since we always look upon the thing which we call our own and which we give away, as being exceedingly valuable. Nevertheless, the amount of the exchange, must be regulated by the value which the recipient sets upon the gifts received. (Pufendorf 1927 edn.: bk 5, ch. 1, para. 9).

In a passage that suggests a distinction between the utility expected and that which is realized, he argued, with regard to the estimation of the value of a commodity by an individual, that 'perhaps it ought not to be fixed at the value which he sets upon it when it is in his hands, but at the value which he set upon it before he had it' (*De Jure*, bk 5, ch. 1, para. 9).

Hutcheson in effect opened his analysis of the problem by pointing out that the 'natural ground of all value or price is some sort of use which goods afford in life', adding that 'by the use causing a demand we mean not only a natural subserviency to our support, or to some natural pleasure, but any tendency to give any satisfaction, by prevailing custom or fancy, as a matter of ornament or distinction' (Hutcheson 1755: II. 53–4). He continued:

But when some aptitude to human use is presupposed, we shall find that the prices of goods depend on these two jointly, the *demand* on account of some use or other which many desire, and the *difficulty* of acquiring, or cultivating for human use. When goods are equal in these respects men are willing to interchange them with each other; nor can any artifice or policy make the values of goods depend on any thing else. When there is no *demand*, there is no price, were the *difficulty* of acquiring never so great: and where there is no *difficulty* or labour requisite to acquire, the most universal *demand* will not cause a price; as we see in fresh water in these climates. Where the demand for two sorts of goods is equal, the prices are as the difficulty. Where the difficulty is equal, the prices are as the demand. (Hutcheson 1755: ii. 54).

Hutcheson then added two points which are reminiscent of Pufendorf in commenting on issues that affect supply price and the rate of exchange. First, he argued:

In like manner by difficulty of acquiring, we do not only mean great labour or toil, but all other circumstances which prevent a great plenty of the goods or performances demanded. Thus the price is encreased by the rarity or scarcity of the materials in nature, or such accidents as prevent plentiful crops or certain fruits of the earth; and the great ingenuity and nice taste requisite in the artists to finish well some works of art, as men of such genius are rare. The value is also raised, by the dignity of station in which, according to the custom of the country, the men must live who provide us with certain goods, or works of art. Fewer can be supported in such stations than in the meaner; and the dignity and expense of their stations must be supported by the higher prices of their goods or services. Some other singular considerations may exceedingly heighten the values of goods to some men, which will not affect their estimation with others. These above mentioned are the chief which obtain in commerce. (Hutcheson 1755: ii. 54–5).

As regards the rate of exchange, Hutcheson commented:

In commerce it must often happen that one may need such goods of mine as yield a great and lasting use in life, and have cost a long course of labour to acquire and cultivate, while yet he has none of those goods I want in exchange, or not sufficient quantities; or what goods of his I want, may be such as yield but a small use, and are procurable by little labour. In such cases it cannot be expected that I should exchange with him. I must search for others who have the goods I want, and such quantities of them as are equivalent in use to my goods, and require as much labour to produce them; and the goods on both sides must be brought to some estimation or value. (Hutcheson 1755: ii. 53).

But although these positions do not differ significantly from those of Pufendorf, Hutcheson does seem to have taken notice of two additional points. First, he seems to suggest, as the above quotation indicates, that goods will exchange at a rate that will be in part determined by the quantity of labour embodied in them (a point later taken up by Smith). Secondly, he noted, in a passage that may have been 'foreshadowed' by Pufendorf, that some commodities 'of great use have no price, either because they are naturally destined for community, or cannot come into commerce but as appendages of something else, the price of which may be increased by them, though they cannot be separately estimated' (Hutcheson 1747 edn.: 200; quoted in Taylor 66).

Money

The discussion of value in exchange led Hutcheson on quite logically to consider the medium of exchange, namely money, and here too he followed an old tradition which had already been commented upon by Pufendorf. In the *De Officio* (bk 1, ch. 14), he noted the inconvenience of exchange by barter:

But after men departed from their primitive simplicity and various kinds of gain were introduced, it was readily understood that common value alone was not sufficient for the transactions of men's affairs and their increased dealings. . .

Hence most nations, attracted by a richer mode of life, have seen fit by convention to impose a value *par excellence* upon a certain thing, in order that the common values of other things might be tested by this, and virtually contained in the same; so that by this medium one could acquire anything that is for sale, and engage conveniently in any sort of dealings and contracts. (Pufendorf 1927 edn.: 72–3).

He added:

For this purpose most nations have decided to employ the nobler and rarer metals. For they possess a very compact substance, so as not to be worn away easily in use, and also they admit of division into many small pieces. And they are no less convenient to keep and to handle, while on account of their rarity, they can equal the value of many other things (Pufendorf 1927 edn.: 73).

Similar points are made in the *De Jure* (bk 5, ch. 1), where Pufendorf elaborated on the need for coinage and the problems of debasement. These passages are interesting not least for the emphasis given to the need for a stable measure of value, and evidence of a search for an invariable standard of value of the kind that money alone could not provide, at least over a long term of years.

Once more, Hutcheson followed suit in explaining the problems of barter and the need to establish a standard or 'common measure' when settling the 'values or goods for commerce':

The qualities requisite to the most perfect standard are these: it must be something generally desired so that men are generally willing to take it in exchange. The very making any goods the standard will of itself give them this quality. It must be portable; which will often be the case if it is rare, so that small quantities are of great value. It must be divisible without loss into small parts, so as to be suited to the values of all sorts of goods; and it must be durable, not easily wearing by use, or perishing in its nature. One or other of these prerequisites in the standard, shews the inconvenience of many of our commonest goods for that purpose. The man who wants a small quantity of my corn will not give me a work-beast for it, and his beast does not admit division. I want perhaps a pair of shoes, but my ox is of far greater value, and the other may not need him. I must travel to distant lands, my grain cannot be carried along for my support, without unsufferable expense, and my wine would perish in the carriage. 'Tis plain therefore that when men found any use for the rarer metals, silver and gold, in ornaments and utensils, and thus a demand was raised for them, they would soon also see that they were the fittest standards for commerce, on all the accounts above-mentioned. (Hutcheson 1755: ii. 55–6).

The familiar arguments concerning the need for coinage and the dangers of debasement follow (Hutcheson 1755: bk 2, ch. 12), while there is also a hint of the need to find an invariable measure of value at least over long periods of time:

We say indeed commonly, that the rates of labour and goods have risen since these metals grew plenty; and that the rates of labour and goods were low when the metals were scarce; conceiving the value of the metals as invariable, because the legal names of the pieces, the pounds, shillings, or pence, continue to them always the same till a law alters them. But a days digging or ploughing was as uneasy to a man a thousand years ago as it is now, tho' he could not then get so much silver for it: and a barrel of wheat, or beef, was then of the same use to support the human body, as it is now when it is exchanged for four times as much silver. Properly, the value of labour, grain, and cattle, are always pretty much the same, as they afford the same uses in life, where no new inventions of tillage, or pasturage, cause a greater quantity in proportion to the demand. 'Tis the metal chiefly that has undergone the great change of value, since these metals have been in greater plenty, the value of the coin is altered tho' it keeps the old names. (Hutcheson 1755: ii. 58).

CONCLUSION

This chapter has pursued two themes. First, I have endeavoured to establish Hutcheson's link to Pufendorf in a manner that confirms a debt to the work of W. L. Taylor. Secondly, the argument has sought to give prominence to the role of subjective judgement as regards the determinants of value in the works of both Pufendorf and Hutcheson.

Edwin Cannan, as we have seen, considered that Hutcheson's emphasis on the utility of the goods to be acquired and on the disutility of effort needed to create the goods to be exchanged, with the attendant emphasis on demand- and supply-side considerations, provided the 'kernel' of the *Wealth of Nations*. Taylor, on the other hand, suggested that Smith's concern with material welfare (Taylor 1965: 193) served to obscure the line of argument set out by Hutcheson. Robertson and Taylor, in fact, concluded that:

It is evident that the *magnum opus* was cast in a mould of a powerful unifying conception. Now within this framework it is evident that the measurement, in real terms, of the wealth of nations, and in particular of its progress, would seem to call for some unvarying standard of value which would enable valid comparisons to be made through time . . . for this reason, if for no other, it does not appear inexplicable that Adam Smith no longer paid so much attention to the lines of argument taken over from Hutcheson, which had served well enough in the *Lectures*. (Robertson and Taylor 1957, 194–5).

What Robertson and Taylor did not note was that Smith's preoccupation with a real measure of value may also have owed much to Hutcheson. These subjects are further developed in Chapter 7.

Readers of the *Wealth of Nations* and *The Theory of Moral Sentiments* will need no reminding that Smith did not conceive of welfare as measurable in real terms alone. In Smith's view, happiness is a state of mind and he was well aware of the social and psychological costs of economic growth (*WN* v. i. f. 60). Indeed, it is this perspective that returns us to the form of argument stated in the opening section, where it was noted that both Hutcheson and Smith emphasized that men desire to be approved of and that this approval was itself a source of satisfaction. As we have seen (in Chapter 3 above), Smith used this argument in disposing of Mandeville's 'licentious doctrine'. He argued in effect that the pursuit of gratification is not inconsistent with *propriety*—and, indeed, should be consistent with it. Again Hutcheson concurred:

there is no necessary vice in the consuming of the finest products, or the wearing of the dearest manufactures by persons whose fortunes can allow it consistently with all the duties of life. But what if men grew generally more frugal and abstemious in such things? More of these finer goods could be sent abroad. (Hutcheson 1755: ii. 320; cf. Taylor 1965: ch. 4).

A mercantilist to the last?

REFERENCES

Blackstone, W. T. (1975), *Francis Hutcheson and Contemporary Ethical Theory* (Athens, Ga).

Brown, V. (1987), 'Value and Property in the History of Economic Thought: An Analysis of the Emergence of Scarcity', *Oeconomia*, 7.

Campbell, T. D. (1982), 'Francis Hutcheson', in *The Origins and Nature of the Scottish Enlightenment*, ed. R. H. Campbell and A. S. Skinner (Edinburgh).

Campbell, W. F. (1967), 'Adam Smith's Theory of Justice, Prudence and Beneficence', *American Economic Review*, 57.

Cannan, E. (1896), *Adam Smith's Lectures on Justice, Police, Revenue and Arms* (Oxford).

Hume, David (1955 edn.), *Economic Writings*, ed. E. Rotwein (London).

Hutcheson, Francis (1725), *Inquiry into the Original of our Ideas of Beauty and Virtue*, 2nd edn. (London).

——(1742), *Philosophie Moralis Institutio Compendiaria, Ethices et Jurisprudentiae Naturalis Elementa continens, Libri Tres* (2nd edn. 1745); published as *A Short Introduction to Moral Philosophy in Three Books, containing the Elements of Ethics and the Law of Nature* (Glasgow).

——(1755), *A System of Moral Philosophy in Three Books, written by the late Francis Hutcheson, LL.D., Professor of Moral Philosophy in the University of Glasgow. Published from the original MS, by his son Francis Hutcheson, M. D. to which is prefixed Some Account of the Life, Writings, and Character of the Author, by The Reverend William Leechman, D. D., Professor of Divinity in the same University* (Glasgow).

Hutchison, T. (1988), *Before Adam Smith: The Emergence of Political Economy 1662–1776* (Oxford).

Kaye, F. B. (ed.) (1924), *The Fable of the Bees* (Oxford).

McCosh, J. (1875), *The Scottish Philosophy from Hutcheson to Hamilton* (Princeton).

Macfie, A. L. (1967), *The Individual in Society* (London).

Meek, R. L. (1976), 'New Light on Adam Smith's Lectures on Jurisprudence', *History of Political Economy*, 8.

Naldi, N. (1993), 'Gershom Carmichael on Demand and Difficulty of Acquiring', *Scottish Journal of Political Economy*, 40.

Norton, D. F. (1976), 'Francis Hutcheson in America', *Studies on Voltaire and the Eighteenth Century*, ed. T. Besterman, 154.

Palgrave, R. H. I. (1899), *Dictionary of Political Economy* (London).

Pesciarelli, E. (1986), 'On Adam Smith's Lectures on Jurisprudence', *Scottish Journal of Political Economy*, 33.

Pufendorf, Samuel von (1682), *De Officio et Civis Juxta Legem Naturalem Libri Duo.*

——(1688 edn), *De Jure Naturae et Gentium Libri Octo.* Both Pufendorf works were translated in *Classics of International Law* (Oxford); the *De Officio* was translated by Frank Gardiner Moore in 1927; the *De Jure* by C. H. and W. A. Oldfather in 1934.

Raphael, D. D. (1947), *Moral Sense* (Oxford).

——(1969), *British Moralists 1650–1800* (Oxford).

Robbins, C. (1954), 'When is it that Colonies may turn Independent: An Analysis of the Environment and Politics of Francis Hutcheson', *William and Mary Quarterly*, 11.

———(1968), *The Eighteenth Century Commonwealth Man* (New York).

Robertson, H. M., and Taylor, W. L. (1957), 'Adam Smith's Approach to the Theory of Value', *Economic Journal*, 67.

Scott, W. R. (1900), *Francis Hutcheson, His Life, Teaching and Position in the History of Philosophy* (Cambridge).

———(1932), 'Francis Hutcheson', *Encyclopaedia of the Social Sciences*, E. R. A Seligman, vii.

———(1937), *Adam Smith as Student and Professor* (Glasgow).

Taylor, W. L. (1965), *Francis Hutcheson and David Hume as Predecessors of Adam Smith* (Durham, NC).

Teichgraeber, R. F. (1986), *Free Trade and Moral Philosophy: Rethinking the Sources of Adam Smith's Wealth of Nations* (Durham, NC).

Winch, D. (1978), *Adam Smith's Politics: An Essay in Historiographic Revision* (Cambridge).

6
The Development of a System: Adam Smith and the Physiocrats

INTRODUCTION

Smith's *Theory of Moral Sentiments* confirms the importance of the rules of justice as a basic requirement of an orderly society and also provides us with some understanding of basic human drives, i.e. of the complex psychology of the so-called 'economic man' (see Chapter 3 above). The treatment of history, as contained in his *Lectures on Jurisprudence*, on the other hand, provides an account of those processes that resulted in the emergence of the 'present establishments' to be found in contemporary Europe, i.e. an understanding of the 'nature and causes' of the stage of commerce, that institutional structure with which Smith as an economist was primarily concerned.

However, a *formal* analysis of economic phenomena is to be found elsewhere. Smith's early writings on economics (apart from two short fragments on the division of labour) are contained in the two sets of lecture notes currently available to us and in the document first discovered by W. R. Scott and described by him as an 'Early Draft' of the *Wealth of Nations*. The latter document belongs to the same broad period as the Lectures, which relate respectively to the sessions 1762–3 and 1763–4. There are of course differences between these documents. The first set of lecture notes on economic topics (i.e. LJ(A)) is less complete than the second, and excludes, for example, the discussion of Law's Bank, interest, exchange, and the causes of the slow progress of opulence. On the other hand, the topics covered in LJ(A) (which correspond approximately to sections 1–12 of part 2 in Cannan's account) are typically handled with much greater elaboration; this is especially true of the treatment of the division of labour, the theory of price, and the problem of velocity. The second set of lecture notes (i.e. LJ(B)) is not only more complete in respect of coverage, but more highly polished, eschewing the passages of recapitulation with which Smith usually began his

Some of the material in this paper was first published under the title of 'The Development of a System' in the *Scottish Journal of Political Economy*, 23 (1976). Section 1 of the original argument is omitted. In the present chapter, the treatment of physiocratic doctrine, is illustrative; it is not intended to provide a strictly accurate commentary on Quesnay's *Analyse*.

lectures. The Early Draft, on the other hand, while often seeming to follow the argument of *LJ*(A) rather than *LJ*(B), features a coverage of the subject which matches that of the latter, although the topics are often handled only in note form. There are, however, two outstanding exceptions. The treatment of the origins and nature of the division of labour is much more elaborate in the Early Draft than in either version of the lectures (although the limitation imposed by the extent of the market is not mentioned),[1] and has the striking feature of beginning with a long polemic on the subject of inequality. Secondly, it is evident that the treatment of the causes of the slow progress of opulence is sometimes rather more elaborate than in *LJ*(B). But in all this there is no evidence of a major shift of analytical perspective, thus making it possible for us to take *LJ*(B), i.e. the Cannan version (Cannan 1896), as providing a reasonable guide to Smith's system of economic analysis in the form in which it existed just before his visit to France.

The account that Smith provides in *LJ*(B) is concerned with an *economic system* featuring the activities of agriculture, manufacture, and commerce (*LJ*(B) 210) where these activities are characterized by a division of labour (*LJ*(B) 211–23), with the patterns of exchange facilitated by the use of money (*LJ*(B) 235–43). There are three main features of the central analysis: the treatment of the division of labour, the analysis of price and allocation, and the exposure of the mercantile fallacy. We may take these in turn, examining each topic with the minimum degree of elaboration that is consistent with the purpose of this chapter.

The division of labour is central to the analysis. It is by reference to this institution that Smith explains the growth in opulence that is associated with the development of the arts under the stimulus of the 'natural wants' of man (*LJ*(B) 209–11). Smith here rehearses points that have now become familiar, explaining the increase in productivity in terms of improved dexterity, the saving of time otherwise lost in passing from one function to another, and the scope given to the use of machines. But the second aspect of the argument is equally important, in the sense that Smith draws attention in two ways to the high degree of interdependence that follows from the division of labour. First, it is pointed out that in the modern state even a relatively simple product such as the labourer's woollen coat is the creation of a large number of different workmen including the wool-gatherer, the spinner, the dyer, weaver, tailor, etc.—not to mention the different processes involved in the manufacture of the tools required. Secondly, it is emphasized that in such a situation every man in effect acquires the goods he needs through exchange (*LJ*(B) 218–22). It is interesting to note that Smith gave less

---

[1] The development of Adam Smith's ideas on the division of labour is explored in Meek and Skinner (1973).

prominence to the problem of *value* in the *Lectures on Jurisprudence* as compared with the *Wealth of Nations*, where the influence of Hutcheson is most marked (see Chapters 5 and 7 in this volume).

As in the *Wealth of Nations*, Smith's handling of price theory is among the most successful aspects of the *LJ*(B) study, featuring as it does a clear distinction between natural and market price together with an examination of their interdependence. *Natural price* is defined in effect as the supply price of a commodity, where the latter refers to labour cost:

A man then has the natural price of his labour when it is sufficient to maintain him during the time of labour, to defray the expence of education, and to compensate the risk of not living long enough and of not succeeding in the business. When a man has this, there is sufficient encouragement to the labourer and the commodity will be cultivated in proportion to the demand. (*LJ*(B) 227).

Market price, on the other hand, is the price that may prevail at any given point in time and will be determined, Smith argues, by the 'demand or need for the commodity', its abundance or scarcity in relation to the demand (a point that is used to explain the 'paradox' of value), and, finally, the 'riches or poverty of those who demand' (*LJ*(B) 227–8). Smith then went on to suggest that, although the two prices were logically distinct, they were also 'necessarily connected'. Thus, in the event of market price rising above the natural level, the reward of labour in this employment will rise above its natural (long-run equilibrium) rate, leading to an inflow of labour and an expansion in supply (and vice versa). In equilibrium, therefore, the market and natural price will be the same, a point that allowed Smith to go on to argue that 'whatever police' tends to prevent this coincidence will 'diminish public opulence' (*LJ*(B) 230). The familiar examples that contributed to keep the market above the natural price include taxes on industry, monopolies, and the exclusive privileges of corporations—all of which affect price either through their impact on the supply of the commodity or on the flow of labour to a specific employment. Similarly, Smith criticized policies such as the bounty on corn, which kept the market below the natural price.

These examples refer to particular cases, but Smith may be said to have added a further dimension to the argument by showing an understanding of the fact that the economic system can be seen under a more general aspect. This much is evident in his objection to particular regulations of 'police' on the ground that they distorted the use of resources by breaking 'what may be called the natural balance of industry' and interfering with the 'natural connexion of all trades in the stock' (*LJ*(B) 233–4). He concluded: 'Upon the whole, therefore, it is by far the best police to leave things to their natural course' (*LJ*(B) 235).

The third main aspect of the argument relates to the issue of money, which is introduced at this point perhaps because it provides an easy means of transition to the discussion of a particular branch of 'police' that attracted Smith's attention—the mercantile system. The subject is approached by way of a discussion of the role of money as the instrument of exchange, which enables Smith to demonstrate that natural opulence does not consist in money, and to expose the absurdity of policies that were designed to prohibit the free exportation of specie. The policy is shown not merely to involve an error, but also to have pernicious effects with regard to the use of resources—once again returning to the general theme stated in connection with the theory of allocation. The advantages of free trade are thus suggested to complement those of domestic economic freedom, and the argument closes with the claim that all policies in restraint of trade, whether based on misunderstanding or national jealousy (a point more than a little reminiscent of Hume), should be rooted out:

> From the above considerations it appears that Brittain should by all means be made a free port, that there should be no interruption of any kind made to forreign trade, that if it were possible to defray the expences of government by any other method, all duties, customs, and excise should be abolished, and that free commerce and liberty of exchange should be allowed with all nations and for all things. (LJ(B) 269).

While this account of Smith's early work on economics is necessarily brief, it may be sufficient to confirm that Smith had in fact acquired a sophisticated grasp of the interdependence of economic phenomena before his departure for France in 1764. The same account also suggests that Smith had succeeded in producing an organized, systematic discourse, which also had the merit of presenting his policy views as the logical outcome of an underlying understanding of economic laws. It certainly seems likely that a man who had developed the level of interest in, and knowledge of, economic problems that is disclosed in the *Lectures* and the *Theory of Moral Sentiments* would be well equipped to appreciate the significance of what the physiocrats were trying to do—a group whose classical texts were already in existence before Smith completed his last lecture course, and whose primary source, Quesnay's *Tableau Economique*, had already gone through several editions before *The Theory of Moral Sentiments* appeared.[2]

THE PHYSIOCRATIC SYSTEM

Although Smith's first visit to Paris was for a period of only ten days, he was resident there continuously from December 1765 until the following

[2] See especially Meek and Kuczynski (1972).

October. He thus came into contact with the Physiocratic School when it was virtually at the zenith of its powers, and it is now well known that he had ready access to the literary salons of the time.[3] We have it on his own authority that he was acquainted with Turgot, enjoying the happiness, 'I flattered myself, even of his friendship; and esteem'.[4] Smith was also known to Quesnay, whom he described as 'one of the worthiest men in France',[5] while in addition we learn from Dugald Stewart that 'Mr Smith had once an intention (as he told me himself) to have inscribed to him his "Wealth of Nations"' (Stewart III. 12).

Smith recognized Quesnay as the main physiocratic figure, and as the founder of a numerous sect whose members all followed his doctrines without 'sensible variation'. In fact, Smith could have come in contact with Quesnay's work before leaving for France, in the shape of the articles 'Fermiers' (January 1756) and 'Grains' (November 1757); both were published in the *Encyclopédie*, which Smith purchased for Glasgow University Library while Quaestor. The second of the two articles may be particularly important since it was here that Quesnay drew attention to Cantillon's recognition of certain 'fundamental truths'. It is at least quite possible that Cantillon, as Professor Meek has suggested, was 'one of the main *theoretical* influences' working on Quesnay (Meek 1962: 267), and it is now well known that Mirabeau too had made considerable use of the *Essai* (1755) when preparing his *Ami des Hommes* (1756). In practice, however, Smith refers to the 'arithmetical formularies' of the 'Oeconomical Table' as a major source of Quesnay's views, and to some 'subsequent formularies' which consider the working of the system 'in different states of restraint and regulation' (*WN* IV. ix. 27). This reference would suggest that Smith may have made use of Quesnay's articles on the first and second 'economic problems' and, if so, that he was relying on Dupont's *Physiocratie* where the latter problem first appeared (Meek 1962: 265). Smith also cited the *Philosophie Rurale* (1763), a joint production of Quesnay and Mirabeau, together with Mercier de la Rivière's *Natural and Essential Order of Political Societies* (1767), a 'little book' which provided the 'most distinct and best connected account' of the doctrine

---

[3] The facts are recorded in Rae (1895: ch. 14). The rise of the school is traced in Meek (1962). Smith's interest in the movement is undoubted; his library contained e.g. works by Mirabeau, Mercier de la Rivière, and Le Trosne. Smith also possessed a run of the *Journal de l'Agriculture* and of the *Ephemerides du citoyen*, which included at least the first two parts of Turgot's *Reflections on the Formation and Distribution of Riches*, written in 1766.

[4] Letter 248, addressed to La Rochefoucauld, dated 1 Nov. 1785. Links between Turgot and Smith are traced by Peter Groenewegen (1969).

[5] Quesnay attended the Duke of Buccleugh in his capacity as a doctor while the latter was in France. In letter 97, addressed to Lady Frances Scott, dated 15 Oct. 1766, Smith, having made the remark quoted in the text, went on to describe Quensay as 'one of the best physicians that is to be met with in any country. He was not only the physician but the friend and confident of Madame Pompadour a woman who was no contemptible judge of merit'.

(*WN* IV. ix. 38). While Cannan was no doubt correct in suggesting that Smith's report on physiocracy did not obviously 'follow any particular book closely', still, Quesnay would appear to be the dominant source.

It is not appropriate to offer a thorough critique of physiocratic teaching in an essay that is intended primarily to interpret Smith's account of it. This is in any event a task that has been exhaustively addressed by Ronald Meek, to whom we are indebted not merely for his 'essays' (1962) but also for the translations of the main texts.

The simpler question considered here is what kind of model Smith was likely to have found as a result of his contacts in France, bearing in mind the state of knowledge that was represented by the *Lectures* and that attained by the time he came to write book II of the *Wealth of Nations*. What Smith is likely to have found is something that differs markedly from the content of his course in Glasgow but without being inconsistent with it: a macroeconomic model that is noteworthy for its formality even if it was in many respects incomplete.

Quesnay's purpose was both practical and theoretical. As Meek has indicated, Quesnay announced his purpose in a letter to Mirabeau which accompanied the first edition of the *Tableau*. 'We must not lose heart', he wrote, 'for the appalling crisis will come, and it will be necessary to have recourse to medical knowledge' (Meek 1962: 18). The position was clarified in a further letter to Mirabeau which was written in 1758: 'I have tried to construct a fundamental *Tableau* of the economic order for the purpose of displaying expenditure and products in a way which is easy to grasp, and for the purpose of forming a clear opinion about the organisation and disorganisation which the government can bring about' (Meek 1962: 108). The statement is significant in that it confirms the importance of government action in the context of a relatively underdeveloped economy which needed urgent support for the agrarian sector, a reform of the mercantile policies associated with Colbert, and in particular changes in the financial sector and in respect of fiscal policy. But Quesnay's statement also announced a clear understanding of the point that governments can act only on the basis of a knowledge of economic laws. Or, as Meek as put it, 'With the physiocrats, for the first time in the history of economic thought, we find a firm appreciation of the fact that areas of decision open to policy makers in the economic sphere have certain limits, and that a theoretical model of the economy is necessary to define these limits' (Meek 1962: 370).

The model in question seeks to explore the interrelationships between output, the generation of income, expenditure, and consumption—or, in Quesnay's words, a 'general system of expenditure, work, gain and consumption' (Meek 1962: 374)—which would expose the point that 'the whole magic of a well ordered society is that each man works for others, while believing that he is working for himself' (p. 70). As Meek puts it, 'In this circle of economic activity, production and consumption appeared as mutually interdependent variables, whose action and interaction in any economic period, proceeding according to certain socially determined laws, laid the basis for a repetition of the process in the next economic period' (p. 19). It would come as no surprise to Smith to discover that Quesnay made heavy use of an analogy drawn from Harvey's discovery of the circulation of the blood.

Perhaps the easiest way of introducing the issues involved, bearing in mind the restricted purposes of this argument, is to consider the argument of the *Analyse* (1766)—interestingly, the very work on which Quesnay was engaged when Smith was in Paris. In this model Quesnay identified two main sectors of activity, agriculture and manufacture, together with three major socio-economic groups: the farmers, the proprietors of land, and those engaged in manufacture. The *farmers* were defined as the productive class, since it was assumed that only agriculture was capable of generating surpluses. The *proprietors* were defined as the distributive class, a group that subsists on rent as its only form of income. The *manufacturers* were defined as important, since the goods they created were essential to the system, but also as sterile, since their activity was not assumed to generate any surpluses.

Having come thus far, Quesnay introduced the concept of *avances* for which these classes may be responsible. The most interesting *avances* are those that involve the farmers and manufacturers. These are the *avances primitives*, or investment in *fixed* capital, and the *avances annuelles*, or investment in *circulating* capital. This decisive step already carries us well beyond Smith's *Lectures*.

Quesnay then proceeded to identify the assumptions of the model. These are both qualitative and quantitative. The *qualitative* assumptions are set out in the *Tableau* (Meek 1962: 109–14) and were to reappear, with further additions, in *The General Maxims for the Government of an Agricultural Kingdom* (pp. 231–62). Quesnay assumed, *inter alia*, that the whole revenue of the system would enter circulation, and that there was a constant level of population with no movement between the sectors, no barriers to trade in corn or in manufactured products, a single tax (on the agricultural surplus), and a large-scale (capital-using) farming sector.

The *quantitative* assumptions include the statement that the annual net produce in the agrarian sector was 2 million *livres* (5 million gross). It was assumed that the total output of the manufacturing sector was 2 million *livres* and (implicitly) that the money supply was also 2 million *livres*.

Quesnay then proceeded to develop his model in terms of an exercise in period analysis. In following out the logic of the argument, let us abstract from the complications presented by the government sector, by the presence of mercantile groups, and by the fact that the proprietors as a class have important economic functions. Let us further assume, for the sake of simplicity, that at the beginning of the period in question the proprietors have no resources saved out of income generated in the period $(t - 1)$; that the farmers possess the entire stock of money at the beginning of the period t together with 2 millions worth of food produced in the period $(t - 1)$ and 1 million worth of raw materials. The manufacturing class is assumed to hold 2 millions worth of manufactured goods produced in the period $(t - 1)$ and available for sale in the current period.

The 'magic of a well-ordered society' can now be illustrated in terms of a series of steps. First, the farmers transmit rent to the proprietors of land (2 millions), thus giving that class an income which can be used to make purchases of the primary and manufactured products that are necessary to sustain life in the current period. Let us assume that the proprietors transmit 1 million to the farmers in exchange for food and 1 million to the manufacturing sector, thus reducing the stocks of goods that were available for sale at the beginning of period t. Assume further that the farmers transmit 1 million to the manufacturing sector in exchange for commodities, thus eliminating the stocks of goods held by this group.

This means in effect that the whole supply of money has moved from the farmers to the proprietors and is now held by the sterile class. This class is now in a position to purchase food (1 million), and raw materials (1 million) thus eliminating the stocks of commodities held by the farmers and at the same time returning the whole stock of money to this sector. The proprietors thus end the period with no unspent income and no accumulation of commodities. The farmers hold the stock of money, while the agrarian and manufacturing sectors are able to replace the goods used up in period t by virtue of current productive activity. Period $(t + 1)$, on these assumptions, is then able to open under conditions identical to those that obtained at the beginning of period t.

The model has a deliberately abstract quality but also a number of deficiencies. There is no clear analysis of the division of labour, as Smith understood the term, and no analysis of the problem of price determination and the allocation of resources. There is no formal allowance made for profit, nor is there a division between capitalists and wage labour— to name but a few issues of importance. But there is present a model of the economy, which represents the working of the (macroeconomic) process as one that involves a series of withdrawals from the market which are matched in turn by a continuous process of replacement—all in the context of a capital-using system. Smith could hardly have failed to be struck by this model, or by the transformation effected by Turgot, who in effect made good the great bulk of the deficiencies in Quesnay's account (Meek 1973).

The 'Reflections' (see Meek 1973: 119–82) describes the second model that was being worked up in 1766. In a valuable commentary, Meek has pointed out that Turgot was one of those who employed a three-stage approach (see Chapter 4 above) but added a fourth in the shape of a modern capital-using system (Meek 1973: 14–33). In developing this model, Turgot accepted the wisdom of Quesnay's emphasis on the importance of capital and also the master's division of the economy into two main sectors and three socio-economic groups.

But Turgot further developed Quesnay's vision of the 'magic of a well-ordered society' not just by emphasizing the importance of fixed and circulating capital, but also by developing these concepts in the context of his discussion of both agriculture and manufactures. He also distinguished clearly between entrepreneurs and wage labour operating in both sectors. Society finds itself, so to speak,

sub-divided into two orders: that of the Entrepreneurs, Manufacturers, and Masters who are all possessors of large capitals which they turn to account by setting to work, through the medium of their advances, the second order, which consists of ordinary Artisans who possess no property but their own hands, who advance nothing but their daily labour, and who receive no profit but their wages. (Meek 1973: 153).

Turgot was then able to identify three factors of production and to distinguish between three categories of return (rent, wages, and profit). In addition to clarifying the relationship between savings and investment, he also identified five uses of capital: namely, in respect of the purchase of land, commerce, manufacturers, agriculture, and capitals, which are lent at interest, together with those forces that determine the rates of return in each of these employments (Meek 1973: 170–1). It was in the course of this analysis that Turgot successfully deployed a doctrine which Smith would have recognized, that of net advantage, while also recognizing that 'the products of these different employments mutually limit one another, and in spite of their inequality are kept in a kind of equilibrium' (p. 172). He also noted the 'influence of the rate of interest on all remunerative enterprises' (p. 173).

These facts are interesting when we compare the content of the *Lectures* with the macroeconomic model that was developed in the *Wealth of Nations* book II, and when we recall Smith's account of what physiocratic teaching was designed to convey (*WN* IV. 9). Certainly, his account of the 'agricultural system' would suggest a close understanding of Quesnay's position but also familiarity with the work of 'revisionists' such as Baudeau and Turgot.[6]

Smith's account of the physiocratic system begins with the now time-honoured statement of the different classes that feature in the model— proprietors, cultivators, manufacturers, and merchants—and thus draws attention to the main sectors of the economy together with the functions of the various groups that are involved. The *proprietors*, for example, are stated to be responsible for the *avances foncieres*, that is, for expenses devoted to the improvement of land, buildings, drains, enclosures, and 'other ameliorations, which they may either make or maintain upon it, and by means of which the cultivators are enabled, with the same capital, to raise a greater produce, and consequently to pay a greater rent' (*WN* IV. ix. 6). Smith went on to note that this enhanced payment need not be regarded as rent properly so called, stating that 'This advanced rent may be considered as the interest or profit due to the proprietor upon the expence or capital which he thus employs' (IV. ix. 6).

The second class, that of the *cultivators*, is divided into two sections, farmers and country labourers (IV. ix. 5), with the former having responsibility for two types of advance, original (or primitive) and annual. Smith defines the former in terms of investment in the instruments of husbandry, in the stock of cattle employed, and in the maintenance of the farmer's family, servants, and cattle 'during at least a great part of the first year of his occupancy' (IV. ix. 7). The annual expenses were said to consist in covering, for example, the cost of the seed annually used up, the wear and tear of the instruments of husbandry, and the annual maintenance of the farmer's servants and cattle. Smith went on to observe that the produce that remains to the farmer after the payment of rent would have to be sufficient to replace to him the whole of his annual expenses together with the ordinary profits of stock, and to replace within 'a reasonable time' or the period of the lease the whole of the original expenses together with a rate of return on capital equal to the ordinary or usual rate of profit. It is thus suggested that profit is the relevant form of return as far as the undertaker engaged in farming is

[6] The term is Meek's; see e.g. his essay on the 'Physiocratic Concept of Profit' in *Economics of Physiocracy*. Professor Gianni Vaggi has confirmed to me that Smith's description of Quesnay's model is not very accurate and that his account of the model owes more to the followers than to the master. Professor Vaggi has drawn my attention, in this regard, to Smith's treatment of profit, and to his use of the concepts of *avances souveraigns* and *avances foncières*.

concerned, and that it also accrues to the proprietor in respect of his *avances foncières*. In addition, the latter also receives a distinct form of return in the shape of rent properly so called, which is 'no more than the neat produce which remains after paying in the compleatest manner all the necessary expences which must be previously laid out in order to raise the gross, or the whole produce' (IV. ix. 7). It is because the advances of the proprietors and farmers are capable of generating this 'neat produce' that they are described, Smith comments, as productive expenses.

As far as the third class is concerned, there is a division between *manufacturers* and *merchants* and, in terms of the latter groups, between employers and labourers. The employers emerge as being responsible for certain advances, which include 'materials, tools, and wages' (IV. ix. 10), so that the goods produced must be sufficient to repay the maintenance which the employer advances to himself, 'as well as the materials, tools and wages which he advances to his workmen'. Wages thus emerge as the payment that accrues to the workmen, and profit as the fund that 'is destined for the maintenance of their employer' (IV. ix. 10). The difference, however, between this type of activity and that carried on by the farmers is, of course, that the latter generates not only a profit on capital invested, but also a neat produce which accrues as rent. Smith duly went on to report that 'The expence, therefore, laid out in employing and maintaining artificers and manufacturers, does no more than continue, if one may say so, the existence of its own value, and does not produce any new value' (IV. ix. 10). Hence the 'humiliating' description of this class, together with that of the merchants, as unproductive—that is, literally unproductive of a neat produce.

At the same time, however, Smith pointed out that the physiocratic system did make allowance for the fact that the manufacturing sector could contribute to economic growth, but only through 'parsimony', or, 'as it is expressed in this system, by privation, that is, by depriving themselves of a part of the funds destined for their own subsistence' (IV. ix. 13). In contrast to the farmers, 'They annually reproduce nothing but those funds. Unless, therefore, they annually save some part of them, unless they annually deprive themselves of the enjoyment of some part of them, the revenue and wealth of their society can never be in the smallest degree augmented by means of their industry' (IV. ix. 13).

But in fact, Smith went further than the enumeration of the classes and their functions in drawing attention to a salient feature of the analysis: namely, the interdependence that was shown to exist between all the relevant groups in the system. The point is evident in Smith's emphasis on the replacement of the various advances by virtue of the purchases by all groups of the agrarian and manufactured goods that were produced within any annual period. The same point was made quite explicit in another way, when he drew attention to the fact that the main purpose of Quesnay's 'Oeconomical Table' was to show 'In what manner . . . the sum total of the annual produce of the land is distributed among the three classes above mentioned, and in what manner the labour of the unproductive class, does no more than replace the value of its own consumption' (IV. ix. 27).

Interestingly enough, Smith also chose to emphasize the issue of interdependence by focusing attention on the position of the unproductive class, which was shown to be ultimately dependent on the 'two other classes', whose purchases finally pay the wages of the labourers employed and the profits that accrue, while furnishing it 'both with the materials of its work and with the fund of its subsistence, with the corn and cattle which it consumes while it is employed about that work' (IV. ix. 14). At the same time, Smith indicates that one purpose of the model was to show that the proprietors and farmers were interdependent, and that both in turn depended on the 'sterile' group for the manufactured products they required. He also indicated that the productive class would benefit from the *sectoral* division of labour postulated in the model, which 'increases the productive powers of productive labour, by leaving it at liberty to confine itself to its proper employment, the cultivation of land' (IV. ix. 15). The basic analysis also served to suggest, as Smith went on to note, that the interests of the different classes did not conflict. He thus observed that 'It can never be the interest of the proprietors and cultivators to restrain or to discourage in any respect the industry of merchants, artificers and manufacturers', since 'The greater the liberty which this unproductive class enjoys, the greater will be the competition in all the different trades which compose it, and the cheaper will the other two classes be supplied' (IV. ix. 16). Similarly, it can never be the interest of the unproductive class to oppress the other two, since the greater the agricultural surplus, the 'greater must likewise be the maintenance and employment of that class', leading to the conclusion that 'The establishment of perfect justice, of perfect liberty, and of perfect equality, is the very simple secret which most effectually secures the highest degree of prosperity to all the three classes' (IV. ix. 17).

Having stated these basic principles, Smith then proceeded to illustrate their application in a relatively neglected area of physiocracy—international trade—at least to the extent of showing that the pattern of interdependence that exists between classes in the domestic case also applies to different nations. Thus, for example, in speaking of mercantile states such as Holland and Hamburg, it is pointed out that their labourers are just as surely maintained by the proprietors and cultivators as any other:

The only difference is, that those proprietors and cultivators are, the greater part of them, placed at a most inconvenient distance from the merchants, artificers, and manufacturers whom they supply with the materials of their work and the fund of their subsistence, are the inhabitants of other countries, and the subjects of other governments. (*WN* IV. ix. 18).

Thus, it can never be the interest of a landed nation to 'discourage or distress the industry of such mercantile states by imposing high duties upon their trade': first, because the nation that follows this policy, 'by raising the price of all foreign goods and of all sorts of manufactures . . . necessarily sinks the real value of the surplus produce of its own land' (*WN* IV. ix. 20); secondly, because the nation thus acting 'raises the rate of mercantile and manufacturing profit in proportion to that of agricultural profit, and consequently either draws from agriculture a part of the capital which had before been employed in it, or hinders from going to it a part of what would otherwise have gone to it' (IV. ix. 25). It therefore follows that 'The most effectual expedient . . . for raising the value of that surplus product, for encouraging its increase, and consequently the improvement and cultivation of their own land, would be to allow the most perfect freedom to the trade of all . . . mercantile nations' (IV. ix. 20).[7]

But there was another and equally interesting reason for this policy, at least as reported by Smith: namely, that a landed nation whose growth was sustained through concentration on agriculture would eventually find itself able to 'justle out' the manufacturers and merchants of those nations on which it might originally have relied, a point of some relevance in the light of Smith's analysis of Britain's relationship with the American colonies. The argument rests on two propositions which are more than a little reminiscent of Smith's own thesis regarding the 'natural progress of opulence'. First, the

continual increase of the surplus produce of their land, would, in due time, create a greater capital than what could be employed with the ordinary rate of profit in the improvement and cultivation of land; and the surplus part of it would naturally turn itself to the employment of artificers and manufacturers at home. (WN IV. ix. 22).

Secondly,

[this] continual increase both of the rude and manufactured produce of those landed nations would in due time create a greater capital than could, with the ordinary rate of profit, be employed either in agriculture or in manufactures. The

---

[7] It is noted at *WN* (IV. ix. 49) that 'Those systems, therefore, which preferring agriculture to all other employments, in order to promote it, impose restraints upon manufactures and foreign trade, act contrary to the very end which they propose, and indirectly discourage that very species of industry which they mean to promote. They are so far, perhaps, more inconsistent than even the mercantile system.'

surplus of this capital would naturally turn itself to foreign trade, and be employed in exporting, to foreign countries, such parts of the rude and manufactured produce of its own country, as exceeded the demand of the home market. (*WN* IV. ix. 23).

While Smith's account is an interesting record of what he understood physiocracy to be, there were, of course, many points on which he disagreed with its teaching. He criticized it, for example, for seeming to have advanced the view that a society could 'thrive and prosper only under a certain precise regimen, the exact regimen of perfect liberty and perfect justice' (*WN* IV. ix. 28), and he rejected the thesis that artificers, manufacturers, and merchants could be regarded as unproductive (IV. ix. 29–37), a proposition that is described as the 'capital error of this system'. Smith was also a critic of of the idea of a single tax, an argument that was further developed in V. ii. c. 2–7. In addition, Smith drew attention to the superior application of the division of labour in manufactures and to the point that parsimony was the route to the achievement of net savings and thus growth for all classes in the system, not merely the manufacturing group (IV. ix. 34). But, at the same time, there was obviously a great deal with which the Smith of the *Lectures on Jurisprudence* could agree, and he duly concluded that:

in representing the wealth of nations as consisting, not in the unconsumable riches of money, but in the consumable goods annually reproduced by the labour of the society; and in representing perfect liberty as the only effectual expedient for rendering this annual reproduction the greatest possible, its doctrine seems to be in every respect as just as it is generous and liberal. (*WN* IV. ix. 38).

CONCLUSION

The task of reaching some conclusions with regard to Smith's sources of ideas or inspiration helps to focus attention not just on these sources but also on the critical importance of his early writings. For, as Edwin Cannan noted, and subsequent discoveries have confirmed, some knowledge of Smith's early work on economics 'enables us to follow the gradual construction of the work almost from its very foundation, and to distinguish positively between what the original genius of its author created out of British materials on the one hand and French materials on the other' (Cannan 1896: p. xxiv). Perhaps the issues are less clear-cut than Cannan implied, although it surely can be said with confidence that the early writings on economics provide a valuable record of an edifice whose basic outlines survive in the *Wealth of Nations* itself.

Such topics as the division of labour, value, the discussion of money, and allocation all find their place in book I of the *Wealth of Nations*, albeit with the analysis of money now preceding that of price, and the doctrine of net advantages being accorded a separate section (as indeed was the discussion of impediments to the working of the allocative mechanism), while the treatment of banking was to find a place in book ɪɪ. The critique of the 'mercantile fallacy' is still the dominant feature of the opening chapters of book ɪᴠ. This pattern is repeated when we consider those sections of the *Lectures on Jurisprudence* that have not been examined in any detail here. The discussion of interest and exchange, for example, was to find a place in book ɪɪ of the *Wealth of Nations*, while the section dealing with the slow progress of opulence was to reappear in a more elaborate form as the main theme of book ɪɪɪ. Taxation is of course featured in the concluding sections of the *Wealth of Nations*, while in addition Smith's comments on the social consequences of the division of labour and the section on 'arms' were to find their echoes in the analyses of defence and education. There are also interesting omissions from the *Wealth of Nations*, such as the thesis of natural wants, the treatment of stock-jobbing, and 'Mr. Law's Bank'. Yet the overwhelming impression left from a comparison of the *Wealth of Nations* and *LJ*(B), such as that undertaken by Edwin Cannan in his edition of the latter work (Cannan 1896), is of a pattern of gradual development in a basic scheme whose outlines were already clear by 1763.

Moreover, particular doctrines are present in the *Lectures*, in addition to those noted above, which were later to acquire an added significance. It is already stated in the *Lectures*, for example, that 'Agriculture is of all other arts the most beneficent to society' (*LJ*(B) 289). The concept of stock is also mentioned in a variety of contexts—in the discussion of the natural balance of industry, and the sections on interest and taxation. The necessity for the prior accumulation of stock is also noted in connection with the division of labour, with perhaps the clearest statement occurring where Smith remarks that 'till some stock be produced there can be no division of labour, and before a division of labour take place there can be very little accumulation of stock' (*LJ*(B) 287). Nor was the issue of growth ignored—a point that can be seen in the discussion of 'natural wants' and their association with the division of labour, and with the development of the arts. Similarly, the discussion of the 'slow progress of opulence' in the *Lectures* throws a great deal of light on factors that influence the growth process, such as transport, legal impediments, and the changing attitudes to commercial activity.

But, at the same time, it is evident that there is a great deal missing from the *Lectures* when compared with the *Wealth of Nations*, and it is this fact that makes Smith's assessment of physiocracy so interesting, especially since many of the features that are absent from the *Lectures* were features that Smith himself associated with physiocratic analysis. In this connection, Smith noted, as we have seen, the use of a clear separation of classes, together with the distinction drawn between employers and employed, and between categories of return such as rent, wages, and profit. Again, it is noteworthy that Smith underlined the physiocratic emphasis on capital, while drawing attention to the point that the rate of return on capital in different employments would tend to equality. It is certainly possible that Smith himself may have been led to clarify his own views as to the role of capital accumulation in the process of developing his criticism of the physiocratic position on unproductive labour, and clearly probable, as Cannan suggested, that he was led to introduce these concepts together with a theory of distribution into his own work as a result of his contact with the School.[8] Donald Winch has reminded me that Dugald Stewart's sympathetic treatment of the Physiocrats influenced, among others, Francis Horner. In particular, Professor Winch has drawn my attention to the following passage from the latter's work:

That Smith did not precisely distinguish the real import of the economical system, is now confessed, we believe, even by those who agree with him in rejecting it. We are further satisfied that he derived a much larger portion of his reasonings from them, than he himself perhaps recollected; that his principles on the formation and distribution of riches approached more nearly to those of Quesnay, than he was himself aware; and that, to have recognised an entire coincidence, it was only necessary for him to have followed out his analysis a few steps further. (Fetler 1957: 73).

A further point, which may have received rather less attention, arises from the fact that Smith evidently associated the thesis of the 'natural progress of opulence' with physiocratic teaching, because this particular thesis may help to explain two important changes in the *Wealth of Nations* as compared with the *Lectures*. First, there is the point that the thesis is stated at the beginning of book III of the *Wealth of Nations* as a direct development of the discussion of the 'different employments of capital' with which the preceding book had concluded. This in turn may explain Smith's decision to use material drawn from the lectures on public jurisprudence in this place—that is, as a record of the inversion of a 'natural order' which seemed to be suggested by the history of Europe from the fall of the Western (Roman) Empire to the present

---

[8] See, e.g. Cannan (1896: xxvii–xxix) and Cannan (1904: pp. xxxvii–xxxix). However, Dugald Stewart has stated that 'it appears from a manuscript of Mr Smith's now in my possession, that the foregoing analysis or division (rent, wages, profit) was suggested to him by Mr Oswald of Dunnikier' (Stewart 1856: ix. 6). While making this point, Meek has also drawn attention to the fact that a similar division was stated by Hume in a letter to Turgot dated September 1766 (Meek 1967: 29); see generally pp. 28–32, where Meek offers some interesting speculations as to the probable influence of physiocratic thought with regard to distribution. For a more detailed analysis of the content of Quesnay's work (and its possible influence on Smith), see G. Vaggi's excellent account (1987).

day. Secondly, it is worth noting that Smith's critique of mercantilism in the *Wealth of Nations* acquires an added dimension from the level of debate contained in *LJ*(B) in that the later version was largely dominated by the desire to prove that mercantile policy had had the effect of artificially diverting the use of capital from more to less productive uses. It is indeed somewhat remarkable that the analogy of the invisible hand is employed in the *Wealth of Nations* in exactly this, essentially dynamic, context (*WN* IV. ii. 9). But perhaps the really important contrasts between the *Wealth of Nations* and the *Lectures on Jurisprudence* are to be seen not merely in relation to specific doctrines, but rather in terms of the system of thought, and the economic model of which these doctrines were the components.

It is now widely recognized that the basic model of the *Tableau* represented an advance in economic theory so considerable as to justify comparison with Harvey's discovery of the circulation of the blood.[9] J. A. Schumpeter not unaptly described it as marking 'the great breach', and went on to point out that 'Only with the help of such an analysis was it possible for further knowledge of the economic life process of society to develop and were scholars enabled to survey all the general factors and their functions as well as all the elements which have to be considered in every individual problem as far as it is purely economic' (Schumpeter 1954*a*: 43).[10] Elsewhere, Schumpeter noted that the model opened up possibilities for numerical theory, and that it provided a means of conceptualizing the working of complex series of interrelated functions, while representing the 'first method ever devised in order to convey an *explicit* conception of the nature of economic equilibrium' (Schumpeter 1954*b*: 241–3). But one need not agree with Schumpeter when he went on to state that Smith 'almost certainly . . . did not fully grasp the importance of the *tableau économique*' (1954*b*: 232).

At first sight, Smith's treatment of the *Tableau* was slight, for it is seemingly dismissed as 'some arithmetical formularies' (*WN* IV. ix. 27), which may indeed have jarred on a man well known for his distrust of 'political arithmetick' (IV. v. b. 30). In addition, Smith can hardly be said to have done justice to the basic model as represented, for example, by Quesnay's *Analyse* (1766) with its careful statement of the qualitative and quantitative assumptions that were to be employed in demonstrating how a system with a particular level of production would function and sustain itself. Yet at the same time, it seems unlikely that a man like Smith, who was so acutely conscious of the role of analogy and system in scientific thought, would fail to be struck by these qualities

---

[9] Henry Higgs, for example, remarked in his edition of Cantillon's *Essai* that 'I would put Cantillon's analysis of the circulation of wealth, trite as it may now appear, on the same level of priority as Harvey's study of the circulation of the blood' (Higgs 1931: 388).
[10] See generally ch. 2, 'The Discovery of the Circular Flow of Economic Life'.

in physiocracy: an impression that is borne out by the fact that Smith's account of the system manifestly succeeds in conveying the *purpose* of the model, by demonstrating the interdependence of economic phenomena at the macroeconomic level. There is, perhaps, no irony in the passage where Mirabeau is cited as having placed the discovery of the *Tableau* at least on a par with the invention of writing and money (*WN* IV. ix. 38), and even some generosity in Smith's conclusion: 'This system, however, with all its imperfections is, perhaps, the nearest approximation to the truth that has yet been published upon the subject of political oeconomy, and is upon that account well worth the consideration of every man who wishes to examine with attention the principles of that very important science' (IV. ix. 38).

That Smith benefited from his own examination of the system may be seen both in terms of the basic model that he employed, and with regard to specific doctrines, whose use served to transform an older apparatus while at the same time taking Smith well beyond the boundaries of physiocratic teaching as a whole. Perhaps two examples can usefully be cited here.

First, it may be worth noting that, although the theory of price and allocation that is developed in the *Wealth of Nations* relies on distinctions already established in the *Lectures*, supply price is now defined in terms of the 'ordinary or average' rate of payment for rent, profit, and wages. In this way, Smith made allowance for the existence of the three factors of production, and also gave his analysis an explicitly static aspect by treating the rates of return as given and the factors as stocks rather than flows, at least in the short run. At the same time, the earlier analysis of allocation is transformed by the central role given to profit, a role which, as R. L. Meek has noted, finally exposed the real significance behind Smith's earlier, intuitive, preoccupation with the 'natural balance of industry' (Meek 1967: 31–2).

It is certainly clear that the division into wages, profit, and rent had struck Smith forcibly and that it still possessed some novelty—a point that may be seen in the attention given to warning his readers against confusion among them (*WN* I. vi). The second point relates to the discussion of macroeconomic problems, and here again a number of issues may be noted. First, there is the fact that, not only did the distinction between wages, profit, and rent transform the older discussion of allocation, it also provided Smith with a means of proceeding directly from the treatment of price to problems of a macro kind. Thus, having pointed out that in equilibrium the price of each commodity must resolve itself into three parts, he went on to note that:

it must be so with regard to all the commodities which compose the whole annual produce of the land and labour of every country, taken complexly. The whole price or exchangeable value of that annual produce, must resolve itself into the same three parts, and be parcelled out among the different inhabitants of the country, either as the wages of their labour, the profits of their stock, or the rent of their land. (*WN* II. ii. 2).

Secondly, in examining the functioning of the economy from this point of view, Smith produced an argument which gives a great deal of prominence to the different employments of capital and to the distinction between fixed and circulating capital (points that may owe much to Turgot). But it is perhaps in his treatment of the 'division of stock' from the standpoint of *society at large* (*WN* II. ii), rather than from that of the individual entrepreneur, that physiocratic influence is to be seen at its strongest. For it is here that Smith divides the stock of society into fixed and circulating capital, where the latter included goods in process and those ready for sale during a particular period but which remain at the outset in the hands of the manufacturers, farmers, and merchants who compose the system. In this way, Smith presented the functioning of the economy in terms of a process of *withdrawal* (through purchase) from the circulating capital of society, which was matched by the *replacement* of the goods thus used up, by virtue of current productive activity. It is surely this kind of perspective on the working of the system which shows just how clearly Smith had grasped the significance of what the physiocrats were trying to do.

REFERENCES

Campbell, R. H., and Skinner, A. S. (1982), *Adam Smith: A Short Biography* (London).

Cannan, E. (ed.) (1896), Adam Smith's *Lectures on Justice, Police, Revenue and Arms* (London).

——(ed.) (1904), Adam Smith's *The Wealth of Nations* (London).

Fetter, F. W. (ed.) (1957), *The Economic Writings of Francis Horner* (London).

Groenewegen, P. D. (1969), 'Turgot and Adam Smith', *Scottish Journal of Political Economy*, 16.

Higgs, H. (1897), *The Physiocrats* (London).

——(ed.) (1931), Cantillon's *Essai sur la nature du commerce en generale* (London).

Hutchison, T. W. (1988), *Before Adam Smith* (Oxford).

Meek, R. L. (1962), *The Economics of Physiocracy* (London).

——(1967), *Economics and Ideology and Other Essays* (Cambridge).

——(1973), *Turgot on Progress, Sociology and Economics* (Cambridge).

——Kuczynski, M. (1972), *Quesnay's Tableau Économique* (London).

——and Skinner, A. S. (1973), 'The Development of Smith's Ideas on the Division of Labour', *Economic Journal*, 83.

Rae, J. (1895), *Life of Adam Smith* (London).

Schumpeter, J. A. (1954*a*), *Economic Doctrine and Method* (London).

——(1954*b*), *History of Economic Analysis* (London).

Skinner, A. S. (1979), *A System of Social Sciences: Papers Relating to Adam Smith* (Oxford).

——(1992), 'Adam Smith, Self-Love', *Revue européenne des sciences sociales*, 30.

Stewart, D. (1980), 'Account of the Life and Writings of Adam Smith' (1793), ed. I. S. Ross, in *Essays on Philosophical Subjects*, ed. D. D. Raphael and A. S. Skinner (Oxford).

——(1856), *Works*, ed. W. Hamilton (Edinburgh).

Teichgraeber, R. (1987), 'Less Abused than I had Reason to Suspect: The Reception of the *Wealth of Nations* in Britain, 1776–1790', *Historical Journal*, 30.

Vaggi, G. (1987), *The Economics of Francois Quesnay* (London).

Zallio, F. (1990), 'Adam Smith's Dual Circulation Framework', *Royal Bank of Scotland Review*, 116.

PART IV

7

A Conceptual Sytem

Although Smith's model, in its post-physiocratic form, has several distinct elements, the feature on which he continued to place most emphasis was the *division of labour*. In terms of the content of the model outlined in previous chapters, a division of labour is of course implied in the existence of distinct *sectors* or types of productive activity. But Smith also emphasized the fact that there was specialization by types of employment, and even within each employment. To illustrate the basic point, he chose the celebrated example of the pin; a very 'trifling manufacture' which none the less required some eighteen processes for its completion.

In Smith's hands, the argument was important for two main reasons. First, he was at some pains to point out that the division of labour (by process) helped to explain the relatively high productivity of labour in modern times, a phenomenon he ascribed to:

1. the increase in 'dexterity' which inevitably results from making a single, relatively simple operation 'the sole employment of the labourer';
2. the saving of time which would otherwise be lost in 'passing from one species of work to another';
3. the associated use of machines which 'facilitate and abridge labour, and enable one man to do the work of many' (WN I. i. 5).

He further observed that the existence of specialization (by employment) necessarily involves a high degree of interdependence, in that each separate manufacture tends to rely on the output of other industries for different goods and services. It thus follows that the individual consumer who purchases a single commodity must at the same time acquire, in effect, the separate outputs of a 'great variety of labour'. Smith added:

If we examine . . . all these things, and consider what a variety of labour is employed about each of them, we shall be sensible that without the assistance and co-operation of many thousands, the very meanest person in a civilized

The argument of this chapter is only intended to convey an impression of the *structure* of Smith's system.

country could not be provided, even according to, what we very falsely imagine, the easy and simple manner in which he is commonly accommodated. (*WN* I. i. 11).

However, the aspect of this discussion that is most immediately relevant is the light it throws on the necessity of exchange. As Smith observed, once the division of labour is established, our own labour can supply us with only a very small part of our wants. He thus noted that even in the barter economy the individual can best satisfy the whole range of his needs by exchanging the surplus part of his own production, receiving in return the products of others. Where the division of labour is thoroughly established, it is to be expected that each individual is in a sense dependent on his fellows, and that 'Every man thus lives by exchanging, or becomes in some measure a merchant'. (*WN* I. iv. 1)

This observation brought Smith directly to the problem of value, where he returned to an area which, interestingly, had been more a feature of Hutcheson's lectures (see Chapter 5 above) than of his own. Here it is noteworthy that he employed the analytical (as distinct from historical) device of the barter economy. However, despite the attempt to be 'perspicuous', these passages remain somewhat difficult, largely because Smith uses a single term in handling two distinct but related problems:

The word VALUE, it is to be observed, has two different meanings, and sometimes expresses the utility of some particular object, and sometimes the power of purchasing other goods which the possession of that object conveys. (*WN* I. iv. 13).

The first problem concerns the forces that determine the *rate* at which one good, or units of one good, may be exchanged for another; the second is concerned basically with the means by which we can measure the value of the total *stock* of goods created by an individual, and which is used in exchange for others. We may take these issues in turn.

As regards the rate of exchange, Smith isolated two relevant factors: the usefulness of the good to be acquired, and the 'cost' incurred in creating the commodity to be given up. The first of the relevant relationships is obviously that existing between 'usefulness' and value. The elements of Smith's argument become apparent in his handling of the famous paradox, namely that:

The things which have the greatest value in use have frequently little or no value in exchange; and, on the contrary, those which have the greatest value in exchange have frequently little or no value in use. Nothing is more useful than water: but it will scarce purchase anything. A diamond, on the contrary, has scarce any value in use; but a very great quantity of other goods may frequently be had in exchange for it. (*WN* I. iv. 13).

The solution to this paradox can be stated in two stages, where the first involves an explanation as to why two such goods have *some* value, and the second an explanation as to why the two goods have *different* values.

Smith's handling of the first part of the problem is based on his recognition of the fact that both goods are considered to be 'useful' although noting that the 'utilities' of each are qualitatively different. In the former case (water) we place a value on the good because we can use it in a practical way, while in the latter (diamonds) we place a value on the good because it appeals to our 'senses', an appeal which, as Smith observed, constitutes a ground 'of preference', or 'source of pleasure'. He concluded: 'The demand for the precious stones arises altogether from their beauty. They are of no use, but ornaments' (*WN* I. xi. c. 32). The utilities of the two goods thus emerge as being qualitatively different, although the significant point is seen to be that both have *some* value precisely because they represent sources of satisfaction to the individual.

Smith was then left with the second part of the initial problem, namely the explanation as to why the two goods have different values. Here again, the answer provided, while simple, is clear, embodying the argument that merit (value) is a function of scarcity. As Smith put it, 'the merit of an object which is in any degree useful or beautiful, is greatly enhanced by its scarcity' (I. xi. c. 31). Even more specifically, he remarked: 'Cheapness is in fact the same thing with plenty. It is only on account of the plenty of water that it is so cheap as to be got for the lifting, and on account of the scarcity of diamonds (for their real use seems not yet to be discovered) that they are so dear' (*LJ*(B) 105–6).

Smith introduced the second major element in the problem by observing that the *rate* at which the individual will exchange one good for another must be affected not only by the utility of the good to be acquired, but also by the 'toil and trouble' involved in creating the good exchanged. In this connection, he recognized that, in acquiring the means of exchange (goods in the barter case), the individual must undergo the 'fatigues' of labour and thus 'lay down' a 'portion of his ease, his liberty, and his happiness' (*WN* I. v. 7).

In dealing with the rate of exchange, Smith may be seen to have placed most emphasis on the supply side of the problem, and explicitly to have argued that in the case of the barter economy 'the proportion between the quantities of labour necessary for acquiring different objects seems to be the only circumstance which can afford any rule for exchanging them for one another' (I. vi. 1). Thus, he suggested that, if it takes twice the labour to kill a beaver as it does to kill a deer, then 'one beaver should naturally exchange for . . . two deer', an argument that may owe something to Hutcheson's emphasis on labour embodied. Smith left the analysis in this form although it will be apparent that the rate of exchange that he specified could obtain only where the perceived ratios of the utilities and disutilities are acceptable to the respective hunters. These are of course subjective judgements whose presence helps to confirm Cannan's opinion that the 'germ' of the *Wealth of Nations* is to be found in Hutcheson's treatment of value.

This is one way of looking at the problem of exchange value, which clearly shows a parallel with Hutcheson; but Smith seems to have treated it not as an end in itself, but as a means of elucidating those factors which govern the value of *the whole stock of goods* that the individual creates, and proposes to use in exchange. It is of course the presence of this argument in the *Wealth of Nations* that helps to confirm Taylor's judgement to the effect that the treatment of value was domi- nated by a concern with the measurement of welfare (see Chapter 5 above). Looking at the problem in this way, Smith went on to argue that:

The value of any commodity . . . to the person who possesses it, and who means not to use or consume it himself, but to exchange it for other commodities, is equal to the quantity of labour which it enables him to purchase or command. Labour, therefore, is the real measure of the exchangeable value of all commod- ities. (*WN* I. v. 1).

Smith's meaning becomes clear when he remarks that the value of a stock of goods must always be in proportion to 'the quantity . . . of other men's labour, *or what is the same thing, of the produce* of other men's labour, which it enables him to purchase or command. The exchange- able value of every thing must always be precisely equal to the extent of this power' (*WN* I. v. 3; italics supplied). In other words, Smith is here arguing that the real value of the goods that the workman has to dispose of (in effect, his income) must be measured by the quantity of goods (expressed in terms of labour units) that he can command, and which he receives once the whole volume of (separate) exchanges has taken place.

If we remain for the moment with the primitive state, we may clarify the conclusion just mentioned, and at the same time show a connection between this and the preceding analysis. In the case of the barter economy, it will be recalled that the individual is assumed to create a single (complete) product, which then becomes his personal (dis- posable) property. Now if, as Smith suggested, the *rate* of exchange between goods is always equal to the ratio of the labour embodied in them, then it follows that the exchangeable value of the whole *stock* of goods must be equal to the labour required to make it. In other words, the labour embodied in the stock of goods made by the individual must be equal to the labour embodied in the goods received, i.e. the quantity of goods which the original stock enables the possessor to purchase or command. Given this, it will be apparent that the argu- ment thus far has two important features. First, Smith argues that in the barter economy the labour that the individual expends, and which is embodied in the goods he creates, must exchange for, or command, an equal quantity. In short, in this stage, labour embodied equals labour commanded, the essential premises being that *all* goods exchange at a given (previously defined) rate and that labour is the sole factor of production. Secondly, Smith suggests that the extent to which the individual can satisfy his needs through exchanging his produce for that of others must be determined by the quantity of other men's output (in labour units) that he receives in exchange. This is one way of measuring the economic welfare (command over goods) of individuals, and one that indicates the usefulness of measuring welfare in *real* terms.

But Mark Blaug, in a definitive treatment of this topic, has noted that:

> Nowadays we assume that an increase in real income is tantamount to an improvement in welfare. But Adam Smith tried to go deeper, associating improvements with a reduction in the sacrifices required to obtain a slab of real income. Labour is irksome and toil and trouble is the ultimate scarce factor of production . . . The 'real value' of a commodity is its labour price, meaning by labour not a certain number of man-hours but units of disutility, the psychological cost of work to the individual, and meaning by value esteem value rather than exchange value. (Blaug 1962:49).

It is evident that in the modern economy labour is no longer the sole factor of production, and that in 'this state of things, the whole produce of labour does not always belong to the labourer' (*WN* I. vi. 7). This means of course that the labour commanded by virtue of our possession of a stock of goods must always exceed the (direct) labour embodied in them, by virtue of the allowance that must be made for the contribution of capital and land. In short, the equality between labour embodied and labour commanded appears to be relevant to the primitive (barter) economy and to no other. However, Smith did not consider that the recognition of this point did any violence to his second result: namely, that the real value of *income* may be expressed in terms of the produce of other men's labour (measured in labour units) which it enables the recipient to purchase or command (*WN* I. vi. 9).

As Smith observed, a clear difference between the barter and modern economies is to be found in the fact that, while in the former goods are exchanged for goods, in the latter goods are exchanged for a sum of money, which may then be expended in purchasing other goods. Under such circumstances the individual, as Smith saw, very naturally estimates the value of his receipts (received in return for undergoing the 'fatigues' of labour) in terms of money, rather than in terms of the quantity of goods he can acquire by virtue of his expenditure. However, Smith was at some pains to insist that the real measure of welfare (that is, our ability to satisfy our wants) was to be found in 'the money's worth' rather than the money, where the former is determined by the quantity of products (labour 'commanded') that either individuals or groups can purchase. On this basis, Smith went on to distinguish between the nominal and the real value of income, pointing out that, if the three original sources of (monetary) revenue in modern times are wages, rent, and profit, then the real value of each must ultimately be measured 'by the quantity of labour which they can, each of them, purchase or command' (*WN* I. vi. 9).

The distinction between real and money income being established, the remainder of chapter 5 is largely concerned with a defence of the labour unit as the only stable basis on which the real value of income may be established both at any one point in time and over time. Smith thus began a (perhaps vain) search for an absolute measure of value: a search perhaps prompted by Hutcheson and to be continued by Ricardo and Marx.

PRICE

It will be apparent from the previous argument that Smith regarded rent, wages, and profit as the types of return payable to the three 'great constituent orders' of society, and as the price paid for the use of the factors of production. The revenues that accrue to individuals and groups in society, and permit them to purchase commodities, thus appear to be costs incurred by those who create commodities. These points were made quite explicitly by Smith when he remarked:

As the price or exchangeable value of every particular commodity, taken separately, resolves itself into some one or other or all of those three parts; so that of all the commodities which compose the whole annual produce of the labour of every country, taken complexly, must resolve itself into the same three parts, and be parcelled out among different inhabitants of the country, either as the wages of their labour, the profits of their stock, or the rent of their land. (*WN* I. vi. 17).

This argument obviously raises the problem of price and its determinants, and it is to this area of analysis that we now turn.

To begin with, Smith assumed the existence of given 'ordinary' or 'average' rates of wages, profit, and rent, rates that may be said to prevail within any given society or neighbourhood, during any given (time) period. This assumption is of considerable importance, for two main reasons. First, it indicates that, in dealing with the problem of price, Smith was implicitly using the analytical device of a static system, and working in terms of a given (stable) stock of factors together with a given (stable) level of aggregate demand for them. Secondly, the assumption of given rates of return is important in that these rates determine the supply price of commodities.[1]

With these two points forming Smith's major premises, he proceeded to examine the determinants of price, and to produce a discussion which seems to involve two distinct, but related, problems. First, he set out to explain the forces that determine the prices of particular commodities, elucidating in the process the nature of partial equilibrium. Secondly, he would appear to have used the above analysis as a means of explaining the phenomenon of general interdependence, and thus those forces that determine the manner in which a given stock of factors of production is allocated between different uses or employments.

In dealing with the first aspect of the problem, Smith implicitly examines the case of a single commodity manufactured by a number of sellers, opening the analysis by establishing a distinction between 'natural' and 'market' price. *Natural price* is now defined as that amount which is 'neither more nor less than what is sufficient to pay the rent of the land, the wages of labour, and the profits of the stock . . . according to their natural rates' (*WN* I. vii. 4). In other words, where natural price prevails, the seller is just able to cover his costs of production, including a margin for 'ordinary or average' profit. By contrast, *market price* is defined as that price which may prevail at any given point in time, being regulated 'by the proportion between the quantity which is actually brought to market, and the demand of those who are willing to pay the natural price of the commodity', the 'effectual demanders' (I. vii. 8). These two 'prices' are interrelated, the essential point being that, while in the short run the market and natural prices may diverge, in the long run they will tend to coincide. Natural price thus emerges as an *equilibrium* price, which will obtain when the commodity in question is in fact sold at its cost of production. The latter point may be illustrated by examining the consequences of divergences between the two prices.

If, for example, the quantity offered by the seller was less than that which the consumers were prepared to take at a particular natural price, the consequence would be a competition among the consumers to procure some of a relatively limited stock. Under such circumstances, Smith argued that the 'market' will rise above the 'natural' price, the extent of the divergence being determined by 'the greatness of the deficiency' and varying 'according as the acquisition of the commodity happens to be of more or less importance' to the buyer (I. vii. 9). In

---

[1] Smith's argument suggests in effect that in the long run manufactures could be produced at constant cost. This means that the position of the cost curve facing the firm will be determined by factor costs. With a given (horizontal) cost 'curve', the position of the demand curve will then determine the *amount* produced, with *price* determined by cost of production.

making the latter point, Smith took due note of the fact that, where a relative shortage occurs of goods that are 'necessaries' of life, the extent of the divergence between the two prices (in effect the demand and supply prices) would be greater than that which would occur for luxuries.

Under such circumstances, the price received by the seller must exceed the natural price, with the result that rates of return accruing to factors in this employment also rise above their 'ordinary' level. The consequence of such a divergence between the returns paid in a particular employment and the 'natural' rates prevailing must then be an inflow of resources to this relatively profitable field, leading to an expansion in the supply of the commodity, and a return to that position where the commodity is sold at its natural price. Given a relative shortage of the commodity in the market, Smith concluded: 'The quantity brought thither will soon be sufficient to supply the effectual demand. All the different parts of its price will soon sink to their natural rate, and the whole price to its natural price' (I. vii. 4).

Smith's second case is one in which the quantity brought to market exceeds that which the consumers are willing to take at a particular (natural) price. Under these circumstances, he argued, the supply offered cannot be disposed of at the natural price, so that part of the total output must be sold 'to those who are willing to pay less, and the low price which they give for it must reduce the price of the whole' (I. vii. 10). In such a case, the market must fall below the natural price with the degree of divergence determined by the extent of the excess supply. The extent of the divergence will vary according to the degree of competition generated among the sellers and 'according as it happens to be more or less important to them to get immediately rid of the commodity' (I. vii. 10). Once again, Smith noted that the type of good involved would be important as regards the competition engendered by a relative excess, and observed that over-supply of a perishable commodity 'will occasion a much greater competition than in that of durable commodities' (I. vii. 10). However, given some divergence between market and natural price, the consequence in this case must be that the rates of return payable to factors in this employment fall below their 'ordinary' rates, thus prompting labourers and entrepreneurs to 'withdraw a part of their labour or stock from this employment. The quantity brought to market will soon be no more than sufficient to supply the effectual demand. All the different parts of its price will rise to their natural rate, and the whole price to its natural price' (I. vii. 13). Taking the two cases of divergence, it thus becomes apparent that the price paid by the consumers in purchasing a particular quantity of some commodity will tend to coincide with that price which the seller requires to cover his costs for a specific level of output. In short, the 'natural' price emerges as the equilibrium or 'central' price, 'to which the prices of all commodities are continually *gravitating*'.[2]

Smith also observed that the result attained, namely that commodities in the long run are sold at their cost of production, can hold good only where there is perfect liberty (as distinct from perfect competition). The cost of production solution is, in short, only to be expected where free competition prevails.

The first stage of the discussion established that, in the case of any one commodity, equilibrium will be attained where the good is sold at its natural price, and where each of the relevant factors is paid for at its natural rate. Under these circumstances, equilibrium obtains precisely because there can be no tendency for resources to increase or decrease in this particular type of employment. Now it is evident that if this process, and this result, holds good for all commodities taken separately, it must also apply to all commodities 'taken complexly', at least where a competitive situation prevails. That is, where the conditions that form the assumptions of the partial equilibrium case are satisfied *over the whole economy*, a position of equilibrium will be attained where each different type of good is sold at its natural price, and where each factor in each employment is paid at its natural rate. The economy can then be said to be in a position of 'balance', since where the above conditions are satisfied there can be no tendency to move resources within or between employments. Where the necessary conditions are not satisfied (for example as a result of changes in tastes). they will naturally tend to be re-established as a result of simultaneous adjustments in the factor and commodity markets, which are analogous to those considered in the 'partial' case.

It will be observed that departure from, and reattainment of, a position of *general* equilibrium depends upon the essentially self-interested actions and reactions of consumers and producers.[3] Smith's treatment of price and allocation thus provides one of the best examples of his emphasis on 'interdependence' and one of the most dramatic applications of his analogy of the invisible hand.

While this argument would appear to express the logic of Smith's treatment, he did modify the conclusions reached in two important respects. First, he observed that in the real world the conditions necessary for the attainment of equilibrium (as previously defined) need not be satisfied in fact, placing most emphasis on the problems presented by

---

[2] It is worth noting that Smith's interest was in the processes by virtue of which positions of equilibrium *tended* to be attained, rather than in the state of equilibrium *per se*.

[3] However, cf. WN I. vii. 17, where Smith discusses the problems of supply with special reference to agriculture.

current 'regulations of police'. Of these, he singled out monopoly powers, since the 'price of monopoly is upon every occasion the highest which can be got' (*WN* I. vii. 27), and thus unlikely to be regulated by cost of production. He was also a bitter critic of the privileges of corporations, which effectively served to hinder the movement of capital between areas; of the Poor Laws, which had a similar effect with respect to labour; and of the Statutes of Apprenticeship, which artificially controlled the numbers of workmen in particular types of employment (see Chapter 8 below). Smith deplored all such regulations, both because they were violations of man's 'natural liberty', and because they broke 'what may be called the natural balance of industry' (*LJ*(B) 233), thus constraining productive activity in an unnatural and less beneficial channel (*LJ*(B) 319). It was the responsibility of the government to ensure that the impediments to the 'obvious and simple' state of natural liberty were removed; a state which, once attained, would, *inter alia*, optimize the efficiency with which resources were allocated (see Chapter 8 below).

Secondly, while Smith certainly conceived of general equilibrium in terms of a situation where there was no tendency for resources to move between employments, he also recognized that a position of 'balance' need not involve an equality between monetary rates of return. The point follows directly from Smith's recognition of the fact that employments differ qualitatively and that such differences may serve to explain why, even in a position of 'balance', different money rates prevail. As Smith put it, 'certain circumstances in the employments themselves . . . either really, or at least in the imaginations of men, make up for a small pecuniary gain in some, and counter-balance a great one in others' (*WN* I. x. a. 2).[4] Thus, for example, he noted that money wage rates would tend to vary between different types of employment according to the difficulty of learning the trade, the constancy of employment, and the degree of trust involved. Similarly, he observed that both wages and profits would vary with differences in the agreeableness of the work, and with the probability of success in particular fields. In short, he was suggesting that money rates of return would tend to equality only within employments of similar kinds, and that over the whole economy the relevant balance would be one involving net advantages (I. x. a. 1).[5] It will be seen that his argument involves an important modification to the definition of (general) equilibrium previously employed, and that the modified result will hold good only where labour and stock are free to move between employments.

[4] See especially Rees (1975) and Phelps-Brown (1976).
[5] The other necessary assumptions are: 'First, the employments must be well known and long established in the neighbourhood; secondly, they must be in their ordinary, or what may be called their natural state; and, thirdly, they must be the sole or principal employments of those who occupy them' (*WN* I. x. b. 40).

Before proceeding to the next stage of the argument, it may be useful to make two points, both of which relate back to *The Theory of Moral Sentiments* while at the same time bearing upon the present discussion of the allocative mechanism. The treatment of the doctrine of net advantages is connected with the argument advanced in *The Theory of Moral Sentiments* to the effect that men are motivated by a desire to be approved of. In the present context, the argument suggests that, where a profession is widely admired, public approbation may become a part of the reward. On the other hand, Smith's analysis also suggests that men may be induced to enter and to remain in particular professions only if public disapprobation is compensated by an appropriate monetary reward. For example, we find Smith arguing that:

> To excel in any profession, in which but few arrive at mediocrity, is the most decisive mark of what is called genius or superior talents. The publick admiration which attends upon such distinguished abilities, makes always a part of their reward; a greater or smaller in proportion as it is higher or lower in degree. It makes a considerable part of that reward in the profession of physick; a still greater perhaps in that of law; in poetry and philosophy it makes almost the whole. (*WN* I. x. b. 24).

On the other hand, there are talents whose exercise 'for the sake of gain, is considered, whether from reason or prejudice, as a sort of publick prostitution' (*WN* I. x. b. 25). In such cases, the reward must 'be sufficient, not only to pay for the time, labour, and expence of acquiring the talents, but for the discredit which attends the employment of them as the means of subsistence' (I. x. b. 25). The 'exhorbitant' rewards of players and opera singers 'are founded upon these two principles; the rarity and beauty of the talents, and the discredit of employing them in this manner' (I. x. b. 25).

As Smith remarked elsewhere, the 'trade of a butcher is a brutish and an odious business; but it is in most places more profitable than the greater part of common trades' (I. x. b. 2). He went on to note that 'Disagreeableness and disgrace affect the profits of stock in the same manner as the wages of labour', citing as an example the profits of the inn-keeper who 'exercises neither a very agreeable nor a very creditable business' (I. x. b. 4). It is an intriguing argument, suggesting as it does that in some employments public disapprobation can, and must, be compensated by an appropriate (and determinate) monetary reward.

The presence of an argument that reminds us of a link with *The Theory of Moral Sentiments* also confirms that there is a further dimension to Smith's treatment of the 'economic man' (see Chapter 3 above), which in effect suggests that choices may be subject to the scrutiny of our fellows. The traditional treatment of the allocative process, which recognizably builds upon Smith's results, presents a simpler picture. Rational eco-

nomic man, acting as producer, maximizes efficiency by so arranging the
use of factors as to bring into equality their weighted marginal productivities. The rational consumer maximizes satisfaction by so arranging
his purchases as to bring to equality the weighted marginal utilities of
the products he chooses. In neither case is concern expressed as to the
consequences these decisions may have for the individual or for other
people—or, indeed, of the public reaction to them.

Seen in this light, Smith's perspective generates real complications.
The producer who seeks to make the best use of resources may contribute to economic efficiency and yet attract unfavourable judgement if,
for instance, the wages paid or the conditions of employment offered are
perceived by the spectator to involve some degree of exploitation. The
consumer, in choosing what he believes to be the 'best' use of available
resources, could do so in a way that attracts a charge of impropriety
from the spectator and may also reflect the presence of a defective
telescopic faculty (cf. *WN* v. ii. g. 4; v. ii. k. 50). Our choice of butcher,
brewer, or baker may be affected by judgements as to their behaviour on
matters other than quality or price. Whom we buy from is as interesting
a decision as what we buy. Such concerns open up complex questions
and suggest that Smith's emphasis upon the central issue of propriety
may find some interesting applications in addressing the wider questions of choice in the sense that 'economic' choices may be socially
constrained.

In an interesting commentary on this theme, Etzioni has noted the
need to recognize 'at least two irreducible sources of valuation or utility;
pleasure and morality'. He added that 'Utility theory does not recognise
the distinct standing of morality as a major, significant, source of valua-
tions, and hence as an explanation of behaviour', before going on to
suggest that his own 'deontological multi-utility model' is 'closer to the
other Adam Smith; the author of the *Theory of Moral Sentiments*' (Etzioni
1988: 21–4).

DISTRIBUTION

Abstracting from the fact of legislative obstacles and qualitative differences in employments, it will be recalled that Smith's theory of price was
built up on the assumption of given rates of factor payment. Following
on from this argument, Smith's next task was to elucidate the forces that
determine the *level* of 'ordinary or average' rates of return during any
given time period, and over time, applying to the problem the simple
'demand and supply' type of analysis just considered. We may take the
relevant issues in turn, reviewing them only in such detail as may be
necessary for the present argument.

Wages

Smith observed that payment for the use of the factor labour was a
feature of modern society, a payment made by those classes who require
the factor (undertakers, farmers) and which is necessary to compensate
the disutility of work. The process of wage determination may then be
viewed as a kind of bargain or contract:

What are the common wages of labour depends every where upon the contract
usually made between . . . two parties, whose interests are by no means the
same. The workmen desire to get as much, the masters to give as little as
possible. The former are disposed to combine in order to raise, the latter in
order to lower the wages of labour. (*WN* I. viii. 11).

In Smith's judgement, the balance of advantage in determining the
terms of this 'contract' must generally lie with the 'masters', the reason
being that, while the law permitted their 'combinations', it prevented
those of the workers. However, Smith was careful to point out that the
bargaining strength of the two parties would itself be affected by
demand and supply relationships, irrespective of legal privileges.
Thus, for example, where labour is relatively abundant, wage rates
will tend to be low, partly because individuals will have to compete
for such employment as is available, and partly because, while in 'the
long-run the workman may be as necessary to his master as his master is
to him . . . the necessity is not so immediate' (I. viii. 2). On the other
hand, where labour is relatively scarce, 'The scarcity of hands occasions
a competition among masters, who bid against one another, in order to
get workmen, and thus voluntarily break through the natural combination of masters not to raise wages' (I. viii. 17).

Having come thus far, Smith clarified the argument by pointing out
that wage rates may be relatively high or low, depending on the available supply of labour and the size of the funds (or capital stock) available
for its purchase. He did not in fact set out to define some upper limit for
wages, but he did suggest that the lowest limit, in the long term, must be
determined by the needs of subsistence, since 'A man must always live
by his work, and his wages must at least be sufficient to maintain him.
They must even upon most occasions be somewhat more; otherwise it
would be impossible for him to bring up a family, and the race of such
workmen could not last beyond the first generation' (I. viii. 15). In
Smith's analysis, the importance of the 'subsistence wage' lies in the
fact that it constitutes the long-run supply price of labour, the argument
being in effect that over time labour may be produced at constant cost,
leading to the conclusion that the subsistence wage could be regarded as
a kind of 'natural' or equilibrium rate. Smith in fact made use of three

cases to illustrate an argument that is analogous to the previous treatment of equilibrium price.

To begin with, it will be apparent that in a position of long-run equilibrium the demand for, and supply of, labour must be such that a particular level of population is in receipt of a subsistence wage. Under such circumstances, we find a position of equilibrium in the sense that there can be no tendency for population to increase or diminish, a condition that will obtain so long as there is no change in the size of the wages fund. This is Smith's example of the stationary state, as illustrated by the experience of China. Secondly, Smith examined a case, again starting from a position of equilibrium, where there is a fall in the demand for labour either in any one year, or continuously over a number of years.

Under such circumstances, the actual wage rate paid must fall below the subsistence rate, resulting in a fall in population until the level is such as to permit subsistence wages to be paid. This example represents Smith's 'declining' state, the cases cited being Bengal and certain East Indian colonies, areas where the decline in the wages fund had led to want, 'famine, and mortality', until 'the number of inhabitants . . . was reduced to what could easily be maintained by the revenue and stock which remained' (I. viii. 26).

Finally, we have Smith's 'advancing state', where an increase, or series of (annual) increases, in the size of the wages fund causes rates in excess of the subsistence level to be paid at least for as long as it takes to increase the level of population—an increase which, Smith said, would inevitably follow from the higher standard of living involved. However, he also pointed out that the feature of the 'advancing state' would be a continuous improvement in the demand for labour, thus making it possible for high wage rates to be paid over a number of years, and at least for as long as the *rate* of increase in the demand for labour exceeded the rate of increase in supply. Smith considered the case of North America to be a good example of the trend, but allowed that many European countries, including Great Britain, showed the same tendency, albeit to a lesser degree. In the case of Britain, for example, Smith pointed out that real wages had increased during the eighteenth century and that as a matter of fact they were well above subsistence level at the time of writing (I. viii. 28). It is interesting to observe that Smith felt that high wages were to be approved of, on the grounds of both equity and the improved productivity of labour that results.[6]

---

[6] 'It is but equity, besides, that they who feed, cloath and lodge the whole body of the people, should have such a share of the produce of their own labour as to be themselves tolerably well fed, cloathed and lodged' (*WN* I. viii. 36). For Smith's views on the causes of the increase in productivity that high wages involve, see WN I. viii. 44).

Now while this argument runs in terms of an analysis of equilibrium similar in kind to that used in dealing with the theory of (commodity) price, it will be apparent that it examines adjustments very much longer-term in character than those so far considered. On the other hand, the argument is important as regards the static aspects of Smith's analysis in the sense that it helps to elucidate the forces that determine the level of wages during the course of a single time period, such as a year, and thus the level of the 'ordinary or average' rates which Smith took as given in handling the problem of price. What has been said so far serves to show that in any one time period (such as a year) wage rates may be equal to, above, or below the subsistence rate, that such rates are a function of the size of the wages fund and the level of the working population, and that particular rates, once established, will remain stable so long as there is no change in any of the relevant aggregates.

Profit

As far as profit is concerned, it is interesting to observe that Smith did not consider this form of return to be the reward payable for undertaking the managerial function of 'inspection and direction' but rather the compensation for the trouble taken, and the risks incurred, in combining the factors of production. As he put it, 'As soon as stock has accumulated in the hands of particular persons, some of them will naturally employ it in setting to work industrious people, whom they will supply with materials and subsistence, in order to make a profit by the sale of their work, or by what their labour adds to the value of the materials' (I. vi. 5).

Looked at in this way, the profits that accrue to individual producers must obviously be affected by the selling price of the commodity and costs of production (including wages). Profits are thus likely to be particularly sensitive to changes in the direction of demand, together with the 'good or bad fortune' of rivals and customers—facts that make it difficult to speak of an 'ordinary or average' rate of return (I. ix. 3). However, Smith did suggest that the rate of interest would provide a reasonably accurate index of profit levels at any one time, basically on the ground that the rate payable for borrowed funds would reflect the profits to be gained from their use: 'It may be laid down as a maxim, that wherever a great deal can be made by the use of money, a great deal will commonly be given for the use of it; and that wherever little can be made by it, less will commonly be given for it' (I. ix. 4).

In this connection Smith was careful to argue that the rate of interest payable would be in proportion to the 'clear or neat' profit, rather than *gross* profit—that is, to the profit remaining after making allowance for the necessary risk premium required by the entrepreneur (I. ix. 18).

At least as a broad generalization, Smith felt able to suggest that the rate of profit accruing at any one point in time, other things remaining equal, and with wage rates given, would be determined by the quantity of stock available, taken in conjunction with the volume of business to be transacted by it, or the extent of the outlets for profitable investment. It thus followed that over time the rate of profit would tend to decline, partly in consequence of the gradual increase of stock, and partly because of the increasing difficulty of finding 'a profitable method of employing any new capital'. As he wrote in another passage, 'When the stocks of many rich merchants are turned into the same trade, their mutual competition naturally tends to lower its profit; and when there is a like increase of stock in all the different trades carried on in the same society, the same competition must produce the same effect in them all' (ɪ. ix. 2). It then follows that 'the diminution of profit is the natural effect of . . . prosperity' (ɪ. ix. 10).

In the long term, Smith concluded that, just as wages would sink towards subsistence levels, so profit would progressively decline until the rate of 'clear' profit was just sufficient to meet the necessary interest payments, including a risk premium for the lender (ɪ. ix. 22). Smith however observed that two sets of circumstances might serve to reverse the associated trend of profits. First, he suggested that a declining state (such as Bengal) would feature a gradual reduction in capital stock and thus a tendency to *increased* rates of profit. Secondly, he pointed out that even in advancing states the tendency for profits to fall might be reversed or temporarily halted, owing to the acquisition of new investment outlets, or of new territories as a result of conquest or colonization. For example, in the case of Great Britain, Smith pointed out that the acquisitions made after 'the late war' (with France) must necessarily have increased the rate of profit, despite the advancing tendency of the country, since so 'great an accession of new business to be carried on by the old stock, must necessarily have diminished the quantity employed in a great number of particular branches, in which the competition being less, the profits must have been greater' (ɪ. ix. 12).

However, the basic points that Smith was endeavouring to establish seem clear. If we look at the long-term trends of the economy, the tendency is for profits (like wages) to fall. If we look at the economy at a particular point in time (say a single year), then it appears that the 'ordinary or average' rate of profit prevailing must be a function of the quantity of stock, and of the 'proportion of business' to which it can be applied. However, Smith made an important qualification to the latter point when he indicated that, even where the quantity of stock remains the same (say, in two different time periods), other things remaining equal, the rate of profit will also be related to the prevailing wage rate. Thus for example, if labour is relatively abundant in relation to a given capital stock (that is, the wages fund), the rate of profit will be higher, and wage rates lower, than they will be where labour is relatively scarce.

Rent

Smith formally defined rent as the 'price paid for the use of land' (*WN* I. xi. a. 1), a price paid because land is of itself productive, part of the property of individuals, and (presumably) scarce. Looking at the question in this way, Smith was careful to argue that rent constitutes a surplus in the sense that it accrues to the owner of land independently of any effort made by him, so that the proprietors emerge as 'the only one of the three orders whose revenue costs them neither labour nor care, but comes to them, as it were, of its own accord' (I. xi. 8). Moreover, Smith suggested that rent payments are akin to a 'monopoly price', at least in the broad sense that they are generally the highest that can be got in the 'actual circumstances of the land' (I. xi. a. 1). The reference to 'actual circumstances' is important, since Smith recognized that rent payments would vary with both the fertility and the situation of the land involved.

Smith generally took the view that land used for the production of human food would always yield a rent, and indeed he computed that rent would be of the order of one-third of the gross produce. Moreover, he suggested that in the long term rent payments would tend to increase, at least absolutely, owing to the increased use of the available stock of land that the growth of population inevitably involves. 'The extension of improvement and cultivation tends to raise it directly. The landlord's share of the produce necessarily increases with the increase of the produce' (I. xi. 2). He added that the real value of the landlords' receipts would also tend to increase over time, since all 'those improvements in the productive powers of labour, which tend directly to reduce the real price of manufactures, tend indirectly to raise the real rent of land' (I. xi. 4).

However, two aspects of Smith's argument would appear to be of particular importance in the present context. First, the analysis serves to suggest that at any point in time, or during any given annual period, rent payments will be a function of the proportion of the fixed stock of land used, where the latter is in turn a function of the level of population. Secondly, his argument indicates that, during any given annual period, rent payments will be related not only to the fertility of the soil, but also to the prevailing rates of wages and profit:

Rent, it is to be observed . . . enters into the composition of the price of commodities in a different way from wages and profit. High or low wages and profit, are the causes of high or low price; high or low rent is the effect of it. It is because high or low wages and profit must be paid, in order to bring a particular commodity to market, that its price is high or low. But it is because its price is high or low; a great deal more, or very little more, or no more, than what is sufficient to pay those wages and profit, that it affords a high rent, or a low rent, or no rent at all. (*WN* I. xi. a. 8).

While we will have occasion to return later to Smith's theory of distribution taken as a whole, two of its features may be worth emphasizing before going further. First, in explaining the forces that determine rates of return, the argument throughout has a short-run element, linking it to the theory of price, at least in so far as Smith was concerned to elucidate those forces that determine the 'ordinary or average' rates of return that prevail in any given annual period. It will be observed that in this case Smith treated factors of production as fixed stocks, and that he suggested a certain interdependence with respect to the rates of return prevailing in the course of a single year. As we have seen, rent payments are affected by the prevailing rates of profit and wages, while, in addition, profits are affected by existing wage levels.

Secondly, the argument just reviewed also has a dynamic element, at least in the sense that Smith was concerned with long-run trends in rates of return, treating factors as flows rather than stocks. Once again, it will be recalled that these trends are interrelated and that they apparently depend on the process of capital accumulation. Thus, Smith suggests that profits will decline as the size of the capital stock increases; that high rates of accumulation will generate high market wage rates, leading to an increase in the level of population, a movement back towards subsistence levels, and changes in rent payments which reflect the inevitable increase in the output of food. However, it is interesting to note that at this stage of the argument no explanation is offered as to the *source* of the increase in capital, an omission that is rectified in the predominantly macroeconomic analysis of book II.

MACROECONOMICS

The great commerce of every civilized society, is that carried on between the inhabitants of the town and those of the country. It consists in the exchange of rude for manufactured produce, either immediately, or by the intervention of money, or of some sort of paper which represents money. . . . The gains of both are mutual and reciprocal, and the division of labour is in this, as in all other cases, advantageous to all the different persons employed in the various occupations into which it is subdivided. (*WN* III. i. 1).

The purpose of book II was to explain the nature of the relationship between the productive sectors and—the dominant theme—the causes of economic growth. But before proceeding to the discussion of these topics, it may be useful to recall the psychological assumptions upon which the analyses are based (see Chapter 3 above). It was in *The Theory of Moral Sentiments*, more than in the *Wealth of Nations*, that Smith offered an explanation of the psychological forces that motivate mankind, drawing attention once more to the desire for approval. As Smith remarked,

> Though it is to supply the necessities and conveniences of the body, that the advantages of external fortune are originally recommended to us, yet we cannot live long in the world without perceiving that the respect of our equals, our credit and rank in the society we live in, depend very much upon the degree in which we possess, or are supposed to possess, these advantages. The desire of becoming the proper objects of this respect, of deserving and obtaining this credit and rank among our equals, is, perhaps, the strongest of all our desires, and our anxiety to obtain the advantages of fortune is accordingly much more excited and irritated by this desire, than by that of supplying all the necessities and conveniences of the body, which are always very easily supplied. (*TMS* vi. i. 3).

As Smith had noted earlier in the book, the advantages which we propose 'by that great purpose of human life which we call bettering our condition' are to be 'observed, to be attended to, to be taken notice of with sympathy, complacency, and approbation' (*TMS* i. iii. 2. 1).

Smith recognized that the pursuit of *place* and wealth was a basic human drive which was linked to the desire to better our condition, 'a desire which, though generally calm and dispassionate, comes with us from the womb, and never leaves us till we go into the grave' (*WN* ii, iii, 28); a drive that involves 'unrelenting industry' (*TMS*, iv. 1, 8) and sacrifices which are supported by the approbation of our fellows. 'The habits of oeconomy, industry, discretion, attention and application of thought, are generally supposed to be cultivated from self-interested motives, and at the same time are apprehended to be very praiseworthy qualities, which deserve the esteem and approbation of every body' (iv, 2, 8). Hence, he continued, 'that eminent esteem with which all men naturally regard a steady perseverance in the practice of frugality, industry and application, though directed to no other purpose than the acquisition of fortune'. He added that it 'is the consciousness of this merited approbation and esteem which is capable of supporting the agent in this tenour of conduct', since normally the 'pleasure which we are to enjoy ten years hence interests us so little in comparison with that which we may enjoy today' (iv. 2. 8).

Smith developed this theme in a passage that was added to the sixth edition of *The Theory of Moral Sentiments*:

> In the steadiness of his industry and frugality, in his steadily sacrificing the ease and enjoyment of the present moment for the probable expectation of the still

greater ease and enjoyment of a more distant but more lasting period of time, the prudent man is always both supported and rewarded by the entire approbation of the impartial spectator, and of the representative of the impartial spectator, the man within the breast. (*TMS* VI. i. 11).

It is not difficult to see in this argument an anticipation of modern concerns with sociological factors as they affect economic behaviour—or even an anticipation, however rudimentary, of a kind of life-cycle hypothesis whereby the behaviour of the individual actively seeking to better his condition is first dominated by frugality before he can enjoy the conspicuous consumption that is the possible outcome of success.

Period Analysis

At a formal level, it can be stated that the 'static' and 'dynamic' themes that are present in the theory of distribution, as outlined in the preceding section, are continued in the second book. The 'static' or, more accurately, the short-run dimension is addressed in Smith's attempt to illustrate the working of the economy as a system, in the context of a model wherein all magnitudes are dated, before going on to consider the performance of the economy over time. These areas of analysis may be seen to be interrelated, while in addition both are connected with the previous treatment of price and distribution. We may take these issues in turn.

Smith's analysis of the 'circular flow' may be seen as a direct development of certain results already stated in connection with the theory of price. To begin with, it will be recalled that costs of production are incurred by those who create commodities, thus providing individuals with the means of exchange. It therefore follows that, if the price of each good in a position of equilibrium comprehends payments made for rent, wages, and profit, according to their natural rates, then 'it must be so with regard to all the commodities which compose the whole annual produce of the land and labour of every country, taken complexly' (*WN* II. ii. 2). On this basis, Smith concluded that 'The whole price or exchangeable value of that annual produce, must resolve itself into the same three parts, and be parcelled out among the different inhabitants' (II. ii. 2). If, for the moment, we ignore the problem of distribution (that is, of a given level of income between rent, wages, and profit), the result that Smith was endeavouring to establish may be stated to involve a relationship between aggregate output and aggregate income. In his own words, 'The gross revenue of all the inhabitants of a great country, comprehends the whole annual produce of their land and labour' (II. ii. 5).[7] It will be evident that a particular level of income, created by a particular level of aggregate output, represents that power to purchase goods which is available to all the members of 'a great society'.

Smith then went on to observe that this level of purchasing power would be divided into two funds, consumption and saving. In fact, Smith offered no formal explanation of the forces that would determine the actual distribution of aggregate income or purchasing power between these two uses at any particular point in time. He did however suggest that proprietors and labourers would tend to devote a high proportion of their income to consumption, the latter by virtue of the size of their receipts in relation to their basic needs, and the former by virtue of the habits of 'expence' associated with that class. The problem of balancing future against present enjoyments thus appeared to be relevant mainly for the entrepreneurial groups, groups whose functions and objectives dispose them to frugality, at least while they are actively engaged in the pursuit of fortune.

But Smith did clarify the problems here considered from the standpoint of expenditure. For example, he noted that the proportion of annual income earmarked for consumption, taking all groups 'complexly', would be used to purchase commodities that were either perishable or durable in character. He also noted that this type of expenditure could involve the purchase of services, services of a kind that do not directly contribute to the annual output of commodities in physical terms and which thus cannot be said to contribute to the level of income associated with it. Smith formally described such labour as 'unproductive', but did not deny that such services were useful. For example, he pointed out that the services of 'players, buffoons, opera singers, and musicians' have a certain value because they represent sources of satisfaction to those who pay for them. Similarly, he pointed out that the services provided by governments, which are paid for out of taxes, have a value, the reason being that society could not subsist without them. However, all such services are by definition unproductive: 'The sovereign . . . with all the officers both of justice and war who serve under him, the whole army and navy, are unproductive labourers. They are the servants of the publick, and are maintained by a part of the annual produce of the industry of other people' (*WN* II. iii. 2).

---

[7] As J. B. Say (1767–1832) observed, 'products are raised by the productive means at the command of mankind, that is to say, by human industry, capital and natural powers and agents. The products thus raised form the revenue of those possessed of the means of production, and enable them to procure such of the necessaries and comforts of existence, as are not furnished gratuitously, either by nature or their fellow creatures' (Say 1821: ii. 21). James Mill (1773–1836) repeated this argument (Mill 1966, edn: 135), as did John Stuart Mill (1806–1873) (Mill 1848: bk III, ch. 14, 'Of Excess of Supply').

With regard to *savings*, Smith identified two sources and two uses. For example, he identified the agrarian, trading, and manufacturing interests as groups wherein 'the owners themselves employ their own capitals' (II. iv. 5), as distinct from the monied interest who may lend either for the purpose of consumption or of production. Interest is defined as:

the compensation which the borrower pays to the lender, for the profit which he has an opportunity of making by the use of the money. Part of that profit naturally belongs to the borrower, who runs the risk and takes the trouble of employing it; and part to the lender, who affords him the opportunity of making this profit. (*WN* I. vi. 18).[8]

Smith went on to argue that the undertaker or entrepreneur engaged in agriculture, manufacture, or trade could employ his own or borrowed resources for productive purposes, and divided their capitals into two categories, both of which are reminiscent of physiocratic teaching. *Fixed capital* was defined as that portion of savings used to purchase 'useful machines' or to improve, for example, the productive powers of land, the characteristic feature being that goods are created, and profits ultimately acquired, by using and retaining possession of the investment goods involved. *Circulating capital* was defined as that portion of savings used to purchase investment goods other than 'fixed implements', such as labour power or raw materials, the characteristic feature being that goods are produced through temporarily 'parting with' the funds so used. Smith made three points in the context of this discussion:

1. 'Every fixed capital is both originally derived from, and requires to be continually supported by, a circulating capital' (*WN* II. i. 24).
2. 'No fixed capital can yield any revenue but by means of a circulating capital' (II. i. 25); while in addition,
3. 'different occupations require very different proportions between the fixed and circulating capitals employed in them' (II. i. 6).

While these points are important of themselves, they were to gain added significance when Smith moved to the next stage of his argument: the development of his version of the 'circular flow', where, again following the physiocratic lead, he examined the functioning of the system in a given time period. Taking the economic system as a whole, Smith suggested that the total stock of society could be divided into three categories:

---

[8] The role played by the rate of interest in contributing to a balance between savings, investment and consumption was more clearly stated by J. S. Mill: 'The rate of interest will be such as to equalize the demand for loans with the supply of them. It will be such, that exactly as much as some people are desirous to borrow at that rate, others shall be willing to lend. If there is more offered than demanded, interest will fall; if more is demanded than offered, it will rise; and in both cases, to the point at which the equation of supply and demand is re-established' (Mill 1848; 1965 edn.: 647).

There is, first, that part of the total stock which is reserved for immediate consumption, and which is held by *all* consumers (capitalists, labour, and proprietors) reflecting purchases made in previous time periods. The characteristic feature of this part of the total stock is that it affords no revenue to its possessors since it consists in 'the stock of food, cloaths, household furniture, etc. which have been purchased by their proper consumers, but which are not yet entirely consumed (*WN* II. i. 12).

Secondly, there is that part of the total stock which may be described as 'fixed capital' and which will be distributed between the various groups in society. This part of the stock, Smith suggested, is composed of the 'useful machines' purchased in preceding periods but currently held by the undertakers engaged in manufacture, the quantity of useful buildings and of 'improved land' in the possession of the 'capitalist' farmers and the proprietors, together with the 'acquired and useful abilities' of all the inhabitants (II. i. 13–17), that is, human capital.

Thirdly, there is that part of the total stock which may be described as 'circulating capital' and which again has several components, these being:

1. the quantity of money necessary to carry on the process of circulation. (In this connection, Smith observed that: 'The sole use of money is to circulate consumable goods. By means of it, provisions, materials, and finished work, are bought and sold, and distributed to their proper consumers. The quantity of money, therefore, which can be annually employed in any country must be determined by the value of the consumable goods annually circulated within it' (*WN* II. iii. 23));[9]
2. the stock of provisions and other agricultural products that are available for sale during the current period, but are still in the hands of either the farmers or merchants;
3. the stock of raw materials and work in process held by merchants, undertakers, or those capitalists engaged in the agricultural sector (including mining, etc.);

[9] Smith defines money as the great wheel of circulation at *WN* II. ii. 14, 23 and shows his appreciation of the importance of the velocity of circulation at *WN* II. ii. 22. J. B. Say also noted that in the modern economy goods are sold for money, which then serves as the instrument which allows other purchases to be made. 'Money performs but a momentary function in this double exchange; and when the transaction is finally closed, it will always be found, that one kind of produce has been exchanged for another' (Say 1821: i. 167). Say was, however, aware (1821: ch. 16) of a point made by James Mill, who noted that in periods of uncertainty: 'there is a general disposition to hoard: a considerable portion therefore, of the medium of exchange is withdrawn from circulation, and the evils of a scarcity of money are immediately felt; the prices of commodities fall, and the value of money rises; those who have goods to sell, and those who have debts to pay, are subject to losses; and calamity is widely diffused' (Mill 1966 edn.: 290). Smith was aware of the problems inherent in a 'dual circulation' model, featuring a sophisticated credit structure (cf. Zallio 1990).

4. the stock of manufactured goods (consumption and investment goods) created during the previous period, but remaining in the hands of undertakers and merchants at the beginning of the period examined (*WN* II. i. 19–22).

The logic of the process can be best represented by artificially separating the activities involved much in the manner of the physiocratic model with which Smith was familiar. Let us suppose that, at the beginning of the time period in question, the major capitalist groups possess the total net receipts earned from the sale of products in the previous period, and that the undertakers engaged in agriculture open by transmitting the total rent due to the proprietors of land for the current use of that factor. The income thus provided will enable the proprietors to make the necessary purchases of consumption (and investment) goods in the current period, thus contributing to reduce the stocks of such goods with which the undertakers and merchants began the period.

Secondly, let us assume that the undertakers engaged in both sectors, together with the merchant groups, transmit to wage labour the content of the wages fund, thus providing this socio-economic class with an income that can be used in the current period. It is worth noting in this connection that the capitalist groups transmit a fund to wage labour which formed a part of their *savings*, providing by this means an income that is available for current *consumption*. Thirdly, the undertakers engaged in agriculture and manufactures will make purchases of consumption and investment goods from each other, through the medium of retail and wholesale merchants, thus generating a series of expenditures linking the two major sectors. Finally, the process of circulation may be seen to be completed by the purchases made by individual undertakers within their own sectors. Once again, these purchases will include consumption and investment goods, thus contributing still further to reduce the stocks of commodities that were available for sale when the period under examination began, and which formed part of the circulating capital of the society in question.

Given these points, we can represent the working of the system in terms of a series of flows whereby money income, accruing in the form of rent, wages, and profit, is exchanged for commodities in such a way as to involve a series of withdrawals from the 'circulating' capital of society. As Smith pointed out, the consumption goods withdrawn from the existing stock may be entirely used up within the current period, used to increase the stock 'reserved for immediate consumption', or used to replace the more durable goods, for example furniture or clothes, that had reached the end of their lives in the course of the same period.

Similarly, the undertakers, as a result of their purchases, may add to their stocks of raw materials and/or their fixed capital, or replace the machines that had finally worn out in the current period, together with the materials used up as a result of current productive activity. Looked at in this way, the 'circular flow' could be seen to involve purchases that take goods from the circulating capital of society, which is in turn matched by a continuous process of *replacement* by virtue of current production of materials and finished goods - where both types of production require the use of the fixed and circulating capitals of individual entrepreneurs. It is an essential part of Smith's argument that all available resources will normally be used:

In all countries where there is tolerable security, every man of common understanding will endeavour to employ whatever stock he can command in procuring either present enjoyment or future profit. If it is employed in procuring present enjoyment, it is a stock reserved for immediate consumption. If it is employed in procuring future profit, it must procure this profit either by staying with him, or by going from him. In the one case it is a fixed, in the other it is a circulating capital. A man must be perfectly crazy who, where there is tolerable security, does not employ all the stock which he commands, whether it be his own or borrowed of other people, in some one or other of those three ways. (*WN* II. i. 30).

Smith elaborated on this argument in drawing attention to the point that the differing ways in which the entrepreneurial classes employ their capitals were interdependent. Defined in this manner,

A capital may be employed in four different ways: either, first, in procuring the rude produce annually required for the use and consumption of the society; or, secondly, in manufacturing and preparing that rude produce for immediate use and consumption; or, thirdly, in transporting either the rude or manufactured produce from the places where they abound to those where they are wanted; or, lastly, in dividing particular portions of either into such small parcels as suit the occasional demands of those who want them. (*WN* II. v. 1).

It is the expenditure of the consumers on particular commodities that in effect replaces the outlays of those who retail them, just as the capital of the retailer replaces, together with its profits, that of the wholesale merchant from whom he purchases goods, thereby enabling him to continue in business (*WN* II. v. 9). In turn,

The capital of the wholesale merchant replaces, together with their profits, the capitals of the farmers and manufacturers of whom he purchases the rude and manufactured product which he deals in, and thereby enables them to continue their respective trades. (*WN* II. v. 10).

At the same time,

> Part of the capital of the master manufacturer is employed as a fixed capital in the instruments of his trade, and replaces, together with its profits, that of some other artificer of whom he purchases them. Part of his circulating capital is employed in purchasing materials, and replaces, with their profits, the capitals of the farmers and miners of whom he purchases them. But a great part of it is always, either annually, or in a much shorter period, distributed among the different workmen whom he employs. (*WN* II. v. 11).

The farmer, needless to say, performs similar (and reciprocal) functions with regard to the manufacturing sector.

The Sources of Growth

In choosing to examine the working of the economy during a given time period such as a year, Smith gave his model a broadly static character although it is obviously one that included a time dimension. At the same time, he did not seek to formulate *equilibrium* conditions (as Quesnay had done) for the model, at least in the sense that he did not try to develop an argument that used specified assumptions of a quantitative kind as a means of showing the conditions that must be satisfied before the following time period could open under conditions identical to those prevailing in the period actually examined. Indeed, Smith's lack of concern not with macro-statics, but with macro-static *equilibrium*, was to some extent announced by the allowance made for the fact that goods are 'used up' at different rates.[10]

Nor, in dealing with the 'flow', did Smith suggest that the level of output attained during any given period would be exactly sufficient to replace the goods used up during its course. On the contrary, he argued that output levels attained in any year would be likely to exceed previous levels, an important reminder that his predominant concern was with economic growth. In this connection, Smith noted that the 'annual produce of the land and labour of any nation can be increased in its value by no other means, but by increasing either the number of its productive labourers, or the productive powers of those labourers who had before been employed' (*WN* II. iii. 32). He also observed that both the above sources of increased output required an 'additional capital' devoted either to increasing the size of the wages fund or to purchasing 'machines and instruments which facilitate and abridge labour', an

---

[10] This interesting preoccupation, which suggests that the level of activity may fluctuate as a result of variations in the replacement cycle of consumption *and* of investment goods, was partially anticipated by Sir James Steuart (1767: ch. 26).

additional capital that can be acquired only through net savings. 'By what a frugal man annually saves, he not only affords maintenance to an additional number of productive hands, for that or the ensuing year, but like the founder of a public workhouse, he establishes as it were a perpetual fund for the maintenance of an equal number in all times to come' (II. iii. 19).

It will be observed that net savings attained during the course of a single annual period will lead to higher output and income, where the latter becomes available during the course of the period examined. The argument can be extended from this point, in that higher levels of output and income attained in any one year make it possible to reach still higher levels of savings and investment in subsequent years, thus generating further increases in output and income. Once started, the process of capital accumulation and thus economic growth may be seen as self-generating, indicating that Smith's 'flow' is to be regarded as a spiral (whose dimensions will vary because of variations in the rate of replacement of commodities) rather than as a circle of given dimensions. This indeed is the burden of Smith's argument in book II, a fact that helps to explain some of its recurrent themes.

First, Smith frequently argued that net savings will always be possible during each annual period:

Whatever a person saves from his revenue he adds to his capital, and either employs it himself in maintaining an additional number of productive hands, or enables some other person to do so, by lending it to him for an interest, that is, for a share of the profits. As the capital of an individual can be increased only by what he saves from his annual revenue or his annual gains, so the capital of a society, which is the same with that of all the individuals who compose it, can be increased only in the same manner. (*WN* II. ii. 15).

Secondly, Smith emphasized that:

Parsimony, by increasing the fund which is destined for the maintenance of productive hands, tends to increase the number of those hands whose labour adds to the value of the subject upon which it is bestowed. It tends therefore to increase the exchangeable value of the land and labour of the country. It puts into motion an additional quantity of industry, which gives an added value to the annual produce. (*WN* II. iii. 17).

Thirdly, Smith suggested, in passages that are reminiscent of Turgot, that savings once made will always be used either to make purchases of investment goods, such as fixed capital, or to employ additional quantities of productive labour, i.e. circulating capital. 'What is annually saved is as regularly consumed as what is annually spent, and nearly in the same time too; but it is consumed by a different set of people' (*WN* II. iii. 18).[11]

Smith's basic theme is that economic growth depends upon the accumulation of capital, and he went on from this point to draw attention to those factors that affect its *rate*.

The Rate of Growth:

First, Smith pointed to the incidence of commercial failure in observing that every 'injudicious and unsuccessful project in agriculture, mines, fisheries, trade, or manufactures, tends . . . to diminish the funds destined for the maintenance of productive labour' (*WN* II.. iii. 26).

Secondly, he drew attention to the fact that the support of productive assets, e.g. fixed capital, must absorb 'a certain portion' of the available resources (II. ii. 7). 'The undertaker of some great manufactory who employs a thousand a year in the maintenance of his machinery, if he can reduce this expence to five hundred, will naturally employ the other five hundred in purchasing an additional quantity of materials to be wrought up by an additional number of workmen' (II. ii. 7).

Thirdly, he drew attention to the advantages of paper money:

the machines and instruments of trade, etc. which compose the fixed capital, bear this . . . resemblance to that part of the circulating capital which consists in money; that as every saving in the expence of erecting and supporting these machines, which does not diminish the productive powers of labour, is an improvement in the neat revenue of the society; so every saving in the expence of collecting and supporting that part of the capital which consists in money, is an improvement of exactly the same kind. (*WN* II. ii. 24).

He added that:

When paper is substituted in the room of gold and silvery money, the quantity of the materials, tools and maintenance, which the whole circulating capital can supply, may be increased by the whole value of the gold and silver which used to be employed in purchasing them. (*WN* II. ii. 39).

[11] J.B. Say recognized that an act of saving would *not* lead to a reduction in the level of effective demand, 'provided the thing saved be reinvested or restored to productive employment' (Say 1821: 115). His position echoes that stated by Smith and was repeated by James Mill when he remarked that: 'Every particle of the annual produce of a country falls as revenue to somebody. But every individual in the nation uniformly makes purchases, or does what is equivalent to making purchases, with every farthings worth which accrues to him. All that part which is destined for mere consumption is evidently employed in purchases. That too which is employed as capital, is not less so' (Mill 1966 edn.: 136). This particular piece of the classical orthodoxy was repeated by J. S. Mill; 'The person who saves his income is no less a consumer than he who spends it: he consumes it in a different way; it supplies food and clothing to be consumed, tools and materials to be used, by productive labourers' (Mill 1844: 48).

In addition, Smith noted that the rate of growth would be affected by the extent to which resources were used to support productive rather than unproductive labour:

According . . . as a smaller or greater proportion . . . is in any one year employed in maintaining unproductive hands, the more in the one case and the less in the other will remain for productive, and the next years produce will be greater or smaller accordingly; the whole annual produce, if we except the spontaneous productions of the earth, being the effect of productive labour. (WN II. iii. 3).

Elsewhere, Smith drew attention to the size of the government sector, since the 'whole, or almost the whole public revenue, is in most countries employed in maintaining unproductive hands' (WN II. iii. 30).

The basic principles just stated led Smith to a further refinement of the argument in stating that the rate of growth would also be affected by the area of investment to which a specific injection of capital was applied.[12] More specifically, it was Smith's contention that the four main fields of investment that were mentioned in the account of the 'flow' would support, directly or indirectly, different quantities of productive labour. For example, the *retailer* replaces the stock of the merchant from whom he purchases goods, thus supporting a certain quantity of productive labour even though the retailer himself may be the only productive labourer directly employed. In the same way, the *wholesaler* replaces the capitals of the farmers and merchants with whom he does business, and 'of whom he purchases the rude and manufactured produce which he deals in, and thereby enables them to continue their respective trades' (II. v. 10). Both indirectly and directly, the wholesale merchant supports a larger number of productive hands than the retailer.

Smith went further in noting that different kinds of wholesale trade would vary in their contribution to the maintenance of productive labour at the domestic level. In this connection, he asserted that the home trade of consumption was to be preferred since it only served to replace domestic capitals. The foreign trade of consumption was ranked second in that the exchange of domestic for foreign goods at least replaced *some* domestic capitals. The carrying trade was held to replace foreign capitals only and thus to make a limited contribution to domestic industry.

If the wholesale trade is preferred to the retail, *manufactures* emerge as still more important, since investment in this area will indirectly support a relatively larger amount of productive labour by replacing the capitals of those who supply machinery and materials, while at the same time tending directly to employ a relatively significant number of men. But undoubtedly, Smith's preference was for agriculture: 'No equal capital

---

[12] On this subject, see WN II. v.

puts into motion a greater quantity of productive labour than that of the farmer'—leading to the conclusion that, 'Of all the ways in which a capital can be employed, it is by far the most advantageous to the society' (II. v. 12).

Smith advanced two additional propositions which *seem* to follow from the argument just stated. First, he asserted that, where the total stock available is insufficient for all three main purposes (agriculture, manufacture, and trade), the growth rate will be maximized by first concentrating on agriculture. He believed as a matter of fact that the rate of growth in Europe was lower than it might be and that 'Agriculture . . . is almost every where capable of absorbing a much greater capital than has ever yet been employed in it' (II. v. 37). By contrast, 'It has been the principal cause of the rapid progress of our American colonies towards wealth and greatness, that almost their whole capitals have hitherto been employed in agriculture' (II. v. 21). Secondly, he argued that a certain *sequence* of investment would generally be preferred, in part because of differences in the degree of security involved. He therefore concluded: 'According to the natural course of things . . . the greater part of the capital of every growing society is, first, directed to agriculture, afterwards to manufactures, and last of all to foreign commerce' (III. i. 8).

While these two propositions are logically distinct, they were to provide Smith with apparently significant weapons in his critique of mercantilism in general, and of the colonial relationship with America in particular (see Chapter 9 below). Smith also commented on the role of 'manners' in a style reminiscent of Hume (see Chapter 10 below), noting that: 'The proportion between capital and revenue . . . seems every where to regulate the proportion between industry and idleness. Wherever capital predominates, industry prevails; wherever revenue, idleness' (II. iii. 13).

As we have seen, Smith commented on the phenomenon of conspicuous consumption not only on the part of the proprietors, but also by those that had attained riches. While drawing attention to the fact that the poor are unlikely to be able to spend a significant proportion of their income in a prodigal manner, he noted that this type of expenditure, generated from such a source, could be significant when taken in the aggregate at any one point in time and over time. But in a modern society, which presents opportunities for accumulation, there would be a tendency for frugality to predominate, thus contributing further to the process of accumulation. Smith concluded that, 'Though the principle of expence, therefore, prevails in almost all men upon some occasions, and in some men upon almost all occasions, yet in the greater part of men, taking the whole course of their life at an average, the principle of frugality seems not only to predominate, but to predominate very greatly' (II. iii. 28).

Smith also noted that some modes of expense are more favourable than others with respect to the opulence of the individual and of the nation. 'The houses, the furniture, the cloathing of the rich, in a little time, become useful to the inferior and middling ranks of the people' (II. iii. 39). In a passage that once again calls attention to our concern with the judgement of society, he added that:

The expence, too, which is laid out in durable commodities, is favourable, not only to accumulation, but to frugality. If a person should at any time exceed in it, he can easily reform without exposing himself to the censure of the publick. To reduce very much the number of his servants, to reform his table from great profusion to great frugality, to lay down his equipage after he has set it up, are changes which cannot escape the observation of his neighbours, and which are supposed to imply some acknowledgement of preceding bad conduct. (*WN* II. iii. 40).[13]

Finally, it must be recalled that Smith's theory of growth is linked not only to the thesis of accumulation, but also to the oldest part of the whole edifice, namely his treatment of the division of labour. The point is a simple one: namely, that as the process of economic growth unfolds, so in turn the increasing size of the market gives greater scope to the division of labour, thus increasing productivity and at the same time giving greater scope to technical change in the shape of the flow of invention (*WN* I. i), so that the economy he describes is one subject to increasing returns.

These arguments taken as a whole would seem to suggest that developed economies could enjoy an increasing rate of growth, thereby giving 'rich' countries such as England (II. iii. 36) an overwhelming advantage as compared with the 'poor'. But Smith did not elaborate upon an argument that had so preoccupied Hume and Steuart (see Chapters 10 and 11 below). Nor did Smith examine the consequences of differing rates of growth in the context of international trade.

Smith's treatment of accumulation completes the earlier analysis of long-run trends in the rates of wages, profit, and rent, by providing an explanation of the motor force involved. It is the process of accumulation that helps to explain the progressive increase in the level of population and the corresponding increase in the quantity of land used for cultivation. It is the same process that explains the tendency for wages to reach

[13] Cf. *TMS* III. i. 3. 18, VI. i. 6, and *LJ* (A) i. 124–5. See also n. 34 to *WN* II. iii. As Sir James Steuart remarked, 'The desires which proceed from the affections of his mind, are often so strong as to make him comply with them at the expence of becoming incapable of satisfying those which his animal oeconomy necessarily demands' (Steuart 1966 edn.: 271 and *n*).

subsistence levels as well as the declining rate of profit and of interest as stated in the first book.[14]

CONCLUSIONS

It will be apparent that the concept of the philosophical or analytical system as a kind of 'imaginary machine' is particularly apt as a description of Smith's contribution to theoretical economics. As Hans Jensen has put it, Smith provided a model of 'conceptualised reality' (1984: ii. 194). As we have seen, Smith's argument makes it possible to proceed from one area of analysis to another in a fairly clear and logical order—from the analysis of price to that of distribution, from the analysis of distribution to the treatment of the 'circular flow', and thus to the explanation of growth. Moreover, it is apparent that Smith advances through the work by dealing with distinct logical problems in a particular sequence, and in a form that successfully demonstrates the interdependence of economic phenomena. Now it is certainly *not* true that Smith's 'system' is a perfect, logical whole, just as it is probably not true to suggest that his handling of particular problems is always superior to that found in the works of contemporaries. What *is* true is that the form and content of Smith's 'imaginary machine' shows a grasp of the interdependence of economic

---

[14] Attention has been drawn above to the way in which early classical economists such as J. B. Say and James Mill formally developed aspects of Smith's position—e.g. the relationship between output and income (n. 7), the role of money (n. 9), and the relationship between saving and investment (nn. 8 and 11). The positions described were associated with the belief that the economy would tend towards full employment in particular time periods, a belief that was supported by reliance on self-equilibrating mechanisms (such as the theory of allocation) and by the preoccupation with economic growth. But it was David Ricardo who gave a sharper focus to Smith's analysis of growth by integrating the theories of accumulation and distribution while providing a new perspective on the labour theory of value. In Smith's case, net savings attained in a given time period, and over time, would enhance the level of demand for labour, which in turn could lead to wage rates that exceeded the natural (subsistence) rate—with consequent effects on the level of population in the long run. Where the level of population rises as a result of sustained levels of accumulation, the demand for food also rises, increasing the level of land use and rent payments. In developing a more formal version of this argument, Ricardo introduced the theory of differential rent, arguing in effect that land was fixed in quantity, and of differing fertility. If we assume a constant subsistence wage, constant technique, a closed economy, and that land of the best quality is used first, it follows that a particular level of demand for food will determine the position of the extensive margin. Ricardo also argued that the value of corn will be regulated by the quantity of labour bestowed on its production on that quality of land which, at the margin, pays no rent. It follows, given the assumptions made, that, as the extensive margin is pushed outwards under pressure of population, then the value of corn must rise, thus limiting the capacity for further accumulation until a theoretical limit is reached beyond which no further accumulation is possible. In this way, Ricardo suggested that there would be a *progression* from the advancing to the stationary (as distinct from separately *identifying*, as Smith had done, the advancing, stationary or declining states). For a succinct statement of Ricardo's position see Baumol (1962), but especially Blaug (1962, 1985).

phenomena that was not equalled by other great system-builders of the period, with the possible exception of Turgot. It is indeed in this respect that the true measure of Smith's contribution is to be found. As Professor Viner has pointed out, the source of Smith's originality lies in his 'detailed and elaborate application to the wilderness of economic phenomena of the unifying concept of a co-ordinated and mutually dependent system of cause and effect relationships which philosophers and theologians had already applied to the world in general' (Viner 1928: 116, 118).

Interestingly enough, the basic point at issue was grasped by writers much closer to the event than Professor Viner. Governor Pownall of Massachusetts, who was one of Smith's most trenchant critics, was none the less quick to appreciate that the *Wealth of Nations* constitutes 'an INSTITUTE OF THE PRINCIPIA *of those laws of motion*, by which the operations of the community are directed and regulated, and by which they should be examined'.[15] Writing a little later, Dugald Stewart also noted that 'it may be doubted, with respect to Mr Smith's Inquiry, if there exists any book beyond the circle of the mathematical and physical sciences, which is at once so agreeable in its arrangement to the rules of a sound logic, and so accessible to the examination of ordinary readers' (Stewart IV. 22).[16] These were certainly compliments that Smith would have appreciated, conscious as he was of the value of systems which connect together 'in the fancy those different movements and effects which are already in reality performed' (Astronomy IV. 19), and of the 'beauty of a systematical arrangement of different observations connected by a few common principles' (*WN* V. i. f. 25; see Chapter 2 above).

The two pillars of Smith's success may be represented as the analytical system and the associated advocacy of free trade. Yet, as Teichgraeber has indicated, Smith's advocacy of freedom of trade did 'not register any significant victories during his life time' (Teichgraeber 1987: 338), echoing a point already made by Raschid (1982: 83). Indeed, Raschid has argued that when success did come it was largely because Smith's policy prescriptions were peculiarly relevant to British interests (1982: 82).

---

[15] *A Letter from Governor Pownall to Adam Smith, LL.D. F.R.S., being an Examination of Several Points of Doctrine . . .*, 1776: 41; *Corr.* Appendix A: 354.

[16] Dugald Stewart described Smith elsewhere as 'a genius which was destined not only to extend the boundaries of science, but to enlighten and reform the commercial policy of Europe' (Stewart I. 3). His emphasis may have been more policy-orientated than analytical. He may have read the *WN* as being concerned primarily 'to ascertain the general principles of justice and of expediency, which ought to guide the institutions of legislators on these important articles' (*WN* IV. 7). In emphasizing the key issue of free trade, Stewart concluded that 'Such are the liberal principles which . . . ought to direct the commercial policy of nations; and of which it ought to be the great object of legislators to facilitate the establishment' (IV. 18).

In the same vein, Teichgraeber's research suggests that, although there were contemporary admirers (such as Dugald Stewart), there 'is no evidence to show that many people explored his arguments with great care before the first two decades of the nineteenth century' (Teichgraeber 1987: 339). He concluded: 'It would seem that at the time of his death Smith was widely known and admired as the author of the *Wealth of Nations*. Yet it should be noted too that only a handful of his contemporaries had come to see his book as uniquely influential' (Teichgraeber 1987: 363).

But if Smith's analytical contribution was understood by only a few at the time of his death, the situation was soon to change. The point is implied in Hollander's exhaustive work (1973) and further elaborated in Dennis O'Brien's excellent account of classical economics (1975). In a later work, O'Brien (1976) noted the *longevity* of Smith's paradigm, a point also made by Boulding (1971), who found in Smith's work the basis of modern economics. It was this perception in the early nineteenth century that did most to consign the work of Smith's predecessors to oblivion precisely because it led to the belief that the history of the discipline dated from 1776.

Donald Winch quotes an important passage from J.B. Say, Smith's committed disciple, who, after an extensive historical review, none the less concluded that: 'Whenever the *Inquiry into the Wealth of Nations* is perused with the attention it so well merits, it will be perceived that until the epoch of its publication, the science of political economy did not exist' (Say 1836: pp. xxxvii–xxxix). Scant wonder that Dupont de Nemours, who edited some of Quesnay's writings under the significant title, *The Origin and Progress of a New Science* (1767), should have been moved to sharp protest: 'This idea that occurs to you to *reject* us, and which you do not hide well, my dear Say, does not do away with the fact that you are through the branch of Smith a grandson of *Quesnay*, a nephew of the great Turgot' (McLain 1977: 201).

As Hutchison has eloquently argued, from an analytical point of view 'the losses and exclusions which ensued after 1776, with the subsequent transformation of the subject and the rise to dominance of the English classical orthodoxy were immense' (Hutchison 1988: 370). The use of the historical method in addressing theoretical issues was one such loss. So too was the concern with unemployment and the model of primitive accumulation, while in addition the classical orthodoxy, as developed by Ricardo and James Mill, showed little interest in the problems of differential rates of growth or undeveloped economies (see Chapters 10 and 11 below).

Ironically, the conventional perception of Smith's contribution also suffered as a result of the developing orthodoxy, at least for a season. Here attention might be drawn to Smith's concern with *processes* of adjustment rather than with equilibrium *states*, and to his emphasis on imperfect knowledge. It may be suggested that the rigorous logic of the classical system as developed by Ricardo, unintentionally (for Ricardo expected serious students to read the *Wealth of Nations*) helped his successors to lose sight of Smith's broad perspective on the working of the economy. The reference is again to the issue of shape, in this case to Smith's concept of the circular flow with its focus on process analysis, where all magnitudes are dated and set in the context of an environment where all sectors and socio-economic groups are horizontally and vertically integrated.

More serious still was the fact that the classical orthodoxy made it possible to think of economics as quite separate from ethics and history, thus obscuring Smith's true purpose. In referring to these problems, Terence Hutchison, in a telling passage, has commented that Adam Smith was unwittingly led by an invisible hand to promote an end that was no part of his intention, that 'of establishing political economy as a separate autonomous discipline' (Hutchison 1988: 355). Professor Macfie made a related point when noting that: 'It is a paradox of history that the analytics of Book I, in which Smith took his own line, should have eclipsed the philosophical and historical methods in which he so revelled and which showed his Scots character' (Macfie 1967: 21).

REFERENCES

Baumol, W. J. (1962), *Economic Dynamics* (London).

Blaug, M. (1962), *Economic Theory in Retrospect* (London; 4th edn. 1985).

Boulding, K. (1971), 'After Samuelson, Who Needs Adam Smith?' *History of Political Economy*, iii; reprinted in Wood (1984: iii. 247–55).

Brown, M. (1988), *Adam Smith's Economics* (London).

Dwyer, J. (1992), 'Virtue and Improvement: The Civic World of Adam Smith', in *Adam Smith Reviewed*, ed. P. Jones and A. S. Skinner (Edinburgh).

Eltis, W. (1984), *The Classical Theory of Economic Growth* (London).

Etzioni, A. (1988), *The Moral Dimension: Towards a New Economics* (London).

Hollander, S. (1973), *The Economics of Adam Smith* (Toronto).

Hutchison, T. W. (1988), *Before Adam Smith: The Emergence of Political Economy, 1662–1776*, (Oxford).

Jeck, A. (1994), 'The Macro-Structure of Adam Smith's Theoretical System', *European Journal of the History of Economic Thought*, 3.

Jensen, H. (1984), 'Sources and Contours of Adam Smith's Conceptualised Reality on the *Wealth of Nations*', in Wood (1984).

Macfie, A. L. (1967), *The Individual in Society* (London).

McLain, J. J. (1977), *The Economic Writings of Dupont de Nemours* (Newark Del.).

McNally, D. P. (1988), *Political Economy and the Rise of Capitalism: A Re-interpretation* (Berkeley).

Mill, James (1966), *Selected Economic Writings*, ed. D. N. Winch (Edinburgh).

Mill, John Stuart (1844), *Essays on Some Unsettled Questions on Political Economy* (London).

——(1948), *Principles of Political Economy*, ed. V. W. Bladen and J. M. Robson (Toronto, 1965).

Oakley, A. (1994), *Classical Economic Man: Human Agency and Methodology in the Political Economy of Adam Smith and J. S. Mill* (Aldershot).

O'Brien, D. P. (1975), *The Classical Economists* (Oxford).

——(1976), 'The Longevity of Adam Smith's Vision', *Scottish Journal of Political Economy*, 23; reprinted in Wood (1984: iii. 377–94).

O'Driscoll, G. P., (ed.) (1979), *Adam Smith and Modern Political Economy* (Ames, Iowa).

Phelps-Brown, E. H. (1976), 'The Labour Market', in *The Market and the State*, ed. T. Wilson and A. S. Skinner (Oxford).

Raschid, S. (1982), 'Adam Smith's Rise to Fame: A Re-examination', *The Eighteenth Century; Theory and Interpretation*, 23.

Rees, A., (1975), 'Compensating Wage Differentials', in Skinner and Wilson (1975).

Reid, G. R. (1989), *Classical Economic Growth* (Oxford).

Samuelson, P. A. (1977), 'A Modern Theorist's Vindication of Adam Smith', *American Economics Association, Papers and Proceedings*, 67; reprinted in Wood (1984: iii. 498–509).

Say, J. B. (1821), *Treatise on Political Economy*, trans. C. R. Prinsep (London).

——(1836), *A Treatise on Political Economy*, trans. Clement Biddle (Philadelphia; reprinted by Augustus Kelley, New York, 1967).

Schumpeter, J. A. (1954), *A History of Economic Analysis* (London).

Skinner, A. S. (1967), 'Say's Law: Origins and Content', *Economica*, 34.

——(1969), 'Malthus, Lauderdale and Say's Law', *Scottish Journal of Political Economy*, 16.

——and Wilson, T. eds. (1975), *Essays on Adam Smith* (Oxford).

Steuart, Sir James (1767), *Principles of Political Economy*, ed. A. S. Skinner (Edinburgh, 1966).

Teichgraeber, R. (1987), 'Less Abused than I Had reason to Expect': The Reception of the *Wealth of Nations* in Britain, 1776–1790', *Historical Journal*, 30.

Urquhart, R. (1994), 'Reciprocating Monads', *Scottish Journal of Political Economy*, 41.

Viner, J. (1928), 'Adam Smith and Laisser-Faire', in *Adam Smith 1776–1926* (Chicago.

——(1965), *Guide to John Rae's Life of Adam Smith* (New York).

Werhane, P. H. (1991), *Adam Smith and His Legacy for Modern Capitalism* (Oxford).

Wood, J. C. (1984), *Adam Smith: Critical Assessments* (Beckenham).

Zallio, F. (1990), 'Adam Smith's Dual Circulation Framework', *Royal Bank of Scotland Review*, 166.

PART V

8

The Role of the State

INTRODUCTION

Smith's contribution to the field of political economy was designed to explain the working of a set of institutional arrangements, that he regarded as the last of four stages of economic development, and to elucidate the 'laws of motion' that governed its operations.

The laws of motion, once stated, were designed to show that the control of resources could be left to the market and to explain the source of their increase. This perspective led directly to the demand that governments ought not to interfere with the economy, a claim which, while it may owe a good deal to Hume, is also a dominant feature of Smith's *Lectures on Jurisprudence* and perhaps one of those 'leading principles' for which he claimed some degree of originality in a paper delivered in 1755. Dugald Stewart informs us that Smith expressed himself 'with a good deal of that honest and indignant warmth, which is perhaps unavoidable by a man who is conscious of the purity of his own intentions, when he suspects that advantages have been taken of the frankness of his temper' (Stewart IV. 25).

The same sentiments appear in the *Wealth of Nations*, albeit expressed with even greater force, when Smith calls upon the sovereign to discharge himself from a duty 'in the attempting to perform which he must always be exposed to innumerable delusions, and for the proper performance of which no human wisdom or knowledge could every be sufficient; the duty of superintending the industry of private people, and of directing it towards the employments most suitable to the interest of the society' (WN IV. ix. 51).

In the words of a later commentator, Lord Robbins, Smith bequeathed to his successors in the Classical School an opposition to conscious paternalism, a belief that 'central authority was incompetent to decide on a proper distribution of resources'. Robbins also noted that Smith had developed an important argument to the effect that economic freedom 'rested on a two fold basis: belief in the desirability of freedom of choice

The argument of this chapter is based upon the original version of 1979 but also draws on Skinner (1986, 1988). I have also incorporated material from Skinner (1991). A fuller version of the argument in respect of 'Education as a Public Service' is published in Copley and Sutherland (1995).

for the consumer and belief in the effectiveness, in meeting this choice, of freedom on the part of the producers'. (Robbins 1953:12).

Reform

A major task of the state is thus to ensure that the conditions of economic freedom are in fact satisfied, so far as possible, by sweeping away all legal and institutional impediments to it. Broadly speaking, these impediments can be reduced to four main categories.

First, there is the problem that, in every society subject to a process of transition, 'Laws frequently continue in force long after the circumstances, which first gave occasion to them, and which could alone render them reasonable, are no more' (*WN* III. ii. 4). In such cases, Smith suggested that arrangements that were once appropriate but are now no longer so should, ideally, be removed, citing as examples the laws of succession and entail, laws that had been appropriate in the feudal period but now had the effect of limiting the sale and improvement of land.

Secondly, Smith drew attention to certain institutions which had their origin in the past but still commanded active support, for example the privileges of corporations with regard to the governance of trades and the control of apprenticeship. Such regulations were criticized on the ground that they were both impolitic and unjust: unjust in that controls over qualification for entry to a trade were a violation of 'this most sacred property which every man has in his own labour' (I. x. c. 12); impolitic in that regulations of apprenticeship constitute no guarantee of competence.

Smith emphasized that such regulations adversely affect the operation of the market mechanism, and pointed out in this connection that 'The statute of apprenticeship obstructs the free circulation of labour from one employment to another, even in the same place. The exclusive privileges of corporations obstruct it from one place to another, even in the same employment' (I. x. c. 42). In a very similar vein, he commented on the problems presented by the Poor Laws and Laws of Settlement, and he summarized his appeal to government in these words:

break down the exclusive privileges of corporations, and repeal the statute of apprenticeship, both of which are real encroachments upon natural liberty, and add to these the repeal of the law of settlements, so that a poor workman, when thrown out of employment either in one trade or in one place, may seek for it in another trade or in another place, without the fear either of a prosecution or of a removal. (*WN* IV. ii. 42).

Thirdly, Smith objected to positions of privilege, such as monopoly powers, that he regarded as essentially creatures of the civil law. The institution is again represented as impolitic and unjust: unjust in that a monopoly position was one of privilege and advantage, and therefore 'contrary to that justice and equality of treatment which the sovereign owes to all the different orders of his subjects' (*WN* IV. viii. 30); impolitic in that the prices at which goods so controlled are sold are 'upon every occasion the highest that can be got'. 'The monopolists, by keeping the market constantly under-stocked, by never fully supplying the effectual demand, sell their commodities much above the natural price, and raise their emoluments, whether they consist in wages or profit, greatly above their natural rate' (I. vii. 26). He added that monopoly is 'a great enemy to good management' (I. xi. b. 5), and that it had the additional defect of restricting the flow of capital to the trades affected because of the legal barriers to entry that were involved.

Finally, we may usefully distinguish Smith's objection to monopoly in general from his criticism of one expression of it: namely, the mercantile *system*, that he described as the 'modern system' of policy, best understood 'in our own country and in our own times' (IV. 2). Here Smith considered regulations that defined the trade relations between one country and another and which, he felt, often reflected the state of animosity between them. In this context he examined a policy that sought to produce a net inflow of gold by means of such 'engines' as bounties on exportation, drawbacks, and controls over imports.

In particular, Smith insisted that this pattern of infringement of liberty was liable to 'that general objection which may be made to all the different expedients of the mercantile system; the objection of forcing some part of the industry of the country into a channel less advantageous than that in which it would run of its own accord' (IV. v. a. 24). The belief that regulation will always distort the use of resources by breaking the 'natural balance of industry' dates back to Smith's days as a lecturer in Glasgow and represents his main criticism both of monopoly in general and of its manifestation in mercantile policy as a whole. The general position is usefully summarized in the following statement:

No regulation of commerce can increase the quantity of industry in any society beyond what its capital can maintain. It can only divert a part of it into a direction into which it might not otherwise have gone; and it is by no means certain that this artificial direction is likely to be more advantageous to the society than that into which it would have gone of its own accord. (WN. IV. ii. 3).

The functions of the state are therefore something other than minimal: Smith here calls for the abolition of institutions and customs which are remnants of the past, for the abolition of positions of monopoly and privilege, and, finally, for a major reform of national policy. All this is done in the name of liberty and economic efficiency, and must be done before the system of *economic* liberty is to be realized in its entirety: 'All systems either of preference or of restraint . . . being thus completely taken away, the obvious and simple system of natural liberty establishes itself of its own accord' (*WN* IV. ix. 51).

Specific Economic Policies

Even in the absence of the problems just discussed, there is still, on Smith's own admission, a wide range of governmental activity which may be necessary if the economy is to function efficiently. In this connection Smith was quite prepared to justify modifications to the general principle of non-intervention.[1] For example, he advocated the use of stamps on plate and linen as the most effectual guarantee of quality (*WN* I. x. c. 13), the compulsory regulation of mortgages (v. ii. h. 17), the legal enforcement of contracts (I. ix. 16), and government control of the coinage.

In addition, Smith defended the granting of temporary monopolies to groups of merchants who were prepared to undertake the great risks involved in establishing a new branch of trade, and like privileges to the inventors of new machines and to the authors of new books (v. i. e. 30). In special circumstances, and for the sake of the community, he was prepared to support bounties on the exportation of corn (IV. v. b. 39) and a moderate tax on the exportation of wool (IV. viii. 29). He advised governments that, where they were faced with taxes imposed by others, retaliation could be in order, especially if this policy had the effect of procuring 'the repeal of the high duties or prohibitions complained of. The recovery of a great foreign market will generally more than compensate the transitory inconveniency of paying dearer during a short time for some sorts of goods' (IV. ii. 39). Smith also noted:

it may sometimes be a matter of deliberation, how far, or in what manner it is proper to restore the free importation of foreign goods, after it has been for some time interrupted . . . when particular manufactures, by means of high duties or prohibitions upon all foreign goods which can come into competition with them, have been so far extended as to employ a great multitude of hands. Humanity may in this case require that the freedom of trade should be restored only by slow gradations, and with a good deal of reserve and circumspection. (IV. ii. 40).

Two broad areas of intervention may be of particular interest, in the sense that they involve wider issues of general principle. First, Smith advocated the use of taxation, not simply as a means of raising revenue, but as a means of controlling certain activities, and of compensating for what would now be known as a defective telescopic faculty (i.e. a failure to perceive our long-run interest). In the name of the public interest,

---

[1] The classic account is still that provided by Viner (1928: § 5)

Smith supported taxes on the retail sale of alcoholic beverages in order to discourage the multiplication of alehouses (*WN* v. ii. g. 4) and differential rates on ale and spirits in order to reduce the sale of the latter (v. ii. k. 50). To take another example, he advocated taxes on those proprietors who demanded rents in kind rather than cash, and on those leases that prescribe a certain form of cultivation. In the same vein, we find Smith arguing that the practice of selling a future revenue for the sake of ready money should be discouraged on the ground that it reduced the working capital of the tenant and at the same time transferred a capital sum to those who would use it for the purposes of consumption (v. ii. c. 12), rather than saving.

The examples are few, but the basic principle involved is extremely important and capable of wide application. Smith is here suggesting that the state is justified in intervening to offset the consequences of ignorance, lack of knowledge, or lack of forethought on the part of individuals or groups of individuals.

Smith was also well aware, to take a second point, that the modern version of the 'circular flow' depended on paper money and on credit—in effect, a system of 'dual circulation' involving a complex of transactions linking producers and merchants, dealers and consumers (*WN* II. ii. 88), transactions that would involve cash at the level of the household and credit (at the level of the firm).[2] It is in this context that Smith advocated control over the rate of interest, set in such a way as to ensure that sober people are universally preferred, as borrowers, to 'prodigals and projectors' (II. iv. 15).[3] He was also willing to regulate the small note issue in the interests of a stable banking system. To those who objected to this proposal, he replied that the interests of the community required it, and concluded that 'the obligation of building party walls, in order to prevent the communication of fire, is a violation of natural liberty, exactly of the same kind (with) the regulations of the banking trade that are here proposed' (II. ii. 94).

Although Smith's monetary analysis is not regarded as being among the strongest of his contributions, it should be remembered that the witness of the collapse of major banks in the 1770s was acutely aware of the problems generated by a sophisticated credit structure. It was in this context that Smith articulated a very general principle, namely that 'those exertions of the natural liberty of a few individuals, which might

[2] The point has been elaborated upon notably by Zallio (1990).

[3] In his *Defence of Usury*, Jeremy Bentham objected to Smith's argument regarding regulation of the rate of interest on the ground that it was inconsistent with his general position (*Corr.* app. C). Dugald Stewart concurred: 'It is a remarkable circumstance, that Mr Smith should, in this solitary instance, have adopted, on such slight grounds, a conclusion so strikingly contrasted with the general spirit of his political dicussions, and so manifestly at variance with the fundamental principles which, on other occasions, he has so boldly followed out, through their practical applications' (Stewart IV. 28. n. J).

endanger the security of the whole society, are, and ought to be, restrained by the laws of all governments; of the most free, as well as of the most despotical' (II. ii. 94).

PUBLIC SERVICES AND PUBLIC WORKS

Defence

The treatment of defence is clearly related to the discussion of the stages of history, an important part of the argument being that a gradual change in the economic and social structure had necessitated the formal provision of an army. Thus, for example, in primitive stages such as those of hunting and pasture, almost the whole male community is fitted and available for war by virtue of their occupations and the mode of subsistence that happens to prevail, while the same is also basically true of the stage of agriculture. In short, the provision of this necessary service is costless until the stage of commerce, or civilization, is reached. It is in this context that the form of economic organisation, the greater complexity of modern war (*WN* v. i. a. 9, 10), and the high costs associated with the introduction of fire-arms lead to a situation where the 'wisdom of the state' (v. i. a. 14) must arrange for provision.

Of the options open to government, Smith preferred a standing army to a militia as likely to be more effective. While admitting the political dangers that such armies present, as exemplified by those commanded by Caesar and Cromwell, Smith noted that:

where the sovereign is himself the general, and the principal nobility and gentry of the country the chief officers of the army; where the military force is placed under the command of those who have the greatest interest in the support of the civil authority, because they have themselves the greatest share of that authority, a standing army can never be dangerous to liberty. (*WN* v. i. a. 41).

On the contrary, he added, such an army

may in some cases be favourable to liberty. The security which it gives to the sovereign renders unnecessary that troublesome jealousy, which, in some modern republicks, seems to watch over the minutest actions, and to be at all times ready to disturb the peace of every citizen . . . That degree of liberty that approaches to licentiousness can be tolerated only in countries where the sovereign is secured by a well-regulated standing army. It is in such countries only, that the publick safety does not require, that the sovereign should be trusted with any discretionary power, for suppressing even the impertinent wantonness of this licentious liberty. (*WN* v i. a. 41).

Having determined the preferred form of *organization*, Smith concluded that this essential service would have to be paid for. Since the expense involved was laid out 'for the benefit of the whole society', it ought to be defrayed 'by the general contribution of the whole society, all the different members contributing, as nearly as possible, in proportion to their respective abilities' (*WN* v. i. i. 1).

Justice

As far as the organization of the essential service of justice is concerned, it was Smith's contention that the separation of powers was a basic prerequisite for effective and equitable provision:

When the judicial is united to the executive power, it is scarce possible that justice should not frequently be sacrificed to, what is vulgarly called, politics. The persons entrusted with the great interests of the state may, even without any corrupt views, sometime imagine it necessary to sacrifice to those interests the rights of a private man. But upon the impartial administration of justice depends the liberty of every individual, the sense that he has of his own security. In order to make every individual feel himself perfectly secure in the possession of every right which belongs to him, it is not only necessary that the judicial should be separated from the executive power, but that it should be rendered as much as possible independent of that power. The judge should not be liable to be removed from his office according to the caprice of that power. The regular payment of his salary should not depend upon the good-will, or even upon the good oeconomy of that power. (*WN* v. i. b. 25).

As Alan Peacock has pointed out, Smith's *efficiency criteria* are clearly distinguished from the basic issue of *organization*, the argument being, in effect, that the services provided by attorneys, clerks, or judges should be paid for in such a way as to encourage productivity. (Peacock 1975). Indeed, Smith ascribed the 'present admirable constitution of the courts of justice in England' to the use of a system of court fees that had served to encourage competition between the Courts of King's Bench, Chancery, and Exchequer (*WN* v. i. b. 20, 21). A further interesting and typical feature of the discussion is found in Smith's argument that, although justice is a service to the whole community, none the less, the costs of handling specific causes should be borne by those who give occasion to, or benefit from, them. He therefore concluded that the 'expense of the administration of justice . . . may very properly be defrayed by the particular contribution of one or other, or both of those two different sets of persons, according as different occasions may require, that is, by the fees of court' (v. i. i. 2), rather than by a charge on the general funds.

Public Works

Emphasis should also be given to Smith's contention that a major responsibility of government must be the provision of certain public works and institutions for facilitating the commerce of the society which were 'of such a nature, that the profit could never repay the expense to any individual or small number of individuals, and which it, therefore, cannot be expected that any individual or small number of individuals should erect or maintain' (*WN* v. i. c.1). In short, he was concerned to point out that the state would have to take steps to provide public works and services which the profit motive alone could not guarantee; the problem of market as distinct from government failure (see e.g. West 1976).

As in the case of justice, Smith considered that public works such as highways, bridges, and canals should be paid for by those who use them and in proportion to the wear and tear occasioned. At the same time, he argued that the consumer who pays the charges generally gains more from the cheapness of carriage than he loses in the charges incurred:

The person who finally pays this tax, therefore, gains by the application, more than he loses by the payment of it. His payment is exactly in proportion to his gain. It is in reality no more than a part of that gain which he is obliged to give up in order to get the rest. It seems impossible to imagine a more equitable method of raising a tax. (*WN* v. i. d. 4).

In addition, Smith suggested that tolls should be higher in the case of luxury goods so that by this means 'the indolence and vanity of the rich is made to contribute in a very easy manner to the relief of the poor, by rendering cheaper the transportation of heavy goods' (*WN* v. i. d. 5).

Smith also defended the principle of direct payment on the ground of efficiency. Only by this means, he contended, would it be possible to ensure that services are provided where there is a recognizable need. Only in this way, for example, would it be possible to avoid building roads through a desert for the sake of some private interest, or to prevent the construction of a great bridge 'thrown over a river at a place where nobody passes, or merely to embellish the view from the windows of a neighbouring palace: things which sometimes happen, in countries where works of this kind are carried on by any other revenue than that which they themselves are capable of affording' (v. i. d. 6).

Smith further argued that, while governments must be responsible for establishing major public works, care should be taken to ensure that services were administered by such bodies, or under such conditions, as made it in the interest of individuals to do so effectively (cf. Rosenberg 1960). He tirelessly emphasized the point, already noticed in the discussion of justice, that in every trade and profession 'the exertion of the greater part of those who exercise it, is always in proportion to the necessity they are under of making that exertion' (v. i. f. 4). On this ground, he approved of the expedient used in France, whereby a construction engineer was made a present of the tolls on a canal for which he had been responsible—thus ensuring that it was in his interest to keep the canal in good repair. In fact, Smith used a number of such devices, advocating, for example, that the administration of roads would have to be handled in a different way from that of canals because they are passable even when full of holes. Here he suggested that the 'wisdom of parliament' would have to be applied to the appointment of proper persons, with 'proper courts of inspection' for 'controuling their conduct, and for reducing the tolls to what is barely sufficient for executing the work to be done by them' (v. i. d. 9).

Smith recognized that such services could not always be paid for by those who used them, arguing that in such cases 'local or provincial expenses of which the benefit is local or provincial' ought, so far as possible, to be no burden on general taxation, it being 'unjust that the whole society should contribute towards an expense of which the benefit is confined to a part of the society' (v. i. i. 3). But here again it is argued, in the interest of efficiency, that such services 'are always better maintained by a local or provincial revenue, under the management of a local and pro- vincial administration, than by the general revenue of the state, of which the executive power must always have the management' (v. i. d. 18).

It is also worth noting that, even where recourse has to be made to general taxation, Smith argued that such taxes should be imposed in accordance with the generally accepted canons of taxation; that so far as possible such taxes should avoid interference with the allocative mechanism; and that they ought not to constitute disincentives to the individual effort on which the working of the system was seen to depend.

It will be apparent that Smith's treatment of public works and services is informed throughout by a particular set of principles of public finance. As we have seen, Smith typically explains the nature of each service and why it is required. He contends that the state will have to ensure provision where market forces fail to do so, recognizing that major public works may well require central funding. He also argues that public services should be paid for by those who benefit from them (although not necessarily at an economic rate) and that they should be organized wherever possible in such a way as to induce efficient delivery.

EDUCATION AS A PUBLIC SERVICE

'Domestic education is the institution of nature; public education, the contrivance of man. It is surely unnecessary to say, which is likely to be the wisest' (*TMS*, vi. ii. 1. 10).

Smith returned to this theme in the *Wealth of Nations* when he observed that those 'parts of education . . . for the teaching of which there are no publick institutions are generally the best taught' (*WN* v. i. f. 16). He went on to suggest that:

Were there no publick institutions for education, no system, no science would be taught for which there was not some demand; or which the circumstances of the times did not render it, either necessary, or convenient, or at least fashionable to learn. A private teacher could never find his account in teaching, either an exploded and antiquated system of a science acknowledged to be useful, or a science universally believed to be a mere useless and pedantick heap of sophistry and nonsense. (*WN* v. i. f. 46).

He then proceeded to pose the central question:

Ought the publick, therefore, to give no attention, it may be asked, to the education of the people? Or if it ought to give any, what are the different parts of education which it ought to attend to in the different orders of the people? and in what manner ought it to attend to them?. (*WN* v. i. 48).

The answer is affirmative—there must be a system of public education—for reasons connected with the probable impact of the division of labour. Smith observed first, that:

In the progress of the division of labour, the employment of the far greater part of those who live by labour, that is, of the great body of the people, comes to be confined to a few simple operations; frequently to one or two. But the understandings of the greater part of men are necessarily formed by their ordinary employments. The man whose whole life is spent in performing a few simple operations, of which the effects too are, perhaps, always the same, or very nearly the same, has no occasion to exert his understanding, or to exercise his invention in finding out expedients for removing difficulties which never occur. He naturally loses, therefore, the habit of such exertion, and generally becomes as stupid and ignorant as it is possible for a human creature to become. The torpor of his mind renders him, not only incapable of relishing or bearing a part in any rational conversation, but of conceiving any generous, noble, or tender sentiment, and consequently of forming any just judgment concerning many even of the ordinary duties of private life. (*WN* v. i. f. 50).

He added that, in every improved and civilized society, 'this is the state into which the labouring poor, that is, the great body of people, must necessarily fall, unless government takes some pains to prevent it' (*WN* v. i. f. 50).

Secondly, Smith drew attention to the contrast between the modern commercial stage, where all goods and services command a price, and the more primitive stages of hunting, pasture, and agriculture. In the latter three cases, all male members of the society were likely to be involved in martial exercise and in military action, whereas the 'number of those who can go to war, in proportion to the whole number of the people, is necessarily much smaller in a civilised, than in a rude state of society' (v. i. a. 11). The problem for Smith was that of a decline in 'martial spirit' in modern society:

a coward, a man incapable either of defending or of revenging himself, evidently wants one of the most essential parts of the character of a man. He is as much mutilated and deformed in his mind, as another is in his body, who is either deprived of some of its most essential members, or has lost the use of them. He is evidently the more wretched and miserable of the two; because happiness and misery, which reside altogether in the mind, must necessarily depend more upon the healthful or unhealthful, the mutilated or entire state of the mind, than upon that of the body. (*WN* v. i. f. 60).

Thirdly, Smith drew attention to the social problems associated with the isolation that could follow from the growth of cities and/or manufactures. In contrast to the man of better condition, whose conduct is exposed to scrutiny by his fellows in the manner suggested by the analysis of *The Theory of Moral Sentiments*,

A man of low condition on the contrary, is far from being a distinguished member of any great society. While he remains in a country village his conduct may be attended to, and he may be obliged to attend to it himself. In this situation, and in this situation only, he may have what is called a character to lose. But as soon as he comes into a great city, he is sunk in obscurity and darkness. His conduct is observed and attended to by nobody, and he is therefore very likely to neglect it himself, and to abandon himself to every sort of low profligacy and vice. (*WN* v. i. g. 12).

As Smith noted, one possible reaction to the difficulty could be through membership of small societies or religious groups, whose standards of conduct, however, might be disagreeably rigorous or 'unsocial'.

In dealing with the first problem, Smith suggested that, while the relatively poor cannot be as well educated as people of rank and fortune, 'the most essential parts of education, however, to read, write and account, can be acquired at so early a period of life, that the greater part even of those who are to be bred to the lowest occupations, have time to acquire them before they can be employed in those occupations' (*WN* v. i. f. 54). He noted that the public could facilitate this process by establishing schools on the Scottish model, 'where children may be taught for a reward so moderate, that even a common labourer can afford it'; and he commented in a characteristic passage, whose implications we shall examine later, that the master should be 'partly, but not wholly paid by the publick; because if he was wholly, or even principally paid by it, he would soon learn to neglect his business' (v. i. f. 55).

It is to be noted that Smith advocated a policy that would encourage the poor to send their children to school, but also that he supported *compulsion*: 'The publick can impose upon almost the whole body of the people the necessity of acquiring those most essential parts of education, by obliging every man to undergo an examination or probation in them before he can obtain the freedom in any corporation, or be allowed to set up any trade either in a village or town corporate' (v. i. f. 57).

It is also to be noted that the poor were to be compelled to act in this way since they typically lacked either incentive or inclination to provide an education for their children. The poor, he observed, have little time to spare for education; as soon as children 'are able to work, they must apply to some trade by which they can earn their subsistence' (v. i. f. 53). In a telling passage in the *Lectures*, Smith noted that 'a boy of six or seven years of age at Birmingham can gain his threepence or sixpence a day, and parents find it to be in their interest to set them soon to work. Thus their education is neglected' (*LJ*(B) 329–30).

Secondly, Smith advocated compulsory military exercises as a means of offsetting the problem of a decline in martial spirit. While he recognized that a people trained in the martial arts could be useful for the purposes of defence, he supported the policy largely on welfare grounds:

Even though the martial spirit of the people were of no use towards the defence of the society, yet to prevent that sort of mental mutilation, deformity and wretchedness, that cowardice necessarily involves in it, from spreading themselves through the great body of the people, would still deserve the most serious attention of government; in the same manner as it would deserve its most serious attention to prevent a leprosy of any other loathsome and offensive disease, though neither mortal nor dangerous, from spreading itself among them; though, perhaps, no other publick good might result from such attention besides the prevention of so great a publick evil. (*WN* v. i. f. 60).

Finally, Smith argued that the problems presented by the disagreeable and unsocial morals often associated with small, and especially religious, sects could be offset by two remedies:

The first of those remedies is the study of science and philosophy, which the state might render almost universal among all people of middling or more than middling rank and fortune; not by giving salaries to teachers in order to make them negligent and idle, but by instituting some sort of probation, even in the higher and more difficult sciences, to be undergone by every person before he was permitted to exercise any liberal profession, or before he could be received as a candidate for any honourable office of trust or profit . . . Science is the great antidote to the poison of enthusiasm and superstition; and where all the superior ranks of people were secured from it, the inferior ranks could not be much exposed to it. (*WN* v. i. g. 14).

In this connection, Smith's preference was probably for the classical programme of physics, moral philosophy, and logic (*WN* v. i. f. 23).

The second of Smith's remedies was found in the frequency and gaiety of public diversions:

The state, by encouraging, that is by giving entire liberty to all those who for their own interest would attempt, without scandal or indecency, to amuse and divert the people by painting, poetry, musick, dancing; by all sorts of dramatic representations and exhibitions, would easily dissipate, in the greater part of them, that melancholy and gloomy humour that is almost always the nurse of popular superstition and enthusiasm. Publick diversions have always been the object of dread and hatred, to all the fanatical promoters of those popular frenzies. The gaiety and good humour which those diversions inspire were altogether inconsistent with that temper of mind, which was fittest for their purpose, or which they could best work upon. Dramatick representations besides, by frequently exposing their artifices to publick ridicule, and sometimes even to publick execration, were upon that account, more than all other diversions, the objects of their peculiar abhorrence. (*WN* v. i. g. 15).

Some passages cited in this section have encouraged those with an eye to the role of the state to identify support for 'National Health' and perhaps something akin to an Arts Council among Smith's recommendations. But it is more important for our present purpose to make Smith's advocacy of a *compulsory* programme of higher education. It is also significant that Smith's advocacy of such a programme was rooted in a perceived need to offset the social costs of the division of labour, and that in particular the programme was intended not only to preserve a capacity for moral judgment, but also to support the individual in his role as a citizen:

Though the state was to derive no advantage from the instruction of the inferior ranks of people, it would still deserve its attention that they should not be altogether uninstructed. The state, however, derives no inconsiderable advantage from their instruction. The more they are instructed, the less liable they are to the delusions of enthusiasm and superstition, which, among ignorant nations, frequently occasion the most dreadful disorders. An instructed and intelligent people besides are always more decent and orderly than an ignorant and stupid one. They feel themselves, each individually, more respectable, and more likely to obtain the respect of their lawful superiors, and they are therefore more disposed to respect those superiors. They are more disposed to examine, and more capable of seeing through, the interested complaints of faction and sedition, and they are, upon that account, less apt to be misled into any wanton or unnecessary opposition to the measures of government. In free countries, where the safety of government depends very much upon the favourable judgment which the people may form of its conduct, it must surely be of the highest importance that they should not be disposed to judge rashly or capriciously concerning it. (*WN* v. i. f. 61).[4]

It will be noted that this argument, taken as a whole, suggests that unproductive labour (see Chapter 7 above) may be indirectly productive of benefit.

---

[4] Of the voluminous literature on the problems associated with the division of labour, see Winch (1978), and also Heilbroner (1975), Lamb (1973), Rosenberg (1965), West (1964); see also Brown (1988).

THE ORGANIZATION OF PROVISION: A CASE STUDY

As to the organization of educational provision, Smith's analysis of principles which are of general application refers primarily to the universities and may well reflect the content of a letter addressed to William Cullen in September 1774. Cullen had written to Smith seeking his opinion on proposals from the Royal College of Physicians of Edinburgh. The petition suggested that doctors should be graduates, that they should have attended university for at least two years, and that they should present themselves for examination. The proposals from the College followed a scandal that revealed the laxity of some Scottish medical schools, a matter that was brought to a head by the dismissal of an Edinburgh graduate from his post at the London Hospital (Rae 1895).

While confirming his view that in 'the present state of the Scotch universities I do most sincerely look upon them as, in spite of their faults, without exception the best seminaries of learning that are to be found anywhere in Europe', Smith none the less rejected the proposals from the Royal College. As he wrote to Cullen, 'There never was, and I will venture to say there never will be, a University from which a degree could give any tolerable security, that the person upon whom it had been conferred, was fit to practise physic' (*Corr.* 176). But the most telling argument was based on the advantage of competition:

You propose, I observe, that no person should be admitted to examination for his degrees unless he brought a certificate of his having studied at least two years in some University. Would not such a regulation be oppressive upon all private teachers, such as the Hunters, Hewson, Fordyce, etc.? The scholars of such teachers surely merit whatever honour or advantage a degree can confer, much more than the greater part of those who have spent many years in some Universities, where the different branches of medical knowledge are either not taught at all, or are taught so superficially that they had as well not be taught at all. When a man has learnt his lesson very well, it surely can be of little importance where or from whom he has learnt it. (*Corr.* 143).

While the reaction of Dr Cullen may be imagined, the letter is an important document, since it may well form the basis of that section in the *Wealth of Nations* where he examined issues of a more general nature. The key question Smith addressed was this: if universities are appropriate agencies for the provision of higher education, then what conditions have to be met if efficiency is to be assured? The answers emerge in the course of Smith's critique of the contemporary situation.

One problem of fundamental importance, identified by Smith, refers to the supply of talent to the universities:

In countries where church benefices are the greater part of them very moderate, a chair in a university is generally a better establishment than a church benefice. The universities have, in this case, the picking and chusing of their members from all the churchmen of the country, who, in every country, constitute by far the most numerous class of men of letters. Where church benefices, on the contrary, are many of them very considerable, the church naturally draws from the universities the greater part of their eminent men of letters. (*WN* v. i. g. 39).

Thus, Smith argued, we can explain the lack of eminent teachers, especially on the arts side, in Roman Catholic countries and in England; while in Protestant countries such as Germany, Holland, Sweden, and Scotland 'the most eminent men of letters whom those countries have produced, have, not all indeed, but the far greater part of them, been professors in universities' (*WN* v. i. g. 39).

But even where the universities can attract professors of quality, it is necessary to provide appropriate stimuli on the ground that it 'is the interest of every man to live as much at his ease as he can' (v. i. f. 7). Smith objected to a situation where high salaries might be paid irrespective of competence or industry. As he observed, in some universities 'the teacher is prohibited from receiving any honorary or fee from his pupils, and his salary constitutes the whole of the revenue which he derives from his office. His interest is, in this case, set as directly in opposition to his duty as it is possible to set it' (v. i. f. 7).

There were other problems that could affect academic efficiency. Smith objected to the fact that the privileges of graduation 'necessarily force a certain number of students to [attend some] universities, independent of the merit or reputation of the teachers' (v. i. f. 11), while in addition specific endowments often force students to attend particular colleges. He added:

If in each college the tutor or teacher, who was to instruct each student in all arts and sciences, should not be voluntarily chosen by the student, but appointed by the head of the college; and if, in case of neglect, inability, or bad usage, the student should not be allowed to change him for another, without leave first asked and obtained; such a regulation would not only tend very much to extinguish all emulation among the different tutors of the same college, but to diminish very much in all of them the necessity of diligence and of attention to their respective pupils. (*WN* v. i. f. 13).

Smith drew attention to a further point of an organizational nature. He was conscious of the fact that there were dangers in the privilege of self-government. In referring to the behaviour of the individual academic, he noted that:

If the authority to which he is subject resides in the body corporate, the college, or university, of which he himself is a member, and in which the greater part of the other members are, like himself, persons who either are, or ought to be teachers; they are likely to make a common cause, to be all very indulgent to one another, and every man to consent that his neighbour may neglect his duty, provided he himself is allowed to neglect his own. In the university of Oxford, the greater part of the publick professors have, for these many years, given up altogether even the pretence of teaching. (*WN* v. i. f. 8).

Institutional structures that did not provide adequate stimuli to the academic could, Smith argued, also have adverse effects on the quality and the content of what was taught:

several of those learned societies have chosen to remain, for a long time, the sanctuaries in which exploded systems and obsolete prejudices found shelter and protection, after they had been hunted out of every other corner of the world. In general, the richest and best endowed universities have been the slowest in adopting . . . improvements, and the most averse to permit any considerable change in the established plan of education . . . improvements were more easily introduced into some of the poorer universities, in which the teachers, depending upon their reputation for the greater part of their subsistence, were obliged to pay more attention to the current opinions of the world. (*WN* v. i. f. 34).

In sum, an efficient system of higher education requires: a state of free competition between established institutions and private teachers; a capacity effectively to compete in the labour market for men of letters; freedom of choice for the student as between teachers, courses, colleges or schools, and the capacity to be competitive and sensitive to market forces, even if these forces are not always of themselves sufficient to ensure the provision of the basic infrastructure.

But perhaps the most intriguing aspect of Smith's argument is the emphasis he gives to the performance of the teacher, and his insistence that income should always be related to the capacity to attract and to sustain student numbers:

In some universities the salary makes but a part, and frequently but a small part of the emoluments of the teacher, of which the greater part of the emoluments of the teacher arises from the honoraries or fees of his pupils. The necessity of application, though always more or less diminished, is not in this case entirely taken away. Reputation in his profession is still of some importance to him, and he still has some dependency upon the affection, gratitude, and favourable report of those who have attended upon his instructions; and these favourable sentiments he is likely to gain in no way so well as by deserving them, that is, by the abilities and diligence with which he discharges every part of his duty. (*WN* v. i. f. 6).

This is an interesting statement when we consider the emphasis that Smith gave to the point that all our actions are subject to the scrutiny of our fellows, together with the stress he placed (in *The Theory of Moral Sentiments*) on our natural desire not just to be praised, but to be *praiseworthy.* However, as the statement just quoted, and indeed the whole tenor of the discussion, suggests, Smith believed that the diligence of the teacher can be relied on only where the stated efficiency criteria are met.

The argument may simply represent Smith's attempt to be logically rigorous; but, on the other hand, his bleak conclusion seems to have been arrived at after careful consideration. As Smith remarked to Cullen, 'I have thought a great deal upon this subject and have enquired very carefully into the constitution and history of several of the principal Universities of Europe.' If the Scottish universities were among the best, this was only because 'the salaries of the Professors are insignificant. There are few or no bursaries and exhibitions, and their monopoly of degrees is broken in upon by all other Universities, foreign or domestic.' In speaking of the Edinburgh medical school in particular, he concluded, 'I require no other explication of its present acknowledged superiority over every other society of the same kind in Europe' (*Corr.* 143).

But if Smith thought that the 'Scotch' universities in general, and the University of Glasgow in particular, satisfied these criteria, not everyone agreed. University education at the time provoked an adverse reaction from those who were concerned with the need to introduce cheap courses in the sciences to a wider public. The spirit of this criticism is neatly caught in the title of a work by William Thom, Minister of Govan, and an arch-critic of Smith's University, in a *Letter to J——— M———— Esq., on the Defects of an University Education and its unsuitableness to a Commercial People: with the Expediency and Necessity of Erecting at Glasgow an Academy for the Instruction of Youth.* Thom was apparently convinced that university education was insufficiently 'vocational', and that it could be forced to move in this direction through competition to be provided by alternative academies (see Withrington 1970).

But Thom would probably have agreed with Smith's assertion that the beneficiary of a service should pay for it whenever possible. In the case of education, Smith recognized that there is a benefit to the individual, but also to the state, where the latter is expressed in terms of investment in human capital and in terms of the capacity of the individual to act as a responsible citizen. Smith's position was necessarily somewhat ambiguous:

The expence of the institutions of education and religious instruction is beneficial to the whole society, and may, therefore, without injustice, be defrayed by the general contribution of the whole society. This expence, however, might perhaps with equal propriety, and even with some advantage, be defrayed altogether by those who receive the immediate benefit of such education and instruction, or by the voluntary contribution of those who think they have occasion for either the one or the other. (*WN* v. i. i. 5).

It seems likely that Smith would have supported the arrangements he envisaged for elementary education where there is a combination of modest private, and a more significant public, contribution.

GOVERNMENT AND CONSTRAINT

Given the significance of the functions of government, it is important to be reminded of the point that Smith was sensitive to the constraints that would face them.

Some of the constraints that affect governments arise from the nature of the economic laws that Smith set out to elucidate and on the basis of which he was to make his general policy recommendations. Smith confirmed a point that was also central to Steuart's *Principles* and to the latter's wide-ranging discussion of economic policy, namely, that the 'statesman' is neither 'master to establish what oeconomy he pleases, or, in the exercise of his sublime authority, to overturn at will the established laws of it, let him be the most despotic monarch upon earth' (Steuart 1966, 16; cf. Hirschman 1977).

Governments, while bound by the laws of political economy, are by the same token faced with the necessity of understanding them and of being capable of implementing policies that are appropriate to particular cases. This obviously places a considerable burden of responsibility on governments, and requires an advanced level of knowledge to handle even the moderately restricted list of functions that Smith seems to have suggested. Moreover, Smith noted that knowledge, especially as applied to particular cases, was always likely to be imperfect, a point that is especially important in the discussion of taxation and debt—areas where the government is particularly liable to offend the people and to be constrained by the necessity of preserving some 'degree of confidence in the justice of government' (*WN* v. iii. 7).

But perhaps the most striking and interesting constraints arise when it is recalled that for Smith the fourth economic stage could be seen to be associated with a particular form of social and political structure, which determines the outline of government and the context within which it must function (see Chapter 4 above). It may be recalled in this connection that Smith associated the fourth economic stage with the advent of freedom in the 'present sense of the term': that is, with the elimination of the relation of direct dependence that had been a characteristic of the feudal/agrarian period. Politically, the significant and associated development appeared to be the diffusion of power consequent on the emergence of new forms of wealth, which, at least in the peculiar circumstances of England, had been reflected in the increased significance of the House of Commons and in the emergence of a situation where liberty was secured 'by an assembly of the representatives of the people, who claim the sole right of imposing taxes' (*WN* IV. vii. b. 51). Smith was far from equating political with personal liberty, nor did he suggest that absolutism was incompatible with the fourth economic stage.[5] But what he did seem to recognize was that 'free governments', especially of the kind that had been confirmed by the Revolution Settlement, now operated within a relatively sensitive political and economic environment. A number of points may be offered by way of illustration.

First, it is interesting to note how often Smith referred to the constraints presented by the 'confirmed habits and prejudices' of the people, and of the necessity of adjusting legislation to what 'the interest, prejudices, and temper of the times would admit of' (*WN* IV. v. b. 40, 50, 53; v. i. g. 8). Smith returned to this point in *The Theory of Moral Sentiments*, where it is stated that, when the statesman

cannot conquer the rooted prejudices of the people by reason and persuasion, he will not attempt to subdue them by force . . . He will accommodate, as well as he can, his public arrangements to the confirmed habits and prejudices of the people; and will remedy as well as he can, the inconveniences which may flow from the want of those regulations which the people are averse to submit to. When he cannot establish the right, he will not disdain to ameliorate the wrong; but like Solon, when he cannot establish the best system of laws, he will endeavour to establish the best that the people can bear. (*TMS* VI. ii. 2. 16).

Secondly, Smith makes the point that, while all governments are subject to the above constraints in some degree, 'free' governments are likely to be particularly sensitive to public opinion. He made this point quite explicitly in the Memorandum on the American War written in 1778, where he commented on the limited options open to a government which, even 'in times of the most profound peace, of the highest public prosperity, when the people had scarce even the pretext of a single grievance to complain of, has not always been able to make itself respected by them' (*Corr.* 383; see Chapter 9 below).

Thirdly, Smith drew attention to the fact that government itself was a complex instrument. In this connection, he felt that the management of Parliament through the distribution of offices was 'a necessary feature of the British mixed government' (cf. *WN* IV. vii. c. 69; see Forbes 1975: 183), a point that is in turn linked to the fact that the pursuit of office was itself a 'dazzling object of ambition', a competitive game with as its object the attainment of 'the great prizes which sometimes come from the wheel of the great state lottery of British politicks' (*WN* IV. vii. c. 75). Smith added,

---

[5] This point has been elaborated by Forbes (1975: 179–201).

in a passage that reflects the psychological assumptions of *The Theory of Moral Sentiments* (I. iii. 2, 'Of the Origin of Ambition'), that:

Men desire to have some share in the management of publick affairs chiefly on account of the importance that it gives them. Upon the power that the greater part of the leading men, the natural aristocracy of every country, have of preserving or defending their respective importance, depends the stability and duration of every system of free government. (*WN* IV. vii. c. 74).

In *The Theory of Moral Sentiments*, Smith also noted that many groups whose activities impinge on the working of government are chiefly devoted to the maintenance of their own power, making the general point that:

Every independent state is divided into many different orders and societies, each of which has its own particular powers, privileges, and immunities. Every individual is naturally more attached to his own particular order or society, than to any other. His own interest, his own vanity, the interest and vanity of many of his friends and companions, are commonly a good deal connected with it. He is ambitious to extend its privileges and immunities. He is zealous to defend them against the encroachments of every other order or society. (*TMS*, VI. ii. 2. 7).

In fact, this point leads on to another that was greatly emphasized by Smith, namely that the same economic forces that had served to elevate the House of Commons to a superior degree of influence had also served to make it an important focal point for sectional interests—a development that could seriously affect the legislation that was passed and thus affect that extensive view of the common good that ought ideally to direct the activities of Parliament.[6]

It is recognized in the *Wealth of Nations* that the landed, monied, manufacturing, and mercantile groups all constitute special interests that could impinge on the working of governments. Smith referred frequently to their 'clamorous importunity', and in speaking of the growth of monopoly pointed out that government policy 'has so much increased the number of some particular tribes of them, that, like an overgrown standing army, they have become formidable to the government, and upon many occasions intimidate the legislature' (*WN* IV. ii. 43). Indeed, Smith went further in suggesting that the legislative power possessed by employers generally could seriously disadvantage other classes in the society (see especially Samuels 1973).

As he put it, 'Whenever the legislature attempts to regulate the differences between masters and their workmen, its counsellors are always the masters. When the regulation, therefore, is in favour of the

---

[6] This point has led West (1976) to emphasize the problem of government (as distinct from market) failure.

workmen, it is always just and equitable; but it is sometimes otherwise when in favour of the masters' (*WN* I. x. c. 61; cf. I. viii. 12, 13). Smith thus insisted that any legislative proposals emanating from this class

ought always to be listened to with the greatest precaution, and ought never to be adopted till after having been long and carefully examined, not only with the most scrupulous, but with the most suspicious attention. It comes from an order of men, whose interest is never exactly the same with that of the publick, who have generally an interest to deceive and even to oppress the publick, and who accordingly have, upon many occasions, both deceived and oppressed it. (*WN* I. xi. p. 10).

Important as the role of government may be, Smith was clearly aware of the pressures operating upon a necessarily imperfect instrument.

SMITH AND ECONOMIC LIBERALISM

The celebration to mark the fiftieth anniversary of the *Wealth of Nations* showed wide and continuing acceptance of the doctrine of economic liberty, a point already emphasized by Dugald Stewart. In 1876, at a dinner held by the Political Economy Club to mark the centenary of the book, one speaker identified free trade as the most important consequence of the work done by 'this simple Glasgow professor'. It was also predicted that 'there will be what may be called a large negative development of Political Economy tending to produce an important beneficial effect; and that is, such a development of Political Economy as will reduce the functions of government within a smaller and smaller compass'. It is hardly surprising that a contemporary leader in *The Times* could claim that 'the time is not yet distant when the supremacy of Adam Smith's teaching shall surpass his largest hopes'.[7]

Nor is the late George Stigler's famous claim, uttered a hundred years later on the occasion of the Glasgow conference, lightly to be dismissed: 'Adam Smith is alive and well and living in Chicago.'

Yet it is important to recall that the agenda for action by governments was determined largely by Smith's choice of the problems to be addressed. He was not, for example, concerned (as Sir James Steuart had been) to analyse or to consider the socio-economic problems that are likely to be involved in the transition *from* a primitive version of the exchange economy *to* the relatively elaborate capital-using system which actually attracted his attention (see Chapter 11 below). Nor was he concerned with the problem of regional imbalance or underdeveloped economies generally. Moreover, his views on economic adjustments were

---

[7] This material is drawn from Black (1976).

relatively long-run, a position that allowed him to discount certain areas of concern. As Schumpeter once remarked of the German economist, von Justi, 'He was much more concerned than A. Smith with the practical problems of government action in the short run vicissitudes of his time and country'. (Schumpeter 1954: 172; cf. Thompson 1991: chs. 4 and 5).

This was not Smith's position. Yet, given this, the list of government functions is, as we have seen, quite impressive, serving to remind the modern reader of two important points. First, Smith's list of recommended policies was longer than some popular assessments suggest. Smith emphatically did not think in terms of 'anarchy plus the constable', to use Carlyle's phrase. As Jacob Viner has observed, 'Adam Smith was not a doctrinaire advocate of laisser-faire. He saw a wide and elastic range of activity for government, and he was prepared to extend it even further if government, by improving its standard of competence, honesty, and public spirit, showed itself entitled to wider responsibilities'. (Viner, in Wood 1984: i. 64).

Second, it is important to recall the need to distinguish between the *principles* that Smith used in justifying intervention (that may be of universal validity) and the specific *agenda* he offered (which may reflect his understanding of the situation he actually confronted at the time of writing). The principles that justify intervention are, after all, wide-ranging in their implications. On Smith's argument, the state should regulate activity to compensate for the imperfect knowledge of individuals; it is the state that must continuously scrutinize the relevance of particular laws and institutions, the state that has a duty to regulate and control the activities of individuals who might otherwise prove damaging to the interest of society at large; and the state that must make adequate provision for public works and services, including education, in cases where the profit motive is likely to prove inadequate.

In dealing with public works, Smith illustrated the issue of market failure. His preference was undoubtedly for a competitive environment, so structured as to ensure that the efficiency criteria he identified could be met. Where competitive forces work effectively, his position suggests that there will be no need for further (external) scrutiny. But where the market for public services either fails or operates only partially, as a result of a *perceived* inability to introduce or sustain the arrangements needed to ensure efficient delivery, then, as we have seen, Smith's argument may be interpreted to suggest the need for steps to be taken, which could involve the introduction of other control mechanisms. If the universities (or any other public service) cannot be rendered capable of self-regulation as a result of meeting his stated efficiency criteria, the implication would seem to be that the 'wisdom of Parliament' would have to be deployed in setting up 'proper courts of inspection' for 'controuling their conduct' (*WN* v. i. d. 9)—as in the case of public roads. It is not only Cullen who might feel tempted to 'box Smith's ears' for what he had written (*Corr.* 179 and n.).[8]

If the key principle is that intervention is a function of market failure in terms both of the provision and the *organization* of a public service, then it is little wonder that Professor Macfie could remark that under certain conditions the strategies that can be culled from the *Wealth of Nations* could be interpreted to 'suggest a formidable state autocracy; a socialist spread of controls that would make some modern socialists' eyes pop.' (Macfie, in Wood 1984: i. 348).

Alec Macfie was, of course, indulging his dry ironic wit. But the same perspective helps to explain Eric Roll's judgement that Smith and Keynes 'would find much common ground in respect of the broad principles that should guide the management of the economy'. (Roll, in Wood 1984: ii. 154).

Smith would surely have had sympathy with Keynes's reading of a different situation, which led him to defend an *enlargement* of government activity 'both as the only practicable means of avoiding the destruction of economic forms in their entirety and as the condition of the successful functioning of individual initiative.' (Keynes 1936: 380). The last point serves to remind us once again of the importance of Smith's treatment of education.

It is worth emphasizing that Smith supported *compulsory* education for particular groups in society. Education at the level of the school is to be regarded as compulsory for *all* members of society, although Smith offered an implicit distinction between vocationally orientated instruction for the lower orders and university education for all those who aspired to an honourable office of trust or of profit. Compulsion of this sort would seem to indicate a major modification to the claim to individual freedom, although it must be remembered that Smith's discussion of education in general is to be seen against the background of his analysis of the social consequences of the division of labour. The real significance of what Robert Heilbroner has called the 'dark side' of the *Wealth of Nations* can be fully appreciated only when seen against the background of Smith's ethics (see Heilbroner 1975). Readers of *The Theory of Moral Sentiments* will be familiar with the argument that a capacity for moral judgement requires the exercise of faculties and propensities such as imagination, sympathy, and reflection—qualities

---

[8] Smith warned his readers of the dangers of 'extraneous jurisdictions' in noting that 'The person subject to such a jurisdiction is necessarily degraded by it, and instead of being one of the most respectable, is rendered one of the meanest and most contemptible persons in the society. It is by powerful protection only that he can effectually guard himself against the bad usage to which he is at all times exposed: and this protection he is most likely to gain, not by ability or diligence in his profession, but by obsequiousness to the will of his superiors, and by being ready, at all times, to sacrifice to that will the rights, the interest, and the honour of the body corporate of which he is a member' (*WN* v. i. f. 9).

of mind that are likely to be eroded in the context of the modern economy unless preventative steps are taken.

Smith's concern with isolation and mental mutilation can be interpreted as part of another contemporary debate, which was concerned with the ideals of civic humanism and the extent to which modern man could attain something approaching the classical concept of citizenship (see Winch 1978; Hont and Ignatieff 1983). But we are also reminded of the revision of liberalism undertaken by the Oxford idealists in the nineteenth century, and of T. H. Green's distinction between negative and positive freedom. In a lecture delivered in 1880 on the subject of 'Liberal Legislation and Freedom of Contract', Green defined negative freedom as freedom from restraint, and positive freedom as a 'power or capacity of doing or enjoying something worth doing or enjoying', recognizing that the condition of positive freedom could be obtained only with the assistance of the state. (Green 1906: 3, 370–1).

Points such as these remind us of E. R. A. Seligman's warning to readers of the 1910 edition of the *Wealth of Nations*: namely, that they should avoid 'absolutism' and respect the point that recent 'investigation has emphasised the principles of relativity'. (Seligman 1910). It is not appropriate uncritically to translate Smith's policy *prescriptions* from the eighteenth to the twentieth century—moreover, it is quite inconsistent with Smith's own teaching. Smith's work was marked by relativity of perspective-dominant features of the treatment of scientific knowledge in the essay on 'Astronomy', and of the analysis of rules of behaviour in the ethics (see Chapters 2 and 3 above).

REFERENCES

Black, R. D. C. (1976), 'Smith's Contribution in Historical Perspective', in T. Wilson and A. Skinner (eds.), *The Market and the State: Essays in Honour of Adam Smith* (Oxford), pp. 42–63.

Blaug, M. (1975), 'The Economics of Education in English Classical Political Economy', in *EAS*.

Brown, M. (1988), *Adam Smith's Economics: Its Place in the Development of Economic Thought* (Beckenham).

Copley, S. and Sutherland, K. (1995), (eds.) *Adam Smith's Wealth of Nations: New Interdisciplinary Essays* (Manchester).

Cropsey, J. (1975), 'Adam Smith and Political Philosophy', in *EAS*.

Forbes, D. (1975), 'Sceptical Whiggism, Commerce and Liberty', in *EAS*.

Green, T. H. (1906), *Works*, ed. R. L. Nettleship, (London).

Haakonssen, K. (1981), *The Science of a Legislator: The Natural Jurisprudence of David Hume and Adam Smith* (Cambridge).

Heilbroner, R. L.(1975), The Paradox of Progress: Decline and Decay in the *Wealth of Nations'*, in *EAS*.

Hirschman, A. O. (1977), *The Passions and the Interests* (Princeton).

Hont, I. and Ignatieff, M. (1983), *Wealth and Virtue: The Shaping of Political Economy in the Scottish Enlightenment* (Cambridge).

Keynes, J. M. (1936), *The General Theory of Employment, Interest and Money* (London).

Lamb, R. (1973), 'Adam Smith's Concept of Alienation', *Oxford Economic Papers*, 25; reprinted in Wood (1984: i. 478–88).

Macfie, A. L.(1967), 'The Moral Justification of Free Enterprise: A Lay Sermon on an Adam Smith Text', *Scottish Journal of Political Economy*, 14; reprinted in his *Individual in Society* (London, 1967).

Muller, J. Z. (1993), *Adam Smith in His Time and Ours* (New York).

Peacock, A. T. (1975), 'The Treatment of the Principles of Public Finance in the *Wealth of Nations'*, in *EAS*.

Rae, J. (1895), *Life of Adam Smith*, (London).

Ricketts, M. (1978), 'Adam Smith on Politics and Bureaucracy', in *The Economics of Politics*, IEA Readings, 18.

Robbins, L. (1953), *The Theory of Economic Policy in English Classical Political Economy* (London).

Roll, E. (1976), 'The *Wealth of Nations* 1776–1976', *Lloyds Bank Review*, 119; reprinted in Wood (1984: ii. 146–55).

Rosenberg, N. (1960), 'Some Institutional Aspects of the *Wealth of Nations'*, *Journal of Political Economy*, 18; reprinted in Wood (1984: iii. 105–20).

——(1965), 'Adam Smith on the Division of Labour: Two Views or One? *Economica*, 32; reprinted in Wood (1984: iii, 171–183).

——(1990), 'Adam Smith as a Social Critic', *Royal Bank of Scotland Review*, 166.

Samuels, W.(1973), 'Adam Smith and the Economy as a System of Power', *Review of Social Economy*, 31.

Schumpeter, J. A. (1954), *History of Economic Analysis* (London).

Seligman, E. R. A. (1910), (ed.),*Wealth of Nations* (London).

Skinner, A. S. (1979), *A System of Social Science: Papers Relating to Adam Smith* (Oxford).

——(1986), 'Adam Smith: Then and Now', in R. D. C. Black (ed.), *Ideas in Economics* (London).

——(1988), 'Adam Smith and Economic Liberalism', *Hume Occasional Papers*, 9.

——(1991), 'Adam Smith: Education as a Public Service', University of Glasgow *Discussion Papers in Economics*, no. 9117.

——(1995), 'Adam Smith and the Role of the State', in Copley and Sutherland (op. cit.).

Steuart, Sir James (1767), *Principles of Political Economy* ed. Skinner, A. S. (Edinburgh).

Stone, R. (1992), 'Public economic Policy: Adam Smith on What the State Should and Should Not Do', in *Adam Smith's Legacy*, ed. Michael Fry (London).

Thompson, E. P. (1991), *Customs in Common* (Harmondsworth).

Viner, J. (1928), 'Adam Smith and Laisser-Faire', *Journal of Political Economy*, 35; reprinted in Wood (1984: i, 143–67).

West, E. G. (1964), 'Adam Smith's Two Views on the Division of Labour', *Economica*, 31; reprinted in Wood (1984: iii, 162–70).

————(1975), 'Adam Smith and Alienation: Wealth Increases, Men Decay?' in *EAS*.

————(1976), 'Adam Smith's Economics of Politics', *History of Political Economy*, 1.

Winch, D. (1978), *Adam Smith's Politics: An Essay in Historiographic Revision* (Cambridge).

————(1983), 'Science and the Legislator: Adam Smith and After', *Economic Journal*, 93.

Witherington, D. (1970), 'Education and Society in the Eighteenth Century', in *Scotland in the Age of Improvement*, ed. N. T. Phillipson and R. Mitchison (Edinburgh).

Wood, J. C. (1984), *Adam Smith: Critical Assessments*, 4 vols. (Beckenham).

Zallio, F. (1990), 'Adam Smith's Dual Circulation Framework', *Royal Bank of Scotland Review*, 166.

9
Mercantilist Policy:
The American Colonies

INTRODUCTION

Smith's interest in the American question goes back to his time in Glasgow as student (1737–40) and professor (1751–64). He witnessed a particularly rapid rate of commercial development in and around the city, based largely on tobacco, which led in turn to major initiatives in manufacturing and banking. These were interesting developments, which recall Smith's reference to the good fortune enjoyed by those observers who live in 'a mercantile town, situated in an unimproved country' (WN III. iv. 3). Quite apart from his contacts with great merchants like Andrew Cochrane, founder of perhaps the first Political Economy Club, Smith could hardly help notice that Glasgow's emergence as a major commercial centre was the result of the city's geographical position. This relationship of geography to commercial activity provided a classic modern example of the historical progression that is so dominant a feature of his treatment of the origins of 'present establishments' in Europe as developed in book III of the Wealth of Nations.

Smith's success as a professor brought him further important contact with the American question, in the generous shape of Charles Townshend. Townshend had married the widowed countess of Dalkeith in 1755 and was sufficiently impressed by Smith's Theory of Moral Sentiments (1759) to make the author tutor to the young Duke of Buccleugh. The post permitted Smith to travel in France between 1764 and 1766, and he was thus able to make contact with the Physiocrats (see Chapter 6 above). On his return to London in 1766, he appears to have had at least two relevant exchanges in the increasingly fraught legislative environment. First, he was asked by Lord Shelburne for advice on the Roman colonial model, but was able to offer little comfort: 'Being in some measure little independent republics they naturally followed the interests which their peculiar situation pointed out to them' (Corr. 101).

This paper draws on the arguments of two previous attempts: an article first published in the *Journal of the History of Ideas*, 37 (1976) and reprinted in Skinner (1979), and 'Adam Smith: The Demise of the Colonial Relationship with America', in *The Treaty of Paris in a Changing States System*, ed. Prosser Gifford (Washington, 1985). An alternative treatment may be found in Skinner (1990).

Secondly, during the same period he annotated a document on the Sinking Fund, which had been prepared by Townshend (*Corr.* 302).

Finally, it should be observed that when Smith returned to London in 1773 to finish work on the *Wealth of Nations*, the delay in completing the book was attributed by some, notably David Hume, to his growing preoccupation with the American problem. Hume wrote in February 1776 to complain: 'By all Accounts, your Book has been printed long ago; yet it has never yet been so much as advertised. What is the Reason? If you wait till the Fate of America be decided, you may wait long' (*Corr.* 149).

That Smith's interest in the American question caused the delay is certainly plausible. The colonies are scarcely mentioned in the lectures delivered in 1762–3, but they feature in what is almost a separate monograph in the *Wealth of Nations*, in the form of the long, three-part chapter 7 of book IV. In this place, Smith reviewed the options open to the British government during the mid-1770s, passages that led Hugh Blair to complain that Smith had given the issues involved: 'a representation etc. which I wish had been omitted, because it is too much like a publication for the present moment. In Subsequent editions when publick Measures come to be Settled, these pages will fall to be omitted or Altered' (*Corr.* 151). Blair was correct, only in in the sense that the monograph does contain a good deal of comment on contemporary events. This fact probably led Alexander Wedderburn, a former pupil and at the time Solicitor-General in Lord North's administration, to seek his old professor's advice in the aftermath of the surrender at Saratoga.[1] Wedderburn, it may be recalled, had been responsible for the hostile examination of Benjamin Franklin before the Privy Council, a critical exchange which moved David Hume to remark in a letter to Smith that Wedderburn's treatment of the distinguished colonist had been 'most cruel' (*Corr.* 140).

STATE OF THE CONFLICT

One possible solution to current difficulties was military victory and the restitution of existing institutional arrangements. But as Smith wryly pointed out, the difficulty in such a solution 'arises altogether from the resistance of America' (*Corr.* App. B: 381). Having little confidence in a military solution, Smith wrote to William Strahan in June 1776: 'The American campaign has begun awkwardly. I hope, I cannot say that I

---

[1] The 'Memorandum' is dated 1778 and was first published by G. H. Guttridge (1932–3). It has been edited by David Stevens and is now included in Smith's *Correspondence* as Appendix A.

expect, it will end better. England, tho' in the present times it breeds men of great professional abilities in all different ways, great lawyers, great watch makers and Clockmakers, etc. etc., seems to breed neither Statesmen nor Generals' (*Corr.* 158).

If such a judgement is somewhat harsh, given the difficulties faced by British commanders in the field, called upon as they were to conciliate and to conquer, perhaps Smith was more insightful when he noted that, while a professional standing army like Great Britain's was always likely to be the superior of a militia, experience suggested that this was not always true when the latter was long in the field: 'Should the war in America drag out through another campaign, the American militia may become in every respect a match for that standing army, of which the valour appeared, in the last war, at least not inferior to that of the hardiest veterans of France and Spain' (*WN* v. i. a. 27).

Yet even if victory were possible, the outcome, he advised, would still be basically unworkable. A military government, he wrote, 'is what of all others, the Americans hate and dread the most. While they are able to keep the field, they will never submit to it; and if, in spite of their utmost resistance, it should be established, they will, for more than a century to come, be at all times ready to take arms in order to overturn it.' He went on:

After so complete a victory . . . after having, not only felt their own strength, but made us feel it, they would be ten times more ungovernable than ever; factious, mutinous and discontented subjects in time of peace; at all times, upon the slightest disobligation, disposed to rebel; and, in the case of a French or Spanish war, certainly rebelling. (*Corr.* App. B: 383).

Besides, he concluded:

By our dominion over a country, which submitted so unwillingly to our authority, we could gain scarce anything but the disgrace of being supposed to oppress a people whom we have long talked of, not only as our fellow subjects, but as of our brethren and even as of our children. (*Corr.* App. B: 381).[2]

A second option open to the British government was simplicity itself—voluntary withdrawal from the conflict and recognition of America as a separate state. The advantages of such a bold course were, in Smith's opinion, immense. At one stroke, Britain would be free of the crushing burden of expenditure needed to defend the colonies and could

---

[2] Sir James Steuart offered an interesting variation on this argument, having first confirmed his view that force would not secure the American colonies. Steuart firmly believed that 'force will never persuade except from fear' and that if 'force may give subjects to a state . . . it will not give citizens'. He concluded that 'it is hardly possible by any force we can send against the colonies, to overcome the general spirit of the people which pushes them to resistance. Steuart also advocated freedom of trade with the colonies. (Raynor and Skinner 1994: 759). See Ch. 11 below, n. 17.

avoid further conflict with France and Spain, at least in the New World. As Smith wrote in the *Wealth of Nations*, 'By thus parting good friends, the natural affection of the colonies to the mother country, which, perhaps, our late dissensions have well nigh extinguished, would quickly revive' (*WN* IV. vii. c. 66).

Even if the two countries were to part with some evidence of bad feeling, Smith advised Wedderburn, 'the similarity of language and manners would in most cases dispose the Americans to prefer our alliance to that of any other nation' (*Corr.* App. B: 383). Yet withdrawal from the conflict was unlikely: 'Such sacrifices, though they might frequently be agreeable to the interest, are always mortifying to the pride of every nation, and what is perhaps of still greater conse-quence, they are always contrary to the private interest of the governing part of it' (*WN* IV. vii. c. 66). He further elaborated this point in his Memorandum of 1778:

[T]ho' this termination of the war might be really advantageous, it would not, in the eyes of Europe, appear honourable to Great Britain; and when her empire was so much curtailed, her power and dignity would be supposed to be proportionably diminished. What is of still greater importance, it could scarce fail to discredit the government in the eyes of our own people, who would probably impute to maladministration what might, perhaps, be no more than the unavoidable effect of the natural and necessary course of things. (*Corr.* App. B: 383).

He continued:

A government which, in times of the most profound peace, of the highest public prosperity, when the people had scarce even the pretext of a single grievance to complain of, has not always been able to make itself respected by them, would have everything to fear from their rage and indignation at the public disgrace and calamity, for such they would suppose it to be, of thus dismembering the empire. (*Corr.* App. B: 383).[3]

Smith was not above an exercise in the politics of the cabinet in suggesting that Great Britain might restore Canada to France and Florida to Spain, thus rendering 'our colonies the natural enemies of these two monarchies and consequently the natural allies of Great Britain'. As he noted: 'Those splendid, but unprofitable acquisitions of the late war, left our colonies no other enemies to quarrel with but their own mother country. By restoring those acquisitions to the (ancient) masters, we should perhaps revive old enmities, and probably old

---

[3] Hume concurred: in a letter of 1775 addressed to Strahan, he observed that 'the worst effect of the Loss of America, will not be the detriment of our Manufactures, which will be a mere trifle . . . but to the Credit and Reputation of Government, which has already but too little authority. You will probably see a Scene of Anarchy and Confusion open'd at home' (Livingston 1990: 145).

friendships' (*Corr.* App. B: 383). Smith, tongue in cheek, also suggested a strategy that was even more remarkable, a strategy that would have involved reaching an accommodation with the Americans while misleading the British public as to its ultimate results (*Corr.* App. B: 384).

But for Smith the most likely outcome was also the most expensive: partial military defeat could mean the loss of all or some of the 'thirteen united colonies' and the retention of Canada. The Memorandum must have made bleak reading for the Solicitor General, but it would have seemed bleaker still had he known how accurately Smith had forecast the events of 1783.

However, Smith's realism was a source of comfort to some. When Sir John Sinclair of Ulbster complained of lack of progress in the war and exclaimed that 'if we go on at this rate, the nation *must be ruined*, Smith dryly replied, 'Be assured my young friend, that there is a great deal of *ruin* in a nation' (*Corr.* 221). His grasp of economic realities also permitted him to assure William Eden that in the long run there was little to fear from the (temporary) loss of American commerce (*Corr.* 233), a position he shared with Hume.

But while Smith's analyses of contemporary events in the *Wealth of Nations* and the Memorandum are undoubtedly interesting, there is another side to the argument. Smith's real purpose in the *Wealth of Nations* was to produce a searching critique of the mercantile system by exposing the inconsistencies of policy with regard to the American colonies. With this end in view, he offered an examination of the thinking behind the regulating acts of trade and navigation before proceeding to explain why current policy must change, offering a rational solution to the problems that were in due course bound to be exposed as well as to those that were unfolding as he sat in London.[4]

Smith's preferred solution, as we shall see, was Union and the creation in effect of an Atlantic Economic Community.

THE REGULATING ACTS

In describing the objectives of colonial policy, Smith concentrated mainly on its economic aspects and duly reported on the extensive range of restrictions that Britain had imposed on trade and manufactures, domestic as well as American. To begin with, the regulating acts of navigation required that trade between the colonies and Great Britain had to be carried on in British ships, and that certain classes of commodity were to be confined initially to the market of the mother country. These, so-called

[4] For comment, see especially Benians (1923), Fay (1934), Koebner (1961), Winch (1965, 1978), and Stevens (1975).

'enumerated' goods were of two types: those that were either the peculiar produce of America or were not produced in Britain, and those goods that were produced in Britain but in insufficient quantities to meet domestic demand. Examples of the first type were molasses, coffee, and tobacco; of the second, naval stores, masts, pig-iron, and copper. The first broad category of goods was not of a kind that could harm British industry, and here the object of policy, as reported by Smith, was to ensure that British merchants could buy more cheaply in the colonies with a view to supplying other countries at higher prices, and at the same time establishing a useful carrying trade.

In the second case, the objective was to ensure essential supplies and, through the careful use of duties, to discourage imports from other countries 'with which the balance of trade was supposed to be unfavourable' (*WN* IV. vii. b. 35). Smith also took notice of another feature of British policy, namely, that the production of the more 'advanced or more refined manufactures' was discouraged in the colonies (IV. vii. b. 40). Thus, woollen manufactures were forbidden, and, although they were encouraged to export pig-iron, the colonists were prevented from erecting slitt-mills which might have led ultimately to the development of manufactures competitive with those of Great Britain.

There was a certain ingenuity in these arrangements in that the colonial relationship could be seen to benefit both parties at least in the short run. For example, the relationship with the colonies, as defined by the regulating acts, had the effect of creating a self-supporting economic unit whose main components provided complementary markets for each other's products, and in addition helped to minimize gold flows abroad (IV. viii. 15). By the same token, the colonial relationship gave Britain access to strategic materials, and also contributed to national defence, through the encouragement given to her mercantile marine.

Smith also argued that there were considerable opportunities for economic growth within the framework of the colonial relationship. In this connection, he placed greatest emphasis on American experience, and drew attention to three factors which contributed to explain her rapid rate of expansion. First, Smith isolated what may be described as 'institutional' forces in pointing out that the colonies possessed political institutions derived from the British model, which encouraged economic activity by guaranteeing the security of the individual (IV. vii. b. 51).

In the same way, he pointed out that the colonists had brought to an underdeveloped territory the habit of subordination and a 'knowledge of agriculture and of other useful arts' (IV. vii. b. 2), the legacy of the more developed economies from which they had often come. Smith also emphasized that certain features were absent from the colonies, of a kind that contributed to slow up the rate of growth in Europe—for example high rents, tithes, and taxes, together with legal arrangements such as laws of entail which hindered the sale of lands to those whose object was to improve them.

Secondly, he drew attention to the economic situation of the colonial territories in pointing out that 'A new colony must always for some time be more under-stocked in proportion to the extent of territory, and more under-peopled in proportion to the extent of its stock, than the greater part of other countries' (I. ix. 11). This meant that the rates of both wages and profits were likely to be high, thus contributing to a level of activity which explained the 'continual complaint of the scarcity of hands in North America. The demand for labourers, the funds destined for maintaining them, increase, it seems, still faster than they can find labourers to employ' (I. viii. 23).

Thirdly, Smith argued that the legislative arrangements governing trade with the mother country had contributed most materially to colonial development even though this had not always been the motive behind them. In this connection, he drew attention to the fact that 'the most perfect freedom of trade is permitted between the British colonies of America and the West Indies', thus providing a 'great and extensive market' for their products (IV. vii. b. 39). In addition, the relative freedom of trade in non-enumerated commodities provided a further market for the primary products involved, while Britain also gave preferential treatment to American products that were confined to her own domestic market. Again, Britain provided a large European market (albeit indirectly) for the enumerated items—for example goods like tobacco which were largely re-exported.

Taken as a whole, the colonial policy had the effect of encouraging what Smith described as 'Agriculture . . . the proper business of all new colonies; a business which the cheapness of land renders more advantageous than any other' (IV. vii. c. 51). This point is of great importance, since on Smith's argument agriculture was the most productive of all forms of investment, capable of generating large surpluses which could sustain further growth. He even argued that the restrictions imposed on the introduction of manufactures had benefited the colonies by ensuring that they bought from the cheaper European markets and therefore avoided diverting any part of the available capital into less productive employments. He concluded:

Unjust, however, as such prohibitions may be, they have not hitherto been very hurtful to the colonies. Land is still so cheap, and, consequently, labour so dear among them, that they can import from the mother country, almost all the more refined or more advanced manufactures cheaper than they could make them for themselves. Though they had not, therefore, been prohibited from establishing such manufactures, yet in their present state of improvement, a regard to their own interest would, probably, have prevented them from doing so. (WN, IV. vii. 44).

As Donald Winch has pointed out, the experience of America is one of the rare examples where the actual and the 'natural' progress of opulence actually coincide.

There is no doubt as to the buoyancy of Smith's tone in describing the growth rate of North America, a country where the benefits available, natural, artificial, and accidental, were such as to prompt the conclusion that, 'though North America is not yet so rich as England, it is much more thriving, and advancing with much greater rapidity to the further acquisition of riches' (I. viii. 23).

At the same time, it cannot be said that Smith minimized the benefits to Britain from the standpoint of economic growth. In this connection, he pointed out that Britain (together with her neighbours) had as a matter of fact acquired, through the control of the colonies, a 'new and inexhaustible market' which had given occasion to 'new divisions of labour and improvements of art'. Indeed, it can be said that Smith's assertion of benefit accruing to Great Britain as a result of the colonial relationship simply reflects his own grasp of the gains from trade (IV. i. 32).

Smith's argument seems designed to suggest that the colonial relationship had both contributed to, and proved compatible with, a relatively high rate of growth in both the colonies and the mother country.

THE CONTRADICTIONS OF THE SYSTEM

The relationship between the mother country and the colonies is thus represented as beneficial to the two parties, both as regards the politico-economic objectives of the regulating acts and the stimulus given to economic growth. But at the same time, Smith evidently believed that there were contradictions inherent in the colonial relationship which must begin to manifest themselves over time. For example, while Smith took pains to emphasize the great stimulus given to the growth of the colonies, he also pointed out that the high and rapid rate of growth which they had attained must ultimately come into conflict with the restrictions imposed on colonial trade and manufactures, restrictions that could be regarded as the 'principal badge of their dependency' (*WN* IV. vii. c. 64) and as a 'manifest violation of one of the most sacred rights of mankind'. He also pointed out that, 'In their present state of improvement, those prohibitions, perhaps, without cramping their industry, or restraining it from any employment to which it would have gone of its own accord, are only impertinent badges of slavery ... In a more advanced state they might be really oppressive and insupportable' (IV. vii. b. 44). Smith quite clearly considered that *in the long run* some change must come in the colonial relationship for the reason just stated, although he did place most emphasis on the more immediate problems faced by Britain herself, as providing the stimulus for change.

As far as Great Britain was concerned, Smith contended that, although the colony trade was 'upon the whole beneficial, and greatly beneficial' (IV. vii. c. 47), still the rate of growth was necessarily lower than it would have been in the absence of the regulating acts. He quite clearly believed that, 'If the manufactures of Great Britain . . . have been advanced, as they certainly have, by the colony trade, it has not been by means of the monopoly of that trade, but in spite of the monopoly' (IV. vii. c. 55). Smith advanced a number of points in support of this contention. First, he suggested that the monopoly of the colony trade had inevitably increased the volume of business to be conducted by a relatively limited amount of British capital and, therefore, the prevailing rate of profit. In this connection, he argued that high rates of profit would affect the improvement of land (IV. vii. c. 58) and the frugality of the merchant classes (IV. vii. c. 61), while ensuring that available capital would be partly drawn, and partly driven, from those trades where Britain lacked the monopoly (that is, drawn by the higher profits available in the colony trade, and driven from them by a poorer competitive position).

But Smith especially emphasized that the pattern of British *trade* had been altered in such a way that her manufactures, 'instead of being suited, as before the act of navigation, to the neighbouring market of Europe, or to the more distant one of the countries which lie round the Mediterranean sea, have, the greater part of them, been accommodated to the still more distant one of the colonies' (IV. vii. c. 22). Smith's point was that the existing legislation had drawn capital from trades carried on with a near market (Europe), and diverted it to trade carried on with a distant market (America), while forcing a certain amount of capital from a direct to an indirect foreign trade—with consequent effects, he alleged, on the rate of return, the employment of productive labour, and, therefore, the rate of economic growth.

Smith added that the pattern of British trade had been altered in such a way as to make her unduly dependent on a single (though large) market:

Her commerce, instead of running in a great number of small channels, has been taught to run principally in one great channel. But the whole system of her industry and commerce has thereby been rendered less secure; the whole state of her body politick less healthful, than it otherwise would have been. In her present condition, Great Britain resembles one of those unwholesome bodies in which some of the vital parts are overgrown, and which, upon that account, are liable to many dangerous disorders scarce incident to those in which all the parts are more properly proportioned. (*WN* IV. vii. c. 43).

But Smith's account of the problem facing Great Britain is largely dominated by that of fiscal need. In Smith's opinion, Britain's needs seemed to be growing more rapidly than her resources, and he noted in this connection that by January 1775 the national debt had reached the then astronomical figure of £130 million (absorbing £4.5 million in interest charges), much of which was due to the acquisition of the colonial territories.

This was a matter of some moment, since it meant that a country whose rate of growth had been adversely affected by the colonial relationship had to face a large and probably growing tax burden which would itself affect the rate of economic expansion, and thus compound the problem. Smith concluded that Great Britain must in the course of time either solve the fiscal problem or abandon it, in the latter case accommodating 'her future views and designs to the real mediocrity of her circumstances' (WN v. iii. 92).

A RATIONAL SOLUTION: THE PROJECT OF EMPIRE

It was Smith's contention that 'The rulers of Great Britain have, for more than a century past, amused the people with the imagination that they possessed a great empire on the west side of the Atlantic. This empire, however, has hitherto existed in imagination only. It has hitherto been, not an empire, but the project of an empire . . . If the project cannot be completed, it ought to be given up' (WN v. iii. 92). Yet Smith believed that the project of empire could be completed and that the tensions actual and potential that were present in the existing colonial relationship could be resolved by the creation of an Atlantic Economic Community which would establish 'an immense internal market for every part of the produce of all its different provinces' (v. iii. 72).

Smith made a number of important points in connection with this thesis. First, he argued that Great Britain both could and should tax the colonies, partly as a means of relief from the growing burden of the national debt and partly as a means of making the colonies pay for benefits received from the imperial connection. It is worth noting that Smith did not defend colonial taxation on the ground that Britain had planted the colonies; on the contrary, he pointed out that they had been originally peopled largely as the result of religious persecution (IV. vii. b. 61). Nor did he suggest that taxation was justified on the ground that the mother country had originally invested in their improvement; on the contrary, he insisted that policy to regulate the colonies had been implemented only after the original colonists had made significant economic progress (IV. vii. b. 63). He simply argued:

It is not contrary to justice that both Ireland and America should contribute towards the discharge of the publick debt of Great Britain. That debt has been contracted in support of the government established by the Revolution, a government to which the protestants of Ireland owe, not only the whole authority which they at present enjoy in their own country, but every security which they possess for their liberty, their property, and their religion; a government to which several of the colonies of America owe their present charters, and consequently their present constitution, and to which all the colonies of America owe the liberty, security, and property which they have ever since enjoyed. That publick debt has been contracted in the defence, not of Great Britain alone, but of all the different provinces of the empire; the immense debt contracted in the late war in particular, and a great part of that contracted in the war before, were both properly contracted in defence of America. (*WN* v. iii. 88).

Having made a point that commanded a good deal of support in contemporary Britain, Smith went on to consider how such a policy might be implemented and what its consequences might be. To begin with, he suggested that the colonies might be taxed by their own assemblies, a proposition no sooner stated than rejected on the ground that colonial assemblies could not be supposed to be the proper judges of the needs of the empire as a whole (*WN* iv. vii. c. 70). Secondly, he suggested that taxes might be levied by requisition, which was the current practice, 'the parliament of Great Britain determining the sum which each colony ought to pay, and the provincial assembly assessing and levying it in the way that suited best the circumstances of the province' (iv. vii. c. 71). Such a system had some obvious advantages in Smith's opinion, especially in that it left the central and colonial governments with important and appropriate areas of control. But this solution too was rejected, partly because he felt that the mother country might face some difficulty in actually extracting the revenue required (a point confirmed by British experience during the war with France), and partly because central control of taxation might have adverse repercussions as a result of its political consequences in America itself. Taxation by requisition and without representation would, Smith felt, effectively reduce the power and status of the colonial assemblies, and, therefore, that of 'all the leading men of British America' who,

like those of other countries, desire to preserve their own importance. They feel, or imagine, that if their assemblies, which they are fond of calling parliaments, and of considering as equal in authority to the parliament of Great Britain, should be so far degraded as to become the humble ministers and executive officers of that parliament, the greater part of their importance would be at an end. (*WN* iv. viii. c. 74).

Smith noted that the Americans 'have rejected therefore, the proposals of being taxed by parliamentary requisition, and like other ambitious and high-spirited men, have rather chosen to draw the sword in defence of their own importance' (*WN* IV. vii. c. 74).

Smith concluded that the British government should retain the right of assessment but extend the British system of taxation to all the colonies. The concluding sections of the *Wealth of Nations* were largely concerned with the technical problems of this aspect of harmonization, and Smith saw no reason to suppose that the major British taxes (land tax, stamp duties, customs, and excise) could not be successfully applied to both America and Ireland. He added that such a change of policy would require a form of union that would give the colonies representation in the British parliament and in effect create a single state:

This, however, could scarce, perhaps, be done, consistently with the principles of the British constitution, without admitting into the British parliament, or if you will into the states-general of the British Empire, a fair and equal representation of all those different provinces, that of each province bearing the same proportion to the produce of its taxes, as the representation of Great Britain might bear to the produce of the taxes levied upon Great Britain. (*WN* v. iii. 68).

Indeed Smith believed that:

there is not the least probability that the British constitution would be hurt by the union of Great Britain with her colonies. That constitution, on the contrary, would be completed by it, and seems to be imperfect without it. The assembly which deliberates and decides concerning the affairs of every part of the empire, in order to be properly informed, ought certainly to have representatives from every part of it. (*WN* IV. vii. c. 77).

As to the colonists,

Instead of piddling for the little prizes which are to be found in what may be called the paltry raffle of colony faction; they might then hope, from the presumption which men naturally have in their own ability and good fortune, to draw some of the great prizes which sometimes come from the wheel of the great state lottery of British politicks. (*WN* IV. vii. c. 75).

He added that union would also deliver the colonists 'from those rancourous and virulent factions which are inseparable from small democracies . . . [and] which have so frequently divided the affections of their people, and disturbed the tranquility of their governments, in their form so nearly democratical'. Indeed, Smith believed that the colonists would regret the loss of this opportunity (*Corr.* 384).

What Smith had in mind was an incorporating union of the kind introduced by the Act of 1707 and which was later extended to Ireland. But the union that Smith envisaged was distinctive in that he foresaw the eventual transfer of power from Westminster to the former colonies. It was Smith's view that America's progress 'in wealth, population and improvement' had been, and would continue to be, so rapid that 'in the course of little more than a century, perhaps, the produce of American might exceed that of British taxation. The seat of empire would then naturally remove itself to that part of the empire which contributed most to the general defence and support of the whole' (*WN* IV. vii. c. 79).

The belief that America would in the long run prove to be the dominant influence also attracted a good deal of support. Thomas Pownall, for example, had already noted that America would become the major partner in his proposed 'grand marine dominion', and so too had Smith's friend Benjamin Franklin, both in his *Observations* and in correspondence with Lord Kames:

Scotland and Ireland are differently circumstanced. Confined by the sea, they can scarcely increase in numbers, wealth and strength, so as to overbalance England. But America, an immense territory, favoured by Nature with all advantages of climate, soil, great navigable rivers, and lakes, etc. must become a great country, populous and mighty; and will, in less time than is generally conceived, be able to shake off any shackles that may be imposed on her, and perhaps place them on the imposers. (Ross 1972: 340–1).

The implications of this position began to attract the attention of economists in the early part of the nineteenth century (Romani 1993).

SOME CHARACTERISTICS OF SMITH'S CRITIQUE

It is now widely recognized that Smith's treatment of the colonial question is in reality a major critique of mercantile policy which has as its centrepiece the analysis of the relationship with America, a relationship that had brought the mercantile system 'a degree of splendour and glory which it could never otherwise have attained to' (*WN* IV. vii. c. 81). It was William Robertson, rather than Hugh Blair, who took Smith's measure when he wrote that:

None of your friends, however, will profit more by your labours and discoveries than I. Many of your observations concerning the Colonies are of capital importance to me. I shall often follow you as my Guide and instructor. I am happy to find my own ideas concerning the absurdity of the limitations upon the Colony trade established much better than I could have done myself. (*Corr.* 153).

To the economist, Smith's critique is interesting not least because of the emphasis on real, rather than on monetary, factors. His analysis of the long-run causes of change in the nature of the imperial relationship would appear to rest on two trends: the relatively slow rate of growth attained by Britain in the face of self-imposed costs and restrictions, and the relatively high rate attained in America, which in part at least had *resulted from* these restrictions. It is also evident that Smith's explanation of British economic performance at the time rests very heavily on his thesis of the natural progress of opulence and the consequent belief that any derangement of the natural balance of industry would slow down the rate of growth. In particular, it would appear that Smith made much of the point that the colonial trade transferred capital from a near to a distant market where the rate of return was slower, and that he relied heavily on the (relative) decline in Britain's taxable capacity, as the source of her problems. However, there is remarkably little by way of verification of these critical points. As Koebner has pointed out, Smith 'did not take the trouble to check' many of his suppositions (Koebner 1961: 229–30).

A similar criticism was voiced by a contemporary of Smith's, Governor Pownall of Massachusetts. The Governor questioned Smith's assertion that the rate of return was slower in the American trade than in the European trade and insisted that the matter of diversion of stock from Europe to America was 'a matter of fact, which must not be established by an argument *a priori*—but on an actual deduction of facts. . . . I did not find the latter in your book. . . .' (Pownall 1776: 41; *Corr.* App. A: 369). Pownall made an even shrewder point when he recognized that Smith was using theses established in one part of the book as proven principles in another. For example, he recognized the central importance of Smith's views on the productivities of investment:

In that part, however, which explains the different effect of different employments of capital . . . I will beg to arrest your steps for a moment, while we examine the ground whereon we tread: and the more so, as I find these propositions used in the second part of your work as data; whence you endeavour to prove, that the monopoly of the colony trade is a disadvantageous commercial institution. (Pownall 1776: 23; *Corr.* App. A: 354).

The Governor also drew attention to the *style* of Smith's argument in the course of a discussion of Britain's potential losses arising from the colonial relationship:

It strikes me as material, and I am sure, therefore, you will excuse me making in this place, one remark *on the manner* of your argument, and how you *stretch your reasoning nicely*. You in words advance upon the ground of *probable reasons for believing* only, you prove by probable suppositions only; yet most people who read your book, will think you mean to set up an absolute proof, and your conclusion is drawn as though you had. (Pownall 1776: p. 40; *Corr.* App. A: 369).

Writing much later, Richard Koebner made a similar point in adverting to the fact that Smith often presents views on the colonial issue in such a way that they appear, at first sight, to be 'unavoidable inferences' from his argument as a whole. As he remarked, 'Adam Smith took care to have his reflections on the American problem organically woven into the context of his great systematic work. They could appear at first sight as unavoidable inferences of [a] consistent and comprehensive argument' (Koebner 1961: 227).

Nor do we need to look far in discovering apparent shortcomings in Smith's treatment of contemporary events. For example, while Smith did emphasize the problems of colonial paper money, he did not give his readers any inkling as to the depth of colonial reaction when the British government was forced to prohibit it in 1764 (WN II. ii, 101; Beer 1933: 180, 187). If he did concentrate attention on the controls introduced by the British Parliament after 1763, he cannot be said to have explained the extent to which these controls were the result of the inability of the colonies to co-operate among themselves (never mind with the British) during the recent major war with France.[5] Again, While Smith did have a good deal to say about the fiscal problem facing Britain after the war, he hardly managed to provide an account of the legislative programme that had been implemented by Grenville, and which had been designed to raise taxes in America: 'for defraying the expense of defending, protecting, and securing the same'.[6]

Moreover, while Smith emphasized the debt owed by the colonists to British political institutions, he did not provide his readers with any guidance as to the widening gulf between the British and colonial interpretation of a common body of constitutional law. On the one hand, there was the colonists' contention, shared by Smith, that there should be 'no taxation without representation', a belief that was aptly illustrated by Franklin's evidence when he appeared before the House of Commons in 1766, where he stated the view of his colleagues in these terms: 'They understood it thus; by the same charter, and otherwise, they are entitled to all the privileges and liberties of Englishmen . . . that one of the privileges of English subjects is, that they are not to be taxed without their common consent' (Morris 1970: 85). On the other hand, there were complications presented by the doctrine of Parliamentary sovereignty. As Beloff put it, 'there was a single tradition of opposition to arbitrary government which went back to the struggles of the seven-

---

[5] Beer has emphasized that the colonies fought among themselves during the war with France and that they also contributed to Britain's difficulties by actively trading with the enemy (Beer 1933: 87). The problems of co-operation also led to the system of levying money by requisition, a system that was largely an expensive failure and contributed to the greatly increased size of the national debt (p. 87). The difficulties faced during the war with France were also evident in the face of the Pontiac Uprising of the 1760s, both contributing to convince the British government 'that Parliamentary taxation was the sole and only means of obtaining from the colonies their just share of the cost of their own defence' (p. 270).

[6] The statement comes from the Revenue (or Sugar) Act of 1764 and is quoted in Rutman (1971: 155). For American reaction to the taxation measures see Morris (1970) and Beloff (1960).

teenth century. In Great Britain it had come to serve as the foundation for a theory of parliamentary sovereignty, in America as the basis of a theory of limited government' (Beloff 1960: 6).

The dilemma is illustrated by the terms of the Declaratory Act of 1766. This Act accompanied the repeal of the Stamp Act but took the opportunity to state, despite the repeal, that the King in Parliament 'had, hath, and of right ought to have, full power and authority to make laws and statutes of sufficient force and validity to bind the colonies and people of America, subjects of the Crown of Great Britain, in all cases whatsoever' (Morris 1970: 87).

It might even be suggested that the state of conflict with America confirmed a contradiction other than the one Smith had identified: namely, the contradiction inherent in the dogma of parliamentary sovereignty which was to Britain affirmation of her freedom from arbitrary power and to the colonists, confirmation of their subjection to it.

It is also relevant to observe that Smith's account of mercantile policy in the context of America gave a great deal of emphasis to the acts of trade and navigation and that he judged the success of the policy in terms of the contribution the colonies could make to imperial revenue and defence. In presenting the matter in this way, Smith obscured the fact that regulations after 1763 marked a major shift from a *mercantile* policy, based on trade regulation, towards an *imperial* policy, based upon territorial aggrandizement and control: 'imperialism not mercantilism . . . was the first cause of the eventual rupture' (Andrews 1924: 122, 128–9). Such a sentiment reflects American opinion at the time and is illustrated by the text of the Continental Association of 1774, whose members found that 'the present unhappy situation of our affairs is occasioned by the ruinous system of colony administration, adopted by the British ministry about the year 1763, evidently calculated for enslaving these colonies, and with them, the British empire' (Morris 1970: 135).

In addition, it should be noted that the regulating acts that were so marked a feature of mercantile policy, and which were regarded by Smith as unjust violations of natural liberty, were not at the time seen in this light by the colonists themselves. As Franklin pointed out in his examination before the House of Commons, 'The authority of Parliament was allowed to be valid in all laws, except such as should lay internal taxes. It was never disputed in laying duties to regulate commerce.' As David Stevens has noted: 'Even when the First Continental Congress convened in 1774, the delegates, whom Dr Johnson was to call 'croakers of calamity' and demigods of independence', showed little opposition to the old system'. In Resolve No. 4 of the Suffolk Resolves, he continued, it was stated that:

We cheerfully consent to the operation of such acts of the British Parliament as are bona fide, restrained to the regulation of our external commerce, for the purpose of securing the commercial advantage of the whole empire to the mother country, and the commercial benefits of its respective members, excluding every idea of taxation internal or external, for raising a revenue on the subjects without their consent. (Stevens 1975: 213).

It is interesting to observe in this connection that neither the Declaration of Colonial Rights and Grievances nor the Declaration of Independence, which included a comprehensive indictment of British policy, contained any critical reference to the acts of trade and navigation. As Oliver Dickinson has pointed out, colonial objections to British policy after 1763 were 'not because they were trade regulations but because they were not laws of that kind' (Dickinson 1951: 295).

THE INTERPRETATION OF SMITH'S PURPOSE

As we have seen, Smith's critique of the mercantile system and his emphasis upon the inevitability of a change in policy at some stage rests heavily on his deployment of theses associated with his treatment of the natural progress of opulence and of the different productivities of capital. This approach is open to the kind of criticism voiced by writers so far apart as Pownall and Koebner.

It is also evident that Smith's account of the colonial problem does not provide the economist as commentator with any real understanding of the fact that the immediate (as distinct from the long-run) source of the difficulty was not rooted in mercantile *policy*. And yet, Smith could write in 1783, the year of the third edition of the *Wealth of Nations* and of peace with America, that 'It is unnecessary, I apprehend, to say anything further, in order to expose the folly of a system which fatal experience has now sufficiently exposed' (*WN* iv. viii. 15). The inference is seemingly unavoidable: namely, that Smith's critique of the mercantile system had been confirmed by the loss of the colonies.

To paraphrase one aspect of the discussion of justice in *The Theory of Moral Sentiments*, the reader is in effect invited to judge 'by the event and not by the design' (*TMS* ii. iii. 3. 2). This interpretation may suggest that Smith's purpose was in part at least rhetorical.

As we have seen, there are two main sides to Smith's argument, which he expounds in turn: the critique of the mercantile fallacy, and the examination of current events. Although these two main sides of the argument are not always linked with the precision we might expect, it is interesting to observe the degree of elaboration that each receives and the juxtaposition in which they are placed, for, by so doing, Smith lent additional weight to each. The analysis of the mercantile fallacy with its emphasis on the natural progress of opulence gains in plausibility from the existence of the difficulties currently faced by Great Britain, just as these difficulties gain an additional dimension from being presented as the inevitable consequence of the fallacy itself. Smith may, in short, have written to *persuade* by producing an argument cast in such a way 'that the several parts, being thus connected, gain a considerable strength by the appearance of probability and connection' (*LRBL* ii. 205). It would seem to be entirely possible that Smith's analysis, developed as it is in terms of a gradually changing focus, was organized in such a way as to attract the agreement of the reader. In the manner of some advocate appealing to the jury, Smith may be seen to have presented his case in such a way that, 'though he can bring proof of very few particulars, yet the connection there is makes them easily comprehended and consequently agreeable, so that when the adversary tries to contradict any of these particulars it is pulling down a fabric with which we are greatly pleased and are very unwilling to give up' (*LRBL* ii. 197).[7]

If this conclusion seems somewhat finely drawn, two points should be borne in mind. First, Smith was the author of a sophisticated series of lectures on rhetoric which were designed to illustrate the powers of the human mind and the manner in which we organize discourse in order to appeal to those whom we wish to teach, persuade, or otherwise influence. Secondly, it may be recalled that Smith was acutely aware of the fact that the connection with America had brought the mercantile system a degree of 'splendor and glory which it could never otherwise have attained to' (*WN* IV. vii. c. 81). This key fact is not denied, so that, even if Smith did regard mercantile policy as but the reflection of the mean and parochial habits of second-rate shopkeepers, he may well have recognized, writing in the early 1770s, that it was necessary to rely on more convincing arguments in disposing of its claims. If Smith did delay publication in order to add to or modify his section on America, it is little wonder. He may well have perceived the exciting possibility of using the difficulties of the moment to 'confirm' the 'truth' of his own principles while at the same time striking a telling blow where he believed it was most needed. In 1776 Smith was still seeking to persuade and still on the offensive; by 1783 he could write *as if* his case had been confirmed by events, and with a

[7] Smith commented at length on the proper style of judicial oration in lect. 28 and made the following interesting point: 'It is in the proper ordering and disposal of this sort of arguments that the great art of an orator often consists. These when placed separately have often no great impression, but if they be placed in a natural order, one leading to the other, their effect is greatly increased' (*LRBL* ii. 197). For comment, see Howell (1975). Smith's lectures show a sophisticated grasp of the problems of communication and contain an analysis of the forms assumed by various sorts of discourse including the scientific forms which reflect the purposes in hand; see e.g. Campbell (1971), and Ch. 1 above.

degree of confidence that would have been inappropriate ten years earlier when he was in London.

America, in short, had acquired the status of an experiment which 'confirmed' Smith's theses, one that could be allowed to remain in the *Wealth of Nations* as a kind of permanent exhibit. Of course, no such conclusion can be established beyond a shadow of doubt, but if the case is plausible it counsels caution in the interpretation of this part of Smith's work.

Without prejudice to this argument, however, there is a further dimension to an essay in persuasion which is more political in character. Smith, arguably, was well aware that the cause of the developing conflict in the 1770s was ultimately to be found in the need for improved tax revenues from the colonies, and therefore that the immediate problem was constitutional and political rather than mercantile in character. Smith was cautious in his statements regarding conflicts of interest that were rooted in the Acts of Trade and Navigation. For example, while he did draw attention to the restrictions imposed upon the colonists, he consistently argued that 'they have not hitherto been very hurtful to the colonies' (WN IV. vii. 44), noting further that *in a more advanced state* 'they might be really oppressive and insupportable' (IV. vii. b. 44).

The fact that mercantile regulations were *not* currently the subject of contention may have opened up a further exciting prospect: namely, the possibility of finding a constitutional solution to immediate problems which would at a stroke solve the economic problem that was still to come. Pownall may have been correct in his assessment of the analytical content of Smith's argument, but that does not dispose of the real point, namely that differential rates of growth in the two countries must at some stage generate a need for change. If the current constitutional crisis had anticipated the economic conflict, the solution remained the same, namely an incorporating union. Nor was this a fanciful thesis. In the early 1770s there were still those who believed that union was a feasible option. The first Continental Congress actually debated and rejected by a narrow margin Joseph Galloway's plan for a 'grand legislative union', a proposal that was essentially a variant of Benjamin Franklin's Albany Plan of 1754.

In Smith's eyes, government was one of the parties immediately to be persuaded of the need for change. The fact that an opportunity had indeed been lost is reflected in one of the most consistent strands of argument in the book, namely, Smith's concern with a political system that was dominated by sectional (commercial) interests.

In the case of the colonial relationship, it was Smith's belief that it had been the product of the 'sneaking arts of underling tradesmen'. He added, 'of the greater part of the regulations concerning the colony trade, the merchants who carry it on, it must be observed, have been the principal advisers. We must not wonder, therefore, if, in the greater part of them, their interest has been more considered than either that of the colonies or that of the mother country' (*WN* IV. vii. b. 49). Like Hume, Smith feared 'the oppression of a mercantile republican empire governed by London' (Livingston 1990: 145). As he acidly remarked in one of the most famous passages in the *Wealth of Nations*, 'To found a great empire for the sole purpose of raising up a people of customers, may at first sight appear a project fit only for a nation of shopkeepers. It is however, a project altogether unfit for a nation of shopkeepers, but extremely fit for a nation whose government is influenced by shopkeepers' (*WN* IV. vii. c. 63). The folly that 'fatal experience' had exposed *in 1783* may in the last analysis have been political rather than economic; a fact of which Smith was well aware.

In this political context, Smith's preference for union raises some interesting questions. Did he have in mind a form of association that would create a single economic and political union, an enormous free trade area of the kind that a later generation was to envisage for Europe, but with the advantage of a common language and culture? Or was the union he envisaged designed to generate a position of global dominance for an Anglo-American empire? Whatever the reason, by the time Smith published the *Wealth of Nations* an opportunity had been lost: 'We, on this side of the water, are afraid lest the multitude of American representatives should overturn the balance of the constitution', he wrote, while those 'on the other side of the water are afraid lest their distance from the seat of government might expose them to many oppressions' (*WN* IV. vii. c. 78). His tone had hardened further in his Memorandum on the American War in 1778: '[I]n their present elevation of spirits,' he advised Wedderburn, 'the ulcerated minds of the Americans are not likely to consent to any union even upon terms the most advantageous to themselves' (*Corr.* App. B: 381). In Britain, he wrote, the plan of union 'seems not to be agreeable to any considerable party of men'. He concluded, sadly, that: 'The plan which, if it could be executed, would certainly tend most to the prosperity, to the splendour, and to the duration of the empire, if you except here and there a solitary philosopher like myself, seems scarce to have a single advocate' (*Corr.* App. B: 382).[8] Had the plan succeeded, might later generations have regarded it as an exercise in enlightened mercantilism?

---

[8] The tenor of the argument suggests that Smith differed from another lone voice, David Hume, who 'alone among the British' had been advocating separation from the colonies from as early as 1768. As Hume remarked in a letter to Baron Mure, 'I am an American in my Principles, and wish we would let them alone to govern or misgovern themselves as they think proper: The Affair is of no consequence or of little consequence to us' (Livingston 1990: 143).

It will be evident from the above that Smith's analyses of the problems and opportunities presented by the relationship with America depends heavily on the issues presented by different rates of growth. This theme, which is also illustrated by his treatment of the growth of cities (see Chapter 4 above), had already attracted the attention of David Hume and Sir James Steuart, writers who, however, put the thesis to more general uses, whose implications were not explicitly examined by Smith.

REFERENCES

Andrews, C. M. (1924), *The Colonial Background of the American Revolution* (New Haven), (rev. edns. 1942 and 1961).

Beer, G. L. (1933), *British Colonial Policy, 1754–1765* (New York).

Beloff, M. (1960), *The Debate on the American Revolution*, 2nd edn. (Cambridge).

Benians, E. A. (1923–5), 'Adam Smith's Project of an Empire', *Cambridge Historical Review*, 1.

Campbell, T. D. (1971), *Adam Smith's Science of Morals* (London).

Dickerson, O. (1951), *The Navigation Acts and the American Revolution* (Philadelphia).

Fay, C. R. (1934), 'Adam Smith and the Doctrinal Defeat of the Mercantile System', *Quarterly Journal of Economics*, 48.

Guttridge, G. H. (1932–3), 'Adam Smith on the American Revolution', *American Historical Review*, 38.

Howell, W. S. (1975), 'Adam Smith's Lectures on Rhetoric: An Historical Assessment', in *EAS*.

Koebner, R. (1961), *Empire* (Cambridge).

Livingston, D. W. (1990), 'Hume, English Barbarism and American Independence', in *Scotland and America in the Age of Enlightenment*, ed. R. B. Sher and J. R. Smitten (Edinburgh).

Morris, R. B. (ed.) (1970), *The American Revolution 1763–1783* (London).

Pownall, T. (1776), *A Letter from Governor Pownall to Adam Smith* in *Corr. Appendix A* (London).

Raynor, D., and Skinner, A. S. (1994), 'Sir James Steuart: Nine Letters on the American Conflict, 1775–1778', *William and Mary Quarterly*, 51.

Romani, R. (1993), 'Early Nineteenth-Century European Views on American Growth: The Smithian Legacy', unpublished paper delivered at the colloque 'Adam Smith et l'economie coloniale' (Paris).

Ross, I. S. (1972), *Lord Kames and the Scotland of his Day* (Oxford).

Rutman, D. B. (1971), *The Morning of America 1603–1789* (Boston).

Skinner A. S. (1979), *A System of Social Science: Papers Relating to Adam Smith* (Oxford).

—— (1990), 'Adam Smith and America: The Political Economy of Conflict', in

Scotland and America in the Age of Enlightenment, ed. R. B. Sher and J. R. Smitten (Edinburgh).
Stevens, D. (1975), 'Adam Smith and the Colonial Disturbances', in *EAS*.
Winch, D. (1965), *Classical Political Economy and the Colonies* (London).
——(1978), *Adam Smith's Politics: An Essay in Historiographic Revision* (Cambridge).

PART VI

10
David Hume: Economic Writings

Psychology

Professor Rotwein's valuable introduction[1] to Hume's *Writings on Economics* (1955) has the great merit, *inter alia*, of reminding students of this subject of the central importance of the *Treatise on Human Nature*, and especially of Hume's conviction that

all the sciences have a relation, greater or less, to human nature; and that, however wide any of them seem to run from it, they still return back by one passage or another. Even *Mathematics*, *Natural Philosophy*, and *Natural Religion*, are in some measure dependent on the science of MAN; since they lie under the cognisance of men, and are judged of by their powers and faculties. (*THN* Introduction, 4).

Hume was convinced that, as 'the science of man is the only solid foundation we can give to this science, this science itself must be laid on experience and observation' (Introduction, 7). He concluded:

We must, therefore, glean up our experiments in this science from a cautious observation of human life, and take them as they appear in the common course of the world, by men's behaviour in company, in affairs, and in their pleasures. Where experiments of this kind are judiciously collected and compared, we may hope to establish on them a science which will not be inferior in certainty, and will be much superior in utility, to any other of human comprehension. (*THN* Introduction, 7).

The novelty of the attempt is reflected in a further passage in which Hume observed

In pretending . . . to explain the principles of human nature, we in effect propose a complete system of the sciences, built on a foundation almost entirely new, and the only one upon which they can stand with any security. (*THN* Introduction, 10).

This chapter was originally published under the title 'David Hume: Principles of Political Economy' in *The Cambridge Companion to Hume*, ed. David Fate Norton (1993). Some modifications have been made in the interest of continuity with other chapters in this collection.

[1] Eugene Rotwein provides the most important commentary on Hume's writings (1955: ix–cxi). His edition also incorporates the relevant correspondence between Hume, Montesquieu, Oswald, Kames, Tucker, Turgot, and Morellet in the period 1740–76 (pp. 187–216).

The argument allowed Hume to state a proposition which was to prove profoundly influential in the eighteenth century:

It is universally acknowledged that there is a great uniformity among the actions of men, in all nations and ages, and that human nature remains still the same in its principles and operations. (EHU viii).

Among these constant principles Hume identified 'action, pleasure and indolence' as essential to human happiness but in practice placed most emphasis on the first (where he makes frequent use of the analogy of the game; cf. *THN* II. iii. x). There is a very direct application in the sphere of economics, where Hume noted that, in 'times when industry and the arts flourish, men are kept in perpetual occupation, and enjoy, as their reward, the occupation itself, as well as those pleasures which are the fruit of their labour' (*Essays*, 270).

Self-Interest and the Pursuit of Gain

Hume did much more than merely isolate the importance of the love of action and the desire for gain, in linking the latter to the concepts of vanity and of pride. As he noted, 'We found a vanity upon houses, gardens, equipages, as well as upon personal merits and Accomplishments' (*THN* II. i. ix. 1), although 'the relation which is esteemed the closest, and which, of all others produces most commonly the passion of pride, is that of *property*'. He went on to observe that 'riches are to be considered as the power of acquiring the property of what pleases' (II. i. x. 1, 3):

The very essence of riches consists in the power of acquiring the pleasures and conveniences of life. The very essence of this power consists in the probability of its exercise, and in its causing us to anticipate, by a *true* or *false* reasoning, the very existence of the pleasure. (*THN* II. i. x. 10).

Hume then used the argument to throw an important light on what Smith was to describe as man's drive to better his condition, and in so doing anticipated Smith's argument that this drive generally has a social reference in as much as it is rooted in the desire for approbation. As he put it:

There are few persons that are satisfied with their own character, or genius, or fortune, who are not desirous of showing themselves to the world, and of acquiring the love and approbation of mankind. (*THN* II. ii. 1. 9).

The position was elaborated when Hume argued that

The *satisfaction* we take in the riches of others, and the *esteem* we have for the possessors, may be ascribed to three different causes. *First*, to the objects they possess; such as houses, gardens, equipages, which, being agreeable in themselves, necessarily produce a sentiment of pleasure in every one that either considers or surveys them. *Secondly*, to the expectation of advantage from the rich and powerful by our sharing their possessions. *Thirdly*, to sympathy, which makes us partake of the satisfaction of every one that approaches us. (*THN* II. ii. v. 1).

In practice, Hume placed most emphasis on the role of sympathy:

Now the pleasure of a stranger for whom we have no friendship, pleases us only by sympathy. To this principle, therefore, is owing the beauty which we find in everything that is useful. How considerable a part this is of beauty will easily appear upon reflection. Wherever an object has a tendency to produce pleasure in the possessor, or, in other words, is the proper *cause* of pleasure, it is sure to please the spectator, by a delicate sympathy with the possessor. Most of the works of art are esteemed beautiful, in proportion to their fitness for the use of man; and even many of the productions of nature derive their beauty from that source, handsome and beautiful, on most occasions, is not an absolute, but a relative quality, and pleases us by nothing but its tendency to produce an end that is agreeable. (*THN* III. iii. i. 8).

While Adam Smith offers a critique of Hume's contention that the 'same principle produces, in many instances, our sentiments of morals, as well as those of beauty' (*TMS* IV), there is no doubt that he accepted (and indeed elaborated upon) Hume's argument in respect of its economic applications.

Self-Interest and Constraint

Again, just as Smith was to do, Hume drew attention to the associated problem of social order which arises from the active pursuit of gain: 'This avidity alone, of acquiring goods and possessions for ourselves and our nearest friends, is insatiable, perpetual, universal, and extremely destructive of society.' He recognized that 'Benevolence to strangers is too weak' adequately to restrain our interested affections, and continued:

There is no passion, therefore, capable of controlling the interested affection, but the very affection itself, by an alteration in its direction. Now this alteration necessarily must take place upon the least reflection; since it is evident that the passion is much better satisfied by its restraint than by its liberty, and that, in preserving society, we make much greater advances in acquiring possessions, than in the solitary and forlorn state which must follow upon violence and an universal licence. (*THN* III. ii. ii. 12, 13).

Hence the importance of justice as a basic precondition of social order:

Here then is a proposition, which, I think, may be regarded as certain, *that it is only from the selfishness and confined generosity of man, along with the scanty provision nature had made for his wants, that justice derives its origin.* (*THN* III. ii. ii. 18).

Hume's conclusion follows in a way that links this argument with the earlier account of sympathy and of the pursuit of gain:

Upon the whole, then, we are to consider this distinction between justice and injustice, as having two different foundations, viz. that of *interest*, when men observe that it is impossible to live in society without restraining themselves by certain rules; and that of *morality*, when this interest is once observed, and men receive a pleasure from the view of such actions as tend to the peace of society, and an uneasiness from such as are contrary to it. It is the voluntary convention and artifice of man which makes the first interest take place; and therefore those laws of justice are so far to be considered as *artificial*. After that interest is once established and acknowledged, the sense of morality in the observance of these rules follows *naturally*, and of itself; though it is certain that it is also augmented by a new *artifice*, and that the public instructions of politicians, and the private education of parents, contribute to the giving us a sense of honour and duty, in the strict regulation of our actions with regard to the properties of others. (*THN* III. ii. vi. 11).

As the reference to politicians perhaps implies, the final condition for social order, and the one that is essential to the conduct of economic affairs, is some system of government. This argument is developed in the *Treatise of Human Nature* (III. ii. viii, 'Of the Origin of Government'). It is essentially a logical argument, although Hume was well aware of the need to provide an institutional and historical dimension.

The Use of History

While it is impossible adequately to review Hume's use of history in the present context, the student of his writings on economics should be aware that the great bulk of Hume's published work was historical and that he was convinced that 'history is not only a valuable part of knowledge, but opens the door to many other parts, and affords materials to most of the sciences'. It is an invention that 'extends our experience to all past ages, and to the most distant nations' (*Essays*, 566). Looked at in this way, historical studies afford invaluable information with regard to the principles of human nature and to the fact that the expression of these principles must be profoundly affected by the socio-economic environment that may happen to exist and by changes in habit, customs, and manners.

To the economist, the most interesting branches of the *History* (1754–62) may initially be found in the appendices and miscellaneous transactions which are introduced throughout the work, but which at the same time conform to a purpose which is also a feature of Voltaire's history of Louis XIV. The purpose of these sections of Hume's *History* was to 'take a general survey of the age, so far as it regards manners, finances, arms, commerce, arts and sciences. The chief use of history is, that it affords materials for disquisitions of this nature; and it seems the duty of the historian to point out the proper inferences and conclusions' (*History*, iv. 140).

Hume applied this procedure to his account of the period from Caesar to Henry VII (1762), the history of the House of Tudor (1759), the period to the Revolution of 1688 (1757), and to the reigns of James I and Charles I (1754). Quite apart from the intrinsic value of the material, Hume's account is informed throughout by an attempt to understand specific policies in their institutional, economic, and political settings.

At the same time, it has to be recognised that the *History* was concerned primarily with the broader theme of the study of civilization and with the interconnections that exist between the growth of commerce, the changing form of government, and liberty. Hume's concern was with the origins and nature of the present establishments in Europe, where the economic dimension was only one part of a wider whole.

The relevance of these positions for the contemporary understanding of Hume's treatment of economic theory and policy will be readily apparent. It should also be recalled that the essay 'Of Refinement in the Arts' is really an 'abridged version' of those aspects of the *History* that we have briefly touched upon in this section (Forbes 1970: 39).

THE ESSAYS

It is usual to identify nine essays, eight of which date from 1752. (The ninth 'Of the Jealousy of Trade', was written in 1758.) They are *essays*, rather than a treatise, which from one point of view can be seen to address separate subjects. Yet it should be noted at the outset that Hume believed economic questions to be amenable to scientific treatment largely as a result of his belief in the constant principles of human nature and the emphasis he gave to self interest. In a famous passage, he asserted that 'it is certain that general principles, if just and sound, must always prevail in the general course of things, though they may fail in particular cases; and it is the chief business of philosophers to regard the general course of things' (*Essays*, 254). He also noted that there are areas of experience where generalization is difficult:

What depends upon a few persons is, in a great measure, to be ascribed to chance, or to secret and unknown causes; What arises from a great number, may often be accounted for by determinate and known causes. (Essays, 112).

Hence the point that the 'domestic and gradual revolutions of a state must be a more proper subject of reasoning and observation than the foreign and violent'. Hence too the argument that it is easier to account for commercial phenomena than for the rise and progress of the sciences:

'Avarice, or the desire of gain, is an universal passion, which operates at all times, in all places, and upon all persons' (*Essays*, 113).

Secondly, it should be observed that the separate essays show a unity of purpose (Rotwein 1955; Hutchison 1988), all of which illustrate the 'fundamental propositions' that have been outlined above. It is this unity of purpose and method that enables us to identify three major themes: historical dynamics, the use of the historical method, and the deployment of both in the treatment of economic development and international trade.

Historical Dynamics and the Exchange Economy

The theme is addressed primarily in the essays 'Of Commerce' and 'Of Refinement in the Arts', where it is suggested that

The bulk of every state may be divided into *husbandmen* and *manufacturers*. The former are employed in the culture of the land; the latter work up the materials furnished by the former, into all the commodities which are necessary or ornamental to human life. As soon as men quit their savage state, where they live chiefly by hunting and fishing, they must fall into these two classes; though the arts of agriculture employ *at first* the most numerous part of the society. (*Essays*, 256).

In an early anticipation of the theory of stages, Hume continued to note that 'Where manufactures and mechanic arts are not cultivated the bulk of the people must apply themselves to agriculture' in a situation where there is little stimulus to change. In this situation, men have no temptation to 'encrease their skill and industry' since they cannot exchange any superfluities for other commodities, as a result of which the 'greater part of the land remains uncultivated. What is cultivated, yields not its utmost for want of skill and assiduity in the farmers.' In contrast, Hume continued,

Everything in the world is purchased by labour; and our passions are the only causes of labour. When a nation abounds in manufactures and mechanic arts, the proprietors of land, as well as the farmers, study agriculture as a science, and redouble their industry and attention. The superfluity, which arises from their labour, is not lost; but is exchanged with manufactures for those commodities which men's luxury now makes them covet. (*Essays*, 261).

In short, Hume was suggesting that there is likely to be a gradual progression to a situation where the two main sectors of activity are fully interdependent, supported by merchants who were described as 'one of the most useful races of men, who serve as agents between those parts of the state, that are wholly unacquainted, and ignorant of each other's necessities' (*Essays*, 300). The argument has its roots in Hume's deployment of the thesis that men have natural wants which gradually extend in a self-sustaining spiral. It was this thesis that Mandeville addressed with such amusing consequences and which drew from Hume the comment that to 'imagine, that the gratifying of any sense, or the indulging of any delicacy in meat, drink, or apparel, is of itself a vice, can never enter a head, that is not disordered by the frenzies of enthusiasm' (*Essays*, 268). Smith concurred (*TMS* vii, ii. 4, see Chapter 3 above).

But there is more to the argument than a concentration on a gradual institutional change; it was also Hume's view that the emergence of what came to be known as the stage of commerce would induce an accelerating rate of change arising from changes in habits and manners[2]—notably by encouraging the desire for gain and by giving progressively increasing scope to man's active disposition. This argument is further supported by a passage from the essay 'Of Interest':

There is no craving or demand of the human mind more constant and insatiable than that for exercise and employment; and this desire seems the foundation of most of our passions and pursuits. Deprive a man of all business and serious occupation, he runs restless from one amusement to another; and the weight and oppression, which he feels from idleness, is so great, that he forgets the ruin which must follow him from his immoderate expences. Give him a more harmless way of employing his mind or body, he is satisfied, and feels no longer that insatiable thirst after pleasure. But if the employment you give him be lucrative, especially if the profit be attached to every particular exertion of industry, he has gain so often in his eye, that he acquires, by degrees, a passion for it, and knows no such pleasure as that of seeing the daily encrease of his fortune. (*Essays*, 300–1).

Hume also made the point that the historical process of economic development had been stimulated by the discovery of gold (*Essays*, 286). It was in this context that he drew attention to the rapid rate of economic growth in the reign of Charles I (*History*, vi. 148), and especially in the period 'from the restoration to the revolution' (vi. 537).

The essays are also remarkable for the emphasis Hume gave to other, non-economic, advantages which accrue from the process of historical development:

the minds of men, being once roused from their lethargy, and put into a fermentation, turn themselves on all sides, and carry improvements into every art and science. Profound ignorance is totally banished, and men enjoy the privilege of rational creatures, to think as well as to act, to cultivate the pleasures of the mind as well as those of the body. (*Essays*, 271).

Hume continued to note that the 'more arts advance, the more sociable men become'; they 'flock into cities; love to receive and communicate

---

[2] The historical variability of moral standards is a feature of the essay 'A Dialogue'; see Rotwein (1955: 19n. and cf. *TMS*, v, 'Of the Influence of Custom and Fashion upon the Sentiments of Moral Approbation and Disapprobation'.

knowledge' (*Essays*, 271). He also emphasized the importance of developments that might be described as sociological and political in character. In a notable passage from the *History*, which described miscellaneous transactions in the reign of Henry VII, Hume observed:

The common people no longer maintained in vicious idleness by their superiors, were obliged to learn some calling or industry, and became both useful to themselves and to others. And it must be acknowledged, in spite of those who declaim so violently against the arts, refinements or what they are pleased to call luxury, that, as much as the industrious tradesman is both a better man and a better citizen than one of those idle retainers, who formerly depended on the great families; as much is the life of a modern nobleman more laudable than that of an ancient baron. (*History*, iii. 76–7).

The theme is elaborated in the essay of 'Refinement of the Arts', where Hume went on to make the point that, 'where luxury nourishes commerce and industry, the peasants by a proper cultivation of the land, become rich and independent; while the tradesmen and merchants acquire a share of the property, and draw authority and consideration to that middling rank of men, who are the best and firmest basis of public liberty' (*Essays*, 277).[3] This development was associated in turn with major constitutional changes, at least in the case of England:

The lower house is the support of our popular government; and all the world acknowledges, that it owed its chief influence and consideration to the encrease of commerce, which threw such a balance of property into the hands of the commons. How inconsistent then is it to blame so violently a refinement in the arts, and to represent it as the bane of liberty and public spirit. (*Essays*, 278).

This environment, buttressed by 'equal laws', further enhanced the possibilities for economic growth.[4] It is interesting to note in this context that Hume offered a critique of egalitarianism:

however specious these ideas of *perfect* equality may seem, they are really, at bottom, *impractical*; and were they not so, would be extremely pernicious to human society. Render possessions ever so equal, men's different degrees of art, care and industry will immediately break that equality. (ECPM iii).

[3] Cf. *History*, iv. 132, where it is remarked in the context of the reign of James I that 'Great riches, acquired by commerce, were more rare, and had not, as yet, been able to confound all ranks of men, and render money the chief foundation of distinction.'
[4] In the essay 'Of Commerce', it is remarked that 'Every person, if possible, ought to enjoy the fruits of his labour, in full possession of all the necessaries, and many of the conveniences of life.' Hume went on to note that 'In this circumstance consists the great advantage of England above any nation at present in the world or that appear in the records of any story.' The link between commerce and liberty is one of the themes developed in the essay 'Of Civil Liberty'.

The Historical or Institutional Method

Hume's interest in the historical process led him quite naturally to develop a distinctive technique in dealing with purely economic questions, a technique that caused him to give prominence to the importance of the institutional background and in particular to the role of customs and manners. While the technique informs all the essays, three in particular may be noted in the present context; the essays on population, on money, and on interest.

In the long essay 'Of the Populousness of Ancient Nations', a work that has scarcely received the attention it deserves, Hume addressed a proposition that had been advanced by Robert Wallace, namely, that population levels had been higher in ancient than in modern times.[5] In dealing with this question, Hume argued that 'there is in all men, both male and female, a desire and power of generation more active than is ever universally exerted' (*Essays*, 381). Therefore, in addressing the question at issue it is necessary to know the 'situation of society' and to compare 'both the *domestic* and *political* situation of these two periods, in order to judge of the facts by their moral causes' (p. 383).

In deciding in favour of modern society, Hume drew attention to the use of slavery in ancient times as 'in general disadvantageous both to the happiness and populousness of mankind' (p. 396), pointing also to the incidence of military conflict and political instability. But perhaps the most striking aspect of the argument is the attention given to the point that 'Trade, manufactures, industry, were no where, in former ages, so flourishing as they are at present in Europe' (p. 416). Population is ultimately limited not just by political factors, but also by the food supply, and this in turn by the type of economic organization prevailing. 'I grant, that agriculture is the species of industry chiefly requisite to the subsistence of multitudes; and it is possible, that this industry may flourish, even where manufactures and other arts are unknown or neglected' (p. 419). But, he added:

The most natural way, surely, of encouraging husbandry, is first, to excite other kinds of industry, and thereby afford the labourer a ready market for his commodities, and a return of such goods as may contribute to his pleasure and enjoyment. This method is infallible and universal; and, as it prevails more in modern government than in the ancient, it affords a presumption of the superior populousness of the former. (*Essays*, 420).

---

[5] Robert Wallace was the author of the *Dissertation on the Numbers of Mankind in Ancient and Modern Times* (1753). Hume claimed to have encouraged Wallace to publish as the result of the appearance of his own essay (Rotwein 1955: 184). Hume also cites Montesquieu, with whom he corresponded on the subject (*Essays*, 379–80). For a summary of the theory of population in this period, see Schumpeter (1954: 250–8).

There is thus no simple relationship between population and the food supply; everything depends on the form of economic organization, on the degree to which sectors of activity are interdependent, and on the degree to which men are motivated by the desire for gain.

The same basic theme emerges in the essay 'Of Money', where Hume rejected the conventional wisdom that money can be regarded as wealth (*Essays*, 281) and stated the famous relationship between changes in the money supply and the general price level.[6] Less familiar is the point that Hume consistently contrasted the situation of a primitive economy with a more sophisticated version. It is, he argued, 'the proportion between the circulating money, and the commodities in the market, which determines the prices' (p. 291). In the primitive economy,

we must consider that, in the first and more uncultivated ages of any state, ere fancy has confounded her wants with those of nature, men, content with the produce of their own fields, or with those rude improvements which they themselves can work upon them, have little occasion for exchange, at least for money, which, by agreement, is the common measure of exchange. (*Essays*, 291).

In a more advanced state of society,

Great undertakers, and manufacturers, and merchants, arise in every commodity; and these can conveniently deal in nothing but specie. And consequently, in this situation of society, the coin enters into many more contracts, and by that means is much more employed than in the former. (*Essays*, 291).

The changed form of economic organization heralds a change in manners by giving greater scope to individual effort, and it must therefore massively increase the supply of commodities that are subject to exchange. Hume thus concluded that, although prices in Europe had risen since the discoveries in the Americas and elsewhere, these prices were in fact much lower than the increase in the money supply might of itself suggest:

And no other satisfactory reason can be given, why all prices have not risen to a much more exorbitant height, except that which is derived from a change of customs and manners. Besides that more commodities are produced by additional industry, the same commodities come more to market, after men depart from their ancient simplicity of manners. And though this increase has not been equal to that of money, it has, however, been considerable, and has preserved the proportion between coin and commodities nearer the ancient standard. (*Essays*, 292).

The essay 'Of Interest', as Hume noted, provides 'an instance of a like fallacy . . . where a collateral effect is taken for a cause, and where a

[6] The initial statement of the relationship occurs in a letter to Montesquieu, dated 10 April 1749 (*HL* i. 136–8). For a summary of the treatment of the quantity theory of money, see Schumpeter (1954: 311–17).

consequence is ascribed to the plenty of money; though it be really owing to a change of the manners and customs of a people', namely, that a large supply of money would be associated with low rates of interest. The argument is that high interest rates arise from three circumstances: 'A great demand for borrowing; little riches to supply that demand, and great profits arising from commerce', while a low rate of interest will reflect the opposite circumstances (*Essays*, 297).

In the primitive economy, Hume contended, there will be little evidence of frugality but often a considerable demand for borrowing for the purpose of consumption, a state of habits and manners that will be consistent with high rates of interest. In the modern economy, there may be high levels of demand for funds to be used for productive purposes, but also an enhanced supply of such funds owing to the fact that

Commerce encreases industry, by conveying it readily from one member of the state to another, and allowing none of it to perish or become useless. It encreases frugality, by giving occupation to men, and employing them in the arts of gain, which soon engages their affections, and removes all relish for pleasure and expence. It is an infallible consequence of all industrious professions, to beget frugality, and make the love of gain prevail over the love of pleasure. (*Essays*, 301).

In short, the increase of commerce 'by a necessary consequence, raises a great number of lenders, and by that means produces lowness of interest' (*Essays*, 302). This is accompanied by a further tendency to reduce the rate of profit: 'when commerce has become extensive, and employs large stocks, there must arise rivalship among the merchants, which diminish the profits of trade'. Hume thus concluded that the most important single factor was not simply the supply of money, but a change in manners and in the form of economic organization. Interest, he concluded, is 'the barometer of the state, and its lowness is a sign almost infallible of the flourishing condition of a people' (p. 303).[7]

The technique just considered counsels caution in offering generalizations in economics in that the way in which economic relationships unfold must be affected by manners and by the institutional structure that prevails. It is therefore important to note Hume's awareness of a further point, namely, that economic relationships will be affected by the condition of an economy even where the institutional structure is given. The point is made consistently but is aptly illustrated by passages from the essay 'Of Money'. As Hume noted,

[7] Rotwein has drawn attention to the fact that both Dudley North and Joseph Massie had already advanced a 'real capital' theory of interest (1955: 49n). Massie published *An Essay on the Governing Causes of the Natural Rate of Interest* (1750). See Hutchison (1988: 239) and Schumpeter (1954: 327–34.

It seems a maxim almost self-evident, that the prices of everything depend on the proportion between commodities and money, and that any considerable alteration in either has the same effect, either of heightening or lowering the price. Encrease the commodities, they become cheaper; encrease the money, they rise in their value. (*Essays*, 290).

A statement of this kind can be interpreted to mean that an increase in the money supply will generate a change in the price level in cases where resources are fully employed, while a similar change in the supply of money could be expected to result in an increase in the output of commodities where there are unemployed resources. Hume's analysis of the process by virtue of which changes in the money supply affect the economy embraces both results and at the same time takes the argument a step further:

Here a Set of manufacturers or merchants, we shall suppose, who have received returns of gold and silver which they sent to CADIZ. They are thereby enabled to employ more workmen than formerly, who never dream of demanding higher wages, but are glad of employment from such good paymasters. If workmen become scarce, the manufacturer gives higher wages, but at first requires an encrease of labour; and this is willingly submitted to by the artisan, who can now eat and drink better, to compensate his additional toil and fatigue. He carries his money to market, where he finds everything at the same price as formerly, but returns with greater quantity and of better kinds, for the use of his family. The farmer and gardener, finding that all their commodities are taken off, apply themselves with alacrity to raising more; and at the same time can afford to take better and more cloths from their tradesmen, whose price is the same as formerly, and their industry only whetted by so much new gain. It is easy to trace the money in its progress through the whole commonwealth; where we shall find, that it must first quicken the diligence of every individual, before it encrease the price of labour. (*Essays*, 286–7).

Hume added that from 'the whole of this reasoning we may conclude, that it is no manner of consequence, with regard to the domestic happiness of a state, whether money be in a greater or less quantity. The good policy of the magistrate consists only in keeping it, if possible, still encreasing; because, by that means, he keeps alive a spirit of industry in the nation, and encreases the stock of labour, in which consists all real power and riches' (*Essays*, 288).

A rather different appreciation of the point was to emerge in the course of the discussion of international trade.

International Trade

The final major theme in Hume's thought relates to the problem of international trade, a theme that, here as elsewhere, unfolds at a number of levels.

To begin with, Hume drew attention to the general benefits of foreign trade. In the essay 'Of Commerce', for example, he made the point that, if 'we consult history, we shall find that in most nations, foreign trade had preceded any refinement in home manufactures, and given birth to domestic luxury'. In the same context he made a point, which also appears in Smith's analysis in book III of the *Wealth of Nations*, when drawing attention to induced changes in taste and to the point that imitation leads domestic manufactures 'to emulate the foreign in their improvements'.[8] The argument was repeated in the essay on the 'Jealousy of Trade':

Compare the situation of Great Britain at present, with what it was two centuries ago. All the arts both of agriculture and manufactures were then extremely rude and imperfect. Every improvement which we have since made, has arisen from our imitation of foreigners; and we ought so far to esteem it happy, that they had previously made advances in arts and ingenuity. (*Essays*, 328).

This sentiment sets the tone of the essay, added in 1758, in which Hume explicitly criticized what he took to be a characteristic feature of mercantile policy:

Nothing is more usual, among states which have made some advances in commerce, than to look on the progress of their neighbours with a suspicious eye, to consider all trading states as their rivals, and to suppose that it is impossible for any of them to flourish, but at their expense. In opposition to this narrow and malignant opinion, I will venture to assert, that the encrease of riches and commerce in any one nation, instead of hurting, commonly promotes the riches and commerce of all its neighbours; and that a state can scarcely carry its trade and industry very far, where all the surrounding states are buried in ignorance, sloth and barbarism. (*Essays*, 328).

In a passage that may well have struck a chord with J. B. Say, who first formulated his famous law in exactly this context (Skinner 1967), Hume continued:

The encrease of domestic industry lays the foundation of foreign commerce. Where a great number of commodities are raised and perfected for the home market, there will always be found some which can be exported with advantage. But if our neighbours have no art or cultivation, they cannot take them; because they will have nothing to give in exchange. In this respect, states are in the same condition as individuals. A single man can scarcely be industrious, where his fellow citizens are idle. (*Essays*, 329).

[8] *History*, iii. 328, refers to the jealousy against foreign merchants in the reign of Henry VIII: 'The Parliament had done better to have encouraged foreign merchants and artizans to come over in greater numbers to England; which might have excited the emulation of the natives, and have improved their skills.'

He went on:

Nor needs any state entertain apprehensions, that their neighbours will improve to such a degree in every art and manufacture, as to have no demand for them. Nature, by giving a diversity of geniuses, climates, and soils to different nations, has secured their mutual intercourse and commerce, as long as they remain industrious and civilised. (*Essays*, 329).

Hume concluded the essay with a passage which must have attracted the attention of Adam Smith:

I shall therefore venture to acknowledge, that, not only as a man, but as a British subject, I pray for the flourishing commerce of Germany, Spain, Italy, and even France itself. I am at least certain, that Great Britain, and all those nations, would flourish more, did their sovereigns and ministers adopt such enlarged and benevolent sentiments towards each other. (*Essays*, 331).

The second aspect of Hume's analysis supports the position just stated on grounds that are essentially technical. Building upon the analysis of the essay 'Of Money', Hume examined the case of two or more economies with no unemployed resources with a view to demonstrating the futility of the mercantile preoccupation with a positive balance of trade. Against this, Hume contended that a net inflow of gold would inevitably raise prices in the domestic economy, while a loss of specie would reduce the general price level elsewhere—thus improving the competitive position in the latter case and reducing it in the former. In the essay 'Of the Balance of Trade', he concluded that 'money, in spite of the absurd jealousy of princes and states, has brought itself nearly to a level' (*Essays*, 314), just as 'All water, wherever it communicates, remains always at a level' (p. 312).

From these principles we may learn what judgement we ought to form of those numberless bars, obstructions, and imposts, which all nations of Europe, and none more than England, have put upon trade; from an exhorbitant desire of amassing money, which will never heap up beyond its level, while it circulates; or from an ill-grounded apprehension of losing their specie, which will never sink below it. Could anything scatter our riches, it would be such impolitic contrivances. (*Essays*, 324).

The third dimension to Hume's treatment of foreign trade is much more complex. It is based upon the premiss that countries have different characteristics and different rates of growth, thus opening up a different and distinctive policy position as compared with those so far considered, one that significantly qualifies the doctrines of free trade and of the specie-flow as a result of formally allowing for variations in economic performance.

The *presence* of an argument that reflects a judgement to the effect that economic conditions are likely to be diverse is not perhaps surprising in a writer such as Hume, whose perspective was Euro-centric rather than Anglo-centric. While critical of Montesquieu's thesis regarding the role of physical factors, Hume was none the less conscious of the fact that different countries could have different factor endowments and that climate could have some influence upon economic activity (*Essays*, 267). But there is also a sense in which the rich country–poor country thesis reflects strands of thought which we have already identified in dealing with the comparative and dynamic branches of Hume's argument.

It is worth recalling in this context that the use of the historical method involved the *comparison* of different economic types, while the dynamic element draws attention to the importance of individual effort and to an accelerating rate of change as institutions and manners themselves change. On the one hand, the reader is reminded of the phenomenon of a 'diversity of geniuses, climate and soil', while on the other attention is drawn to the point that the extent to which men apply 'art, care and industry' may vary in one society over time and between different societies at a given point in time. Other factors that will affect the rate of growth and cause variations in rates of growth in different communities include the form of government and the degree to which public policies such as trade regulations, taxes, and debt are deployed with intelligence.

Hume illustrated this new phase of the problem by referring to the issue of regional imbalance (a concern he shared with Josiah Tucker), citing the case of London and Yorkshire (*Essays*, 354). He also makes the interesting point in the essay entitled 'That Politics May be Reduced to a Science' that, 'though free governments have been commonly the most happy for those who partake of that freedom; yet they are the most ruinous and oppressive to their provinces' (pp. 18–19). The regional dimension is just as relevant to the rich country–poor country debate as is the international, although it was upon the latter that Hume chose to place most emphasis.

Hume's treatment of the performance of the modern economy, especially in the context of the essays 'Of Money' and 'Of Interest', implies that an increase in productivity may give the developed economy an advantage in terms of the price of manufactures. He also recognized that an inflow of gold in the context of a growing economy need not generate adverse price effects. As he observed in a letter to James Oswald, 'I never meant to say that money, in all countries which communicate, must necessarily be on a level, but only on a level proportioned to their people, industry and commodities' (*HL* i. 142–3). He added, 'I agree with you, that the increase of money, if not too sudden, naturally increases people and industry' (*HL* i. 142–3).

Looked at from this point of view, Hume might have agreed with Tucker's belief that 'the poor country, according to my apprehension, can never overtake the rich, unless it be through the fault and mismanagement of the latter' (quoted in Rotwein 1955: 205). Hume had already noted, in the essay 'Of Money', that 'Where one nation has gotten the start of another in trade, it is very difficult for the latter to regain the ground it has lost; because of the superior industry and skill of the former, and the greater stocks, of which its merchants are possessed, and which enable them to trade on so much smaller profits' (*Essays*, 283). But he also observed that the historical increase in the quantity of money which had 'quickened diligence' could also result in a general increase in the price level which could be disadvantageous in the context of international trade. The advantages enjoyed by a relatively advanced economy, he continued,

are compensated, in some measure, by the low price of labour in every nation which has not an extensive commerce, and does not much abound in gold and silver. Manufactures, therefore gradually shift their places, leaving those countries and provinces which they have already enriched, and flying to others, whither they are allured by the cheapness of provisions and labour; till they have enriched these also, and are again banished by the same causes. And, in general, we may observe, that the dearness of everything, from plenty of money, is a disadvantage, which attends an established commerce, and sets bounds to it in every country, by enabling the poorer states to undersell the richer in all foreign markets. (*Essays*, 283–4).

Hume clearly felt that these trends were beginning to manifest themselves in England, which feels 'some disadvantages in foreign trade by the high price of labour, which is in part the effect of the riches of their artisans, as well as of the plenty of money' (*Essays*, 265). The position he was striving to formulate was well put in a letter to Lord Kames in the course of a discussion of the advantages enjoyed by rich countries:

The question is, whether these advantages can go on, increasing trade *in infinitum*, or whether they do not come at least to a *ne plus ultra*, and check themselves, by begetting disadvantages, which at first retard, and at last finally stop their progress.

He continued:

It was never surely the intention of Providence, that any one nation should be a monopoliser of wealth: and the growth of all bodies, artificial as well as natural, is stopped by internal causes, derived from their enormous size and greatness. Great empires, great cities, great commerce, all of them receive a check, not from accidental events, but necessary principles. (*HL* i. 271–2, Letter of 4 March 1758).

Such sentiments echo a point that had already been made in the essay, 'Of Money': 'There seems to be a happy concurrence of causes in human affairs, which checks the growth of trade and riches, and hinders them from being confined entirely to one people' (*Essays*, 283).[9]

The possibilities that Hume outlined are not without their implications for economic policy. A relatively backward economy might, for example, find it in its interest to adopt a policy of protection for infant industries. More advanced economies confronting a general loss of markets might have to adopt a policy of protection in order to sustain the level of employment, a situation that Hume regarded with some equanimity in noting that, 'as foreign trade is not the most material circumstance, it is not to be put in competition with the happiness of so many millions' (*Essays*, 265).

While there is in Hume's writings a marked presumption in favour of free trade, it was also recognized that policy must always be related to the circumstances that prevail, a perspective that is entirely consistent with that adopted in dealing with questions of a more purely analytical nature.

The reference to economic policy in these concluding pages serves to remind us of other aspects of Hume's contribution. As noted in the discussion of 'historical dynamics', Hume's tone is thoroughly optimistic in the sense that he traces a series of institutional changes whose net result is to give increasing scope to man's active disposition and in particular to the pursuit of riches.

This vision of the future is however qualified by the introduction of the classic eighteenth-century thesis of growth and decay, manifesting itself in the belief that mature economies may confront constraints to their further development. A further qualification emerges in the discussion of public credit, which Hume believed to be a characteristic feature of the modern state. In this connection, Hume notes the following dangers, First, 'national debts cause a mighty confluence of people and riches to the capital, by the great sums, levied in the provinces to pay the interest'. Secondly, public stocks, 'being a kind of paper-credit, have all the disadvantages attending that species of money'.[10] Thirdly, holders of this kind of stock 'have no connections with the state' and can enjoy their revenue in any part of the globe'; they are a group liable to

[9] The rich country–poor country issue was the subject of considerable debate. See e.g. James Oswald to Hume, 10 October 1749 (Rotwein 1955: 190–6) where it is argued, *inter alia*, that rich countries are likely to enjoy continuing advantages. Hume took issue with this position in a letter to Oswald dated 1 November 1750 (*HL* i. 142–4). The topic is also addressed in correspondence between Hume and Kames (*HL* i. 270–1) and Josiah Tucker and Kames (Rotwein 1955: 202–4).

[10] Doubts are expressed frequently, e.g. in the essays 'Of Money' (*Essays*, 284) and 'Of the Balance of Trade' (p. 317). These concerns reflect the spectre of John Law (*Money and Trade Considered*, 1705), whose position was echoed in part by Bishop Berkeley (*Querist*, 1735–7). It is interesting to note that both writers were concerned with the problems of underdeveloped economies (Hutchison 1988: 148).

250 *David Hume: Economic Writings*

'sink into the lethargy of a stupid and pampered luxury, without spirit, ambition, or enjoyment'. Fourthly, this form of wealth conveys 'no hereditary authority or credit to the possessor; and by this means, the several ranks of men, which form a kind of independent magistracy in a state, instituted by the hand of nature, are entirely lost; and every man in authority derives his influence from the commission alone of the sovereign'. Hume concluded that circumstances could arise which would offset the political and constitutional advantages that had been emphasized in 'Of Refinement in the Arts':

No expedient remains for preventing or suppressing insurrections, but mercenary armies: No expedient at all remains for resisting tyranny: Elections are swayed by bribery and corruption alone: And the middle power between king and people being totally removed, a grievous despotism must infallibly prevail. (*Essays*, 357–8).

CONCLUSION

It is a now commonplace to suggest that Smith endeavoured to link philosophy, history, and economics as part of the grand plan announced in the closing pages of the first edition of *the Theory of Moral Sentiments* and repeated in the advertisement to the sixth and last edition of that work. But when we take the *Treatise of Human Nature* in conjunction with the *Essays*, it becomes apparent that the outlines of the model had already been established by Hume. As he noted in the advertisement to the *Treatise*, Hume saw a close link between his treatment of the 'Understanding and Passions' and the analysis of 'Morals, Politics and Criticism, which will complete this Treatise of Human Nature'.

It is important to note that Adam Smith had a close knowledge of Hume's philosophy and that Dugald Stewart should have concluded that the 'Political Discourses of Mr Hume were evidently of greater use to Mr Smith than any other book that had appeared prior to his lectures' (Stewart, IV. 24). It is equally noteworthy that Smith should have acknowledged Hume's historical analysis of the links between commerce and liberty. Smith would have agreed with the view that Hume 'deserves to be remembered . . . for his more fundamental attempts to incorporate economics into a broader science of human experience' (Rotwein 1955: p. cxi).

But Smith's formal economic analysis differs from that of Hume (and of Steuart), partly because it was finally developed after the appearance of some of the great systematic performances of the period. Notable among these is Richard Cantillon's *Essai sur la Nature du Commerce en General*, written in the 1730s but not published until 1755. This work was rediscovered by the economist W. S. Jevons in 1881 and has justly been described by its editor, Henry Higgs, as 'A statue silted by the sands of time' (Cantillon 1931: 365). Cantillon's teaching was disseminated, in part, by the Marquis de Mirabeau in the *Ami des Hommes* (1756) and had a profound influence on the Physiocrats (Higgs 1897; Meek 1962; see Chapter 6 above). The most notable of the group include, as we have seen, Quesnay, whose *Tableau Economique* (1757) provided a coherent account of a macroeconomic model, and Turgot, whose *Reflections on the Formation and Distribution of Riches* dates from 1766.

Adam Smith was to object that the members of the Physiocratic School 'all follow implicitly, and without any sensible variation, the doctrine of Mr. Quesnai' (*WN* IV. ix. 38). Perhaps with this in mind, Hume in 1769 wrote to the Abbe Morellet:

I hope that in your work you will thunder them [the Physiocrats], and crush them, and pound them, and reduce them to dust and ashes! They are, indeed, the set of men the most chimerical and most arrogant that now exist, since the annihilation of the Sorbonne. I ask your pardon for saying so, as I know you belong to that venerable body. I wonder what could engage our friend, M. Turgot, to herd among them, I mean, among the economists. (*HL* ii. 205).

But the truth is that writers such as Quesnay and Turgot produced a model of capital-using system wherein all magnitudes were dated and in which a number of sectors of activity were featured. In addition, the relevant socio-economic groups were presented as being fully interdependent. Hume's essays do not compare with the analytical contributions of the Physiocrats.

That being said, it must be noted that Hume made specific contributions in the fields of population and of money (see Vickers 1960), especially in the context of the quantity theory and of the analysis of the specie-flow—where his work 'remained substantially unchallenged until the mid-twenties of this century' (Schumpeter 1954: 367). Hume also succeeded in establishing a relationship between the production of commodities and the level of aggregate demand which is more commonly associated with the work of J. B. Say. Certainly, Hume's analysis of the sectoral division of labour, his treatment of the theory of population, and his consideration of international trade separately and severally prompt a conclusion which, in the words of Say, 'may at first sight appear paradoxical, viz. that it is production which opens a demand for products' (see Chapter 7 above, n. 8).

If the essays do not constitute a single treatise, they do disclose evidence of systematic treatment, as this chapter has endeavoured to show. Here the most important single feature is to be found in the use of history and of the historical method, where Hume consistently sought to link economic *relationships* with the environment and the state of manners. This position was to find another expression in the work of the German Historical School and of the American Institutionalists (cf. Rogin 1956). In the present context, it is also important in that the technique is different from that later adopted by Adam Smith. In Smith's hands, the history of civil society is essential for our understanding of the exchange economy and of the social and political environment it may produce. But here, history is the *preface* to political economy rather than integral to the treatment. In the event, Smith did not use the historical method in dealing with economic questions:

One may say that, despite its pronounced emphasis on economic development, Smith's approach to its more general aspects is less basically genetic or evolutionary than Hume's. . . . With regard particularly to his treatment of the theoretical issues of political economy, Smith clearly exhibits the tendency to abstract from the historical influence which was so characteristic of Ricardo and the later classical economists. (Rotwein 1955: cix; cf. Hutchison 1988: 213–14).

A further point of interest to the modern economist relates to Hume's systematic comparison of different economic states and his concern with the process of transition between them, a procedure that throws an important light on the problems of economic and social development. So too is the concern with international trade where trade takes place between economies with different characteristics and different rates of growth. The argument effectively introduced what Hont has described as the 'rich country–poor country' debate, which was also addressed by, among others, Josiah Tucker, Robert Wallace, and Sir James Steuart (Hont 1983: ch. 11). Such a perspective means that *policy* recommendations must always be related to the circumstances that prevail. Joseph Schumpeter's description of the work done by the contemporary Italian economist Ferdinando Galiani (see Hutchison 1988: ch. 15) thus applies equally to Hume:

One point about his thought must be emphasised . . . he was the one eighteenth-century economist who always insisted on the variability of man and of the relativity to time and place, of all policies; the one who was completely free from the paralysing belief, that crept over the intellectual life of Europe, in practical principles that claim universal validity; who saw that a policy that was rational in France at a given time might be quite irrational, at the same time in Naples . . . (Schumpter 1954: 293–4).

It was this line of thinking that was later to be followed by Sir James Steuart rather than by Smith.

REFERENCES

Arkin, M. (1956), 'The Economic Writings of David Hume: A Re-assessment', *South African Journal of Economics*, 22.

Belgion, M. (1965), *David Hume* (London).

Burton, J. H. (1846), *Life and Correspondence of David Hume* (Edinburgh).

Cantillon, R. (1931), *Essai sur la nature du commerce en general*, ed. H. Higgs (London).

Chamley, P. (1975), 'The Conflict between Montesquieu and Hume: A Study of the Origins of Adam Smith's Universalism', in *EAS*.

Eagly, R. (1970), 'Adam Smith and the Specie Flow Doctrine', *Southern Journal of Political Economy*, 17.

Forbes, D. (ed.) (1970), Hume's *The History of Great Britain: The Reigns of James I and Charles I* (Harmondsworth).

Higgs, H. (1897), *The Physiocrats* (London).

Hont, I. (1983), 'The Rich Country–Poor Country Relationship in Scottish Classical Political Economy', in I. Hont and M. Ignatieff (eds), *Wealth and Virtue: The Shaping of Political Economy in the Scottish Enlightenment* (Cambridge).

Hutchison, T. W. (1988), *Before Adam Smith: The Emergence of Political Economy, 1662–1776* (Oxford).

Johnson, E. A. G. (1937), *Predecessors of Adam Smith: The Growth of British Economic Thought* (New York).

Letwin, W. (1963), *The Origins of Scientific Economics* (London).

Mair, D. (ed.) (1990), *The Scottish Contribution to Modern Economic Thought* (Aberdeen).

Meek, R. L. (1962), *Physiocracy* (London).

Peacock, A. (1990), 'Foreword to Hume's Political Discourses'; reprinted in Mair (1990).

Petrella, F. (1968), 'Adam Smith's Rejection of Hume's Specie Flow Mechanism', *Southern Journal of Political Economy*, 34.

Rogin, L. (1956), *The Meaning of Validity of Economic Theory* (New York).

Rotwein, E. (1955), *David Hume: Economic Writings* (Edinburgh).

——— (1987), 'David Hume', in *The New Palgrave Dictionary of Economics*, ed. J. Eatwell, M. Milgate and P. Newman (London).

Say, J. B. (1821), *Treaties on Political Economy*, trans. C. R. Prinsep (London).

Schumpeter, J. (1954), *History of Economic Analysis* (London).

Skinner, A. S. (ed.) (1966), *Sir James Steuart's Principles of Political Oeconomy* (Edinburgh).

——— (1967), 'Say's Law: Origins and Content', *Economica*, 34.

——— (1990a), 'David Hume: Precursor of Sir James Steuart', *Discussion Papers in Economics*, no. 9003 (Glasgow).

——— (1990b), 'The Shaping of Political Economy in the Enlightenment', *Scottish Journal of Political Economy*, 37.

Spengler, J. J. (1954), 'Richard Cantillon: First of the Moderns', *Journal of Political Economy*, 62.

Taylor, W. L. (1956), 'Eighteenth Century Scottish Political Economy: The Impact on Adam Smith and his Work, of his Association with Frances Hutcheson and David Hume', *South African Journal of Economics*, 24.

———(1965), *Francis Hutcheson and David Hume as Predecessors of Adam Smith* (Durham, NC).

Vickers, D. (1960), *Studies in the Theory of Money, 1660–1776* (London).

Viner, J. (1930), 'English Theories of Foreign Trade before Adam Smith', *Journal of Political Economy*, 38.

11

Sir James Steuart:
Principles of Political Economy

INTRODUCTION

The lives of Steuart and Smith, their careers, and their perspectives on political economy could hardly have been more different. Steuart qualified as a lawyer in 1735, two years before Smith became a student in Glasgow. Having embarked on the Foreign Tour in the same year, Sir James returned to Scotland at the very time that Adam Smith went to Oxford as the Snell Exhibitioner in 1740. By the time Smith left Oxford in 1746, Steuart was already in exile, as a result of his commitment to the Jacobite cause, and when in 1764 the Professor left for France as tutor to the Duke of Buccleuch, Steuart had just returned to Scotland. At this time he was busily engaged in completing his *Principles of Political Economy*, a work that was published within a year of Smith's return from France in 1766. In their later years the two men lived on opposite sides of the country, Smith as a government official based in Edinburgh, and Steuart as a retired country gentleman living in Lanarkshire.

Smith's position with regard to the *Principles* has not emerged with any clarity. While it is known that he owned a copy of the book, he made no mention of it even in respect of areas where Steuart had provided relevant information—notably with regard to the Bank of Amsterdam, about which Smith claimed, in the advertisement to the fourth edition of the *Wealth of Nations*, that 'no printed account had ever appeared to me satisfactory, or even intelligible'. Steuart's interesting account of Law's Bank suffered the same fate, as did his analysis of the Scottish Banks (*Principles*, bk 4, pt 2).

But it is probably unwise to take such speculation too far. Smith provided many examples of what now seems to be a cavalier attitude to authorities, the most notable of which is surely that passage in the *Wealth of Nations* where it is claimed that 'Mr Hume is the only writer who, so far as I know, has hitherto taken notice' of the association between commerce and 'the liberty and security of individuals' (*WN*,

---

This chapter is based upon an account of Steuart's system as set out in Skinner (1966, 1981). The argument includes some additional material which was introduced in Skinner (1988).

III. iv. 4). Quite apart from Steuart, a number of people, including many of Smith's closest friends, must have been either hurt or amused by a claim that Smith never saw fit to qualify.

On the other hand, it has been noted that Smith had 'been heard to observe that he understood Sir James's system better from his conversation than from his volumes' (Rae 1895: 63). But nor is this remark necessarily to be taken other than at face value. Even Elizabeth Mure, an affectionate and admiring relative, of Steuart, commented that the 'eloquence and clearness of comprehension that he showed in conversation does not appear in his works; there is a darkness in his writing, that he could dispel in a moment by words' (Chamley 1965: 116).[1] Lady Mary Wortley Montagu formed a similar opinion (Skinner 1966: p. xli).

It is also known that Smith wrote to William Pulteney on 4 September 1772, to the effect that 'I have the same opinion of Sir James Stewart's [*sic*] book that you have. Without once mentioning it, I flatter myself, that every false principle in it, will meet with a clear and distinct confutation in mine' (*Corr.* 132). Yet such a statement does not preclude recognition of the fact that there were principles in the book which were not incorrect. Reading the work in 1767, the author of the essay on 'Astronomy' could hardly fail to appreciate Steuart's scientific purpose, his concern with the emergence of the 'present establishments in Europe', the successful deployment of the 'theory of stages' which Smith himself had used in his *Lectures*, or the interest shown in the relationship between the mode of subsistence and the patterns of authority and subordination. There is a similar emphasis on the importance of 'natural wants' as a stimulus to economic activity, and the same broadly sociological dimension to a discussion that featured so strongly in Smith's ethics.

In terms of economic analysis, Smith would have confronted a sophisticated theory of population, an advanced theory of the determination of prices, and the same clear grasp of the interdependence of economic phenomenon that marked his own early work in the *Lectures on Jurisprudence*. Other and more general parallels are to be observed in Steuart's awareness of the potential for economic growth and in his appreciation of the contribution made by international trade to the process.

Perhaps none of this is surprising in view of the influence exerted by Hume on his close friends.

---

[1] Elizabeth Mure's correspondent was Steuart's neice, Mrs. Calderwood-Durham. Details of the family history are given in the Coltness Collections (Coltness 1842: 391–407). Biographical materials are also given in Chamley (1963, 1965), Skinner (1966), and the 'Anecodotes of the Life of Sir James Steuart, Baronet', appended to Steuart's *Works* (1805*a*).

INFLUENCES ON STEUART

It is known that David Hume visited Steuart at Coltness, his family home, on a number of occasions, during at least one of which the two men discussed the former's *History* (*Principles*, 1966, edn: 742n.). The work also figures in the one long letter from Steuart to Hume that has survived, a letter that is remarkable for its good humour and familiarity and which attests the 'many proofs which you have given me of your friendship' (Burton 1849: 174). Hume had probably given assistance in the vexed question of Steuart's pardon. He had also read the *Principles* in draft. In a letter dated 11 March 1766, Professor Rouet wrote to Baron Mure that 'George Scott and David Hume have looked into our friend's MS and are exceedingly pleased with it', although Hume was later stated to have been critical of its 'form and style' (Skinner 1966: p. xlv). Hume was arguably justified in his criticism, although as we shall see he may have had good reason to be pleased with many aspects of the general 'philosophy' that underlies the work.

Before I proceed to offer an account of Steuart's contribution, however, it may be useful to consider two points relating to the circumstances under which the book was written. First, it is worth recording that, although Steuart held a commission from Charles Edward, dated 29 December 1746 (Bongie 1986: 148), he gradually withdrew from his association with the Jacobites as support for the 'cause' receded and in the hopes of a return to Great Britain. In the early 1750s he removed to Angouleme, and it was here that he met the members of the exiled Parlement of Paris, including the latter-day Physiocrat so admired by Smith, Mercier de la Rivière. These meetings apparently stimulated his interest in political economy and were continued when he moved to the Capital in the late summer of 1754. Supported by such powerful patronage, Steuart was able to meet Montesquieu and probably Mirabeau, and certainly to renew acquaintance with Mercier de la Rivière, who was to become a valued and supportive friend.[2] The scientific opportunities that might have followed were considerable, but Steuart felt obliged to leave Paris in 1755 to avoid compromising his position as war approached. He was to settle in Tubingen (Skinner 1966: p. xxxix), and

---

[2] Steuart was imprisoned by the French in 1762 as a result of publicly acknowledged satisfaction with the course of the war and of his close knowledge of the state of the French economy (Skinner 1966: p. xliii). His stated satisfaction with regard to the war may have been intended to attract the attention of the French as a means of furthering his cause with the British government. J. E. King records that Steuart had been caught in possession of coded plans for the seizure of Santo Domingo (Haiti), plans that had been prepared by Mercier de la Rivière (1720–93), 'who had a personal pecuniary interest in an English invasion of the island and may also have realised that it would do his friend Steuart no harm in the eyes of London if he were arrested by the French' (King 1988: 24). The authority for this statement is supplied by Chamley (1965: 44–61, 110–11).

it was there that the first two books of the *Principles* were completed by August 1759.[3]

Steuart's isolation, and the date of completion of the first part of his work, are important. While owing a great deal to Mirabeau's *Ami des Hommes* (1756), the fact remains that the *Principles* is essentially pre-Physiocratic in character in the sense that Steuart was apparently unaware of the model that was being developed by Quesnay in the later years of the decade (see Chapter 6 above). Secondly, it should be noted that one of the most important features of Sir James Steuart's career was his extensive knowledge of the Continent. The Foreign Tour (1735–40) and his exile as a result of his association with the Jacobites (1745–63) meant that by the end of the Seven Years' War Sir James had spent almost half of his life in Europe. In this time he mastered four languages (French, German, Spanish, and Italian). These facts may help to explain Joseph Schumpeter's judgement that 'there is something un-English (which is not merely Scottish) about his views and his mode of presentation' (1954: 176n.).

In the course of his travels, Steuart visited a remarkable number of places including Antwerp, Avignon, Brussels, Cadiz, Frankfurt, Leyden, Liège, Madrid, Paris, Rome, Rotterdam, Tübingen, Utrecht, Venice, and Verona. He seems, moreover, consistently to have pursued experiences that were out of the common way. For example, when he settled at Angoulême he took advantage of his situation to visit Lyons and the surrounding country. During his residence in Tübingen, he undertook a tour of the schools in the Duchy of Württemberg. Earlier he had spent no less than fifteen months in Spain, where he was much struck by the irrigation schemes in Valencia, Mercia, and Granada, the mosque in Cordoba, and the consequences of the famine in 'Andalousia' (Andalucia) in the Spring of 1737.[4] In fact, very little seems to have been lost and it is remarkable how often specific impressions found their way into the main body of the *Principles*. In his major book Steuart noted the economic consequences of the Seven Years' War in Germany, the state of agriculture in Picardy, the arrangement of the kitchen gardens round Padua,[5] and the problem of depopulation in the cities of the Austrian Netherlands.

---

[3] The manuscript, one version of which is in the Coltness Papers (Edinburgh University Library), does not differ substantially from the text of 1767. A version of the manuscript was dedicated to Lady Mary Wortley Montagu and is dated 11 August 1759. A second version was dedicated to the Margrave of Baden-Durlach and is dated 31 August of the same year (Chamley 1965:130, 138).

[4] Steuart wrote two interesting letters from Spain, dated 5 and 17 March 1737, addressed to his brother-in-law, Thomas Calderwood, and to his old professor, Charles Mackie (Laing MS, Edinburgh University). The first letter is reprinted in Chamley (1965: 127–9).

[5] Steuart's treatment of land use theory was the subject of the presidential address to the Regional Science Association of the USA given by Martin J. Beckmann (1981); cf. W. J. Stull (1986).

Steuart drew attention to the difficulties under which he laboured in the preface to the *Principles* precisely because he thought they would be of interest to the reader. He pointed out that the 'composition' was the 'successive labour of many years spent in travelling' (1966 edn.: 3–4) during which he had examined different countries 'constantly, with an eye to my own subject':

I have attempted to draw information from every one with whom I have been acquainted: this however I found to be very difficult until I had attained to some previous knowledge of my subject. Such difficulties confirmed to me the justness of Lord Bacon's remark, that he who can draw information by forming proper questions, is already possessed of half the science.

I could form no consistent plan from the various opinions I met with; hence I was engaged to compile the observations I had casually made, in the course of my travels, reading, and experience. From these I formed the following work after expunging the numberless inconsistencies and contradictions which I found had arisen from my separate inquiries. (Steuart 1966 edn.: 5–6).

Steuart wrote very much in the style of a man finding his way through a new field. This, added to the fact that nearly eight years separate the first and last books, presented obvious problems, problems of which Steuart was always conscious but which he viewed with very mixed feelings:

Had I been master of my subject on setting out, the arrangement of the whole would have been rendered more concise; but had this been the case, I should never have been able to go through the painful deduction which forms the whole train of my reasoning and upon which . . . the conviction it carries along with it in a great measure depends. (Steuart 1966 edn.: 5).

But the critical point to note is that Steuart attempted to produce a single great conceptual system, linking the most interesting branches of modern policy, such as 'population, agriculture, trade, industry, money, coin, interest, circulation, banks, exchange, public credit, and taxes' (1966 edn.: 7). He added: 'The principles deduced from all these topics appear tolerably consistent; and the whole is a train of reasoning, through which I have adhered to the connection of subjects as faithfully as I could' (p. 5).

As Paul Chamley has pointed out, Steuart's attempt to produce a systematic treatise confirms that he sought to include economics in the body of organized science, and that as such his purpose conforms to the design of the *Encyclopédie* as described by D'Alembert (Chamley 1965: 50).[6]

---

[6] It should be noted that 'a new methodological order characterises all eighteenth century thought. The value of system, the *esprit systématique* is rather underestimated and neglected; but it is sharply distinguished from the love of system for its own sake, the *esprit de système* (Cassirer 1951: 8). Exactly this point is made by Steuart in the preface to the *Principles* (1966 edn.: 8)

METHODOLOGY

Steuart sought to establish a system of thought whose content met the requirements of Newtonian methodology. The leading feature of his method is objective empiricism. He was thus entirely in accord with Hume, but, like Hume, recognized that the mere collection of facts was not of itself sufficient. The first step on the route to knowledge is the collection and description of facts; the second, the statement of certain 'principles' reached through a process of induction.

Steuart also recognized that the scientist can advance only by concerning 'himself' with *cause* and *consequence*, that is, by thinking deductively. He solved the problem of how to combine the two techniques by using induction to establish his basic hypotheses, or 'principles', and deduction for what Hasbach (1891) described as the 'clarification of phenomena'. Steuart's recommended deployment of the techniques of induction and deduction corresponds closely to Colin McLaurin's (1748) account of the methodology of Sir Isaac Newton, whose 'vast and creative talent' was deeply admired by Steuart (Steuart 1805*a* (henceforth *Works*): vi. 93). McLaurin concluded:

It is evident that, as in mathematics, so in natural philosophy, the investigation of difficult things by the method of *analysis* ought ever to precede the method of composition, or the *synthesis*. For in any other way we can never be sure that we assume the principles that really obtain in nature; and that our system, after we have composed it with great labour, is not mere dream and illusion. (McLaurin 1775 edn.: 9; see Ch. 1 above).

Recognition of the necessity of employing both techniques brought awareness of the problem of subjective preference for purely logical thought. (Steuart 1966 edn.: 6). The problem was widely recognized and the dangers involved often avoided, so that, when speaking of the psychological attractions of deductive thought (of which Smith was well aware), Lord Kames was able to point out that 'It redounds not a little to the honour of some late enquirers after truth that, subduing this bent of nature, they have submitted to the slow and more painful method of experiment' (1779: 23). Kames did not allude to Steuart, but the latter also recognized the dangers of 'long steps of reasoning' (1966 edn.: 19) and deliberately chose a different and more appropriate route to knowledge. Steuart argued that we should proceed 'by the shortest steps when we draw a conclusion from a general proposition and still keep experience and matter of fact before our eyes' (*Works*, ii. 121).

Steuart was quite clear as to the techniques of reasoning to be employed. The rules were simple, if difficult to obey; observation, induction, deduction, verification. There remained the question of the technique to be followed in building up a body of knowledge, and here

Steuart's answer was equally clear. The scientist should begin with the simple (and thus apparently abstract) case and gradually take account of more and more complex (and thus 'realistic') cases. The first objective must be clarity, and Steuart thus recognized that the attainment of the second, relevance, can come about only through the use of abstraction in the early stages of study. He argued that, in building up a body of knowledge, 'Every branch of it must, in setting out, be treated with simplicity and all combinations not absolutely necessary must be banished from the theory' (1966 edn.: 227).However, since the object is relevance, and since the 'more extensive any theory be made, the more it will be useful', it follows that as we proceed 'combinations will crowd in and every one of these must be attended to' (p. 227). Steuart always employed this technique in dealing with a body of knowledge; that is, he would gradually build up his argument in a series of steps which progressively increased in complexity.

At the same time, Steuart recognized that theoretical edifices constructed in this manner present the economist with particular difficulties arising from the nature of the subject matter itself. In Steuart's view, the economist or social scientist can show only 'how consequences *may* follow from one another; to foretell what *must* follow is exceedingly difficult if not impossible' (p. 365). While we can and must establish general principles, these do not provide rules of behaviour that must always hold good. Steuart thus concluded (somewhat ironically, in the context of a critique of Hume's quantity theory), that: 'I think I have discovered that in this, as in every other part of political economy, there is hardly such a thing as a general rule to be laid down' (p. 339).

The procedures that Steuart recommended, and his concern with the problem of prediction, correspond closely with Alfred Marshall's classic statement which was offered more than a hundred years later (Marshall 1890: bk I, ch.3, apps. C and D).[7]

Given the need for a systematic statement of particular principles, established in accordance with the discipline of an appropriate methodology, there remained the problem of establishing a useful 'method' in respect of the *organization* of the discourse as a whole. 'The thing to be done is to fall upon a distinct method . . . by contriving a chain of ideas, which may be directed towards every part of the plan, and which at the same time, may be made to arise methodically from one another' (Steuart 1966 edn.: 28).

Here again, Steuart followed Hume's lead. The 'plan' is contained in the first two books and is based upon a theory of economic development. Steuart's dominant theme was to be change and growth, and it is this that gives his work cohesion:

---

[7] For an account of Steuart's methodology, see Sen (1957); Vickers (1960), and Skinner (1965a, 1967a).

By this kind of historical clue, I shall conduct myself through the great avenues of this extensive labyrinth; and in my review of every particular district, I shall step from consequence to consequence, until I have penetrated into the inmost recesses of my own understanding.' (Steuart 1966 edn. 29).

THE HISTORICAL PERSPECTIVE

Steuart clearly accepted a proposition that had been stated by Aristotle to the effect that: 'If you consider the state—or anything else for that matter—in relation to the origins from which it springs, you will arrive at the clearest understanding of its nature' (*Politics*, I. 1252a). He thus opened his analysis with 'society in the cradle' before going on to trace the origins of, and the process of transition between, the various stages of the progress of man.[8]

In this context, Steuart made use of a theory of stages, now recognized as a piece of apparatus which was central to the work of the Scottish Historical School. He cites, for example, the Tartars and Indians as relatively primitive socio-economic types of organization (1966 edn.: 56) while concentrating primarily on the third and fourth stages, the stages of agriculture and commerce.[9] In the former case, Steuart observed that those who lacked the means of subsistence could acquire it only through becoming dependent on those who owned it; in the latter, he noted that the situation was radically different in that all goods and services command a price. He concluded, in passages of quite striking clarity,

I deduce the origin of the great subordination under the feudal government, from the necessary dependence of the lower classes for their subsistence. They consumed the produce of the land, as the price of their subordination, not as the reward of their industry in making it produce. . . .

I deduce modern liberty from the independence of the same classes, by the introduction of industry, and circulation of an adequate equivalent for every service. (Steuart 1966 edn.: 209).

Steuart was also aware of the political aspect of these changes, and its effect upon the state:

From feudal and military, it is become free and commercial. I oppose freedom in government to the feudal system only to mark that there is not found now that chain of subordination among the subjects, which made the essential part of the feudal form. (Steuart 1966 edn.: 24).

[8] On Steuart's interest in evolution, see Stettner (1945), Grossman (1943), and Chamley (1963).
[9] See Meek (1976). Steuart's analysis of the relationship between the mode of subsistence and patterns of authority and dependence is located primarily in bk II, Ch. 12. Like Smith, Steuart was critical of the contract theory of government.

He continued:

I oppose commercial to military, only because the military governments now are made to subsist from the consequences and effects of commerce; that is, from the revenue of the state, proceeding from taxes. Formerly, everything was brought about by numbers; now numbers of men cannot be kept together without money. (Steuart 1966 edn.: 24).

Steuart noted that the gradual emergence of the stage of commerce had generated new sources of wealth which had affected the position of princes: 'The pre-rogative of Princes, in former times, was measured by the power they could constitutionally exercise over the *persons* of their subjects; that of modern princes, by the power they have over their *purse*' (1966, edn.: 290). He also observed that 'an opulent, bold, and spirited people, having the fund of the Prince's wealth in their own hands, have it also in their own power, when it becomes strongly their inclination, to shake off his authority' (p. 216).

The alteration in the distribution of power which was reflected in the changing balance between proprietor and merchant led Steuart to the conclusion that 'industry must give wealth and wealth *will* give power' (p. 213). In support of this position, he drew attention (significantly in his Notes on Hume's *History*) to the reduced position of the Crown at the end of the reign of Elizabeth—a revolution that appears 'quite natural when we set before us the causes which occasioned it. Wealth must give power; and industry, in a country of luxury, will throw it into the hands of the commons' (p. 213 n.).[10]

It was perhaps for this reason that Steuart's French translator, Seno-vert (1789), advised his readers that, of the advantages to be gained from a reading of the *Principles*, 'Le premier sera de convaincre, sans doute, que la revolution qui s'opere sous nos yeux etait dans l'ordre des choses necessaires' (p. 24 n.).

The Theory of Population

The analysis of the emergence of the exchange economy is not untypical of the period and is intrinsically interesting even if Steuart did consider that it was more properly the province of the science of politics than that of political economy strictly defined. But he also argued that the subjects reviewed above were not 'altogether foreign to this [science], i.e. to economics (Steuart 1966 edn.: 206), illustrating the truth of the remark by deploying the 'stadial' thesis in a purely economic context. The technique finds illustration in a number of fields, and generally involves the use of the stages of society treated as models.

---

[10] Steuart's manuscript writings are detailed in Skinner (1966: 741–3).

The first analytical problem to which Steuart addressed himself, again following Hume, was that of population, where his stated purpose was 'not to inquire what numbers of people were found upon the earth at a certain time, but to examine the natural and rational causes of multiplication' (1966 edn.: 31). In so doing, he stated that the 'fundamental principle' is 'generation; the next is food' (p. 31), from which it follows that, where men live by gathering the spontaneous fruits of the soil (the North American Indian model), population levels must be determined by their extent:

From what has been said, we may conclude, that the numbers of mankind must depend upon the quantity of food produced by the earth for their nourishment; from which, as a corollary may be drawn;

That mankind have been, as to numbers, and must ever be, in proportion to the food produced; and that the food produced will be in compound proportion to the fertility of the climate, and the industry of the inhabitants. (Steuart 1966 edn.: 36–7).

Where some effort is applied to the cultivation of the soil (the agrarian stage), Steuart recognized that the output of food and therefore the level of population would grow. But here again, he drew a distinction between cultivation for subsistence, which was typical of the feudal stage, and the application of industry to the soil, as found in the modern situation where goods and services command a price, and where the potential for economic growth (and therefore population) is greatly enhanced.

Perhaps two major points arising from this argument deserve further notice. To begin with, attention should be drawn to the emphasis that Steuart gives to the interdependent state of the sectors in his model of the exchange economy, recognizing as he did that *'Agriculture among a free people will augment population, in proportion only as the necessitous are put in a situation to purchase subsistence with their labour'* (1966 edn.: 40). Secondly, Steuart gave a good deal of attention to the point that the whole process depended on 'reciprocal' wants, so that there are cases where the limited extent of the latter will constrain economic development and population growth:

Experience everywhere shows the possible existence of such a case, since no country in Europe is cultivated to the utmost: and that there are many still, where cultivation, and consequently multiplication, is at a stop. These nations I consider as being in a *moral incapacity* of multiplying: the incapacity would be *physical*, if there was any actual impossibility of their procuring an augmentation of food by any means whatsoever. (Steuart 1966 edn.: 42).

Although we cannot review the theory in any detail here, it can be said that in Book I we confront a single major theme: the theory of population. This theory, while owing a great deal to David Hume (and possibly to Cantillon), none the less represents one of Steuart's most distinguished contributions and one of the best examples of his capacity for the systematic deployment of diminishing levels of abstraction. The theory also moved Marx to claim that Steuart should be regarded as a major precursor of Malthus (Eltis 1987: 495). But equally characteristic of his mode of argument is the fact that the theory was built up in such a way as to permit him to provide an account of the modern or exchange economy (the last of the 'models' used above), thus gradually widening the scope of the inquiry while still preserving a coherent 'chain of ideas'.

THE EXCHANGE ECONOMY

In dealing with the nature of the exchange economy, it is significant that Steuart made little use of the division of labour in the Smithian sense of the term. On the other hand, he gave great emphasis to the social division of labour in using the basic sectoral division to be found in Cantillon, Hume, Hutcheson, Mirabeau, and Quesnay's *Encyclopédie* articles:

we find the people distributed into two classes. The first is that of the farmers who produce the subsistence, and who are necessarily employed in this branch of business; the other I shall call *free hands*; because their occupation being to procure themselves subsistence out of the superfluity of the farmers, and by a labour adapted to the wants of the society, may vary according to these wants, and these again according to the spirit of the times. (Steuart 1966 edn.: 43).

In both cases productive activity involves what Steuart defines as *industry*, namely, *'the application to ingenious labour in a free man, in order to procure, by means of trade, an equivalent, fit for supplying every want'*. *Trade*, on the other hand, is defined as *'an operation by which the wealth, or work, either of individuals, or of societies, may, by a set of men called merchants, be exchanged, for an equivalent, proper for supplying every want, without any interruption to industry, or any check upon consumption'* (1966 edn.: 146). The whole pattern is carried on through the use of money, also defined, with characteristic care as *'any commodity, which purely in itself is of no material use to man . . . but which acquires such an estimation from his opinion of it, as to become the universal measure of what is called value, and an adequate equivalent for anything alienable'* (p. 44).

For Steuart, the modern system was clearly an exchange economy characterized by a high degree of dependence between forms of activity and the individuals who carried them on, so that the idea or ideal of a free society emerges as involving *'a general tacit contract, from which reciprocal and proportional services result universally between all those who compose it'* (p. 88). Later Steuart was to state an hypothesis of obvious relevance to the situation under review in remarking that 'the principle of self-interest will serve as a general key to this inquiry; and it may, in one sense, be considered as the ruling principle of my subject, and may therefore be traced throughout the whole. This is the main spring . . . (p. 142). But the main underlying theme remains that of the interdependence of economic phenomena, a theme which brought Steuart quite logically to the treatment of price and allocation.

As far as the supply price of commodities is concerned, Steuart noted two elements: 'to wit, the real value of the commodity, and the profit upon alienation'. Real value was defined in such a way as to include three elements:

The first thing to be known of any manufacture when it comes to be sold, is how much of it a person can perform in a day, a week, a month, according to the nature of the work, which may require more or less time to bring it to perfection. . . .

The second thing to be known, is the value of the workman's subsistence and necessary expense, both for supplying his personal wants, and providing the instruments belonging to his profession, which must be taken upon an average as above. . . .

The third and last thing to be known, is the value of the materials, that is the first matter employed by the workman. . . .

These three articles being known, the price of the manufacture is determined. It cannot be lower than the amount of all three, that is, than the real value; whatever it is higher, is the manufacturer's profit. (Steuart 1966 edn.: 160–1).

He went on to note that,

when we say that the balance between work and demand is to be sustained in equilibrio, as far as possible, we mean that the quantity supplied should be in proportion to the quantity *demanded*, that is, *wanted*. While the balance stands justly poised, prices are found in the adequate proportion of the real expense of making the goods, with a small addition for profit to the manufacturer and merchant, (Steuart 1966 edn.: 189).

As far as the *process* of price determination was concerned, Steuart contended that the outcome of the 'contract' would be determined by competition between and *among* buyers and sellers:

'*Double competition* is, when, in a certain degree, it takes place on both sides of the contract at once, or vibrates alternately from one to the other. This is what restrains prices to the adequate value of the merchandize.' (Steuart 1966 edn.: 172).

Thus, for example, if there is a relative shortage of some commodity there may be competition between buyers in order to procure limited supplies, thus causing prices to rise. In the event of an excess supply, e.g. of a perishable commodity such as fish, there will be competition between sellers to rid themselves of excess stocks, thus causing prices to fall below their equilibrium values. Both cases present examples of what Steuart called 'simple competition' prevailing in effect on one side of the 'contract' only, and anticipated Smith's position (see Chapter 7 above).

Three points follow from this argument. First, the attainment of a 'balance' between demand and supply does not of itself indicate a position of equilibrium. Secondly, that the process of bargaining will normally affect both parties to the exchange:

In all markets . . . this competition is varying, though insensibly, on many occasions; but in others, the vibrations are very perceptible. Sometimes it is found strongest on the side of the buyers, and in proportion as this grows, the competition between the sellers diminishes. When the competition between the former has raised prices to a certain standard, it comes to a stop; then the competition changes sides, and takes place among the sellers, eager to profit of the highest price. This makes prices fall, and according as they fall, the competition between the buyers diminishes (Steuart 1966 edn.: 174).

Steuart was thus able to offer a definition of *equilibrium* but also a statement of a *stability* condition, in noting that,

In proportion therefore as the rising of prices can stop demand or the sinking of prices can increase it, in the same proportion will competition prevent either the rise or the fall from being carried beyond a certain length. (Steuart 1966 edn.: 177).

Thirdly, it should be noted that Steuart was aware of the allocative functions of the market. As he put it,

Trade produces many excellent advantages; it marks out to the manufacturers when their branch is under or overstocked with hands. If it be understocked, they will find more demand than they can answer; if it be overstocked, the sale will be slow (Steuart 1966 edn.: 158).

Arguments such as these are obviously broadly 'static' in character, but in fact are to be found in a setting which shows the same preoccupation with long-run dynamics that characterizes the argument of book I, thus presenting the reader with yet another change of focus.

It will be recalled that Steuart's definition of equilibrium required that the balance between supply and demand be such that 'prices are found in the adequate proportion of the real expense of making the goods, with a small addition for profit to the manufacturer or merchant'. It was Steuart's view that this definition, originally applied to particular commodities, must also apply to *all* goods, thus suggesting, as in the case of Smith's *Lectures*, an intuitive grasp of the general interdependence of economic phenomena. Indeed, this perspective seems to dominate Steuart's treatment of the long run, where he argues in effect that the balance of work and demand, taking the economy *as a macro unit*, is likely to change over time with consequent effects on the components of real value and on the relationship between real value and price.

Some causes of change, while important, were easily explained. Steuart recognized that taxes, for example, could affect the prices of commodities. He also drew attention to the tendency for the prices of primary products (subsistence and materials) to rise over time, especially as the result of 'the increase of population, which may imply a more expensive improvement of the soil' (1966 edn.: 198). But the most significant problem, for Steuart, was located on the demand side.

Steuart believed that the long-run macroeconomic trend would be for the balance of demand to *preponderate*, initially generating higher levels of profit, and thus suggesting a tendency for the general price level to rise over time. But he added that the impact on the general price level would be reinforced by another factor: higher profits 'subsisting for a long time . . . insensibly become *consolidated*, or, as it were, transformed into the intrinsic value of the goods' (1966 edn.: 193) in such a way as to become 'in a manner necessary' to their existence. Secondly, and related to the above, Steuart distinguished between *physical* and *political* necessaries, where the former is defined almost in biological terms as 'ample subsistence where no degree of superfluity is implied' (p. 269). He added:

The nature of man furnishes him with some desires relative to his wants, which do not proceed from his animal oeconomy, but which are entirely similar to them in their effects. These proceed from the affections of his mind, are formed by habit and education, and when once *regularly established*, create another kind of necessary, which, for the sake of distinction, I shall call *political*. (Steuart 1966 edn.: 270).

Steuart went on from this point to suggest that the political necessary was 'determined by birth, education or habit' and 'rank' in society, clearly recognizing that it is 'determined by general opinion only, and therefore can never be ascertained justly' (1966 edn.: 271). But he was clear in respect of one point: namely, that there is a tendency for the acceptable definition of the political necessary to rise over time with revised expectations of acceptable standards of living. The importance of this argument was to emerge in a later stage of the exposition.

For the moment, however, the important point to note is that the theses just outlined provide one reflection of Steuart's confidence in respect of the potential for economic growth, which was essentially demand-led. In addressing himself to the modern state in particular, Steuart drew attention to the 'extraordinary flux of money' (p. 309) and to the fact that its institutions had greatly stimulated that 'taste for superfluity and expence' (p. 243) which was associated with 'luxury' in its modern or 'systematical' form, a point he (like Hume) thought to be of greater significance than the discovery of the mines of the New World.[11] The general point at issue is best caught by Steuart's earlier (but recurring) contrast between the feudal and modern systems: 'Men were then forced to labour because they were slaves to others; men are now forced to labour because they are slaves to their own wants' (p. 51).

In the manner of Smith and Hume, it was Steuart's contention that the modern economy had opened up new forms of demand and new incentives to industry. In passages reminiscent of Smith's *Moral Sentiments* (which he may have read), Steuart drew attention to man's love of ingenuity and to the fact that the satisfaction of one level of perceived wants tends to open up others by virtue of a kind of 'demonstration' effect (1966 edn.: 157; cf. *TMS*, IV. 1). But Steuart also gave attention to the supply side in this connection, suggesting that refinements of taste

seem more generally owing to the industry and inventions of the manufacturers (who by their industry daily contrive means of softening or relieving inconveniences, which mankind seldom perceive to be such, till the way of removing them be contrived) than to the taste for luxury in the rich, who, to indulge their ease, engage the poor to become industrious. . . . Here then is the reason why mankind labour though not in want. They become desirous of possessing the very instruments of luxury, which their avarice or ambition prompted them to invent for the use of others. (Steuart 1966 edn.: 157).

As Hume had already pointed out, the institutions of the exchange economy also provided an important stimulus to economic activity in the sense that these institutions had established a situation where 'Wealth becomes *equably distributed;* . . . by *equably distributed* I do not mean, that every individual comes to have an *equal* share, but an equal chance, I may say a certainty, of becoming rich in proportion to his industry (*Works*, ii. 156).

Steuart also argued that the potential for economic growth was almost without limit or certain boundary in the current 'situation of every country in Europe', and especially France, 'at present . . . in her infancy as to improvement, although the advances she has made within a century excite the admiration of the world' (1966 edn.: 137). An equally dramatic confirmation of the general theme is to be found in the chapter on machines, which he considered to be 'of the greatest utility' in 'augmenting the produce or assisting the labour and ingenuity of man' (p. 125). He added:

Upon the whole, daily experience shews the advantage and improvement acquired by the introduction of machines. Let the inconveniences complained of be ever so sensibly felt, let a statesman be ever so careless in relieving those who are forced to be idle, all these inconveniences are only temporary; the advantage is permanent, and the necessity of introducing every method of

---

[11] The role of 'natural wants' in Steuart's work is considered by Eagly (1961).

abridging labour and expence, in order to supply the wants of luxurious mankind, is absolutely indispensable, according to modern policy, according to experience, and according to reason. (Steuart 1966 edn.: 125).

Steuart's confidence in the potential for economic growth was further supported by his appreciation of the opportunities presented by international trade.

DEVELOPMENT AND TRADE

Steuart recognized that trade within and between states would immeasurably increase the possibilities of economic growth through the provision of wider markets. He was thus able to conclude that 'trade has an evident tendency towards the improvement of the world in general' (Steuart 1966 edn.: 119).

He recognized further that trade between nations, like that between men, was based upon the existence of reciprocal needs, so that the cement of international society, like that of civil society, must be of the same kind: 'intercourse tends to unite the most distant nations as well as to improve them: and . . . their mutual interest leads them to endeavour to become serviceable to one another' (p. 217).

In the second book Steuart dropped the assumption of the closed economy. Characteristically, he traced the interrelationship between developed and undeveloped nations in terms of the distinction between active and passive trade, which had already been established by Malachy Postlethwayt (cf. Johnson 1937: 225). Here the purpose was to examine the positive impact of foreign demand on a backward economy in terms of an analysis which anticipated one of Adam Smith's most notable disciples, J. B. Say, who in effect elaborated on an argument that is developed, albeit in a purely historical context, in the *Wealth of the Nations*, book III.[12]

Equally striking is the fact that Steuart treated different states as competitive firms:

The trading nations of Europe represent a fleet of ships, every one striving who shall get first to a certain port. The statesman of each is the master. The same wind blows upon all; and this wind is the principle of self-interest, which engages every consumer to seek the cheapest and the best market. No trade wind can be more general, or more constant than this. (Steuart 1966 edn.: 203)

But Steuart's treatment of international trade takes as its basic premiss the proposition that economic conditions and performance will differ even in the context of the relatively developed nations whose trade he described as 'active'. He was clearly aware of variations caused by

[12] Cf. Say (1821: bk I, ch. 15) and cf. Skinner (1967b).

'natural advantages' such as access to materials, transport, and the nature of the climate (1966 edn.: 238), as befits a close student and admirer of 'the great' Montesquieu (p. 238). To these he added the form of government in arguing that 'trade and industry have been found mostly to flourish under the republican form, and under those which have come nearest to it' (p. 211).[13] But equally important for Steuart were the spirit of a people and 'the greater degree of force' with which 'a taste for refinement and luxury in the rich, an ambition to become so, and an application to labour and ingenuity in the lower classes of men' manifested themselves in different societies at any one point in time and over time.

Steuart also believed that there are likely to be variations in the extent to which the definition of 'political necessary' changes through time and in the rate and extent to which the 'balance' of demand tends to preponderate in different countries. He was acutely conscious of the sheer variety of economic conditions, and indeed noted early in the book that,

If one considers the variety which is found in different countries, in the distribution of property, subordination of classes, genius of people, proceeding from the variety of forms of government, laws, climate, and manners, one may conclude, that the political oeconomy of each must necessarily be different. (Steuart 1966 edn.: 17).

From the point of view of policy, the number of possible 'combinations' opened up by the proposition that growth rates and other characteristics will vary is virtually endless, and it was in recognition of this point that Steuart employed three broad classifications, all of which may derive from Mirabeau's *Friend of Man* (1756) but which generalize on the argument already advanced by Hume: the stages of infant, foreign, and inland trade.

Infant trade represents that situation 'known in all ages, and in all countries, in a less or a greater degree' and which is antecedent to supplying the wants of others. Here the ruling principle

is to encourage the manufacturing of every branch of natural productions, by extending the home-consumption of them; by excluding all competition with strangers; by permitting the rise of profits, so far as to promote dexterity and emulation in invention and improvement; by relieving the industrious of their work, as often as demand for it falls short. And, until it can be exported to advantage, it may be exported with loss, at the expence of the public. (Steuart 1966 edn.: 263).

[13] The quotation continues: 'May I be allowed to say, that, perhaps, one principal reason for this has been, that under these forms the administration of the laws has been the most uniform, and consequently that most liberty has *actually* been there enjoyed: I say actually, because . . . in my acceptation of the term, liberty is equally compatible with monarchy as with democracy: I do not say the enjoyment of it is equally secure under both; because under the first it is much more liable to be destroyed' (Steuart 1966 edn.: 211).

At the same time, Steuart suggested that the statesman must control profit levels so that when the real value of commodities indicates that they are competitive in the international context, trade may begin.

In the case of *foreign trade*, taken as representing the attainment of a competitive stage, the policies recommended are simply designed to retain the capability: here the ruling principles are 'to banish luxury; to encourage frugality; to fix the lowest standard of prices possible; and to watch, with the greatest attention, over the vibrations of the balance between work and demand. While this is preserved, no internal vice can affect the prosperity of it' (1966 edn.: 263).

Inland Trade, on the other hand, represents a situation where a developed nation has lost its competitive edge as a result of the tendency for the balance of work and demand to be disturbed in the historical long run.[14] Here the basic preoccupation must be the maintenance of the level of employment. Steuart also recognized the importance of the balance of payments[15] in advocating a restrictive monetary policy, and concluded that 'I will not therefore say that in every case which can be supposed, certain restrictions upon the exportation of bullion or coin are contrary to good policy. This proposition I confine to the flourishing nations of our own time' (p. 581).[16] But in this case the basic problem was not the level of aggregate demand so much as the need to keep domestic price levels as low as possible with a view to taking advantage of the present and future difficulties of other states. With the possible exception of Holland, it was Steuart's contention that because all nations would suffer the same long-run trends, but at different rates, it followed that, 'as industry and idleness, luxury and frugality, are constantly changing their balance throughout the nations of Europe, able merchants make it their business to inform themselves of these fluctuations, and able statesmen profit of the discovery for the re-establishment of their own commerce' (p. 296).

This possibly endless process of competition and of fluctuating fortunes was only qualified by Steuart by reference to the classic eighteenth-century theme of growth and decay; the belief (shared in some form by, amongst others, Cantillon, Hume, and Smith) that 'no trading state has ever been of long duration, after arriving at a certain height of prosperity. We perceive in history the rise, progress, grandeur, and decline of Sydon, Tyre, Carthage, Alexandria, and Venice, not to come

---

[14] M. A. Akhtar (1979) has presented an interesting macroeconomic model based on the stage of 'inland trade' which makes due use of the part played by government.

[15] For comment on Steuart's clear distinction between the balance of payments and the balance of trade, see Sen (1957: 74ff.) and Viner (1930).

[16] Steuart also believed that the flow of specie from a relatively underdeveloped economy could prove irreversible, arguing that banks should borrow abroad to fund current deficits while continuing to support domestic credit in the interests of development (1966 edn.: 505–20); cf. Eltis (1986).

nearer home. While these states were on the growing hand, they were powerful; when once they came to their height, they immediately found themselves labouring under their own greatness' (Steuart 1966 edn.: 195–6).

While it appears that nations may be expected to go through a series of stages of trade, fluctuating especially between the second and third, this should not distract attention from the point that trade takes place between nations at a given point in time where these nations, and industries and regions within them, are differently circumstanced, thus requiring different strategies in a policy sense in respect of *all* of these areas.

The basic problem reflects Steuart's understanding of the fact that a variety of conditions must prevail. As he put it, 'Were industry and frugality found to prevail equally in every part of these great political bodies, or were luxury and superfluous consumption, everywhere carried to the same height, trade might, without any hurt, be thrown entirely open. It would then cease to be an object of a statesman's care and concern' (1966 edn.: 296).[17]

Given the circumstances outlined, there is a certain realism in Steuart's general conclusion:

Nothing, I imagine, but an universal monarchy, governed by the same laws, and administered according to one plan, well concerted, can be compatible with an universally open trade. While there are different states, there must be different interests; and when no one statesman is found at the head of these interests, there can be no such thing as a common good; and where there is no common good, every interest must be considered separately (1966 edn.: 365).

ASPECTS OF DOMESTIC POLICY

It is sometimes forgotten that Steuart's 'stages of trade' apply not only to national economies, but also to particular industries and regions within them. Indeed it is fair to claim that the state of 'foreign trade' may be interpreted as involving a capacity to compete within the framework of a system of organized markets. The state of 'infant trade' may be re-stated to mean that active policies must be followed in order to ensure that the

[17] On the subject of free trade, there is interesting evidence of some coincidence of view in respect of Steuart's treatment of the American crisis (see Ch. 9, n. 2). Steuart argued that the British government would have a better chance of concluding the conflict by virtue of economic sanctions rather than military force. Steuart argued that if the colonies survived economic sanctions and thereby proved that they were not dependent on Great Britain, they should be given up and a policy of free trade pursued. But even if the colonies failed the test of economic independence, he argued that they should still be given the opportunity of unrestricted trade, a position that must significantly qualify the claim that he is best described as a 'mercantilist'. See Raynor and Skinner (1994: 760).

necessary infrastructure is in place to ensure that markets are properly established while 'industries' are sufficiently developed as to ensure a capacity to compete. A number of examples may be cited in order to illustrate these distinctive themes.

First, attention should be drawn to Steuart's interest in 'that spirit of liberty, which reigns more and more every day, throughout all the polite and flourishing nations of Europe' (Steuart 1966 edn.: 18). He was acutely aware of the current 'revolution' in the affairs of Europe: '*Trade and the Industry* are in vogue: and their establishment is occasioning a wonderful fermentation with the remaining fierceness of the feudal constitution' (p. 215). In fact Steuart, notably in Book I of the *Principles*, directly addressed a problem which is implicit in the analysis of the third book of the *Wealth of Nations*, but which was not explicitly considered by Smith: namely, the policy dimension of the socio-economic process which finally resulted in the emergence of the fourth stage of commerce in an advanced form. Steuart's model may be loosely described as that of 'primitive accumulation', in contrast to Smith, where 'the process of 'primitive accumulation' has now been completed' (Kobayashi 1967: 19).[18] The same point has been made by Perelman in noting that Steuart directly addressed the problems of a primitive version of the stage of commerce (Perelman 1983: 454) in a way which led Marx to appreciate his sensitivity to historical differences in modes of production (p. 467).[19]

There are, however, other dimensions to Steuart's treatment of this general theme. Steuart may, for example, be seen to have used historical experience as a model on the basis of which advice could be offered to the statesman who actually confronted the economic and social problems involved in emergence from the agrarian stage—a condition which obtained in many countries of Europe at the time of writing (Steuart 1966 edn.: 215).

In yet another version of the same argument Steuart suggested that the historical and contemporary record could provide a guide to the problems which would confront a statesman seeking to *induce* change; that is, a guide to the statesman who seeks to adopt a self-conscious policy of economic, and therefore of social, development. It was Steuart's contention that in many cases the transition from a state of 'trifling industry' and subsistence farming would not occur without 'the interposition of the sovereign, and a new plan of administration' (1966 edn.: 96).

[18] Kobayashi (1967) has suggested that Steuart's emphasis on what he calls a model of 'primitive accumulation' may help to explain the popularity of his work in contemporary Ireland and Germany. See also Chamley (1965: 88–9).

[19] A relationship between Steuart and G. W. F. Hegel has been noted, especially by Chamley (1963, 1965). But see especially Waszek (1988).

Steuart was undoubtedly preoccupied with the problem of employment in socio-economic systems in a process of transition:

Pipers, blue bonnets, and oat meal are known in Swabia, Auvergne, Limousin, and Catalonia, as well as in Lochaber: numbers of idle, poor, useless hands, multitudes of children, whom I have found to be fed, nobody knows how, doing nothing at the age of fourteen . . . If you ask why they are not employed, their parents will tell you because commerce is not in the country: they talk of commerce as if it was a man, who comes to reside in some countries in order to feed the inhabitants. The truth is, it is not the fault of these poor people, but of those whose business it is to find out employment for them (Steuart 1966 edn.: 108).[20]

Secondly, and arising from the above, it is worth noting Steuart's interest in the problem of regional imbalance even within the context of a relatively mature economy. Steuart's general interest in regional issues is a marked feature of the *Principles* and was to find further expressions in his *Considerations of the Interest of the County of Lanark in Scotland*, which was first published in 1769 under the name of Robert Frame. This short work was explicitly designed to illustrate general principles by reference to a particular case; namely that of a backward county in which Steuart resided and which supplied corn to the neighbouring city of Glasgow. Steuart was concerned to demonstrate the impact of the city's demand for agricultural products on an undeveloped region (*Works*, v: 321). He also drew attention to the fact that economic development had enhanced local demand, and thus temporarily reduced the supply of food available for sale outside the region.

From the point of view of the city, the fact that local supply was fitful had lent support to the proposed Forth and Clyde Canal, which was intended to link the two coasts and further to improve the market for grain. Steuart clearly welcomed this development, while warning his contemporaries that its short-run effect would be to ruin local agriculture unless steps were taken to further the cause of agricultural improvement and to develop the local infrastructure. In particular he contended that the infant industry argument as developed in his treatment of 'infant trade', and which had been applied to the textiles of the neighbouring town of Paisley, should be extended to agriculture (*Works*, v: 308).

Steuart returned to this theme in the course of the Corn Law debate of

---

[20] Smith was not unaware of the problems faced in backward areas. In a letter dated 4 April 1759, addressed to Lord Shelburne, he congratulated him on his attempt 'to introduce arts, industry and independency into a miserable country, which has hitherto been a stranger to them all. Nothing, I have often imagined, would give more pleasure to Sir William Petty, your Lordship's ever honoured ancestor, than to see his representative pursuing a Plan so suitable to his own Ideas which are generally equally wise and public spirited' (*Corr.* 30). But this was not one of Smith's preoccupations. cf. Viner (1965: 101).

the 1770s. He argued that the proposed reduction in the importation price would not necessarily reduce costs, as the Glasgow merchants suggested, but that it would certainly further discourage local agriculture. Interestingly, Steuart objected to the merchants' reliance on Smith's *authority* (as distinct from Smith's general position) on the grounds that it was at worst politically motivated and at best failed to distinguish between a general principle and a particular application: 'I have had conversations with the *Glasgow Theorists*. I have written to them on the same subject, to no purpose' (*Works*, vi: 379. See Skinner 1966: liv–lv).[21]

Undoubtedly Steuart recognized the power of Smith's message in remarking that '*Smith* has printed in favour of free importation' (Skinner 1966: 738) and that his case (and those of others) was effectively lost. It was an interesting perception, which confirms Steuart's acute appreciation of the power of Smith's message as a general principle and the dangers of its application to specific cases; a point which deserves some elaboration as a representative example of contrasting styles.

E. P. Thompson (1993) reminded his readers of the importance of the 'Digression Concerning the Corn trade' and indeed of the significance which Smith attached to it (WN, IV. v. b. 1). The argument is part of the logical extension of Smith's position and is marked by the claim that 'The unlimited, unrestrained freedom of the corn trade, as it is the only effectual preventative of the miseries of a famine, so it is the best palliative of the inconveniences of a dearth' (WN, IV. v. b. 7).

As Thompson pointed out, the Digression acquired 'oracular authority' and claimed that 'few chapters can have a more palpable influence' (op. cit.: 279, 276). But as Thompson also argued, 'dearth and famine are always in the short run, but not the long. And Adam Smith has only long run remedies' (op. cit.: 278; cf. 283). But the short-run is crucial, as Steuart well knew, thus making it possible for Thompson to claim that Smith's position, ironically, apparently lacked a 'moral imperative'. If Smith argued that high prices of wage goods put the 'inferior ranks of people, upon thrift and good management' (WN, IV. v. b. 3), the fact remains that 'High prices of bread mattered little to the rich, were inconvenient to the middling sort, were painful to the steadily employed labourers, but could threaten the survival of the poor' (Thompson, op. cit.: 285). It was the poor with whom Steuart was, once again, primarily concerned, not to mention the realities of the short-run in the context of a situation where agricultural provision was, to say the least, imperfect.

Yet if Steuart was capable of a strong emotional response to situations

---

[21] Steuart's *Memorial on the Corn Laws*, is dated 10 October 1777. It is reprinted in Chamley (1965: 140–2) and in Skinner (1966: 737–8). See also Steuart's *Dissertation on the Policy of Grain* (1759), in *Works*, V.

of this kind, he was equally capable of a coolly analytical approach to them, notably in *A Dissertation on the Policy of Grain: with a View to a Plan for preventing Scarcity or exorbitant prices in the Common Markets of England*, a piece which was completed in 1759, when Steuart was still resident in Tubingen. In this important document, which Walter Eltis claims to have anticipated the modern recommendations of the EC (1986: 44), Steuart returned once more to the problems presented by a relatively underdeveloped agricultural sector, subject to vagaries of supply, but this time in the context of a national, as distinct from a regional, economy. Once again, Steuart's interest was in the protection of the interests of the 'poor' while seeking to establish an environment which would be consistent with the encouragement of agriculture—all in the context of a concern with short- to medium-run considerations. Seen in this light Steuart disagreed with Smith's later position in so far as he supported the bounty on exportation:

The bounty act had the desired effect of encouraging tillage, of supporting prices at a reasonable height, and of relieving farmers of a superfluous load of plenty in a tract of good years; but it has not produced the same good effect, in preventing the exorbitant rise of prices in years of scarcity: Something still remains to be done, in order to carry this branch of English policy to its full perfection (*Works*, V: 350).

It was Steuart's view that 'the difficulty lies in reconciling the entire liberty of amassing grain in favour of exportation, with the plentiful and ready supply of inland markets' (op. cit.: 354). In this connection Steuart advocated the introduction of a granary scheme, the granary keepers being obliged to receive supplies at a basic minimum price until a total supply (based upon empirical evidence) was secured. Thereafter the granaries would close and should be so organized that 'while prices fluctuate' below a higher (specified) level 'the grain in them be no more allowed to influence the market than it could have done had it been exported' (op. cit.: 357). The granaries should be opened only *above* the specified price, 'but with this restriction, never to be allowed to sell in competition with any corn-dealer . . . who shall bring grain to market below this price' (ibid.). The policy was designed in part to protect the interests of the lower orders. Steuart went on to suggest that 'no person, at least in the beginning of the scheme, be put upon the granary list, but such as are of the lowest classes of the people. . . . such, in a word, who may be supposed to be the most essentially hurt by the high prices of grain' (op. cit.: 358).

Steuart sought a managed market—a combination of the 'two schemes of bounty-money, and granary making' (op. cit.: 359)—in order to protect the interests of the poor, to stabilize prices, and to provide encouragement to agriculture in the context of a situation where supply was variable and regional transport uncertain. In short, he sought to address a situation where the operation of the market in wage goods was imperfect. As Steuart remarked at the outset of this analysis: 'No more is required from good government, but to guard against the two extremes of superfluous plenty and pinching want. The bounty upon exportation has prevented the former, let us now endeavour to find out a remedy for the latter' (op. cit.: 353).

INSTRUMENTS AND CONSTRAINTS

The 'historical clue' which Steuart found in Hume led him to develop an account of the origins of the exchange economy and to elaborate upon the social and political consequences of a new order. As far as the exchange economy is concerned, Steuart was seeking to describe a case where all goods and services command a price and which is marked by a high degree of interdependence both of individuals and sectors of activity. The idea, or ideal, of a 'free society' thus emerges as involving 'a general tacit contract, from which reciprocal and proportional services result universally between all those who compose it' (Steuart, 1966 edn.: 88). It is a telling analogy. There is no doubt that Steuart fully comprehended the operation of market forces, but equally no doubt that he regarded markets, even when fully operational, as being subject to periodical failure. Steuart's position recalls Schumpeter's description of von Justi:

'His laisser-faire policy was laisser-faire plus watchfulness, his private enterprise economy a machine that was logically automatic but exposed to breakdown and hitches which his government was to stand ready to mend . . . his vision of economic policy might look like laisser-faire with the nonsense left out' (1954: 172).

Even more significant, however, is the attention which he gave to the need to ensure that markets could function as efficiently as possible. It was Steuart's belief, as the examples cited above indicate, that the state would have a major role to play in this regard.

The perspective which Steuart adopted follows directly from his interpretation of the conditions which actually confronted him and from his appreciation of the socio-economic conditions which prevailed. Where the necessary preconditions for the successful operation of the 'tacit contract' are *not* met, 'whenever . . . anyone is found upon whom nobody depends, and who depends upon every one, as is the case with him who is willing to work for his bread, but who can find no employment, there is a breach of the contract and an abuse' (1966: 88). In such circumstances the state must intervene simply because there is no alternative agency: 'The state of affairs in Europe, and in England in particular, is changed entirely, by the establishment of universal liberty. Our lowest classes are absolutely free; they belong to themselves' (1966 edn.: 77).

Steuart addressed a series of practical questions which did not engage Smith's attention and it is this perception which explains his distinctive position:

My object is to examine the consequences of what we feel and see daily passing, and to point out how the bad may be avoided, and the good turned to the best advantage (1966 edn.: 75–6).

He added:

In treating every question of political oeconomy, I constantly suppose a states-man at the head of government, systematically conducting every part of it, so as to prevent the vicissitudes of manners and innovations, by their natural and immediate effects or consequences, from hurting any interest within the com-monwealth (Steuart 1966 edn.: 122).

Looking back on the nature of his contribution, and on the reaction of the reviews of 1767, Steuart was to write that 'I frankly acknowledge, that I have, perhaps, on some occasions, been more apt to consider myself in the light of a political matron, than that of a jovial and free born Englishman' (*Works*, iv: 392n.).

But two points should be noted by way of qualification. First it should be repeated that the role of the 'political matron' was not inappropriate given the nature of Steuart's European experience and of the scope of the *Inquiry*. Secondly, we should recall that Steuart never advocated inter-vention for its own sake. As he pointed out in dealing with the problems of 'infant' trade, protection is only justified when accompanied by a scheme to introduce industry while 'the scaffolding must be taken away when the fabric is completed' (*Works*, ii: 235; 1966: lxxvi); that is, when market imperfections have been eliminated, as far as possible.

If most of the problems just considered can be said to be associated with the exchange economy, then so too were the *means* of implementing the appropriate policies. In this connection Steuart drew attention to the role of the public debt, while giving particular emphasis to the fact that 'by the imposition of taxes, and the right employment of the amount of them, a statesman has it in his power to retard or to promote the consumption of any branch of industry' (Steuart 1966 edn.: 332). Steuart also drew attention to the rate of interest as an instrument of economic policy (1966: 462) and to the statesman's capacity to manipulate the money supply, concluding that 'he'

ought at all times to maintain a just proportion between the produce of industry, and the quantity of circulating equivalent, in the hands of his subjects, for the purchase of it; *that, by a steady and judicious administration, he may have it in his power at all times, either to check prodigality and hurtful luxury, or to extend industry and domestic consumption, according as the circumstances of his people shall require the one or the other corrective* . . . For this purpose, he must examine the situation of his country, relatively to three objects, viz. the propensity of the rich to consume; the disposition of the poor to be industrious; and the proportion of circulating money, with respect to the one and the other (Steuart 1966 edn.: 323–4).

In passages reminiscent of Hume, Steuart argued that the modern statesman, by virtue of his capacity to manipulate taxation, public debt, monetary, and fiscal policy, had at his disposal greater sources of power than in any previous age.[22] He added that the modern citizen was in a sense much *more* constrained than his predecessors:

Can any change be greater among free men, than from a state of absolute liberty and independency to become subject to constraint in the most trivial actions? This change has however taken place over all Europe within these last three hundred years, and yet we think ourselves more free than ever our fathers were (Steuart 1966 edn.: 26).

Later he was to remark that

So powerful an influence over the operations of a whole people, vests an authority in a modern statesman, which in former ages, even under the most absolute governments, was utterly unknown. The truth of this remark will appear upon reflecting on the fate of some states, at present in Europe, where the sovereign power is extremely limited, in every *arbitrary* exercise of it, and where at the same time, it is found to operate over the wealth of the inhabitants, in a manner far more efficacious than the most despotic and arbitrary authority possibly can do (Steuart 1966 edn.: 278).

But in practice, Steuart gave a great deal of emphasis to the *constraints* confronting the statesman, in drawing attention, much as Smith had done, to the importance of the 'spirit' of a people as 'formed upon a set of received opinions relative to three objects: morals, government, and manners' (1966 edn.: 22)—opinions of such significance 'that many examples may be found, of a people's rejecting the most beneficial institutions, and even the greatest favours, merely because some circumstance had shocked their established customs' (p. 27). Linked to the above, but separate from it, was Steuart's concern with the subjects' imperfect knowledge of the purposes of particular policies; indeed, he pointed out in the Preface that, although the work may 'seem addressed to a statesman, the real object of the inquiry is to influence the spirit of those whom he governs' (p. 12). He went on to note that 'A people taught to expect from a statesman the execution of plans, big with

---

[22] On public debt and monetary theory, see especially Stettner (1945) and Vickers (1960). Cf. Hume, 'Of Taxes' and 'Of Public Credit'.

impossibility and contradiction, will remain discontented under the government of the best of Kings' (p. 13).

To such constraints must be added those of a broadly constitutional kind, in that the major sources of modern power (for example public debt and taxes) have to be sensitively applied if they are not to be counterproductive. Steuart also noted that the advent of the modern economy had led to a shift in the balance of political power. While recognizing, as Smith was to do, that the institutions of the commercial stage are compatible with both republican and monarchial forms, he observed that he knew of 'no Christian monarchy (except, perhaps, Russia) where either the consent of states, or the approbation or concurrence of some political body within the state, has not been requisite to make the imposition of taxes, constitutional' (p. 290).

But perhaps the most important element in what A. O. Hirschman has described as Steuart's 'deterrence model' of government is the emphasis given to the role of purely economic laws. For Steuart, the statesman 'is neither master to establish what oeconomy he pleases, or, in the exercise of his sublime authority, to overturn at will the established laws of it, let him be the most despotic monarch upon earth' (p. 16). Later he wrote:

The power of a modern prince, let him be by the constitution of his kingdom, ever so absolute, immediately becomes limited so soon as he established the plan of oeconomy which we are endeavouring to explain. If his authority formerly resembled the solidity and the force of the wedge . . . it will at length come to resemble the delicacy of the watch, which is good for no other purpose than to mark the progression of time, and which is immediately destroyed, if put to any other use, or touched with any but the gentlest hand.

As modern oeconomy, . . . is the most effectual bridle ever . . . invented against the folly of despotism; so the wisdom of so great a power never shines with greater lustre, than when we see it exerted in planning and establishing this oeconomy, as a bridle against the wanton exercise of itself in succeeding generations (Steuart 1966 edn.: 278–9).

Earlier in the work he remarked that,

When once a state begins to subsist by the consequences of industry, there is less danger to be apprehended from the power of the sovereign. The mechanism of his administration becomes more complex, and . . . he finds himself so bound up by the laws of his political economy, that every transgression of them runs him into new difficulties (Steuart 1966 edn.: 217).

This point did not go unnoticed.

When the *Principles* was reviewed in 1767, it was in the main criticized for the role ascribed to the statesman. The point was repeated in the reviews of Steuart's *Works* (1805), when the *Monthly* complained that the author had committed a 'capital and injurious mistake' in insisting on the 'statesman's constant superintendence over trade'.[23] Yet the same reviewer perceptively remarked that

a reader of the present day will most prize, in these volumes, their illustration of the influence of political economy on civil government; which places in the strongest light the mischiefs of arbitrary rule, and which exhibit it as not less prejudical to its depositaries than to their subjects. This very momentous question, is no where, to our knowledge, so satisfactory treated.

The reviewer of the Playfair edition of the *Wealth of Nations*, in the same journal, noted that:

Wide as have been the excursions of Dr. Smith into politics and statistics, he never discussed the influence of the true principles of political economy over civil government. This fine subject, however, has been treated by Sir James Steuart with considerable success.

But it is equally important to remember that in referring to the statesman Steuart was not speaking of 'ministers of state, and even such as are eminent for their knowledge in state affairs', nor yet of a particular type of government. As he put it, within the context of the *Principles*, the *statesman* is taken to be a 'general term to signify the legislature and supreme power, according to the form of government'. Moreover, we should note that Steuart abstracted from those particular constraints which arise from the nature of the monarch, or from the types of political pressures to which a legislature might be subject. In sharp contrast to the position adopted by Smith, Steuart spoke only 'of governments which are conducted systematically, constitutionally, and by general laws; and when I mention princes, I mean their councils. The principles I am enquiring into, regard the cool administration of their government; it belongs to another branch of politics, to contrive bulwarks against their passions, vices and weaknesses, as men' (Steuart 1966 edn.: 217).

CONCLUSION

Steuart's statesman is essentially an abstract concept. Ironically, Smith, with his greater emphasis on the role of the market, took a different, and politically more informative, view in emphasizing the significance of pressure groups, and in particular of mercantile pressure groups, as they affect public policy (see Chapter 8 above). But the absence of a political dimension, in the sense in which Smith used the term, also

[23] The *Critical Review* (1767) is representative: 'We have no idea of a statesman having any connection with the affair, and we believe that the superiority which England has at present over all the world, in point of commerce, is owing to her excluding statesmen from the executive part of all commercial concerns' (23: 412).

means that his 'very violent attack' upon this aspect of the mercantile system finds no target in the *Principles* (see Chapter 9 above); nor, perhaps, does it find as many other direct targets as is sometimes thought.

From an analytical point of view, Steuart's *Principles* does not compare with Smith's great conceptual system (see Chapter 7 above) which had so profound an influence on the classical account. Even those writers who have quite properly emphasized the agrarian dimension to Smith's thought (e.g. McNally) do not suggest that the *components* and *structure* of the analytical system did not find continuing relevance under very different economic conditions from those that actually confronted Smith.

But this is not to deny that Steuart's perception of relevant areas of economic policy in the eighteenth century was misplaced in his time, or indeed in any other time where the conditions which he confronted are replicated. Steuart's complex views on economic policy serve to remind us of the wide range of practical problems that Smith's analytical strategy caused him to ignore, thus adding to our appreciation of the content of that strategy. The same perspective also reminds us of Schumpeter's belief that economic *policy* must reflect the conditions that are perceived to prevail (local, national, and international) and of his legitimate doubts with respect to practical principles, such as freedom of trade, which claim universal validity (see Chapter 10 above). When we add Steuart's sensitivity to the problem of method and prediction, we gain some idea of the complexity of the subject that Steuart addressed. It was for these reasons that Terence Hutchison concluded that Steuart's stylistic faults were 'brought about by his intellectual virtues, and by his persistent resistance to oversimplification ... It is easier to write clearly and engagingly when one has a simple system to expound' (Hutchison 1988: 350). Smith may well have ignored the *Principles* when he came to write the *Wealth of Nations*, because there were limited points of contact between two such different systems. As Johnson remarked in reviewing the content of Steuart's work, 'Smith would have had real difficulty in refuting completely a system of economic theory which contained so many elements. Very wisely he rejected the challenge' (Johnson 1937: 210).

It should also be emphasized that, while Smith and others gathered information concerning remote peoples as part of the exercise of establishing a complete *history* of civil society, Steuart exploited an unexpected opportunity with regard to contemporary Europe which was quite unique and unmatched by any Scottish thinker of the time. In the course of his travels he visited, as we have seen, a number of places that would be remarkable even by modern standards, and which is quite astonishing given the problems of communication that prevailed.

It is thus scarcely surprising, in view of the differing analytical contributions, that Dugald Stewart should have recommended his students to *begin* their study of political economy by reading the *Wealth of Nations*, and then to proceed to the *Principles* as a work that contained 'a great mass of accurate details' gleaned through 'personal observation during a long residence on the Continent' (Stewart 1857: ix. 458). Stewart may also have intended his students to appreciate that Steuart's stance was Euro-centric rather than Angle-centric in character.

Steuart was surely a worthy contributor to what he himself described as an 'Augustan age' (1966 edn.: 6). But Donald Winch has remarked with respect to the *Principles* that 'the difficulties in making this part of Smith's context are well known. To put it bluntly, one has to take on board a Jacobite traitor tainted with Continental notions' (Winch 1983: 268).

There is no doubt that Steuart threw in his lot with the Cause, nor that his political ambitions, thwarted by the influential Arniston family, as he thought, prompted this action. As Elizabeth Mure remarked in the letter above (n. 1), 'I look on this as the foundation of all his after conduct, for had that revolution taken place which he wished, he would have been the first man in the state. When their Prince was at Ed^r, he was consulted in everything, he wrote the Manifesto, and several little things in the public papers, and was sent as ambassador to France to negotiate assistance' (Chamley 1965: 116).[24] Steuart, who returned to England in 1763 under the mistaken impression that his imprisonment by the French had been terminated as a result of British intervention, was fortunate to escape prosecution. He was not in fact pardoned until nearly eight years later, which suggests that the authorities continued to take him seriously.

Committed Jabobite he may have been, but a man 'tainted with Continental notions'? This judgement echoes comments made by the reviews of 1767 which accused Steuart of '*imbibing prejudices abroad by*

[24] Elizabeth Mure added: 'Our friend's notions of government would ill suit the rage for freedom (I may call it) that now reigns in this country, and is fast running on to licentiousness. His ambition was to have an active share in a government that he approved of, and [he] was a Jacobite on some whig principles, but not the whole of them.' Elizabeth Mure would not be drawn further despite the evident curiosity of Steuart's relative. 'Were we by the fireside alone, no doubt I could give you more information than most people now alive, but those incidents are improper for a publication' (Chamley 1965: 115). This cautious letter was written *seven* years after Steuart's death in 1780. Steuart's 'whig principles', to which Elizabeth Mure referred, are borne out by his interest in the relationship between economic and political power (see § IV above and Skinner 1965*b*). The same principles may be illustrated by the content of Prince Charles's Manifesto (dated 10 October 1745), in which it was argued that the purpose of the cause was to give 'ample security' to the people and to confirm his father's wish to 're-instate all his subjects in the full enjoyment of their religion, laws and liberties, and that our present attempt is not taken to enslave a free people'. The document added that it was also intended to invite Parliament to address the National Debt, 'now a most heavy load upon the nation' (Taylor 1944: 372–5). I owe this reference to John Gibson.

no means consistent with the present state of England, and the genius of Englishmen' (*Monthly Review*, 36 (1767): 464). Steuart replied, with a logic more attractive, perhaps, to a later age:

Can it be supposed, that during an absence of near twenty years, I should in my studies, have all the while been modelling my speculations upon the standard of English notions? . . . If, from this work, I have any merit at all, it is by divesting myself of English notions, so far as to be able to expose in a fair light, the sentiments and policy of foreign nations, relative to their own situation. (Steuart 1966 edn.: 4–5).

Scottish students of Montesquieu would surely have admired the sentiment, at least.

REFERENCES

Akhtar, M. A. (1978), 'Steuart on Growth', *Scottish Journal of Political Economy*, 25.
——(1979), 'An Analytical Outline of Sir James Steuart's Macroeconomic Model', *Oxford Economic Papers*, 31.
Anderson, G. M., and Tollison, R. D. (1984), 'Sir James Steuart as the Apotheosis of Mercantilism and his Relation to Adam Smith', *Southern Economic Journal*, 51.
Aspromourgos, T. (1995), *On the Formation of Classical Economics: Distribution and Value from William Petty to Adam Smith* (London).
Beckman, J. (1981), 'Land-Use Theory Then and Now: A Tribute to Sir James Steuart', in *Papers, Regional Science Association*, 48.
Black, R. D. C. (ed.) (1986), *Ideas in Economics* (London).
Bongie, L. L. (1986), *The Love of a Prince: Bonnie Prince Charlie in France* (Vancouver).
Burton, J. H. (1849), *Letters of Eminent Persons Addressed to David Hume* (Edinburgh).
Cassirer, E. (1951), *The Philosophy of the Enlightenment* (Princeton).
Chamley, P. (1963), *Economie politique et philosophie chez Steuart et Hegel* (Paris).
——(1965), *Documents relatifs à Sir James Steuart* (Paris).
Checkland, S. G. (1967), 'Adam Smith and the Biographer', *Scottish Journal of Political Economy*, 14.
——(1975), 'Adam Smith and the Bankers', in *EAS*.
Clark, J. M. (1928), 'Adam Smith and the Currents of History', in *Adam Smith, 1776–1926* (Chicago).
Coleman, D. C. (ed.) *Revisions in Mercantilism* (London).
Coltness (1842), *The Coltness Collections*, (Edinburgh).
Cunningham, W. (1891), 'The Progress of Economic Doctrine in England in the Eighteenth Century', *Economic Journal*, 1.

Davie, G. E. (1967), 'Anglophobe and Anglophile', *Scottish Journal of Political Economy*, 14.

Doujon, R. (1994), 'Steuart's Position on Economic Progress', *European Journal of the History of Economic Thought*, 3.

Eagly, R. V. (1961), 'Sir James Steuart and the Aspiration Effect', *Economica*, 28.

Eltis, W. (1986), 'Sir James Steuart's Corporate State', in Black (1986).

——(1987), 'Steuart, Sir James', in *The New Palgrave Dictionary of Economics*, J. Eatwell, M. Milgate, and P. Newman (London).

Grampp, W. D. (1952), 'The Liberal Elements in English Mercantilism', *Quarterly Journal of Economics*, 66.

Grossman, H. (1943), 'The Evolutionist Revolt against Classical Political Economy', *Journal of Political Economy*, 51.

Hasbach, W. (1891), *Untersuchungen über Adam Smith* (Leipzig).

Hirschman, A. O. (1977), *The Passions and the Interests; Political Arguments for Capitalism before its Triumph* (Princeton).

Hont, I., 'The Rich Country–Poor Country Debate in Scottish Political Economy', in I. Hont and M. Ignatieff (eds.) (1983), *Wealth and Virtue: The Shaping of Political Economy in the Scottish Enlightenment* (Cambridge).

Hutchison, T. (1988), *Before Adam Smith* (Oxford).

Johnson, E. A. G. (1937), *Predecessors of Adam Smith* (New York).

Jones, P., (ed.) (1988), *Philosophy and Science in the Age of Enlightenment* (Edinburgh).

Judges, A. V. (1969), 'The Idea of a Mercantile State', in Coleman (1969).

Kames, Henry Home, Lord (1779), *Principles of Morality and Natural Religion* (Edinburgh).

Karayiannis, A. (1994), 'Sir James Steuart on the Managed Market', in *Economic Thought and Political Theory*, ed. D. Reisman (London).

Khalil, E. (1987), 'Sir James Steuart vs Professor James Buchanan: Critical Notes on Modern Public Choice', *Review of Social Economy*, 45.

Kindleberger, C. (1976), 'The Historical Background: Adam Smith and the Industrial Revolution', in T. Wilson and A. S. Skinner (eds.), *The Market and the State: Essays in Honour of Adam Smith* (Oxford).

King, J. E. (1988), *Economic Exiles* (London).

Kobayashi, N. (1967), *Sir James Steuart, Adam Smith and Friedrich List* (Tokyo).

——(1992), 'The First System of Political Economy: An Essay on Political Economy of Sir James Steuart', *Keizai Ronshu*, Daitobunka University.

Letwin, W. (1963), *The Origin of Scientific Economics: English Economic Thought 1660–1776* (London).

Low, J. M. (1952), 'An Eighteenth Century Controversy in the Theory of Economic Progress', *Manchester School of Economic and Social Studies*, 20.

McLaurin, C. (1748), *An Account of Sir Isaac Newton's Philosophical Discoveries* (Edinburgh; 3rd edn. 1775).

McNally, D. (1988), *Political Economy and the Rise of Capitalism: A Re-interpretation* (London).

Marshall, A. (1890), *Principles of Economics* (London).

Meek, R. L. (1967), 'The Rehabilitation of Sir James Steuart', in *Economics and Ideology and Other Essays: Studies in the Development of Economic Thought* (London).

———(1976), *Social Science and the Ignoble Savage* (Cambridge).

Perelman, M. (1983), 'Classical Political Economy and Primitive Accumulation', *History of Political Economy*, 15.

———(1990), 'Sir James Steuart's Absorption and Wealth Approach to the Balance of Payments', *History of Political Economy*, 22.

Raschid, S. (1986), 'Smith, Steuart and Mercantilism: Comment', *Southern Economic Journal*, 52.

Raynor, D., and Skinner, A. S. (1994), 'Sir James Steuart: Nine Letters on the American Conflict, 1775–1778', *William and Mary Quarterly*, 51.

Reisman, D. (ed.) (1984), *Economic Thought and Political Theory* (London).

Roncaglia, A. (1985), *Sir William Petty: The Origins of Political Economy* (New York).

Rotwein, E. (1955), *David Hume: Writings on Economics* (Edinburgh).

Say, J. B. (1821), *Treatise on Political Economy* trans. C. R. Prinsep (London).

Schumpeter, J. A. (1954), *History of Economic Analysis* (London).

Sen, S. R. (1957), *The Economics of Sir James Steuart* (London).

Skinner, A. S. (1965a), 'Economics and the Problem of Method', *Scottish Journal of Political Economy*, 12.

———(1965b), 'Economics and History: The Scottish Enlightenment', *Scottish Journal of Political Economy*, 12.

———(ed.) (1966), *Sir James Steuart: Principles of Political Oeconomy* (Edinburgh and Chicago).

———(1967a), 'Money and Prices: A Critique of the Quantity Theory', *Scottish Journal of Political Economy*, 14.

———(1967b), 'Say's Law: Origins and Content', *Economica*, 34.

———(1979), *A System of Social Science: Papers Relating to Adam Smith* (Oxford).

———(1981), 'Sir James Steuart: Author of a System', *Scottish Journal of Political Economy*, 28.

———(1988), 'Sir James Steuart: Economic Theory and Policy', in *Philosophy and Science in the Scottish Enlightenment*, ed. P. Jones (Edinburgh).

———(1990a), 'David Hume: Precursor of Sir James Steuart?' University of Glasgow *Discussion Papers in Economics*.

———(1990b), 'The Shaping of Political Economy in the Enlightenment', *Scottish Journal of Political Economy*, 37.

Stettner, W. (1945), 'Sir James Steuart on the Public Debt', *Quarterly Journal of Economics*, 59.

Steuart, Sir James (1759), *A Dissertation on the policy of Grain, with a view to a Plan for preventing scarcity or exorbitant prices, in the Common Markets of England*, in Steuart (1805a) (henceforth *Works*), v..

———(1766), *Observations on the Advantages arising to the Public from Good Roads, particularly of the Utility of a short and easy Communication between the Firths of Forth and Clyde; with Remarks on the Present Roads Leading to Glasgow* (Glasgow).

———(1767), *Principles of Political Oeconomy: being an Essay on the Science of Domestic policy in Free Nations*, ed. A. S. Skinner (Edinburgh and Chicago, 1966).

———(1769), *Considerations on the Interest of the County of Lanark in Scotland; which (in several respects) may be applied to that of Great Britain*, in *Works*, v.

——(1770), *Sketch of a Plan for Executing a Set of Roads over the County of Lanark* (Glasgow).

——(1805*a*), *Works, Political, Metaphysical and Chronological*, 6 vols. (London).

——(1805*b*), *Remarks on the proposed Bill for the Improvement of the Roads in the Country of Lanark, by Statute Labour* (Glasgow).

Stewart, D. (1854–60), *Works*, ed. Sir William Hamilton, 10 vols. (Edinburgh).

Stull, W. J. (1986), 'The Urban Economics of Adam Smith', *Journal of Urban Economics*, 20.

Taylor, H. (ed.) (1944), *History of the Rebellion in the Years 1745 and 1746* (Edinburgh).

Thompson, E. P. (1991), *Customs in Common* (Harmondsworth).

Tribe, K. P. (1984), 'Cameralism and the Science of Government', *Journal of Modern History*, 56.

——(1988), *Governing Economy: The Reformation of German Economic Discourse, 1750–1840* (Cambridge).

Vickers, D. (1960), *Studies in the Theory of Money, 1690–1776* (London).

——(1970), 'Sir James Steuart', *Journal of Economic Literature*, 8.

——(1975), 'Adam Smith and the Status of the Theory of Money', in *EAS*.

Viner, J. (1930), 'English Theories of Foreign Trade before Adam Smith', *Journal of Political Economy*, 38.

——(1965), *Guide to John Rae's Life of Adam Smith* (New York).

Waszek, N. (1988), *The Scottish Enlightenment and Hegel's Account of Civil Society* (London).

Wemyss, A. (1988), 'Lord Elcho and the '45', in *The 45: To Gather an Image Whole'*, ed. L. Scott-Moncrieff (Edinburgh).

Winch, D. (1983), 'Adam Smith's Enduring Particular Result', in Hont and Ignatieff, (1983).

Yang, H-S. (1994), *The Political Economy of Trade and Growth: An Analytical Interpretation of Sir James Steuart's Inquiry* (Aldershot).

Index of Authorities